A HISTORY IN DOCUMENTS

A HISTORY IN DOCUMENTS

PIERO WEISS

NEW YORK · OXFORD

OXFORD UNIVERSITY PRESS

2002

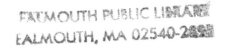

Oxford University Press

Oxford   New York
Athens   Auckland   Bangkok   Bogota   Buenos Aires   Cape Town
Chennai   Dar es Salaam   Delhi   Florence   Hong Kong   Istanbul   Karachi
Kolkata   Kuala Lumpur   Madrid   Melbourne   Mexico City   Mumbai   Nairobi
Paris   São Paulo   Shanghai   Singapore   Taipei   Tokyo   Toronto   Warsaw

and associated companies in
Berlin   Ibadan

Published by Oxford University Press, Inc.
198 Madison Avenue, New York, New York, 10016
http://www.oup-usa.org

Library of Congress Cataloging-in-Publication Data

Opera: a history in documents / [compiled by] Piero Weiss.
    p. cm.
    Includes index
    ISBN 0-19-511637-2—ISBN 0-19-511638-0 (pbk.)
    1. Opera—Sources. I. Weiss, Piero.

ML1700 .O644 2002
782.1'09—dc21   2001032179

Printing number: 9 8 7 6 5 4 3 2 1

Printed in the United States of America
on acid-free paper

For Antonio and Maria

Contents

Preface

This book shares its subtitle with a predecessor, *Music in the Western World: A History in Documents*, compiled by Richard Taruskin and myself. It also shares that book's method, for it presents in chronological order a series of documents chosen to illustrate various aspects of music history. But the history here is that of opera alone; and its more concentrated purview has suggested a slightly different treatment of the sources. They are fewer in number here and longer, and the headnotes and interspersed comments tend to be rather more detailed. This is in line with the more specialized type of course for which this book is intended.

The nature of the selected texts, however, remains varied. Memoirs, letters, histories, polemical writings, reviews, biography, essays, poetry, even a whole short story (Verga's *Cavalleria rusticana*) illustrate the changing attitudes of successive generations and the impact they have had on operatic developments. Certain themes recur, for example the fundamental paradox of opera: *real* people, after all, don't sing when they speak. And so, at the very dawn of operatic history, Jacopo Peri is seen defending the new genre in terms of the prevailing Aristotelian principles of imitation and verisimilitude. Saint-Évremond will have none of it and launches his famous attack on what he sees as the uncomfortable union of speech and song. Metastasio and Gluck (incompatible on the surface but basically of one mind) both aim at recovering the Greek ideal of tragedy, in which melody has an essential part in the catharsis. The romantics suspend their disbelief of opera's unreality for the sake of its emotional impact, while twentieth-century modernists like Busoni and Brecht come out against emotion altogether, indeed against reality, in opera. Other recurring themes grow out of the periodic impulse to reform opera, which very early on proves to be an easy prey to the pretensions of singers and the fickleness of the public. Another thread running through the book involves the struggle of composers to impose their will on the multifarious forces involved in an operatic production.

But thematic cohesiveness is not, cannot be, a major factor in a collection such as this, whose main purpose is to illustrate operatic history from a variety of angles. Well over half the documents collected here are newly translated, many of them for the first time. Yet the coverage is far from complete; and although this disclaimer might be made for almost any anthology (a genre that by its very nature excludes far more than it includes), there is an added consideration here: not every important composer or opera can be meaningfully represented by the existing documents. Among the missing greats, for example, is Rameau, an eloquent writer on practically every musical topic—except opera. I long debated whether to translate his librettist's preface to *Hippolyte et Aricie*, but in the end decided not to: it tells us everything about Pellegrin's "anxiety of influence" with regard to Racine, but practically nothing about Rameau's opera. I could tell of many other such futile searches.

Accordingly, students of opera—and opera lovers at large, for this book is meant for them too—should view this collection as an opportunity for fairly prolonged visits to selected moments of operatic history. My hope is that they will profit from such visits by gaining a closer acquaintance with the spirit that prevailed at those times in the minds of composers, librettists, critics, audiences. Much factual information is to be gleaned here too; but perhaps the most important benefit will be an awareness of how matters really stood then, an awareness that narrative histories can convey only imperfectly.

In the headnotes I have tried to present the essential historical background to each selection. Omissions in the texts are marked with ellipsis points, and the texts' sources are cited at the end of each item, or group of items.

I owe a debt of thanks to Ellen Rosand, who first suggested the book, then read and commented on each of these documents as they emerged from my printer; her encouragement and discerning criticism have been invaluable. Richard Taruskin hovered over my work only in spirit, being absorbed with his own new book; needless to say, I missed his collaboration at every turn. It is a pleasure to acknowledge the influence, without the anxiety, of two such friends.

A HISTORY IN DOCUMENTS

1

THE MEDICI WEDDING FESTIVITIES OF 1589

Opera was born in Florence at the end of the sixteenth century. It derived almost seamlessly from its immediate precursor, the intermedio, or lavish between-the-acts spectacle presented in conjunction with a play on festive occasions. Plays were spoken, and their stage settings were simple: a street backed by palace façades for tragedies, by lower-class houses for comedies; for satyr plays or pastorals, the setting was a woodland or country scene. Meanwhile the ever-growing magnificence of state celebrations in Medici Florence on occasions such as dynastic weddings gave rise to a variety of spectacles involving exuberant scenic displays: naval battles in the flooded courtyard of the Pitti Palace, tournaments in the squares, triumphal entries into the city. These all called upon the services of architects, machinists, costume designers, instrumental and vocal artists. Such visual and aural delights also found their way into the theater—not in plays, with their traditional, sober settings, but between the acts of plays. Intermedi had everything the plays had not: miraculous transformations of scenery, flying creatures (both natural and supernatural), dancing, singing. The plays satisfied Renaissance intellects imbued with classical culture; the intermedi fed the new Baroque craving for the marvelous, the incredible, the impossible. By all accounts, no Medici festivities were as grand and lavish as those held through much of the month of May 1589 in conjunction with the marriage of Grand Duke Ferdinand I and Christine of Lorraine. The intermedi produced between the acts of a comedy on the evening of May 2 were considered to be the highlight of the entire occasion and were repeated, with different plays, on May 6 and 13. Nearly all the main figures we will read about in connection with the birth of opera took part in the extravagant production, which was many months in the making: Emilio de' Cavalieri acted as intermediary between the court and the theater besides being responsible for the actors and musicians and composing some of the music; Giovanni Bardi conceived the scenarios for the six intermedi and saw to it that his highly allegorical allusions were made clear in the realization. Jacopo Peri and Giulio Caccini were among the featured singers, as was the madrigal composer Luca Marenzio, who wrote the music for Intermedio 3, described below. The poet responsible for the musical texts, finally, was Ottavio Rinuccini, who wrote the poetry for the earliest operas; indeed, the subject of

Intermedio 3, the slaying of Python by Apollo, is directly related to that of *La Dafne*, the first opera, in which, after slaying the monster, Apollo falls in love with and pursues the virgin Daphne, who is saved by the goddess Diana and transformed into a laurel. The following description appeared in 1589 in a pamphlet by Bastiano de' Rossi.

INTERMEDIO 3

The hill and the grottoes having disappeared, and the magpies having scattered, croaking and hopping, the scene returned to its original state, and the second act of the play began. At the close of the act, the houses were masked by oaks, turkey oaks, chestnuts, beeches, and other such trees, and the whole stage became a wood. In the midst of the wood was a large, dark, rocky cave, and all the plants around the cave had been parched and rendered leafless by fire. The trees farther from the cave, whose tops seemed to touch the sky, were green and fresh and laden with fruit.

After the appearance of the wood (a wonder in itself), nine couples, men and women, dressed after the Greek fashion, appeared from the left. Each couple differed slightly from the next, whether in the color of their dress, or in their ornaments—these will be described later. No sooner had they arrived on the stage than viols, flutes, and sackbuts struck up, and they began to sing:

> Here is the spot where, drunk with human blood,
>> The monster lay within this gloomy grove,
>> Clouding and blackening the air
>> With its foul breath and its malignant venom.

The words of this and the other madrigals in this Intermedio are by the above-named Ottavio Rinuccini, and the music by Marenzio. While the nine couples on the stage sang this madrigal, nine more couples of men and women entered from the other side and took up the same instruments, singing:

> This is the place where, craving flesh,
>> The fearful worm stands; in this place
>> It spews out fire and flames, hisses, and roars,
>> Destroying grass and flowers;
>> But where's the monster now?
>> Can Jove at last have heard our pleas?

Hardly were these words spoken when a serpent of immense size, portrayed by the poet as the serpent Python, belching flames and black smoke that darkened the air around the cave, thrust its head out of the dark and fearsome cavern. Screened, as it were, by the charred foliage, it failed to see the human beings nearby; it stood preening itself in the sunlight—for the brilliancy of the stage rivaled the Sun itself—and after a while went back into the cave. When those poor wretches saw the cruel beast they sang, in plaintive and melancholy voices, accompanied by the same instruments, a prayer to God, that he might deliver them from their strange and cruel misfortune:

> O miserable ones,
>> Were we then born to slake
>> The hunger of this loathsome beast?
>> O Father, King of Heaven,
>> Look mercifully down
>> On miserable Delos,
>> Imploring you on bended knee,
>> Pleading for help with bitter tears.
>> Send your lightning and your bolt
>> To avenge poor Delos
>> On the ferocious monster that devours her.

While this song was being sung, the serpent thrust its head and neck out of the cave twice more in the same way. When the song was over, it unfurled its small wings, which were of a curious color between green and black and studded with little glinting mirrors, and opened wide its vast mouth, showing three rows of huge teeth and a flaming tongue. Then, hissing and spitting fire and venom, fierce and horrid to behold, the monster caught sight of the wretches in the wood and made one great bound out of the cave to kill and eat them.

No sooner had it emerged into the open than a man with a bow and arrows, dressed as Apollo, appeared from the sky to help them. In this Intermedio, the poet has indeed sought to recreate the Pythian Battle, as described by Julius Pollux, who states that, when the battle was enacted with the ancient music, it was divided into five parts. First, Apollo looked round to see if the place was suitable for a battle, then, in the second part, he confronted the serpent and in the third (in iambics) he fought the battle. The section in iambics also contains what is called the "biting," described below. The fourth, spondaic section represented the death of the serpent and the victory of Apollo. In the fifth section he danced a joyful dance, signifying victory.

APOLLO (*l.*) AND PYTHON (*r.*). *Costume designs by Bernardo Buontalenti for Intermedio 3 in the comedy* La pellegrina, *performed in Florence during the Medici wedding festivities of 1589.* Florence, Biblioteca Nazionale Centrale.

Through the depredations of time, we have lost the ability to perform such things with the musical modes of antiquity; the poet, however, feeling that this battle, reenacted, should give the utmost delight to the audience (as indeed it does), has presented it to the accompaniment of our modern music, doing his utmost, as one highly learned in that art, to imitate and recreate the music of antiquity. He made Apollo descend from the skies, to the utter stupefaction of all who saw it: a ray of light could not have descended more quickly, as he appeared miraculously (for, whatever the mechanism that held him up, it was not visible), his bow in his hand and a quiverful of arrows at his side, dressed in a gleaming robe of gold, in the manner described in Intermedio 1, where he appeared among the seven planets in the heavens. To be sure, his costume was no longer so much covered by flames; and, for greater agility and speed, it had no surrounding rays.

When he had thus arrived on stage, to the music of viols, flutes, and sackbuts, he began the first part of the battle, which is the reconnaissance of the field of battle, and with great skill, but at a distance, he executed a dance around the serpent, leaping, showing himself to the fell serpent in elegant attitudes, expressing his contempt, and the serpent could be seen hissing, beating its wings and gnashing its teeth, hideously bracing itself for the fight.

In the third part he enacted the fight, still dancing and leaping, shooting frequent arrows at the monster, which pursued him around the stage. The monster roared to the sound of the music and gnashed its teeth; striking extraordinary poses, it tore out the arrows that lodged in its back, rending the wounds they caused, and from the wounds flowed vast quantities of dreadful black blood, like ink. Then, with terrifying groans and cries, still tearing at its own flesh and pursuing its assailant, the serpent fell and died. Apollo, joyous and full of pride at its death, danced to music signifying victory, and felicitously expressed his state of happiness and pride; after this dance, he stood beside the dead serpent and set his right foot on its head in triumph.

This done, two of the couples who had been in the wood watching the fight approached, as if incredulous and eager to make sure that the serpent was dead. When they saw it on the ground in a pool of dark, almost black, blood, and Apollo with his foot planted on its head, they began singing and playing dulcet instruments for joy, praising the God and inviting their companions to share their joy. This is what they sang:

> O valiant God,
>> Illustrious and sovereign God,
>> See the foul monster,
>> Slain by your unconquered hand.
>> Dead is the loathsome beast;

Come, rank after rank,

Come, lovely nymphs, and with your song,

Exalt Apollo and his Delos to the skies.

As they sang, the others, who had appeared at the beginning of the Intermedio, and had then withdrawn to the forest to watch the fight from farther off,
came forward to marvel at the dead serpent; when the song was finished, the
serpent was dragged offstage, out of sight. When the serpent was gone, Apollo,
accompanied only by instruments, danced and made merry, and with graceful
movements of his person interpreting the fifth part of the music, which was the
joy of having freed the people of Delphi from so vile and hideous a scourge as
the serpent. When his dance was finished, the people of Delphi surrounding him,
men and women alike, began to rejoice, and he rejoiced with them. They thanked
the God for so great a favor; and, to the accompaniment of lutes, sackbuts, harps,
violins, and cornetts, sweetly sang a carol to these words:

A thousand times, a thousand,

O joyous, happy day!

O blessed homes,

O blessed hills, allowed to see

The fearful serpent

Drained of its life and blood—

Which with malignant venom

Did rob the fields of blooms, the woods of leaves.

Thus singing and dancing in a ring, they returned the way they had come;
the wood disappeared, and the Intermedio came to an end. And because this was
a reenactment of the Pythian Battle in Delos, in the presence of the people of
Delphi, the poet showed us those people, eighteen couples, men and women, in
costumes in the Greek style, leaving the colors to the discretion of the artist.
And because some maintain that Delos was founded by Delphos, son of Nep-
tune, each person was made to carry or wear something connected with the sea.

Aby Warburg, *The Renewal of Pagan Antiquity: Contributions to the Cultural History of the European
Renaissance,* trans. David Britt (Los Angeles: Getty Research Institute for the History of Art and the Hu-
manities, 1999), 376–79.

2

PIETRO BARDI ON THE BIRTH OF OPERA

Opera did not spring from the brains of a few "inventors," though that may be the impression one gathers from documents of its early history. Rather, it emerged from the rich matrix of theatrical practices at Italian courts of the late Renaissance, with an added component. The Florentine intermedi show that almost everything was already in place: a penchant for classical mythological subjects with their abundance of marvelous happenings; elaborate scenery and scenic effects involving "machines" for the realization of those happenings on-stage; plenty of music, both vocal and instrumental, to accompany ballets and pantomimes, and to fill empty intervals in the action. To all of this, the "in-ventors" of opera added the one ingredient that would define the new genre throughout its later history, long after the Greek and Roman deities of early opera and their attendant machines were discarded and forgotten: solo singing of the actors' lines. Yet the revival of classical antiquity had everything to do with the birth of opera. The group of poets, singer-composers, and theorists that gathered at the palace of Giovanni Bardi, Count of Vernio in Florence in the 1570s and 1580s, and who sometimes referred to themselves as a "cam-erata" (loosely, a club or gathering), were fascinated by the miraculous effects of Greek music as told by the authors of antiquity. In their initial phase, un-der the guidance of Bardi and Vincenzo Galilei, they evolved a style of solo singing that tried to replicate the effects of ancient music by projecting the emotional content of the text while avoiding all purely musical procedures. In the 1590s, under the aegis of another wealthy patron of the arts, Jacopo Corsi, this new monodic style, or *stile rappresentativo*, was for the first time applied to the stage, on the theory that the dialogue of ancient drama was sung, not spoken, and that the *stile rappresentativo* would therefore be an ideal equiv-alent of that lost art of dramatic recitation. Pietro Bardi, Giovanni's son, rec-ollected these experiments in a letter written some forty years later to a musical scholar, Giovan Battista Doni. Besides discussing Galilei's contribution, he de-scribes the achievements of Jacopo Peri and Giulio Caccini, the first composers of opera, and their poet, Ottavio Rinuccini. We shall hear from them all in the documents that follow.

My most Illustrious and Revered Patron, most Highly Honored Giovan Battista Doni:

As signor Giovanni, my father, took great pleasure in music, of which in those days he was an esteemed composer, he was always surrounded by the city's most famous men who were well versed in that profession; and inviting them to his house, he thus formed an academy, as it were, both delightful and continuous. Absent all vice and in particular any kind of gaming, the noble Florentine youths were entertained much to their profit, dwelling not only on music but also on discourse and instruction regarding poetry, astrology, and other sciences, which lent varying kinds of usefulness to that agreeable conversation.

Vincenzo Galilei, father of the present famous philosopher and a man of some eminence in those days, became so enamored of this distinguished assembly that, adding to practical music (in which he excelled) also the study of musical theory, he attempted, with the help of those virtuosos and also many a vigil, to extract the essence of the Greek, the Latin, and the most modern authors: so that Galilei became a good theoretical master of all kinds of music.

This great man realized that one of the above academy's principal goals (besides recovering ancient music to the extent that such a thing was possible in so obscure a field) was to improve modern music and lift it somewhat above the miserable condition in which the Goths, chiefly, had plunged it after the loss of [ancient music] and the other noblest sciences and arts. And thus he was the first to demonstrate singing in the *stile rappresentativo*, encouraged and aided on his thorny way, considered at the time almost ridiculous, mainly by my father, who labored towards that noble goal through whole nights and at considerable expense, a thing Vincenzio gratefully acknowledged in his learned book on ancient and modern music. Then he had Dante's Lament of Count Ugolino performed, sung by a good and intelligible tenor over a consort of viols faultlessly played. This novelty, though it generated much envy among professional musicians, pleased the true music lovers. Continuing in so worthy an enterprise, Galilei set to music a part of the Lamentations and Responds of Holy Week, sung in the same manner in devout company. At that time Giulio Caccini, still very young but esteemed as an exceptional and tasteful singer, was a member of my father's gathering [camerata]; feeling an inclination for this new music, he began, entirely under my father's supervision, to sing various *ariette*, sonnets, and other poems to a single instrument; and they provoked wonder in those who heard them. Also living in Florence at that time was Jacopo Peri, who, as Cristofano Malvezzi's prime student in organ and keyed instruments as well as in counterpoint, won much praise by his playing and composing, and was rightly considered second to none among singers in this city. He, competing with Giulio, brought to light the initiative of the *stile rappresentativo* and, avoiding a certain roughness and excessive archaism that could be heard in Galilei's music, he, with Giulio, softened that style; and they made it capable of moving the affections in an unusual way, as both one and the other succeeded in doing in the course of time.

For which reason they both acquired the title of first singers and inventors of this manner of composing and singing.

Peri had more science and, having found the way to imitate familiar speech with few notes and exact diligence, he acquired great fame. Giulio had more grace in his inventions.

The first poem that was sung upon the stage in the *stile rappresentativo* was *La favola di Dafne* by Signor Ottavio Rinuccini, set to music by Peri with few notes and short scenes; it was performed in a small room and sung privately, and I was stunned at this marvel.

It was sung to a consort of instruments, which arrangement was observed also in the other plays. Caccini and Peri bore a heavy debt of gratitude to Signor Ottavio; but even more to Signor Jacopo Corsi, who, fired with enthusiasm but never satisfied by anything but the best in this art, instructed those composers with excellent ideas and admirable doctrine, as was only fitting in such a noble cause. These instructions were carried out by Peri and Caccini in all compositions of this kind, composed by them in various ways. After *Dafne*, many more fables were put upon the stage by the said Signor Ottavio, who, as both poet and teacher, presented them to great applause, with the support of the more than liberal Corsi, whose hand was ever bountiful; and the most famous were *L'Euridice* and *L'Arianna*, besides many shorter fables set to music by the said Giulio Caccini and Jacopo Peri. They had no lack of imitators in Florence, the first center for this sort of music, and in other cities of Italy, especially Rome, who have been and continue to be admired in their *scena rappresentativa*; among the best of whom it seems appropriate to rank Monteverdi.

I am sure that I have but poorly carried out Your Most Revered Lordship's command, not only because of my delay in serving you, but also because I have not satisfied myself, since so few are alive today who can remember the music of those days. Still I believe that, as I serve you with heartfelt affection, so will the truth [be recognized] of those few things I have chosen among the many that one might mention concerning this *musica rappresentativa*, which is so admired today.

But in any case I hope I will be excused by Your Most Revered Lordship's indulgence, to whom, while wishing you the happiest days during the coming Christmas season, I pray that God, Father of all good things, may bestow perfect felicity.

Florence, 16 December 1634.

Your Illustrious and Most Revered Lordship's Very Humble Servant
Pietro Bardi, Count of Vernio.

Angelo Solerti, *Le origini del melodramma* (Turin: Fratelli Bocca, 1903), 143–47. Trans. P.W.

3

L'EURIDICE, THE SECOND OPERA (1600)

La Dafne, a "fable" by Ottavio Rinuccini set to music by Jacopo Peri and Jacopo Corsi, was the first opera. "It was performed in a small room and sung privately," according to Pietro Bardi, who was there (see p. 8 above). It is quite possible that Peri was first apprised of Corsi's and Rinuccini's project "as early as 1594," as he himself states (p. 15 below); but the most informed guess as to its first performance would place it in the carnival season of 1597–98. There are no questions, on the other hand, about the date of the very public première of the second opera, *L'Euridice*. That took place at the Pitti Palace, Florence, on 6 October 1600 in the presence of Maria de' Medici, whose marriage to King Henry IV of France was being celebrated throughout the city in the grandest Medici style. A description of the event appeared in a printed account of the festivities by Michelangelo Buonarroti the Younger (grandnephew of the great artist). Only two stage settings were needed for the short work, but it is evident from the description below that no expense was spared to make them impressive. Elaborate stage effects were nothing new (see pp. 2–7 above), and it is worth noting therefore that, while the sung dialogue of early opera was innovative and experimental, the scenic component had by then reached a high degree of sophistication.

. . . After the wedding, on all the days preceding the departure of the Legate and the Queen [for Paris] there took place various entertainments, and not only by the court. But while the most magnificent spectacles were being prepared, noble and sumptuous ones were also ordered by private and munificent gentlemen for still greater pleasure and more universal display. Wherefore signor Jacopo Corsi had *L'Euridice*, the affecting and gentle fable by signor Ottavio Rinuccini, set to music with all diligence and had the most luxurious and beautiful costumes prepared for the actors; and when offered to Their Highnesses, it was accepted and a noble scene prepared for it at Palazzo Pitti, where it was performed on the evening after that of the royal wedding; and this was its drift:

While Orpheus and Eurydice, wedded lovers, enjoy a tranquil life, she dies, wounded by a serpent hidden in the grass. Orpheus mourns for her, and on

Venus's advice, and led by her to the entrance of Hades, he calls for [Eurydice], singing lamentably; the suavity of the song and Proserpine's advice having moved him to pity, Pluto returns her to him, lovelier than ever: whereupon, loving again they rejoice.

In a worthy hall, beyond the curtains within a great arch with niches on either side (wherein statues, in a pretty conceit of the artist, represented Poetry and Painting), the magnificent apparatus showed the most enchanting woods both in relief and painted, placed in a well-composed arrangement and lit as if by daylight by means of aptly-placed lights within.

But as Hades was to be represented next, the woods were seen to turn into hideous and fearsome rocks which seemed real, over which the twigs appeared leafless and the grass livid. And there, deeper inside, through a fissure in a large cliff, was seen the city of Pluto all ablaze, tongues of flame flaring from the openings of its towers, the air all around turned to a coppery color. After this change the first scene returned, nor were there any further changes. Everything took place with the greatest perfection and to the honor of all who had any share in its direction; and it gave a variety of pleasures both for the mind and for the senses to those who witnessed it.

Angelo Solerti, *Gli albori del melodramma*, Vol. 2 (Milan: Remo Sandron, [1905]), 113. Trans. P.W.

As the first opera to be performed in public, *L'Euridice* was provided with a printed libretto, which Rinuccini dedicated to the new queen. (NB: the appellation "Most Christian" was reserved for the monarchs of France.)

[RINUCCINI'S DEDICATION
OF THE LIBRETTO]

To the Most Christian Maria Medici
Queen of France and Navarre.

It has been the opinion of many, Most Christian Queen, that the tragedies put on the stage by the ancient Greeks and Romans were sung throughout; but that noble mode of declamation, far from having been revived, has to my knowledge not even been attempted by anyone until now; and I believed this was due to the deficiency of modern music, which is so markedly inferior to that of the ancients. But this opinion was wholly dispelled from my mind by Messer Jacopo Peri when, having listened to the intention of Signor Jacopo Corsi and myself, he set to music the fable of *Dafne* (which I had written simply as a trial of what the song of our own day could do), set it so gracefully that those few who heard it were enchanted.

Thus encouraged, and having improved the form of that fable, Signor Jacopo had it performed again at his house, winning the favor not only of the nobility of the whole city but of the most serene Grand Duchess and the very illustrious Cardinals Dal Monte and Montaldo, who heard and praised it.

But much greater favor and good fortune befell L'Euridice, set to music by the same Peri with an admirable artistry never before applied by others; and the benevolence and munificence of the most serene Grand Duke judged it worthy of being performed on a magnificent stage in the presence of Y[our] M[ajesty], the Cardinal Legate, and many Princes and Lords of Italy and France.

And so, having begun to realize how much such plays set to music are appreciated, I have decided to publish these two, so that others more capable than I may strive to add to and improve upon this kind of poetry without needing to envy that of antiquity, so celebrated by the best authors. Some perhaps may think it excessively bold in me to have altered the ending of the fable of Orpheus; but I thought it more seemly to do so on so festive an occasion, having as my justification the example of Greek poets in other fables; indeed, our own Dante dared to affirm that Ulysses was drowned with his ship, even though Homer and the other poets contradict him in their version of the tale. Thus also have I followed the authority of Sophocles in his *Ajax* by changing the place of the action, since it was impossible otherwise to represent the prayers and laments of Orpheus. May Y[our] M[ajesty] see in these trifling exercises my spirit's humble devotion, and may you live long and happily, daily receiving God's ever more abundant grace and favors.

Florence, [4] October 1600.

Y[our] M[ajesty]'s most humble servant,
Ottavio Rinuccini

Angelo Solerti, *Le origini del melodramma* (Turin: Fratelli Bocca, 1903), 40–42. Trans. P.W.

Peri's score of *L'Euridice* was published in February 1601 with a dedication to the queen and a letter to the reader. It will be seen that here and there he quotes literally from Rinuccini's dedication of the libretto, not surprising in view of the two men's close collaboration; the technical remarks involving harmony and counterpoint are probably by Peri himself and not easy to interpret unequivocally. Noteworthy in Peri's account of the birth of opera is his generous acknowledgment of Emilio de' Cavalieri's priority, an allusion to three pastorals that had been staged in Florence in 1590 and 1595 (see the preface

to Cavalieri's *Rappresentatione*, p. 20 below). Giulio Caccini was less generous: he forced his own music on Peri at the first performance because the
singer of Eurydice was his pupil; and, as we shall see, he then rushed to have
his own version of the whole opera printed before Peri could publish his.

[PERI'S DEDICATION OF THE SCORE AND LETTER TO THE READER]

To the Most Christian Maria Medici
Queen of France and of Navarre

Because the new music I composed for the wedding of Your Majesty, Most
Christian Queen, was so favored by your presence, which can not only make up
for all its defects but infinitely surpass all other sources of goodness and beauty,
I feel some confidence in dedicating it to your most glorious name. You may not
recognize in it anything worthy of yourself or at least compatible with the perfection of this new poem, which signor Ottavio Rinuccini, in both the ordering
and the development of this noble fable, has adorned with a thousand graces and
a thousand attractions in a wonderful union of two qualities that rarely go together: gravity and sweetness, thus showing himself to be the equal of the most
famous authors of antiquity, a poet admirable in all his parts. But you will at
least perceive in [my music] the noble quality it has derived from your presence,
when you were pleased to hear it and listen to my singing in the guise of Orpheus. May Your Majesty then be pleased to receive it as being noble and worthy for no reason other than your own greatness, which has done it honor. And
accept in it a most humble expression of my long-standing service, with which,
along with this music, I again dedicate myself to you and pray that God grant
you a full measure of His grace and favor.

Florence, 6 February 1600 [1601].

Your Most Christian Majesty's

Most humble servant
Jacopo Peri

To the Reader

Before I present you (gentle Reader) with this music, I have thought it
proper to acquaint you with what has led me to invent this new manner of song:

for Reason ought to be the source and origin of all human endeavors, and whoever cannot state it with ease must be thought to have acted fortuitously. Although signor Emilio del Cavaliere, exhibiting a remarkable inventiveness, was the first, so far as I know, to let us hear our music upon the stage, nonetheless it pleased the signori Jacopo Corsi and Ottavio Rinuccini (as early as 1594) that I, making a different use of it, should set notes to the fable of *Dafne*, written by Signor Ottavio, simply as a trial of what the song of our own day could do. And so, seeing that it was a question of dramatic poetry, and that therefore it was necessary by means of song to imitate speech (and there is no doubt that no one ever spoke singing), I judged that the ancient Greeks and Romans (whose tragedies, in the opinion of many, were sung throughout upon the stage) used a harmony which, transcending that of ordinary speech, was yet somewhat below the melody of song and took an intermediate form. And this is why we see the iambic occur in those [ancient dramatic] poems, for it does not rise to the heights of the hexameter [of epic poetry], though it is said to advance above the limits of familiar discourse. And so, abandoning all other manners of singing heard until then, I gave myself over wholly to searching for the imitation which these poems require; and I considered that the type of voice which the ancients assigned to singing, which they called diastematic (held back, as it were, and suspended), might be partly hurried, taking a middle course between song's suspended, slow movement and the prompt and rapid pace of speech, and thus made to suit my purpose (as they suited theirs when reading heroic poems and verses), approaching reasoned discourse, which they called continuous: our modern [composers] (though perhaps to a different end) have also used this in their music. I recognized, as well, that in our speech certain words are intoned in such a manner that they allow harmony to be founded on them, passing, in the course of speech, through many others that are not intoned, returning eventually to another [word] capable of a new consonant movement. And having a regard to those modes and those accents that serve us in lamenting, rejoicing, and similar moments, I set the bass moving at the same pace as those accents, now faster, now slower, according to the affections, and held it through dissonances and consonances until, running through various notes, the voice of the speaker arrived at ordinary speech, opening the way to a new consort. And this not only lest the course of the speech strike the ear (stumbling, as it were, while coming across the repeated notes of the commoner consonances) or lest it seem in a way to dance to the motion of the bass, principally in sad or grave things, whereas happier ones require by their nature a livelier motion: but also lest the use of dissonances lessen or cover the advantage we derive from the need to intone every note: which the ancient music perhaps had less need to do. And so, while I would not dare affirm that this was the song used in the Greek and Roman fables, I do believe it to be the only one our music can afford us in adapting itself to our language. Having therefore expressed my opinion to those Gentlemen, I demonstrated for them this new manner of singing, and it pleased them immensely; not only signor Jacopo, who had already composed very beautiful airs for that fable, but signor Pietro Strozzi, signor Francesco Cini, and many other highly expert gentlemen (for music flourishes among the nobles in our day), and [it pleased] also the famous lady who may well be called the Euterpe of our age, signora Vittoria Archilei; who has ever made my music worthy of her singing, adorning it not only with those *gruppi* and those long *giri di voce* both simple and double which spring at all times from her lively imagination (more to obey the custom of our times than because she considers the beauty and forcefulness of our singing to depend on them), but also with those elegant graces that cannot be written down, and when written cannot be learned from the writing. It was heard and commended by messer Giovan Battista Iacomelli, who, excellent in all branches of music, is known as "dal Violino," on which [instrument] he is admirable; and in the three successive years in which it was performed during carnival, it was heard with immense delight and received with general applause by all who were there. But the present *Euridice* has been even more fortunate, not because it was heard by those gentlemen and other worthy men whom I have mentioned, besides Count Alfonso Fontanella and signor Orazio Vecchi, most noble witnesses to my intentions, but because it was performed before so great a Queen and so many famous princes of Italy and of France, and sung by the most excellent musicians of our times. Among whom signor Francesco Rasi, noble of Arezzo, played *Aminta*; signor Antonio Brandi *Arcetro*, and signor Melchior Palandrotti *Pluto*; and behind the scenes the instrumental music was played by gentlemen illustrious for the nobility of their blood and their excellence in music: signor Jacopo Corsi, whom I have mentioned so frequently, played on a harpsichord, and signor Don Grazia Montalvo on a chitarrone, messer Giovan Battista dal Violino on a lira grande, and messer Giovanni Lapi on a large lute. And although I composed it exactly as it is now being published, nonetheless Giulio Caccini (called *Romano*), whose superlative merits are well known to the world, composed the airs for *Euridice* and some for the *Shepherds* and *Nymphs* of the Chorus; and, among the choruses, "*Al canto, al ballo*," "*Sospirate*," and "*Poi che gli eterni imperi*": this because they were to be sung by persons dependent on him, which airs may be read in his [version], composed and printed after my own was performed for Her Most Christian Majesty.

Receive it benignly, therefore, courteous reader; and although I have not here attained the goal I had set for myself, being held back by a regard for its novelty, accept it all the same; and perhaps it will come to pass that on another occasion I shall show you something more perfect than this. Meanwhile, I will deem it a sufficient accomplishment to have opened a path for the genius of others to tread in my footsteps on their way to glory, where it has not been my lot to arrive. And I hope that the use [here made] of dissonances, played and sung without fear, and discreetly (which indeed pleased so many men and so worthy) will not vex you, especially in the sadder and graver airs of *Orpheus, Arcetro,* and *Daphne,* who was played with much grace by Jacopo Giusti, a little boy from Lucca. And live happily.

Jacopo Peri

Ibid., 43–49. Trans. P.W.

Caccini's printed score of *L'Euridice* appeared in January 1601, a few weeks before Peri's. It was performed only once, in December 1602. The letter of dedication, which studiously avoids mentioning Peri's name, announces what would become a seminal treatise on the practice of monody, Caccini's preface to his *Nuove musiche* (1602). In the present letter to Bardi, he expounds a few of his principles but seems mostly concerned with establishing his priority in the "new music."

[CACCINI'S DEDICATION OF HIS VERSION OF *L'EURIDICE*]

To the Most Illustrious Gentleman
Signor Giovanni Bardi of the Counts of Vernio,
Lieutenant General of Both Guards of Our Most Respected Lord

Having set to music the fable of *Euridice* in the *stile rappresentivotivo* and having had it printed, I have felt it a part of my duty to dedicate it to Your Most Illustrious Lordship, to whom I have ever been a particular servant, and to whom I find myself endlessly obliged. In it you will recognize the style used by me on other occasions many years ago, as Your Most Illustrious Lordship is aware, in the eglogue by Sanazzaro "Iten' all'ombra de gli ameni faggi" and in other madrigals of mine of those times: "Perfidissimo volto," "Vedrò 'l mio sol," "Dovrò dunque morire," and similar ones. And this, too, is the manner which, in the years when your Camerata flourished in Florence, you and many other noble connoisseurs asserted the ancient Greeks used in performing their tragedies and other fables employing song. And so the melody of the parts recited in the present *Euridice* is supported by a *basso continuato* in which I have marked the more necessary fourths, fifths, and sevenths, and major and minor thirds, otherwise leaving the placing of the middle parts to the judgment and skill of the player; and I have sometimes tied the bass notes so that under the many passing dissonances contained [in the melody] the bass shall not be struck again, offending the ear. In this manner of singing I have used a certain *sprezzatura* [casualness], which I feel has an aura of nobility and with which I think I have more nearly approached natural speech. Nor have I avoided sequences of two octaves or two fifths when two sopranos, singing with middle parts, engage in passages, thinking their grace and novelty more delightful, especially since, except those passages, all other parts are free of such errors. I had thought on the present occasion to address the reader on the noble manner of singing, the best, in my opinion, in which to exercise oneself, together with some curiosities on the subject, and the new manner of passages and *raddoppiate* invented by me and now for some time used when singing my works by Vittoria Archilei, a singer whose excellence is attested by her widespread fame. But since the present did not seem [the proper time] to some of my friends (whom I cannot and must not disappoint), I have reserved this for another occasion, contenting myself for now with the sole satisfaction of having been the first to entrust to the press this sort of song, and its style and manner, which may be observed in all my other music circulating in manuscript and composed by me more than fifteen years ago at various times, never having used in my music any art other than the imitation of the sentiments underlying the words, while touching upon those notes, impregnated with greater or lesser affection, which I felt to be the best suited for the grace that is most looked for in good singing; which grace and manner of singing Your Most Illustrious Lordship has very often assured me are held in universally high esteem in Rome, where you reside at present. And I beg you meanwhile to receive kindly the result of my good intention and to save me your protection, behind which shield I shall ever hope to find refuge and defense from the dangers that often hover over unprecedented enterprises, knowing you will always be willing to testify that my things have not been unwelcome to a great Prince, who, being in a position to sample all the fine arts, can be their best judge. And so, kissing Your Most Illustrious Lordship's hand, I pray Our Lord to grant you happiness. Florence, 20 December 1600.

Your Illustrious Excellency's
Most Affectionate & Most Obliged Servant
Giulio Caccini

Giulio Caccini detto Romano, *L'Euridice composta in musica in Stile rappresentativo* (Florence: Giorgio Marescotti, 1600), vi–vii. Trans. P.W.

4

CAVALIERI'S *RAPPRESENTATIONE DI ANIMA, ET DI CORPO*

There was much rivalry among the pioneering composers of opera over who was the true "inventor" of the new genre. Cavalieri (see p. 1 above) had as valid a claim as his two main competitors, Peri and Caccini, and Peri even had the good grace to concede him the priority. There is no question, at any rate, as to whose opera was the first to be published. The score of Cavalieri's *Rappresentatione di anima, et di corpo* appeared in September 1600, three months before Caccini's *Euridice*. The work had first been performed that February in the Oratory of St. Philip Neri, Rome, birthplace of the oratorio; and indeed the *Rappresentatione*, because of its *Everyman*-style morality and its many paraphrases of liturgy, may be considered as much an oratorio as an opera. Yet, unlike most later oratorios, it was not performed during Lent; moreover, it was staged. Indeed, the prefatory remarks in the published score, unsigned but most probably by Cavalieri himself, contain invaluable information on the staging, in the form of instructions to stage directors, singers, dancers, and instrumentalists. They are given below, preceded by a letter of dedication signed by the Bolognese editor Guidotti; written in the fulsome style of all such letters, it is nevertheless something more than the usual dedication, for Guidotti is at some pains to establish Cavalieri's claims to precedence in the establishment of wholly sung drama. As a reflection, then, of how conscious the founders of opera were of its importance, the dedication, too, has its historical significance.

To the Most Illustrious and Most Reverend
Cardinal Aldobrandini
Chamberlain of the Holy Church
My Most Honored Master

The desire which I have always had to manifest my gratitude to Signor Emilio del Cavaliere, Roman gentleman, for my many obligations to him has emboldened me to send to press some singular and novel musical compositions of his, made in a style similar to that with which it is said the ancient Greeks and Romans were wont to move the spectators to diverse affections in their scenes and their theaters. And because in certain particular airs of his it seems that he has imitated perfectly their custom (insofar as it is known to us), and since he himself recommends that sometimes a pastoral dialogue be played and sung in the aforesaid ancient manner, I have decided to place at the end of the present work an example in which the singing is to be accompanied by two flutes or two tibiae of ancient fashion, which we call *sordelline*. It is true that, to lend to this kind of affective music all possible perfection, Signor Emilio has judged it proper to employ other instruments, given the quantity we have today, a matter that is taken up in the letter to the reader. Immense applause has universally been bestowed on this Gentleman for succeeding, through his industry and ability, in so happily reviving that ancient custom: as was seen on diverse occasions, particularly in his three pastorals, performed in the presence of Their Most Serene Highnesses of Tuscany: in 1590 *Il satiro*, which was also performed another time; and, the same year, *La disperazione di Fileno*, performed privately; and in 1595 *Il giuoco della cieca*, performed in the presence of the Very Illustrious Cardinals Monte and Mont'Alto and the Most Serene Archduke Ferdinand, eliciting much admiration, and rightly so, for no one had ever seen or heard such a manner [of performance] before: I shall not place among them *La rappresentatione di Anima, et di Corpo*, performed this past February in Rome at the Oratorio della Vallicella to so numerous an audience and to so much applause, manifestly demonstrating how apt this style is also to move to devotion: now therefore I have elected to make this the first of them to appear in print, so that the religious and the secular may derive pleasure from it: and have determined to dedicate it to Your Most Illustrious and Most Reverend Lordship, knowing what a devoted servant Signor Emilio is to you, how great is your love of virtue, and in particular how deep your understanding of music, and that your authority will secure it against any and all opposition. . . .

Rome, 3 September 1600

Your Most Illustrious and Most Reverend Lordship's
Most humble and devoted servant,
Alessandro Guidotti

To the Reader

If one wishes to stage the present work, or other similar ones, and follow the directions of Signor Emilio del Cavaliere; and if one wishes to cause this sort of music, which he has revived, to elicit diverse affections, such as pity and joy, tears and laughter, and others like them, as was effectively shown in *La disper-*

azione di Fileno, a modern scene composed by him, in which Signora Vittoria Archilei, whose excellence in music is well known to all, recited and moved everyone to tears while the character of Fileno moved to laughter; if, I say, one wishes to stage it, it seems necessary that everything be excellent: that the singer have a beautiful voice, with good intonation and solid control, that he sing with affection, both soft and loud, without passages, and in particular that he express well the words so they be understood and that he accompany them with gestures and motions not of the hands alone but of steps too, which are very effective aids in moving the affections. Let the instruments be played well, and let them be more or less numerous in accordance with the place, whether theater or hall; which, to be proportionate to this musical recitation, ought to accommodate not more than a thousand persons, comfortably seated, for the sake of silence and for their own greater satisfaction: for if the performances take place in very large halls, it is not possible for everyone to hear the words, so that the singer will need to force the voice, causing the affection to be lessened; and the overabundance of music, the words not being heard, will have a tedious effect. In order that the instruments not be seen, they should be played behind the scene, and by persons who will constantly support the singer, without divisions, and with full sound [*senza diminuzioni, e pieno*]. And in order to give an idea of which instruments have proved serviceable in such a situation, a lira doppia, a harpsichord, [and] a chitarrone or theorbo together make an excellent effect, as do also a sweet-sounding organ with a chitarrone. And Signor Emilio recommends changing instruments in accordance with the affection of the actor; and he thinks that such musical representations ought not to last longer than two hours and should be distributed in acts; and the characters dressed becomingly and with variety. Passage from one affection to its opposite, as from sad to happy, from fierce to mild, is very moving. When there has been solo singing for a while, it is well to introduce the choruses, and to vary the modes [*i tuoni*] often; and let the singers alternate, now a soprano, now a bass, now a contralto, now a tenor; and let the airs and the [instrumental] music [*le musiche*] not all be similar, but let them be varied with many [different] proportions, such as triple, sextuple, and binary, and adorned with echoes and inventions as much as possible; and especially with dances, for they animate these representations to the highest degree, as in effect all spectators concur; which dances, or morescas, if they are presented in ways that are not common, will have a comely, novel effect: as for example a moresca of combat and a playful or jesting dance: thus in the *Pastorale di Fileno* three satyrs come to blows, and with this pretext engage in combat, singing and dancing to a moresca air. And in the *Giuoco della cieca* four nymphs dance and sing while they cavort around the blindfolded Amaryllis according to the rules of blindman's buff. This is not to say that one ought not in the end, given the proper occasion, to present a formal dance [*un ballo formato*]: but it would be well to have the dance sung by those who dance it and, given a reason for holding instruments in their hands, also played by them, for thus it would be more perfect and out of the ordinary: like that produced by Signor Emilio in the grand comedy performed at the time of the wedding of the most serene Grand Duchess of Tuscany in 1588 [*recte* 1589].

When the composition is divided in three acts, which experience has shown ought to suffice, one might add four theatrical intermedi, arranged so that the first will appear before the proem, and each of the others at the end of its act, observing this procedure: let a full music and harmonious symphony of instruments be played behind the scenes, to the sound of which the motions of the intermedio are to be matched, bearing in mind that it should require no recitation, as none, for example, is required in a representation of the war of the giants against Jove, or in similar subjects. And in each, one might change the scenery in accordance with the subject of the intermedio: which, one must note, cannot involve a descent of clouds, for it would be impossible to coordinate the action with the time of the symphony, whereas moresca and other dance steps would suit it well.

The poem ought not to exceed seven hundred lines, and it should be easy, and filled with versets not only of seven syllables but also of five and eight, and sometimes accented on the antepenult [*sdruccioli*]; and the rhymes should be close for the sake of the music, for this has a graceful effect. And let the utterances and replies not be too long in the dialogues; and let the solo narratives be as short as possible. And there is no doubt that variety in the characters greatly enhances the attractiveness of the stage, a principle closely followed, as one may see, in the pastorals *Il satiro* and *La disperazione di Fileno*, which the very noble Signora Laura Guidiccioni de' Luchesini of Lucca was pleased to write in conformity with Signor Emilio's intentions; as she also took *Il giuoco della cieca* from the Cavalier Guarino's *Pastor fido* and adapted that noble spirit most becomingly according to those intentions.

Directions for producing the present Rappresentatione in singing speech

The words have been placed [again] at the end without the music, with numbers conforming to those found in the music, in order to make it easier to arrange; with those numbers it becomes possible to differentiate the several scenes and the characters who recite alone and in ensembles.

At the beginning, before the curtain is lowered, it will be well to perform a full music with voices doubled and a great quantity of instruments: number 86, the six-voiced madrigal *O Signor santo*, will serve the purpose very well.

When the curtain is lowered, the two youths who are to recite the proem will be onstage: and when they have finished, Time will enter; and the instruments which are to accompany him will sound the first consonance and wait for him to begin.

The chorus must be onstage, in part seated, in part standing, and they shall listen to what is being said, occasionally exchanging their positions and executing movements; and when they are to sing, let them stand up in order to be able to make their gestures, and then return to their places: and since the music for the chorus is in four parts, one might, if so desired, double it, singing now four, now all together, provided, however, the stage can accommodate eight.

It will be appropriate for Pleasure and his two companions to have instruments in their hands when they sing, and let them play their own ritornellos. One of them may have a chitarrone, another a little Spanish guitar, and another a Spanish tambourine, but not a noisy one, and they shall exit while playing the last ritornello.

Body, when he recites the words "Sì che ormai alma mia" with what follows, may remove some vain ornaments, such as a golden necklace, a feather from his hat, or some such things.

The World, and Mundane Life in particular, should be dressed in the richest manner; and when undressed, let the former reveal much poverty and ugliness beneath those clothes; the latter, a skeleton.

The sinfonias and ritornellos may be played with a great quantity of instruments; and a violin playing the soprano part will make an excellent effect.

The ending can be effected in two ways, either with a dance or without; if a dance is not wanted, then one must finish in 8 parts with the verse of number 91, doubling the voices and instruments as much as possible; the verse reads, "Rispondono nel Ciel scettri e corone."

If one wishes to end with the dance, then one should omit the eight-part verse; and as "Chiostri altissimi e stellati" is intoned, let the dance begin reverently and continently; and then let other grave steps follow, interwoven and passed along by all the couples with gravity; in the ritornellos, let four who dance exquisitely do a leaping dance with somersaults and no singing; and thus let it continue in all the stanzas, always varying the dance: and the four master dancers may vary [their steps], now with a galliard, now with a canary, now with a corrente, all of which fit the ritornellos very well indeed. And if the stage is not large enough for the four dancers, let at least two dance; and let that dance be composed by the best master available.

Let the stanzas of the dance be sung by everyone within and without; and let all available instruments be used in the ritornellos.

Angelo Solerti, ed., *Le origini del melodramma: Testimonianze dei contemporanei* (Turin: Fratelli Bocca, 1902), 1–11. Trans. P.W.

5

MONTEVERDI CRITICIZES A LIBRETTO

By the latest count, 127 letters of Monteverdi have survived, a gratifying number for a composer of such importance to the development of Western music
in general and of opera in particular. The present letter, written from Venice
in 1616, three years after he had settled there as Director of Music at St. Mark's,
is addressed to Alessandro Striggio (1573–1630), a diplomat-poet at the court
of the Gonzagas in Mantua and author of the text for Monteverdi's first opera,
Orfeo (1607). In view of the Duke of Mantua's forthcoming wedding, Striggio
had sent him a "maritime fable," asking him whether he would set it to music. It appears the choice, *Le nozze di Tetide* by Scipione Agnelli, was tenta-
tive, and in any case the commission was canceled a few weeks later. But
meanwhile Monteverdi, just barely keeping his temper, reacted to the "little
book" and in so doing preserved for us his views on operatic dramaturgy. Some
of his allusions need to be clarified here. Since this opera was to deal with
sea gods, tritons, sirens, and so forth, Monteverdi foresaw they and the orchestra would need to occupy the lowest portion of the stage, to the detriment
of the acoustics. Further, he would have to set to music the speeches of ab-
stractions such as Zephyrs and Boreals (west and north winds), in contrast to
the speeches of passionate human beings like Orpheus and Ariadne, who had
been the principal characters in his first two operas. Let the singers compose
their own music, Monteverdi concluded, mentioning by name several well-
known singers in the service of the court at Mantua.

Most Illustrious Sir and Honorable Master,

I greatly rejoiced at receiving from Mr. Carlo de Torri your letter and the
little book containing the maritime fable of the wedding of Thetis; you write, Illustrious Sir, that you are sending it to me in order that I may view it diligently
and write you my opinion of it afterwards, since it is to be set to music and used
at the forthcoming wedding of His Serene Highness; I, Illustrious Sir, having no
other desire than to be of some service to H.S.H., shall answer first that I am
ever ready to attend to anything H.S.H. will deign to command me and always
honored to receive without demur whatever H.H. will command. So that, should
H.S.H. approve this, it would in consequence be both very beautiful and much

to my liking. But if you bid me speak, I will obey your orders with all respect and promptness, mindful that what I say is nothing, being a person of little worth in all things and a person who honors all virtue, especially that of the present poet whose name I do not know, and the more so since poetry is not my profession. I would say with all due respect, to obey you since you so command, I would say, then, first and in general that music wants to be mistress of the air and not only of the water. By this I mean that all the concerted music described in this fable is low and close to the ground, much to the detriment of beautiful harmonies, since the harmonies will be placed amid the thicker vapors of the air of the stage so as to be heard by all and performed on the stage; and I leave this to the judgment of your most refined and intelligent taste. For because of this fault, instead of one chitarrone, three will be needed; instead of one harp, there would be need of three and so forth; and instead of a delicate singer's voice, a vehement one would be needed. Besides, a proper imitation of the speech ought in my judgment to rest upon wind instruments, since I should think that the Tritons' and other sea-gods' [accompanying] harmonies belonged to the trombones and cornetts, not to citherns or harpsichords and harps. For this action being a maritime one, it is in consequence outside the city; and Plato teaches that *cithara debet esse in civitate, et thibia in agris* ["the cithara must be in the city, and the aulos in the fields"—see *Republic* 399d]; so that either the delicate [instruments] will be improper or the proper ones not delicate. Besides I see the interlocutors are to be winds, Cupids, little Zephyrs, and Sirens; and many trebles will be needed in consequence. To which, moreover, must be added this, that the winds are to sing—that is, the Zephyrs and Boreals. How, dear Sir, shall I be able to imitate the speech of winds when they don't speak! And how shall I be able to move the affections by their means! Arianna moved, being a woman, and also Orfeo moved, being a man and not a wind. The harmonies imitate their very essence; and not by means of the discourse and stridulous noise of winds and the bleating of sheep, the neighing of horses, and so forth; nor do they imitate the undiscoverable speech of winds. The dances, further, which are scattered throughout this fable are not in dancing meter. And I feel, in my rather deep ignorance, that the whole fable does not move me a whit; and I hardly understand it either, nor do I feel that it brings me by a natural order to any end that moves me. Arianna brings me to a just lament and Orfeo to a just prayer; but this, I know not to what end. And so, Illustrious Sir, what can you expect the music to accomplish in it? Nevertheless I shall always accept it with all reverence and honor, should H.S.H. so command and be pleased, for he is my master without exception. And should H.S.H. command that it be set to music, then, seeing that in it the gods speak more than others and that I like to hear such gods sing gracefully, I would say that the three sisters, that is madam Andriana and the others, could sing [those parts] and also compose them; so could Mr. Rasco his part, Don Francesco likewise, and so too the other gentlemen; thereby imitating Cardinal Montalto, who produced a play for which each person appearing in it composed his own part. For if this were a thing tending towards a single end, such as Arianna and Orfeo, it would indeed require a single hand as well, to attend to the singing speech; and not, as here, to spoken song. And in this respect also, I hold it is too long-winded in every part, from the sirens onward, and [there are also?] some other little arguments. Forgive me, dear Sir, if I have said too much; [it was] not to disparage anything, but out of a desire to obey your commands, so that, if I am ordered to set it to music, you may take my thoughts under consideration. Remember me in all affection, I pray you, to His Most Serene Highness, to whom I humbly bow as the most loyal and humble servant; and I kiss your hands in all affection, Illustrious Sir, praying that God grant you a fullness of joy. From Venice, this 9th December 1616.

I wish you a happy holiday in all affection and am, Illustrious Sir,

Your most Humble and Obedient Servant
Claudio Monteverdi

Piero Weiss, ed., *Letters of Composers through Six Centuries* (Philadelphia: Chilton, 1967), 36–38.

6

SANT'ALESSIO AT THE BARBERINI PALACE, ROME

Opera thrived in Rome in the days when the Barberini family were in power, with one member, Urban VIII, on the papal throne (1623–44) and two nephews prominent cardinals. Cardinal Francesco built the monumental Barberini Palace in the via Quattro Fontane and there presented operas for his invited guests. By 1639, with the palace completed, the space devoted to operatic productions was said to accommodate three thousand or more spectators. The most famous of the Barberini operas was *Sant'Alessio*, with music by Stefano Landi and libretto by Giulio Rospigliosi (later Pope Clement IX), first performed on 18 February 1632 and several times later that season. It was revived in 1634 in a revised and enlarged version to honor the visiting Prince Alexander Charles of Poland, for whom a full score was printed, decorated with plates illustrating the various stage settings. Each scene in this score is prefaced by a summary of the action; when placed together as below, these short summaries amount to a synopsis of the whole libretto.

DRAMATIS PERSONAE

Rome, Prologue
Eufemiano, Father to S. Alessio
Adrasto, Roman Knight
S. Alessio
Wife
Mother
Nurse
Martio ⎫
Curtio ⎭ Pages
Angel
Religion
Demon
Herald
Chorus of Slaves
Chorus of Servants to Eufemiano
Choruse of Angels
Chorus of Demons behind the scenes
Chorus of Demons ⎫
Chorus of Peasants ⎪
Chorus of Young Romans ⎬ who dance
Chorus of Virtues ⎭

PROLOGUE
CHORUS OF SLAVES, ROME

Rome, standing on a trophy of spoils surrounded by several Slaves, having listened to the praises of the Most Serene Prince ALEXANDER CHARLES of Poland & to the general rejoicing over His Highness's arrival, resolves to present him with the experiences of S. Alessio, who among her Citizens was not less conspicuous for the glory of his sainthood than many others have been for their valor in arms. And to indicate how much she esteems ruling over the hearts of men above all other kinds of power, she commands that the above Slaves be freed of their chains.

ACT THE FIRST
FIRST SCENE
Eufemiano, Adrasto

Eufemiano, a Roman Senator and Father to S. Alessio, having met Adrasto, a Roman Knight recently returned from the war, congratulates him upon his return: & coming to speak of the experiences of Alessio, takes this opportunity to tell him of his departure many years earlier; and, lamenting so much adversity, he is pitied with particular affection and consoled by Adrasto.

SECOND SCENE
S. Alessio

S. Alessio, contemplating the vanity of man and the transience of earthly things, desires to be free of the chains of this World and therefore has recourse to God with Prayer.

THIRD SCENE
S. Alessio, Martio and Curtio, Pages

Martio and Curtio, Pages of Eufemiano, seeing S. Alessio and thinking him a Foreign beggar lodging in the Palace out of charity, do not cease mocking him and are heard by S. Alessio with humility and sufferance.

FOURTH SCENE
Demon, Chorus of Demons behind the Scenes, Another Chorus dancing

The Demon having been summoned by the infernal Choruses, which, in the expectation of great victories, make merry with dancing, he undertakes to tempt and seduce the Saint's resolve.

FIFTH SCENE
Mother, Wife, Nurse, Martio, Curtio

The Mother and the Wife of S. Alessio lament his absence, the Nurse vainly attempting to console them; at whose advice they turn to God, praying that He will cause him to prosper wherever he might be.

ADDED SCENE
For the Introduction of a Dance

Having gone to his Master's country estate for diversion, Curtio plans some entertainments, in order to use them later to mock the Pilgrim, whom he plans to

DHORUS OF DEMONS IN LANDI'S SANT'ALESSIO. *Act I, scene 4 of the revised and enlarged version performed in honor of a Polish prince visiting Rome in 1634. Seven such engravings decorate the commemorative score, published that year and dedicated to Cardinal Barberini.*

bring there; and so, having invited some Rustics from those woods, he gives occasion to a pleasant Dance.

ACT THE SECOND

FIRST SCENE
Eufemiano

Eufemiano, imagining the relief felt by the relatives of Adrasto upon his return, laments his own unhappiness, being nearly bereft of hope of ever seeing his Son again.

SECOND SCENE
Demon

The Demon makes known that he has devised a scheme whereby he hopes the Saint will be obliged to reveal himself and thus return to worldly delights.

THIRD SCENE

Wife in pilgrim's costume, Nurse.

The Wife, having resolved to search the whole World for her lost Alessio, appears in pilgrim's costume; and while she is speaking to herself about this intention, she is observed by the Nurse, who without revealing her presence brings the news to the Mother.

FOURTH SCENE

Mother, Wife, Nurse, S. Alessio, Martio, Curtio

The Mother tries in vain to thwart the Wife's intentions; then, stimulated by the example of so intense a love, she resolves to imitate her and to leave with her. S. Alessio, hearing this, commends himself to Divine mercy, then attempts with various reasons to detain them from their proposed journey. The Wife, greatly perplexed, feels more than ever the pain of her Husband's absence and faints.

FIFTH SCENE

S. Alessio

S. Alessio, affected by the miserable travail of his Relations and agitated by various thoughts, considers whether he should manifest himself.

SIXTH SCENE

S. Alessio, Demon under the guise of a Hermit

Amid such thoughts he is met by the Demon, who in the guise of an old Hermit tries with diverse reasons to induce the Saint to reveal himself to his Relatives. He, however, more confused than won over, cannot but doubt that this is a delusion from Hell; wherefore he begs God not to abandon him in his great need.

SEVENTH SCENE

Angel, and S. Alessio

An Angel appears and assures him that the Hermit was the Demon and that the reasons adduced by him were worthy of Sant'Alessio's contempt, for he is called upon by God with special inspiration to follow a path more admirable than imitable. He reveals to him his imminent Death and the magnitude of the reward Heaven has prepared for him; and he exhorts him to await that passage with an intrepid spirit; thus comforted, the Saint invites Death and meditates on the tranquillity found in it by the Just.

EIGHTH SCENE
Demon, and Martio

The Demon returns, resolved to try his hardest to overcome Alessio in the short time remaining to his life. He is joined by Martio, who takes him for a Hermit and wishes to trick him as he is wont to do with S. Alessio. Martio enters into a conversation with him and, growing angry, tries to detain him but is in diverse ways mocked by the Demon.

NINTH SCENE
Religion

Enter Religion, to be present at the devout passing of Alessio: and glorying in the works of one who has now attained his just reward, invites the world to follow in the train of Virtue.

TENTH SCENE
Eufemiano, Adrasto, Herald

As Eufemiano laments his ill fortune with Adrasto, he learns that a voice from Heaven was heard in the Great Church, summoning the World's travailed souls up to the stars: comforted by this, he gathers that he too might at some future time be consoled with the return of his Son; and that no matter what the adversity, one ought never to lose hope.

ACT THE THIRD
FIRST SCENE
Demon, and Chorus of Demons

The Demon, having used all his wiles against the Saint in vain, is confounded and plunges into Hell.

SECOND SCENE
Adrasto, Chorus, Herald

Adrasto, seeing several people walking towards Eufemiano's House, goes with others to discover the reason; and meeting a member of that House, he hears from him of the death and recognition of S. Alessio and is introduced by him into the chamber where his Body lies.

THIRD SCENE

Eufemiano, Wife, Mother, Martio, Curtio, Adrasto,
Chorus of Angels behind the Scenes

His Relatives bitterly lament the death of Alessio; the letter which he wrote before he died is read.

FOURTH SCENE

Chorus of Angels behind the Scenes, Eufemiano, Mother, Wife

The Angels who accompany the Saint's soul persuade his Relatives that they
wrongly grieve in the World over the death of one who is being received in
Heaven with so much jubilation.

FIFTH SCENE

Religion, Chorus of the Virtues, Chorus of Angels

Enter from the Saint's House Religion, accompanied by a Chorus of the Virtues
representing the eight Beatitudes, the means by which Alessio obtained his
Glory; and as his soul rises to Heaven, they remain on earth, Heaven not being
capable of poverty, weeping, suffering, and other acts proper to them. Religion,
rejoicing at Sant'Alessio's accession to Heaven, designates for him the Temple
which the ancient Romans had dedicated to Hercules. Mentioning further that
in due time St. Adalbert Martyr, Patron of the Kingdom of Poland, having spread
the Faith there, would arrive and reside in the convent adjacent to the Church,
Religion departs and goes to consecrate the Temple to Sant'Alessio; and while
the Angels continue to sing, the Virtues celebrate with dances.

Il S. Alessio, dramma musicale (Rome: Paolo Masotti, 1634; reprint, Bologna: Forni, [1970]), passim. Trans.
P.W.

A rare eyewitness account of one of the 1632 performances of *Sant'Alessio*
was set down by Jean-Jacques Bouchard (1606–41), a relatively obscure scholar
and scabrous memorialist, who entered the service of Cardinal Francesco Barberini very soon after his arrival in Rome from France. In his memoirs he refers
to himself in the third person as Orestes and uses Latin for some of his more
risqué observations. He had arrived during the carnival season and entered
wholeheartedly into the spirit of the festivities, *Sant'Alessio* being only one of
many pleasures to which he treated himself. Of course he did not fail to note
the ban on women on the Roman stage, a local phenomenon that gave extra
employment to boys and castratos who played the female roles. The ban was
in force throughout the seventeenth and eighteenth centuries.

On Monday the 23rd [of February 1632], Orestes went at the usual hour for masquerades . . . to the top of a tribune, to throw eggs and watch the masks go by. . . . That day nothing extraordinary appeared except for an open coach quite wrapped in nets for fear of the eggs, and those within it threw water at the passersby using syringes; and a little carriage wholly decorated from top to bottom with flowers, so that one saw nothing of the wood or the wheels, nor the horse itself, which was entirely barded and caparisoned with the same, four young men inside being also entirely dressed in them, a thing infinitely pleasant to see that filled the whole Corso with scent. . . .

From there Orestes went to the spectacle offered by Cardinal Francesco Barberino in his new palace. The Cardinal himself admitted Orestes underneath the scaffolding and, leading him by the hand, bade him sit at his feet on a little bench and commanded Luca Holsteinius to keep close to Orestes and explain the subject to him, intending with this gratuitous favor, which cost him nothing, to make up for the lack of those other [favors] which he would seem to have owed as a result of the recommendations he had received for Orestes. It was one of the finest spectacles ever produced in Rome, people said. Orestes never saw anything so sumptuous, so agreeable. The entire hall was draped in red, blue, and yellow satin with a canopy above of the same material covering the entire hall. The stage had four scenes: the first represented the city of Rome with its palaces; the second Hell, from which emerged a quantity of devils; the third was the mausoleum or tomb of St. Alexis; and the fourth a glory of Paradise where one saw St. Alexis with a quantity of angels. The clouds parted and there appeared a place so resplendent and luminous that one could hardly bear to look at it. The entire spectacle was recited in music with those *stili recitativi* they use in Italy, and one understood all the words as distinctly as if they had been merely spoken. All the voices were excellent, being the elite of the musicians of the Palace and of Rome. The actors who played women or choruses or angels were perfectly beautiful, being either young pages or young castratos *di cappella,* so that muffled sighs were all one heard in the hall, which admiration and desire drew forth from the peacock breasts [*da i petti impavonazzati*]; for the men of the purple, having more authority, behaved with greater freedom, so much so that Cardinals San Giorgio and Aldobrandini, with puckered lips and frequent and sonorous clucking of the tongue, invited those beardless actors to come and be kissed [*protensis labjis et crebris sonorisque popismatibus glabros hos ludiones ad suavia invitabant*]; and the costumes were worthy of note indeed, both for their richness and for the care with which they had been made, having been modeled after [ancient] statuary and medals.

Emanuele Kanceff, ed., *Œuvres de Jean-Jacques Bouchard,* Vol. 1, *Journal,* (Turin: G. Giappichelli, [1976]), 150–52. Trans. P.W.

7

OPERA MOVES TO VENICE AND GOES PUBLIC

In its earliest years opera emerged as an enhancement of festivities designed to glorify the rule of dynasties in city-states or the power of cardinals in Rome. Its arrival in Venice led to a radical transformation in its very essence and a new beginning in its history. Coming from Rome in 1637, what the first opera troupe found upon arriving in Venice was not a dynasty to glorify (unless it was Venice herself) but thriving commerce and, especially during carnival, a teeming international, pleasure-seeking public. Opera took root immediately, on an entirely new basis: in one form or another, the public paid to be admitted to the theater, and the introduction of this new commercial factor speedily had its effect on what the public was offered. Opera very soon learned to adapt itself to the new consumers: scenic effects remained a high priority, but now solo singing grew tremendously in importance. More and more, composers strove to exploit the solo voice in constructing their scores, and star opera singers began to dominate the operatic stage (as they do to this day). It was Venetian opera, in turn, that dominated wherever opera found a new venue, whether in Italy or abroad. And except where supported by kings or other rulers, its economic underpinnings reflected the lessons learned in Venice. The details of operatic production in seventeenth-century Venice are nowhere so clearly described as in the following extracts from a book by the theatrical chronicler Cristoforo Ivanovich published in 1681. Entitled *Minerva al tavolino* (*Minerva at her desk*), it is a catalogue of all the operas produced at Venice's numerous theaters from 1637 to the date of publication, with an appendix (from which we quote) describing the theaters themselves and how they functioned.

*THE INTRODUCTION OF DRAMAS HAS BEEN AN OCCASION FOR BUILDING
SEVERAL THEATERS AND FOR MAKING THE CARNIVAL MORE REMARKABLE*

CHAPTER VI

The novel introduction of musical dramas [*drami in musica*] perfectly suited Venice's temper, inclined as it is towards the tender and the delicate; it would seem the Sirens' song is sweet and gentle only on the waters; and Fable would settle here most agreeably, were it not for the danger that usually accompanies [the Sirens'] song. There were in Venice at that time two theaters which presented plays [*commedie*], namely those at San Cassiano and at San Salvatore; but afterwards there were many more, some of which were used for the presentation now of plays, now of musical dramas, while others presented only dramas. . . . As a consequence, the Carnival became even more remarkable than it had been formerly, every year attracting a considerable number of distinguished foreigners who came to enjoy so delicious and at the same time virtuous an entertainment, one that employs the most exalted minds in both poetry and music, select and exquisite male and female voices, and the most bizarre inventions in its costumes, scenery, machines, flights, and dances. So that, if in earlier days the Carnival had been remarkable only on account of the masks, banquets, and festive assemblies [*ridotti*], it became much more so on account of the plays that were added to it in the two theaters of San Cassiano and San Salvatore; but it has become remarkable to a supreme degree in our own time, in which masks, banquets, festive assemblies, plays, and musical dramas are conjoined, so that entire nights are consumed in an ecstasy of delicious entertainments. And more important, the diversity of the prices of admission facilitates greater attendance. For the nobility and merchants, thanks to their income and commerce, have the means to be continually satisfied, as do the common people, prices being very much lower now than they were before. . . .

HOW MANY THEATERS HAVE EXISTED AND EXIST PRESENTLY IN VENICE,
WITH THE DATES OF THEIR APPEARANCE

CHAPTER IX

. . . The present chapter will serve as a full record of all [the theaters] that have existed in the past and exist at present, in the chronological order of their establishment, and by whom, and for what purpose [they were established]; so that [the reader's] curiosity will have nothing left to wish for, and the task itself shall lack for nothing as to accuracy and thoroughness. The number of theaters, then, is twelve, some of which have been demolished, others shut down, and others opened for annual performances, as will be gathered from the Catalogue of the Dramas, to be drawn up as the present treatise progresses.

THE TWELVE THEATERS ENUMERATED

The first one opened at San Cassiano in the Corte Michela behind the Campanile and served to introduce comedians for the first time through the agency of the famous [masked actor] Scapino. It lasted a few years; but when another [theater], the one presently owned by the heirs of Carlo Andrea Tron, was built in

the same district, the first one was abandoned and only now, having been converted into a few rented apartments, shows some vestiges [of its former state].
The present one, then, has served for the production of plays at first, and then,
in 1637, for the production of *L'Andromeda*, which was the first musical drama
to be heard in Venice. Later it served for both plays and dramas, as will be noted
in its place below. In 1629 it suffered greatly from a fire; however, it was promptly
restored.

The second one, at San Salvatore, built for the performance of plays, owned
by Andrea Vendramin, was also reborn after a fire, in better condition than before. In 1661 it began presenting dramas and continues to do so to this day.

The third one, at Santi Giovanni e Paolo, was opened in 1638 by Giovanni
Grimani. . . . It has always served, and continues to serve today, for the production of musical works [*opere musicali*].

The fourth one, at San Moisè, was opened in 1640 by Almorò Zane; but as
it was small, it served now for dramas, now for plays; it was taken apart in the
year 1681 and served [afterwards] for the display of puppets, while works set to
music [*opere in musica*] were being performed [behind the scenes], as will be
noted elsewhere.

The fifth one was the Novissimo, which opened in 1642 under the patronage of Luigi Michiel and several gentlemen; it was built of wood, and dramas
were sung there [*e si recitò in quello in musica*] until 1646, when it was utterly
destroyed; it stood where the riding school stands at present, behind the Men-
dicanti, towards the Fondamente Nuove.

The sixth, at Santi Apostoli, consisted of two theaters built at different times
within private houses. Diverse dramas were performed there from 1649 to 1652;
but just as these [theaters] appeared, so they disappeared without a hope of being reopened.

The seventh, at Sant'Apollinare, was opened in 1652 under the patronage
of Luigi Duodo, later a procurator of St. Mark, and Marc'Antonio Corraro; it
served for works set to music for a few years, and a few more for plays; now it
is shut down with little hope of being reopened.

The eighth, a theater at the Saloni, with no circle of boxes but with a few
facing the stage, was opened by some academicians for the performance of recited dramas [*drami recitativi*]. . . .

The ninth is at San Samuele, built in 1655 by the above-mentioned
Giovanni Grimani for plays. . . .

The tenth is at Sant'Angelo on the Grand Canal; it was opened in 1677 by
Francesco Santurini on the plot of an old building that was ruined down to its
foundations, an agreement having been made with the owners of the plot that
it would remain at their disposal for seven years, after which it would devolve
to its legitimate buyers in perpetuity. . . .

The eleventh is at San Giovanni Grisostomo, built with admirable speed in
1678 by the Grimani brothers Giovanni Carlo and the abbé Vincenzo, nephews

FOR THE PRICE OF A TICKET. *It was in Venice that it became possible for the first time to attend the opera not as the guest of a noble patron but as a paying customer. The usual arrangement was to own a box at the theater, but one could also gain admission "just for the evening," as evidenced by this ticket for the San Giovanni Grisostomo theater, which, as the handwritten note tells us, cost 4 Lire.* Venice, Biblioteca del Civico Museo Correr.

and heirs to the above-named Giovanni, thus showing that they had inherited not only the magnificence but also the virtuous genius that render more conspicuous their nobility of birth and spirit. The plot was that of an old building that was ruined down to its foundations. It had been the home of Marco Polo, the Venetian nobleman famous for his travels; destroyed by a great fire that consumed some very valuable merchandise, it was inherited by Stefano Vecchia and now purchased by the above-named most noble gentlemen.

The twelfth appeared in Cannaregio and was built in 1680 on the property of Marco Morosini for the purpose of producing works [*opere*] in prose and verse. Here also were produced some little dramas set to music which will be listed in the general catalogue of dramas performed [in Venice].

*THE CUSTOM OF RENTING BOXES, AND THE RIGHTS
ACQUIRED BY THOSE WHO RENT THEM*

CHAPTER X

The most certain profit accruing to every theater consists in the rental of boxes. These number at least one hundred, not counting the upper tiers, which are divided in several orders. Not all [boxes] have the same price, which is determined by the order and the number indicating their location; therefore one cannot accurately assign a value to each [box] because of the variety of locations, which in turn makes the rents variable. These orders of boxes have easy, well-lit access, and each box has its number. The key bears two marks, the number of the order and that of the box, which averts all confusion and helps one to find the box. When a theater is to be built, it is the custom to establish two sources of revenue from the very beginning. The first consists of a gift of money for each box, and this serves to a large extent to cover the construction costs and has been the principal reason why several theaters have been built with such ease and celerity. The second is the yearly rental; every year in which a theater offers performances, this payment is made to meet the theater's expenses and provide ease and comfort to the renter. It is the right, then, acquired by the owner of that box to hold it as his own property, though without the option of yielding it to others; furthermore to keep it for his own use and lend it at will. Two reasons can make it revert to the owner of the theater: when the rent is not paid during a year of performances, or when [the box] is voluntarily relinquished by its owner; in such cases it can pass on to a new tenant. Otherwise, once acquired, it remains the owner's property for life as well as his heirs' after his death; that is, it passes from father to son, from son to father, from brother to brother, and the obligation contracted in the beginning remains in force without any alterations in the manner in which it was met in the past. This custom is founded on several cases argued in courts of law and is punctually observed. The profit from this practice is considerable, as will be mentioned later, in the discussion on a theater's earnings. There are in addition several boxes at the ground level and in the upper tiers, which, because they are inconvenient and of lesser quality, are not all rented out at the beginning, but instead are rented just for the evening or for the year at the pleasure of the owner, who seeks to realize as much as possible for his own benefit.

THE EXPENSES A THEATER MUST SUSTAIN

CHAPTER XIII

A theater, before it earns any profit, must incur many expenses, all of them connected with the performance of the dramas, without which all interest in it would cease completely. The first and most considerable [expense] is that of remunerating the men and women who sing, their pretensions having become excessive, where before they were content to perform for a share of the profit or to receive honest compensation. One must pay the maestro who sets the drama to music; then come the expenses for the costumes, the scenery, the construction of machines, the contract with the choreographer [*mastro de' balli*], the compensation each evening for the stagehands [*gli operarii*] and orchestra players, and for keeping the theater lit. All the above expenses have changed with the times, for when the theaters were just starting, prices were not so high; discretion and honesty were still respected, and the efforts of *virtuosos* were more welcome and appreciated. Today dispositions are so insatiable that loss rather than gain is the rule; and for the most part one spends far more than one gains because of the exorbitant payments to the singers. In earlier days two exquisite voices sufficed, a small number of arias gave pleasure, a few changes of scenery satisfied curiosity; nowadays one unsuitable voice receives more attention than the best voices in Europe. Every scene in the drama is expected to entail a change of scenery, and the invention of the machines must be extravagant. These are the reasons why expenses grow heavier every year; but in reality they do not grow, for payments at the door are becoming less expensive, putting the continuance [of theaters] at risk, unless a better regulation is imposed on the current trends.

Cristoforo Ivanovich, *Memorie teatrali di Venezia*, ed. Norbert Dubowy (Lucca: Libreria Musicale Italiana, 1993), 391–92, 397–401, 401–3, 407–8. Trans. P.W.

8

LULLY IS GRANTED A MONOPOLY ON OPERA IN FRENCH

The French court was indirectly involved in the creation of opera by virtue of the marriage of Maria de' Medici with Henry IV of France in 1600, an event that was marked, as we have seen (pp. 11 ff. above), by the performance in Florence of Peri's *L'Euridice* (1600), the first opera ever to be produced in public. In 1603 and again in 1604–5, after the queen had settled in Paris, Giulio Caccini, along with his singing daughters, was invited to perform for the French court, which was thus exposed directly to the "new music." Staged Italian opera, however, did not reach Paris until the 1640s, when Cardinal Mazarin imported Italian composers, singers, and the great scenographer Giacomo Torelli as part of a general attempt to Italianize French culture. The policy was hugely unpopular, and after seventeen years, during which seven operas were produced at court at exorbitant expense and failed to take root, Italian opera in France was dead. The cardinal himself died in 1661, the year in which Jean-Baptiste Lully, a native of Florence, became a naturalized French citizen and was named superintendent and composer of the chamber music of King Louis XIV. Having witnessed Mazarin's operatic failures, Lully declared that opera was peculiar to Italy and impossible to compose in French. Then Pierre Perrin, a modest but ambitious poet, obtained a monopoly on opera in French and with the composer Robert Cambert proceeded in 1671 to produce *Pomone*, a pastoral that is considered the first French opera. The venture, though financially ruinous for Perrin, appealed to the public. Lully, wasting no time, visited Perrin in debtor's prison and bought him his freedom in exchange for the operatic monopoly. Further disputes by rival claimants were promptly laid to rest by the king himself, who in the letters patent given below assigned to Lully and his descendants the sole right in perpetuity to compose and produce operas in French. By this instrument the king called into being the Académie Royale de Musique, the Paris Opéra's official name for more than a century.

PRIVILEGE IN FAVOR OF THE SIEUR JEAN-BAPTISTE LULLY, SUPERINTENDENT AND COMPOSER OF THE MUSIC OF THE KING'S CHAMBER, TO HOLD A ROYAL ACADEMY OF MUSIC

Louis, by the grace of God King of France and Navarre, to all persons both present and future, greetings. The sciences and arts being the most considerable ornaments of States, We have had no more agreeable diversion since We have brought peace to our peoples than to have them revived by summoning to our presence all those who have acquired the reputation of excelling in them, not only within the breadth of our kingdom but also in foreign countries; and in order to oblige them further to perfect themselves, we have honored them with marks of our esteem and our benevolence; and, as among the liberal arts music occupies one of the first ranks, We had designed to assure its success by means of all its attributes with our letters patent of 28 June 1669, granting to sieur Perrin permission to establish in our good city of Paris and in other cities of our realm Academies of music for the singing in public of theater pieces as is the practice in Italy, in Germany, and in England, for the space of twelve years. But having since then been informed that the pains and care taken by the said sieur Perrin with regard to such an establishment have not fully realized our intention of raising music to the level which We had anticipated, We have thought that, to succeed, it would be better to entrust its direction to a person whose experience and ability were known to Us and who was competent to form pupils, as much to promote good singing and acting upon the stage as to train bands of violins, flutes, and other instruments. For these reasons, being well acquainted with the intelligence and great knowledge acquired by our dear and beloved Jean-Baptiste Lully in the field of music, of which he has given, and gives Us daily, the most agreeable evidence over the several years he has been in our service, leading Us to honor him with the charge of superintendent and composer of the music of our chamber: now therefore We have permitted and granted to the said sieur Lully and do permit and grant to him by these presents, signed in our hand, to establish a Royal Academy of Music in our good city of Paris, which shall be composed of the number and quality of persons which he shall deem suitable, whom We will choose and engage on the strength of the report he shall present to Us, in order that they may perform before Us, whenever it shall please Us, musical pieces which shall be composed both in French verses and in foreign languages, equal and similar to the Academies of Italy; to be held and enjoyed by him throughout his life, and after him by that child of his who shall be endowed with and chosen for the inheritance of the said charge of Superintendent of the music of our chamber; with the power to take as associate any person he shall see fit for the establishment of the said Academy; and in order to defray the great expenses that will be necessary for the said performances, both on account of the theaters, machines, scenery, and costumes, as well as for other necessities, We permit him to present to the public all the pieces he shall have composed, even those which shall have been performed before Us, without, however, the right to use musicians in our employ for the production of said pieces; as also to appropriate such sums as he shall deem necessary to establish guards and other needed personnel at the doors of the places where the said performances shall occur. While we prohibit and forbid very expressly all persons, even the officers of our household, to enter without paying; as also to have any musical piece sung throughout its entirety, whether in French verses or any other language, without the written permission of the said sieur Lully, on pain of a fine of ten thousand livres and confiscation of the theaters, machines, scenery, costumes, and other things thereto pertaining, one third payable to Us, one third to the General Hospital, and the other third to the said sieur Lully; who may also establish particular music Schools in Our good city of Paris and wherever

Jean Baptiste Lully
Sur-intendant de la Musique du Roy.

THE SUPERINTENDENT OF THE KING'S MUSIC.   *This portrait by the Flemish engraver Gérard Edelinck leaves no doubt as to Lully's rank and status at the court of Louis XIV.*

he may find it necessary to do so for the good and advantage of the said Royal Academy; and just as We are founding it on the model of the Academies of Italy, where the gentlemen sing in public without demeaning themselves, We desire, and it pleases Us, that any gentleman and lady may sing in the said pieces and performances of our said Royal Academy without therefore being thought to demean their titles of nobility and privileges, charges, rights, and immunities. We revoke, cancel, and annul by these presents all permissions and privileges which We may hitherto have given and granted, even that of the said sieur Perrin, with regard to the said theatrical musical pieces, no matter what their names, qualities, conditions, and pretexts might be. We thus command our beloved and faithful councilors, those holding our parliamentary court in Paris and others, our relevant dispensers of justice and officers, to have these presents read, published and registered and to let the said beneficiary enjoy and use to the full and peaceably what is herein contained, ending and causing to end all troubles and hindrances to the contrary: for that is our pleasure; and in order that this be a firm and stable commitment in perpetuity, We have caused our seal to be affixed to these presents. Given at Versailles, in the month of May, in the year of grace one thousand six hundred and seventy-two, the twenty-ninth of our reign.

LOUIS

By the King,

COLBERT

Charles Nuitter and Ernest Thoinan, *Les Origines de l'opéra français* . . . (Paris: Librairie Plon, 1886), 237–40. Trans. P.W.

The countersignature on the above document is that of Jean-Baptiste Colbert, the king's powerful minister, through whom Lully channeled his petitions to the king. Having received the letters patent, his next concern was to find quarters for an opera house in which he could produce his future compositions. He had hopes of being assigned suitable space at the Louvre but had to settle at first for a converted tennis court, where in November 1672 he began his new career with a pastoral (actually a medley of pieces from earlier works) entitled *Les Festes de l'Amour et de Bacchus*. His next work, *Cadmus et Hermione*, was also produced there, but when Molière suddenly died in February 1673, Lully quickly requested and obtained his former colleague's theater in the Palais Royal. It was there, and at court, that all his later operas were first produced. In the following letter to Colbert, Lully specifies the changes that need to be made in order to convert Molière's theater into an opera house.

[Paris, early spring 1673]

My Lord is most humbly entreated to inform the King that the Royal Academy of Music requests His Majesty's permission to elevate the part of the hall in the Palais Royal that is above the stage, such elevation being feasible without prejudice to the symmetry of the said Palais, and without touching any of the Apartments that are in the said hall.

It also requests that some beams which are broken and on the point of falling down be changed before the work there is commenced, because it would be impossible to build any machines there with safety.

There are at either side of the Arch of the Stage two stone pillars that serve no function, and that on the contrary greatly obstruct the space for the Scenery: His Majesty is most humbly entreated to grant permission to remove them and make use of the stone for the said elevation of the Stage's walls. All this with the stipulation that the Places and works proposed shall first be visited by the Officers of His Majesty's buildings, and approved by my Lord Colbert.

The Academy being presently under the necessity of paying Rent for the place it now occupies, of restoring it when moving away, of having the hall and the machines conveyed to the Palais Royal, of paying Rent for the Comédiens Italiens and the new Stage, not including the ordinary wages and maintenance of the Academicians, all these expenses are so great that it most humbly requests His Majesty to consider that its establishment or its ruin depends entirely on a new Room in the Palais Royal before the winter.

Jean Baptiste Lully

Piero Weiss, ed., *Letters of Composers through Six Centuries* (Philadelphia: Chilton, 1967), 53–54.

9

THE *GRAND SIÈCLE* ABSORBS THE *TRAGÉDIE EN MUSIQUE*

The seventeenth century is known in France as the Great Century, *le Grand Siècle*, not only because of the splendor brought to it by the Sun King, Louis XIV, whose absolutist rule and dazzling court became a model for all the rest of Europe, but also and especially because of the great poets who thrived under his patronage. Molière (with whom Lully, before he turned to opera, collaborated on several *comédies-ballets*), Corneille, Racine, Boileau, La Fontaine are the brightest stars in France's constellation of seventeenth-century poets, and they were all involved in the gradual, contentious acceptance of opera in their midst. Lully, known generally as Baptiste and malevolently as *le Florentin*, was feared and hated but invulnerable: the king stood by him, and French opera was imposed on the French by royal decree. Who was not invulnerable was Lully's librettist Philippe Quinault. Quinault was no Corneille or Racine; and although his librettos were entitled *tragèdies en musique*, his critics treated them as regular tragedies and found them wanting. (One should note that in the following century, when the librettos of another poet, Metastasio, were universally praised as great tragedies, Quinault's, too, enjoyed unprecedented esteem and served as models for new operas.) Criticism became openly hostile after the première of Lully's and Quinault's second collaboration, *Alceste* (19 January 1674). The fact that it was based (loosely) on Euripides' *Alkestis* drew forth invidious comparisons. Charles Perrault (famous today for his *Histoires ou contes du temps passé*, or Mother Goose stories) published a defense of *Alceste*, Racine a rebuttal, Perrault a surrebuttal, and thus was launched the first in a series of memorable operatic *querelles* (disputes) in French literary history (see, for other examples, the War of the Buffoons, pp. 106-11, and the Gluckist-Piccinnist controversy, pp. 127–29 below). "La querelle d'*Alceste*" focused almost exclusively on literary issues, leaving music out of the discussion; and it was only years later, after Quinault's death, that Perrault brought forward the poet's best defense, namely, that his *tragédies* were *en musique*, i.e. meant to be sung, not spoken:

When he came to write Operas, a certain number of persons of great wit and distinguished merit chose to find them bad and to persuade everyone else to find them so. One day when they were supping together, they all descended on Monsieur de Lulli, who was one of the guests, each holding his glass, and placing the glass against his throat they began shouting, "Give up Quinault, or you are dead." This pleasantry having caused much laughter, the conversation turned serious, and no argument was omitted in order to disgust Lulli with Monsieur Quinault's Poetry; but since they were dealing with a refined and enlightened man, their stratagems in the end came to nothing. They spoke of me at that meeting, and one of those Gentlemen said good-naturedly that it was too bad that I stubbornly kept supporting Monsieur Quinault; that while it was true I was his friend, friendship had its limits, and that since Monsieur Quinault was a drowned man I should only succeed in drowning with him; in a word, that if I had a friend among the present company, that friend ought to bring me a charitable warning. Monsieur D*** [perhaps Pierre de Nyert, a nobleman and singer], who bore me some friendship and at whose house the meal took place, undertook to discharge the errand. After he had made me his salutary remonstrances, and after I had thanked him, I asked him what those Gentlemen found to complain about in the Operas of Monsieur Quinault. They find, said he, that the expressions he uses are too common and too ordinary, and that in the end his style consists of only a certain number of words that keep coming back. I am not astonished, I replied, that those Gentlemen, who know nothing about Music, should talk in this fashion; but you, Monsieur, who know it so perfectly, who know all its refinements, and to whom France owes that purity and delicacy in singing that is still lacking in all other Nations, don't you see that if one were to adhere to what they say, one would write words the Musicians could not sing and the listeners would not understand? You know that the voice, no matter how clear it may be, always swallows up a part of what it sings and that, no matter how natural and common the thoughts and words of an air, something always gets lost. What would be the result if those thoughts were very subtle and nicely chosen, and if the words expressing them were rarely used words of the kind one only finds in grand and sublime Poetry? We should not understand anything at all. In a word that is to be sung, the syllable we hear ought to lead us to guess at the one we have not heard; and in a sentence, some words we have heard ought to lead us to supply those that have escaped our hearing; and finally, a portion of a speech ought to be sufficient to let us understand the whole of it. Now, that cannot be done unless the words, the expressions, and the thoughts are entirely natural, familiar, and in common use; thus, Monsieur, they are blaming Monsieur Quinault for just the point on which he most deserves to be praised, namely, that he has been able, with a certain number of ordinary expressions and perfectly natural thoughts, to write such a quantity of works that are so beautiful and attractive, and all so different from each other. And indeed you can see that Monsieur Lulli has no complaints, persuaded as he is that he will never find words which are more fit to be turned into song and which place his Music in the most favorable light. The truth is that in those days I was almost the only one in Paris who dared declare himself for Monsieur Quinault, so vehemently had the jealousy of several Authors risen up against him and corrupted all the votes of both the Court and the City; but in the end I received satisfaction. Everyone has rendered him justice in recent times, and those who blamed him the most have been obliged by the force of truth to admire him publicly, having recognized that he possessed a particular genius for these kinds of works.

Charles Perrault, *Parallèle des Anciens et des Modernes en ce qui concerne la Poésie*, Vol. 3 (Paris: Coignard, 1692), 238–42. Trans. P.W.

The cabal against Quinault included not only Racine but also La Fontaine and Boileau. Amusingly, when Quinault fell temporarily out of favor with the king in 1677–80, all three poets betrayed a great willingness to become Lully's librettists, much as they despised him personally. La Fontaine actually completed a libretto, *Daphné*, only to see it turned down by Lully, who instead set to music *Proserpine* by Quinault, newly restored to favor. La Fontaine thereupon composed a satire in rhyming verse, here rendered in prose:

LE FLORENTIN

The Florentine
At last reveals
The stuff he's made of:
He resembles those wolves one nourishes, and he's right;
For a wolf must always stay in character,
Just as a sheep must stay in its own.
I had been warned; they said: Look out;
Whoever associates with him is taking a chance:
You don't yet know the Florentine;
He is lewd, he's a sly dog
Who devours everything,
Snatches everything, clutches at everything: his throat's capacious.
Give to him, stuff him, the glutton wants more:
The King himself could hardly satisfy him.

Despite all these warnings, he got me to work.
The lewd man came and woke up
A child of the Nine Sisters; a grizzled child,
Who should never have been
A dupe: but he was, and will ever be.
I feel I was born to be the butt of dirty tricks.
Let another deceiver appear, I'll be as willing as ever.

This one said: Will you write
Presto, presto, an Opera,
But a good one? Your muse's
Success will be assured before a notary.
Here's how we will share
The profits of the affair.

Première Journée.
Alceste, Tragedie en musique, ornée d'entrée de Ballet, representée à Versailles dans la cour de marbre du Chasteau eclairée depuis le haut jusqu'en bas d'une infinité de lumieres.

Dies primus.
Alceste Tragœdia, perpetuo cantu et variis Saltationibus decorata, ja numerose Palatij Versailiarum arcuarijs, utcumque facibus accensis illuminati, exta.

COMMAND PERFORMANCE OF LULLY'S *ALCESTE* AT VERSAILLES. *Seven months after its première, the opera was staged outdoors to help celebrate one of Louis XIV's military victories. The king occupies his usual place, facing the stage at dead center, in front of the rest of the audience.* Paris, photo Bibliothèque nationale de France.

We will divide it in two lots, the money and the songs:
The money will be mine, the music yours:
You will hear your poetry sung, I'll take the guineas:
Gladly will I pay in capers.
I've got eight or ten gags
At my fingertips; that, and the honor
Of working for me, and you're a wealthy man.
Maybe I'm not quoting him exactly;
But if those were not the words he spoke,
They were in his heart. He persuaded me;
Right or wrong, he asked me for
Something sweet, something tender, and similar fiddlesticks,
Little words, the talk of flirtation

Candied with honey; in short, he *Quinault'd* me.
I spared neither care nor pains
To realize his goal and satisfy him:
          My friends were prepared to assist me;
In case of need, I could call on their vein.
          Friends? said the glutton,
          Does one have them?
Those people will deceive you, they'll remove all that's good,
          Will put bad things in its stead.
          That is the Florentine's spirit:
          Suspicious, tremulous, uncertain,
          Never quite sure of his gain,
          Whatever we say we will do.
          I vainly offered him back his word a hundred times;
          The b[ugger] had sworn I'd be amused for six months.
          He missed by two; my friends, by their kindness,
          Spared me them by sending him where I think
          He will go without their help or mine.

There you have the story in broad lines: the details will unfold
          In ways that are worth surmising;
          But I shall carry the consequences for a year;
And I'll resemble the man from Florence,
A man hard to describe, if there's anyone like him in France.
Everyone wishes he were in the bosom of Abraham.
          His architect, his librarian,
          His neighbor, his colleague,
          And his father-in-law,
His wife, and his children, and all of mankind,
          Big or little, in their prayers
          Say in the evening and in the morning:
O Lord, through thy singular mercy for us,
          Deliver us from the Florentine.

Jean de La Fontaine, *Œuvres complètes*, vol. 2, ed. Pierre Clarac (Paris: Éditions Gallimard, Bibliothèque de la Pléiade, [1991]), 613–14. Trans. P.W.

During the time Quinault was out of favor, also Racine and Boileau, avowed enemies of opera, attempted to become librettists. The details of the affair are best left to Boileau himself, who later published what little he had written (the sketch for a prologue) before the project was called off. He prefaced the fragment with the following notice.

NOTICE TO THE READER

Mme de M[ontespan, the King's mistress] and Mme de T[hiange] her sister, tired of M. Quinault's operas, suggested to the King that he have one written by M. Racine, who rather thoughtlessly engaged himself to satisfy them, not remembering at that moment a thing about which he had more than once agreed with me: namely, that it is impossible to write a good opera, because music is incapable of narrating; that in it the passions cannot be painted to the full extent which they require; that besides, [music] cannot always turn truly sublime and courageous expressions into song. That is what I pointed out to him when he told me of his commitment; and he confessed I was right; but he had gone too far to retreat. At that point, indeed, he began to write an opera, whose subject was the fall of Phaethon. He even wrote some verses of it, which he recited for the King, who appeared satisfied. But as M. Racine had embarked on this work with reluctance, he assured me resolutely that he would not finish it unless I worked on it with him, and declared first of all that I was to write the prologue. It was of no use to remind him of my lack of talent for this sort of thing and that I had never written flirtatious verses: he persisted in his resolve and said he would get the King to order me to do it. So I reflected, trying to see what I might be capable of doing, in case I should be absolutely obliged to work on something so completely alien to my genius and inclination. Thus, to test myself, I traced, without telling anybody, not even Racine, the scenario of a prologue; and I wrote out its first scene. The subject of this scene was a dispute between Poetry and Music, who argued over the excellence of their art and in the end were quite ready to part company, when suddenly the goddess of concord, I mean Harmony, descended from heaven with all her charms and graces and reconciled them. She was then to go on and give the reason why she had descended to earth, which was quite simply to amuse the Prince who, in all the universe, was worthiest of being served and to whom she owed the most, since it was he who maintained her in France, where she reigned over all things. She then added that, to prevent that some audacious person, by rising against so great a Prince, should disturb the glory she enjoyed with him, she desired that this very day, with not a moment's delay, there should be presented on the stage the fall of the ambitious Phaethon. Instantly all the poets and all the musicians, following her command, retired and donned their costumes. That was the subject of my prologue, on which I worked for three or four days with some repugnance, at the same time that M. Racine, for his part, with no less repugnance continued to lay out the scheme of his opera, for which I was unstinting with my advice. We were busy with this miserable task, whose outcome was by no means certain, when all of a sudden a happy incident relieved us of our quandary. The incident was this: M. Quinault having come in tears before the King and having pointed out to him what a humiliation he would suffer if he were no longer to work for His Majesty's entertainment, the King, touched with compassion, declared frankly to the ladies I mentioned earlier that he could not make up his mind to let him suffer. *Sic nos servavit Apollo* [thus did Apollo save us]. And so we, Racine and I, returned to our former occupation, and no further mention was made of our opera, whose only remains were a few verses of M. Racine, which were not found among his papers after his death, and which he most likely suppressed from nicety of conscience, since they dealt with love. As for me, since there was not a trace of flirtatiousness in the scene I had composed, not only did I think it improper to suppress it, but I herewith present it to the public, persuaded it will please the readers, who perhaps will not regret seeing how I went about sweetening the gall and vehemence of my satirical poetry in order to take a plunge into the saccharine style. This they will be able to judge from the fragment I present to them here, and I present it to them the more confidently in that, since it is very short, should it not amuse them, it will not allow them enough time to get bored.

Nicolas Boileau, *Œuvres*, ed. G. Mongrédien (Paris: Garnier, 1961), 262–63. Trans. P.W.

10

SAINT-ÉVREMOND'S VIEWS ON OPERA

The writings of Charles de Saint-Évremond (1613–1703), who has been called the most civilized man of his century, enjoyed a great popularity in the early 1700s, undergoing several editions, all of them posthumous. His famous letter on operas (addressed to the second Duke of Buckingham and here given in the English version of 1728) summarizes most of the opinions on the subject current in Paris before the rise of Lully's *tragédies en musique*. Saint-Évremond himself had been obliged to flee Paris in 1661, having compromised

himself politically, and spent the rest of his long life in London. His letter therefore, which may have been drafted as early as 1661 and was probably written mostly in 1669–70, can only have reflected a limited personal experience
of Italian opera. The works he almost certainly saw performed in Paris were
those promoted by Cardinal Mazarin: Sacrati's *La finta pazza* (1645), Cavalli's
Egisto (1646), *Orfeo* (1647) by Luigi Rossi (the composer referred to below as
Luigi), *Le nozze di Peleo e di Teti* (1654) by Carlo Caproli, and Cavalli's *Xerse*
(1660). He also probably knew the *Pastorale d'Issy* (1659), an early precursor
of opera in French, with music by Robert Cambert (who was later to join him
in exile in England). His several references to Lully's operas, therefore, were
later interpolations, based on whatever excerpts he may have heard in London, and "politically correct" in view of Lully's prestigious position at the court
of Louis XIV. The topics broached here by Saint-Évremond were to become
major ones in operatic criticism for the rest of the eighteenth century. The be-
lievability of sung drama had, of course, been the basic aesthetic problem
since opera's beginning, and Saint-Évremond addresses it with great wit, coming down emphatically on the side of the nonbelievers: his definition of opera
("an odd medley of poetry and music," etc.) became a byword in later criticism. Ever present, too, are signs of the tension that existed in France with regard to everything Italian, partly due to the unpopularity of Mazarin, but partly
endemic in French culture; and indeed the relative merits of Italian and French
opera were to be endlessly debated forever afterwards. Finally, Saint-
Évremond's hostility to the "machines" of opera summarizes his essentially rationalistic attitude: the "marvelous," that stock-in-trade of Baroque opera, was
repugnant to the mind of this cultivated precursor of the Enlightenment.

I have long had a desire to tell your Grace my thoughts of Operas, and to
acquaint you with the difference I have observ'd betwixt the Italian and French
way of singing. The occasion I had of speaking of it, at the Duchesse *Mazarins's*,
has rather increased than satisfied that desire; therefore I will gratify it in the
Discourse I now send to your Grace.

I shall begin with great freedom, and tell your Grace, that I am no great admirer of Comedies in Musick, such as now a-days are in request. I confess I am
not displeased with their magnificence; the Machines have something that is surprising; the Musick, in some places, is charming; the whole together seems wonderful: but it must be granted me also, that this wonderful is very tedious; for
where the Mind has so little to do, there the Senses must of necessity languish.
After the first pleasure that surprize gives us, the eyes are taken up, and at length
grow weary of being continually fix'd upon the same object. In the beginning
of the Concerts, we observe the justness of the concords; and amidst all the Varieties that unite to make the sweetness of the harmony, nothing escapes us. But

'tis not long before the Instruments stun us; and the Musick is nothing else to our ears but a confused sound that suffers nothing to be distinguish'd. Now how is it possible to avoid being tir'd with the *Recitativo*, which has neither the charm of singing, nor the agreeable energy of speech? The Soul fatigued by a long attention, wherein it finds nothing to affect it, seeks some relief within it self; and the Mind, which in vain expected to be entertained with the show, either gives way to idle musing, or is dissatisfied that it has nothing to employ it. In a word, the fatigue is so universal, that every one wishes himself out of the house; and the only comfort that is left to the poor spectators, is the hopes that the Show will soon be over.

The reason why, commonly, I soon grow weary at Operas, is, that I never yet saw any which appear'd not to me despicable, both as to the Contrivance of the subject, and the Poetry. Now it is in vain to charm the Ears, or gratify the Eyes, if the Mind be not satisfied; for my Soul being in better intelligence with my mind than with my senses, struggles against the impressions it may receive, or at least does not give an agreeable consent to them, without which, even the most delightful Objects can never afford me any great pleasure. An extravagance set off with Musick, Dances, Machines, and fine Scenes, is a pompous piece of folly, but 'tis still a folly. Tho' the embroidery is rich, yet the ground it is wrought upon is such wretched stuff that it offends the sight.

There is another thing in Operas so contrary to Nature, that I cannot be reconciled to it; and that is the singing of the whole Piece, from beginning to end, as if the Persons represented were ridiculously match'd, and had agreed to treat in Musick both the most common, and most important affairs of Life. Is it to be imagin'd that a master calls his servant, or sends him on an errand, singing; that one friend imparts a secret to another, singing; that men deliberate in council, singing; that orders in time of battle are given, singing; and that men are melodiously killed with swords and darts? This is the downright way to lose the life of Representation, which without doubt is preferable to that of Harmony: for, Harmony ought to be no more than a bare attendant, and the great masters of the Stage have introduc'd it as pleasing, not as necessary, after they have perform'd all that relates to the Subject and Discourse. Nevertheless, our thoughts run more upon the Musician than the Hero in the Opera: *Luigi*, *Cavalli*, and *Cesti*, are still present to our imagination. The mind not being able to conceive of a Hero that sings, thinks of the Composer that set the song; and I don't question but that in the Operas at the Palace-Royal, *Lulli* is an hundred times more thought of than *Theseus* or *Cadmus*.

I pretend not, however, to banish all manner of singing from the Stage: there are some things which ought to be sung, and others that may be sung without trespassing against reason or decency: Vows, Prayers, Praises, Sacrifices, and generally all that relates to the service of the Gods, have been sung in all Nations, and in all times; tender and mournful Passions express themselves naturally in a sort of querulous tone; the expressions of Love in its birth; the

AN OPERATIC MACHINE. *A cloudscape, crowded (l.) and bare (r.), in Giovanni Legrenzi's* Germanico sul Reno *(Venice, 1675). The big wheel turned, and the entire machine moved forward towards the public.* Paris, photo Bibliothèque nationale de France.

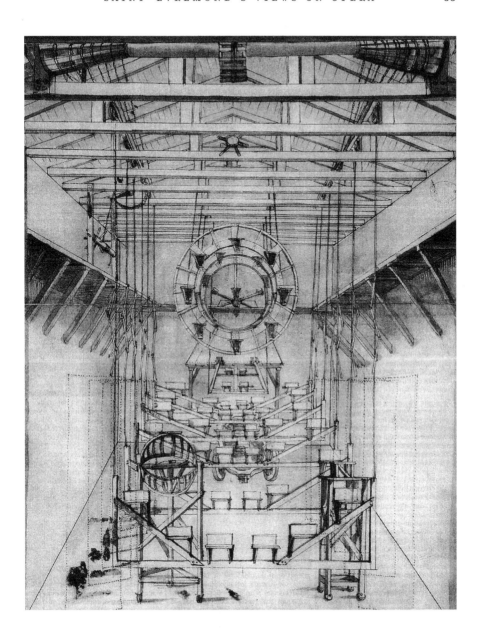

irresolution of a soul toss'd by different motions, are the proper matters for Stanzas, as Stanzas are for Musick. Every one knows that the Chorus was introduc'd upon the Grecian Theatre, and it is not to be denied, but that with equal reason it might be brought upon ours. So far, in my opinion, Musick may be allow'd: all that belongs to Conversation, all that relates to Intrigues and Affairs, all that belongs to Council and Action, is proper for Actors to rehearse, but ridiculous in the mouth of Musicians to sing. The Grecians made admirable Tragedies where they had some singing; the Italians and the French make bad ones, where they sing all.

Would you know what an Opera is? I'll tell you, that is is an *odd medley of Poetry and Musick, wherein the Poet and Musician, equally confined one by the other, take a world of pains to compose a wretched performance.* Not but that you may find agreeable Words and very fine Airs in our Operas; but you will more certainly find, at length, a dislike of the Verses, where the genius of the Poet is so crampt; and be cloy'd with the singing, where the Musician is spent by too long a service.

If I thought myself to be capable of giving counsel to Persons of Quality, who delight in the Theatre, I would advise them to take up their old relish for good Comedies, where Dances and Musick might be introduced. That would not, in the least, hurt the Representation. The *Prologue* might be sung with an agreeable Accompaniment. In the *Intermedes* singing might animate words, that should be as the life of what had been represented. After the end of the Play the *Epilogue* might be sung, or some Reflections upon the finest things in the Play; which would fortify the idea, and rivet the impressions they had made upon the Spectators. Thus you might find enough to satisfy both the Senses and the Mind; wanting neither the charms of singing in a bare Representation, nor the beauty of acting in a long continued course of Musick.

It remains that I give you my advice in general for all the Comedies, where any singing is used; and that is, to leave to the Poet's discretion the whole management of the Piece. The Musick must be made for the words, rather than the Words for the Musick. The Musician is to follow the Poet's directions; only, in my opinion, *Lulli* is to be exempted, who knows the Passions better, and enters farther into the heart of man, than the Authors themselves. *Cambert*, without a doubt, hath an excellent genius, proper for an hundred different sorts of Musick, and all well managed with a just symphony of Voices and Instruments: no *Recitativo* is better understood, nor better diversified than his; but as to the nature of the Passions, and the quality of the Sentiments that are to be expressed, he ought to receive from the Authors those lights which *Lulli* can give them; and submit to be directed, when *Lulli*, thro' the strength of his Genius, may justly be allowed to be the director.

Before I put an end to my Discourse, I will tell your Grace what a small esteem the Italians have for our Operas, and how great a dislike those of Italy give us. The Italians, who apply themselves wholly to the Representation, and take a particular care in expressing things, cannot endure that we should give the name of Opera to a mixture of Dances and Musick, which have not a natural relation, or exact connexion with the Subject. The French, on the other hand, accustom'd to the beauty of their Entries [i.e., ballets], the delightfulness of their Airs, and charms of their Symphony, cannot endure the ignorance, or ill-use of the Instruments in the Operas of Venice, and are weary of a long *Recitativo*, which becomes tedious for want of variety. I cannot properly tell you what this *Recitativo* of theirs is; but I know very well that it is neither singing nor reciting; it is somewhat unknown to the Antients, which may be defined, *an awkward use of Music and Speech*. I confess, I have found things inimitable in the Opera of *Luigi*, both for the expression of the Thoughts, and the charms of the Musick; but the common *Recitativo* was very tiresome, insomuch that the Italians themselves impatiently expected those fine places [i.e., the airs], which in their opinion came too seldom. I shall in a few words sum up the greatest defects of our Operas: one thinks he is going to a Representation, where nothing will be represented; and expects to see a Comedy, but finds nothing of the spirit of Comedy.

So much I thought I might say concerning the different constitution of Operas. As for the manner of singing, which we in France call *Execution*, I think, without partiality, that no Nation can justly vie with us. The Spaniards have admirable pipes; but with their warblings and shakings, they seem to mind nothing in their singing, but to out-rival the Nightingales. The Italian singing is either feign'd, or at least forc'd: for want of knowing exactly the nature or degree of the Passions, they burst out into laughter, rather than sing, when they would express any Joy; if they sigh, you will hear violent sobs form'd in the throat, and not Sighs which unawares escape from the passion of an amorous heart; instead of a doleful tone, they fall into the loudest Exclamations; the Tears of absence, are with them the downright weeping at a funeral; sadness becomes so sorrowful in their mouths, that they roar rather than complain; and sometimes they express a languishing passion, as a natural fainting. Perhaps there may be at present some alteration in their way of singing; and by conversing with us, they may be improved as to the justness of a neat Execution, as we are improved by them, as to the beauties of a stronger and bolder Composition.

I have seen Plays in England, wherein there is a great deal of Musick; but to speak my thoughts with discretion, I could not accustom my self to the English singing. I came too late to find a relish in that which is so different from all others. There is no Nation that affords greater Courage in the men, more Beauty in the women, nor more Wit in both sexes. 'Tis impossible to have every thing; and where so many good qualities are so common, 'tis no misfortune that a good Taste is a rarity there. 'Tis certain that 'tis very rarely to be found: but those persons that have it, possess it in as eminent a degree of niceness and perfection, as any in the world; being distinguish'd from the rest of their Nation, either by an exquisite Art, or by a most happy Genius.

Solus Gallus cantat; none but the Frenchman sings. I will not be so injurious to all other Nations, as to maintain what an Author has publish'd, *Hispanus flet, dolet Italus, Germanus boat, Flander ululat, & solus Gallus cantat* [the Spaniard weeps, the Italian laments, the German roars, the Fleming howls, and none but the Frenchman sings]: I shall leave these pretty distinctions with the Author, and only beg leave to back my opinion by the authority of *Luigi*, who would not endure that the Italians should pretend to sing his Airs, after he had heard them sung by [the French singers] *Nyert, Hilaire*, and the little *Varenne*. On his return to Italy, he made all the Musicians of that Nation his Enemies, by saying openly at Rome, as he had said at Paris, that to make fine Musick, Italian Airs must come out of a French mouth. He made little account of our Songs, except those of *Boisset* [J.-B. Boesset, 1614–85], which he admired, as well as the consort of our Violins, our Lutes, Harpsichords, and Organs: and how would he have been charmed with our Flutes, if they had been then in use? It is most certain, that he was much disgusted with the harshness of the greatest Masters of Italy, when he had once heard the sweet touch, and agreeable manner of the French.

I should be too partial, if I insisted only upon our advantages: therefore I must own, that no people have a slower apprehension both for the true sense of Words, and for humouring the thought of the Composer, than the French. There are but few who less understand the quantity, and who with greater difficulty find out the pronunciation; but when, by long study, they have surmounted all these difficulties, and are Masters of what they sing, nothing comes near them. The same thing happens to us in our instrumental Musick, and particularly in Concerts, where we can pretend to nothing very sure or just, till after an infinite number of Rehearsals; but when once we are perfect in them, nothing can be so just and fine. The Italians, for all their profound skill in Musick, bring their Art to our ears without any sweetness. The French, not satisfied to take away from the skill the first harshness that shews the labour of the Composition, find in the beauty of their Performance, as it were a charm for our Souls, and I know not what that touches, which they carry home to the very Heart.

I forgot to speak to your Grace about *Machines*, so easy it is for man to forget that which he would have laid aside. Machines may satisfy the curiosity of ingenious Men, who love Mathematical Inventions, but they'll hardly please persons of good judgment in the Theatre: the more they surprize, the more they divert the mind from attending to the Discourse; and the more admirable they are, the less Tenderness and exquisite Sense they leave in us, to be touch'd and charm'd with the Musick. The Antients made no use of Machines, but when there was a necessity of bringing in some God; nay, the Poets themselves were generally laughed at for suffering themselves to be reduc'd to that necessity. If men love to be at expences, let them lay out their Money upon fine Scenes, the use whereof is more natural and more agreeable than that of Machines. Antiquity, which expos'd their Gods, even at the gates, and chimney-corners; Antiquity, I say, as vain and credulous as it was, exposed them, nevertheless, but very rarely upon the Stage. Now the belief of them is gone, the Italians, in their Operas, have brought the Pagan Gods again into the world; and have not scrupled to amuse men with these ridiculous vanities, only to make their Pieces look great, by the introduction of that dazzling and surprizing Wonderful. These Stage Deities have long enough abused Italy: but the People there being happily undeceived at last, are disgusted with those very Gods they were so fond of before, and have return's to Plays, which, in truth, cannot pretend to the same exactness, but are not so fabulous, and which with a little indulgence, may pass well enough with men of sense.

It hath happen'd with us as to our Gods and Machines, what happens with the Germans as to our Modes and Fashion: we now take up what the Italians have laid aside; and as if we would atone for the fault of being prevented in the invention, we run extravagantly into a Custom which they brought up preposterously. In truth, we cover the Earth with Deities, and make them dance in troops, whereas they made them descend with discretion, and on the most important occasions. As *Ariosto* carried too far the Wonderful of Poetry, by a vain profusion of Fables, so we strain even Fable it self by a confused assembly of Gods, Shepherds, Heroes, Enchanters, Apparitions, Furies, and Devils. I admire *Lulli*, as well for the diversion of Dances, as for what concerns the Voices and Instruments; but the constitution of our Operas must appear very extravagant to those who are true Judges of the Probable and the Wonderful.

Nevertheless, a man runs a risk of having his Judgment call'd in question, if he dares declare his good taste; and I advise others, when they hear any discourse of Operas, to keep their knowledge a secret to themselves. For my own part, who am past the age and time of signalizing my self in the world by the invention of Modes, and the merit of new Fancies, I am resolv'd to strike in with good Sense, and to follow Reason tho' in disgrace, with as much zeal, as if it were still in as great vogue as formerly. That which vexes me most at this our fondness for Operas, is that they tend directly to ruin the finest thing we have, I mean *Tragedy*, than which nothing is more proper to elevate the Soul, or more capable to form the Mind.

After this long Discourse, let us conclude, that the constitution of our Operas cannot be more faulty than it is. But it is to be acknowledg'd at the same time, that no man can perform better than *Lulli*, upon an ill-conceiv'd Subject; and that it is not easy to out-do *Quinault* in what belongs to his part.

John Hayward, ed., *The Letters of Saint Evremond* (London: Routledge, 1930), 205–17.

11

THE FIRST ENGLISH OPERAS

The Restoration playwright and poet John Dryden (1631–1700) witnessed the birth of opera in England. It happened in 1656, while the Puritans ruled the country and regular theatrical performances were banned. Dryden himself tells us about it in the preface to one of his heroic plays, *The Conquest of Granada by the Spaniards* (1672):

The first light we had of [heroic plays] on the English theatre was from the late Sir William Davenant [1606–67]. It being forbidden him by the rebellious times to act tragedies and comedies, because they contained some matter of scandal to those good people who could more easily dispossess their lawful sovereign than endure a wanton jest, he was forced to turn his thoughts another way, and to introduce the examples of moral virtue writ in verse, and performed in recitative music. The original of this music, and of the scenes which adorned his work, he had from the Italian operas; but he heightened his characters (as I may probably imagine) from the example of Corneille and some French poets. In this condition did this part of poetry remain at his Majesty's return; when, growing bolder, as being now owned by a public authority, he reviewed his *Siege of Rhodes*, and caused it be acted as a just drama.

In its first version, then, *The Siege of Rhodes* by Davenant had been a full-length opera, with music by Henry Lawes, Matthew Locke, and others. It remained without a successor until the restoration of the monarchy in 1660, when Davenant was allowed to run a legitimate theater. Here, with Dryden as collaborator, he produced a version of Shakespeare's *The Tempest* (1667) with added music and musical scenes that went a long way towards establishing that peculiar Restoration genre, the "semi-opera." The next true opera, however, was to be Dryden's own *Albion and Albanius*, which was produced at court in 1685, shortly before Charles II died, and never again. The music, by Luis Grabu, a French-educated Catalan then residing in London, proved to be a total failure. It was published nonetheless, and this gave Dryden the opportunity of writing a preface expounding his views on opera. Of special interest is the distinction he makes between recitative and aria, or "the songish part." *The Siege of Rhodes* had been mostly recitative and choruses, and aria was something new, the word itself not yet adopted into English. Interesting too is his implied disagreement with Saint-Évremond (whose writings he knew well and admired) on at least two issues, "machines" and French vocal music. Unlike Saint-Évremond, Dryden favored machines in opera, and as for French vocal music, he considered it an "impossibility." Other aspects of French opera, such as its mythological prologues, he seems to have tolerated, but his fullest admiration is reserved for Italian music and culture; and in this he anticipates a trend that would dominate operatic life in England for a long time to come.

THE PREFACE TO *ALBION AND ALBANIUS*,

AN OPERA

If wit has truly been defined a propriety of thought and words, then that definition will extend to all sorts of poetry; and amongst the rest, to this present entertainment of an opera. Propriety of thought is that fancy which arises naturally from the subject, or which the poet adapts to it. Propriety of words is the clothing of those thoughts with such expressions as are naturally proper to them; and from both these, if they are judiciously performed, the delight of poetry results. An opera is a poetical tale or fiction, represented by vocal and instrumental music, adorned with scenes, machines, and dancing. The supposed persons of this musical drama are generally supernatural, as gods, and goddesses, and heroes, which at least are descended from them, and are in due time to be adopted into their number. The subject therefore being extended beyond the limits of human nature, admits of that sort of marvellous and surprising conduct which is rejected in other plays. Human impossibilities are to be received as they are in faith; because, where gods are introduced, a supreme power is to be understood, and second causes are out of doors. Yet propriety is to be observed even here. The gods are all to manage their peculiar provinces; and what was attributed to them by the heathens to one power ought not to be performed by any other. Phoebus must foretell, Mercury must charm with his caduceus, and Juno must reconcile the quarrels of the marriage-bed. To conclude, they must all act according to their distinct and peculiar characters. If the persons represented were to speak upon the stage, it would follow of necessity that the expressions should be lofty, figurative, and majestical: but the nature of an opera denies the frequent use of those poetical ornaments; for vocal music, though it often admits a loftiness of sound, yet always exacts an harmonious sweetness; or to distinguish yet more justly, the recitative part of the opera requires a more masculine beauty of expression and sound; the other (which for want of a proper English word) I must call the *songish part*, must abound in the softness and variety of numbers [i.e. meters]; its principal intention being to please the hearing rather

than to gratify the understanding. It appears, indeed, preposterous at first sight
that rhyme, on any consideration, should take the place of reason. But in order
to resolve the problem, this fundamental proposition must be settled, that
the first inventors of any art or science, provided they have brought it to perfection, are, in reason, to give laws to it; and according to their model, all after-
undertakers are to build. Thus, in epic poetry, no man ought to dispute the
authority of Homer, who gave the first being to that masterpiece of art, and en-
dued it with that form of perfection in all its parts that nothing was wanting to
its excellency. . . . Now, to apply this axiom to our present purpose, whosoever
undertakes the writing of an opera (which is a modern invention, though built
indeed on the foundation of ethnic worship), is obliged to imitate the design of
the Italians, who have not only invented, but brought to perfection, this sort of
dramatic musical entertainment. I have not been able, by any search, to get any
light, either of the time when it began, or of the first author. . . . But however
it began, . . . we know that for some centuries the knowledge of music has flourished principally in Italy, the mother of learning and of arts; that poetry and
painting have been there restored, and so cultivated by Italian masters that all
Europe has been enriched out of their treasury; and the other parts of it, in relation to those delightful arts, are still as much provincial to Italy as they were
in the time of the Roman Empire. Their first operas seem to have been intended
for the celebration of the marriages of their princes, or for the magnificence of
some general time of joy. Accordingly, the expenses of them were from the purse
of the sovereign, or of the republic, as they are still practised at Venice, Rome,
and other places, at their carnivals. Savoy and Florence have often used them in
their courts, at the weddings of their dukes; and at Turin particularly was performed [in 1585] the *Pastor Fido*, written by the famous [poet Battista] Guarini
[1538–1612], which is a pastoral opera [actually a play with music] made to sol-
emnize the marriage of the Duke of Savoy. The prologue of it has given the design to all the French, which is a compliment to the sovereign power by some
god or goddess: so that it looks no less than a kind of embassy from heaven to
earth. I said, in the beginning of this preface, that the persons represented in operas are generally gods, goddesses, and heroes descended from them, who are
supposed to be their peculiar care; which hinders not but that meaner persons
may sometimes gracefully be introduced, especially if they have relation to those
first times which poets call the Golden Age; wherein by reason of their innocence, those happy mortals were supposed to have had a more familiar inter-
course with superior beings; and therefore shepherds might reasonably be
admitted, as of all callings the most innocent, the most happy, and who, by reason of the spare time they had, in their almost idle employment, had most leisure
to make verses, and to be in love; without somewhat of which passion, no opera
can possibly subsist.

'Tis almost needless to speak of that noble language in which this musical
drama was first invented and performed. All who are conversant in the Italian

cannot but observe that it is the softest, the sweetest, the most harmonious, not only of any modern tongue, but even beyond any of the learned. It seems indeed to have been invented for the sake of poetry and music; the vowels are so abounding in all words, especially in terminations of them, that, excepting some few monosyllables, the whole language ends in them. Then the pronunciation is so manly, and so sonorous, that their very speaking has more of music in it than Dutch poetry and song. . . . This language has in a manner been refined and purified from the Gothic, ever since the time of Dante, which is above four hundred years ago; and the French, who now cast a longing eye to their country, are not less ambitious to possess their elegance in poetry and music: in both which they labour at impossibilities. 'Tis true, indeed, they have reformed their tongue, and brought both their prose and poetry to a standard; the sweetness, as well as the purity, is much improved by throwing off the unnecessary consonants which made their spelling tedious, and their pronunciation harsh. But, after all, nothing can be improved beyond its own species, or farther than its original nature will allow; as an ill voice, though ever so thoroughly instructed in the rules of music, can never be brought to sing harmoniously, nor many an honest critic ever arrive to be a good poet, so neither can the natural harshness of the French, or their perpetual ill accent, be ever refined into perfect harmony like the Italian. The English has yet more natural disadvantages than the French; our original Teutonic consisting most in monosyllables, and those encumbered with consonants, cannot possibly be freed from those inconveniences. The rest of our words, which are derived from the Latin chiefly, and the French, with some small sprinkling of Greek, Italian, and Spanish, are some relief in poetry, and help us to soften our uncouth numbers; which, together with our English genius, incomparably beyond the trifling of the French, in all the nobler parts of verse, will jointly give us the pre-eminence. But, on the other hand, the effeminacy of our pronunciation (a defect common to us, and the Danes), and our scarcity of female rhymes, have left the advantage of musical composition for songs, though not for recitative, to our neighbours.

Through these difficulties I have made a shift to struggle in my part of the performance of this opera; which, as mean as it is, deserves at least a pardon, because it has attempted a discovery beyond any former undertaker of our nation; only remember, that if there be no North-East Passage to be found, the fault is in nature, and not in me; . . . so I may thus far be positive, that if I have not succeeded as I desire, yet there is somewhat still remaining to satisfy the curiosity, or itch of sight and hearing. Yet I have no great reason to despair; for I may, without vanity, own some advantages which are not common to every writer; such as are the knowledge of the Italian and French language, and the being conversant with some of their best performances in this kind; which have furnished me with such a variety of measures, as have given the composer, Monsieur Grabut, what occasions he could wish to show his extraordinary talent in diversifying the recitative, the lyrical part, and the chorus. . . .

'Tis no easy matter in our language to make words so smooth, and numbers so harmonious, that they shall almost set themselves, and yet there are rules for this in nature, and as great a certainty of quantity in our syllables, as either in the Greek or Latin. But let poets and judges understand those first, and let them begin to study English. When they have chawed awhile upon these preliminaries, it may be they will scarce adventure to tax me with want of thought and elevation of fancy for this work; for they will soon be satisfied that those are not of the nature of this sort of writing. The necessity of double rhymes, and ordering of the words and numbers for the sweetness of the voice, are the main hinges on which an opera must move; and both of these are without the compass of any art to teach another to perform, unless nature in the first place has done her part, by enduing the poet with that nicety of hearing, that the discord of sounds in words shall as much offend him as a seventh in music would a good composer. I have therefore no need to make excuses for meanness of thought in many places. The Italians, with all the advantages of their language, are continually forced upon it; or rather affect it. The chief secret is in the choice of words; and by this choice I do not here mean elegancy of expression, but propriety of sound, to be varied according to the nature of the subject. . . .

The same reasons which depress thought in an opera have a stronger effect upon the words, especially in our language; . . . I am often forced to coin new words, revive some that are antiquated, and botch others; as if I had not served out my time in poetry, but was bound apprentice to some doggerel rhymer, who makes songs to tunes, and sings them for a livelihood. 'Tis true, I have not been often put to this drudgery; but where I have, the words will sufficiently show that I was then a slave to the composition, which I will never be again: for 'tis my part to invent, and the musician's to humour that invention. I may be counselled, and will always follow my friend's advice where I find it reasonable; but will never part with the power of the militia.

I am now to acquaint my reader with somewhat more particular concerning this opera, after having begged his pardon for so long a preface to so short a work. It was originally intended only for a prologue to a play of the nature of the *Tempest*; which is a tragedy mixed with opera, or a drama written in blank verse, adorned with scenes, machines, songs, and dances, so that the fable of it is all spoken and acted by the best of the comedians; the other part of the entertainment to be performed by the same singers and dancers who are introduced in this present opera. It cannot properly be called a play, because the action of it is supposed to be conducted sometimes by supernatural means, or magic; nor an opera, because the story of it is not sung. But more of this at its proper time. But some intervening accidents having hitherto deferred the performance of the main design, I proposed to the actors to turn the intended prologue into an entertainment by itself, as you now see it, by adding two acts more to what I had written. The subject of it is wholly allegorical; and the allegory itself so very obvious that it will no sooner be read than understood. 'Tis divided, according to the plain and natural method of every action, into three parts. For even Aristotle himself is contented to say simply that in all actions there is a beginning, a middle, and an end; after which model all the Spanish plays are built.

The description of the scenes and other decorations of the stage I had from Mr. Betterton, who has spared neither for industry, nor cost, to make this entertainment perfect nor for invention of the ornaments to beautify it.

To conclude, tho' the enemies of the composer are not few, and that there is a party formed against him of his own profession, I hope, and am persuaded, that this prejudice will turn in the end to his advantage. For the greatest part of an audience is always uninterested, though seldom knowing; and if the music be well composed, and well performed, they who find themselves pleased will be so wise as not be imposed upon, and fooled out of their satisfaction, The newness of the undertaking is all the hazard. When operas were first set up in France, they were not followed over eagerly; but they gained daily upon their hearers, till they grew to that height of reputation which they now enjoy. The English, I confess, are not altogether so musical as the French; and yet they have been pleased already with the *Tempest,* and some pieces that followed, which were neither much better written nor so well composed as this. If it finds encouragement, I dare promise myself to mend my hand by making a more pleasing fable. In the meantime, every loyal Englishman cannot but be satisfied with the moral of this, which so plainly represents the double restoration of his Sacred Majesty.

John Dryden, *Of Dramatic Poesy and Other Critical Essays,* ed. G. Watson, 2 vols. (London: Dent, 1962), 1:157–58, 2:34–42.

12

HANDEL'S *RINALDO* AT THE HAYMARKET THEATRE

Italian opera came to England in 1706 with Giovanni Bononcini's *Trionfo di Camilla* (Naples, 1696), translated into English and performed by an English cast at London's Drury Lane Theatre. Its success was immediate and lasting, but the next few attempts at opera in English were failures. It was not long before Italian singers infiltrated the English casts. *Camilla* in 1707 featured two Italians (one of them a castrato), who sang their parts in Italian while the others continued to sing theirs in English. "At length," wrote Joseph Addison in *The Spectator*, "the Audience grew tir'd of understanding Half the Opera, and therefore to ease themselves intirely of the Fatigue of Thinking, have so order'd it at Present that the whole Opera is perform'd in an unknown Tongue." This acerbic remark was prompted by the success of *Rinaldo*, Handel's first London opera, which was produced at the Queen's Theatre in the Haymarket on 24 February 1711 with an all-Italian cast. It was the first Italian opera written expressly for the London stage, and Nicolini (Nicolò Grimaldi), the great alto singer and remarkable actor, starred in the title role. Aaron Hill, who functioned briefly as the theater's manager, drafted the opera's scenario after Tasso's *Jerusalem Delivered*. He dedicated the libretto to Queen Anne and also wrote the preface. Giacomo Rossi, who provided the Italian versification of Hill's scenario, then addressed the reader, in the florid manner typical of Italian librettists of the period.

[HILL'S DEDICATION TO THE QUEEN]

Madam,

Among the numerous Arts and Sciences, which now distinguish the Best of Nations under the Best of Queens; Musick, the most engaging of the Train, appears in Charms we never saw her wear till lately; when the Universal Glory of your Majesty's Illustrious Name drew hither the most celebrated Masters from every part of *Europe*.

In this Capacity for Flourishing, 'twere a publick Misfortune, shou'd OPERA's for want of due Encouragement, grow faint and languish: My little Fortune and my Application stand devoted to a Trial, whether such a noble Entertainment, in its due Magnificence, can fail of living, in a City, the most capable of *Europe*, both to relish and support it.

Madam,

This OPERA is a Native of your Majesty's Dominions, and was consequently born your Subject: 'Tis thence that it presumes to come, a dutiful Entreater of your Royal Favour and Protection; a Blessing, which having once obtain'd, it cannot miss the Clemency of every Air it may hereafter breathe in. Nor shall I then be longer doubtful of succeeding in my Endeavour, to see the *English* OPERA more splendid than her MOTHER, the *Italian*.

[HILL'S PREFACE]

When I ventur'd on an Undertaking so hazardous as the Direction of OPERA'S in their present Establishment, I resolv'd to spare no Pains or Cost, that might be requisite to make those Entertainments flourish in their proper Grandeur, that so at least it might not be my Fault, if the Town should hereafter miss so noble a Diversion.

The Deficiencies I found, or thought I found, in such *Italian* OPERA'S as have hitherto been introduc'd among us, were, *First*, That they had been compos'd for Tastes and Voices, different from those who were to sing and hear them on the *English* Stage; And *Secondly*, That wanting the Machines and Decorations, which bestow so great a Beauty on their Appearance, they have been heard and seen to very considerable Disadvantage.

At once to remedy both these Misfortunes, I resolv'd to frame some Dramma, that, by different Incidents and Passions, might afford the Musick Scope to vary and display its Excellence, and fill the Eye with more delightful Prospects, so at once to give Two Senses equal Pleasure.

I could not chuse a finer Subject than the celebrated Story of *Rinaldo* and *Armida*, which has furnish'd OPERA'S for every Stage and Tongue in *Europe*. I have, however, us'd a Poet's Privilege, and vary'd from the Scheme of Tasso, as was necessary for the better forming a Theatrical Representation.

It was a very particular Happiness, that I met with a Gentleman so excellently qualify'd as Signor *Rossi*, to fill up the Model I had drawn, with Words so sounding and so rich in Sense, that if my Translation is in many Places led to deviate, 'tis for want of Power to reach the Force of his Original.

Mr. *Hendel*, whom the World so justly celebrates, has made his Musick speak so finely for its self, that I am purposely silent on that Subject; and shall only add, That as when I undertook this Affair, I had no Gain in View, but That of the Acknowledgement and Approbation of the Gentlemen of my Country; so No Loss, the Loss of That excepted, shall discourage me from a Pursuit of all Improvements, which can possibly be introduc'd upon our *English* Theatre.

THE POET TO THE READER

Behold, gentle Reader, the Birth of a few Evenings, which, though it be the offspring of the Night, is not the abortive of Darkness, but will make itself known to be the Son of *Apollo*, with a certain ray of *Parnassus*. The Haste in bringing it to Light was due to an attempt to satisfy the Nobility with uncommon Things; and a virtuous Urge prevailed within me (not indeed with regard to the Perfection of the Opera but only to the Brevity of the Time), for Mr. *Hendel*, the *Orpheus* of our Century, in setting it to Music, scarcely gave me the Time to write, and to my great Astonishment I saw an entire Opera put to music by that sublime Genius in only two Weeks, and to the highest Degree of Perfection. Welcome, I beg of you, discerning Reader, this hasty Task of mine, and if it does not deserve your Praise, at least do not deprive it of your Indulgence, which I should rather call Justice, given the Limitation of Time. And if some are not pleased, I regret it; but let them consider that their Disgust will arise from themselves and not from my Composition, which, finally, is prompted by the Willingness with which it respects every Person and can satisfy each one.

Facsimile of the original libretto in Ellen T. Harris, ed., *The Librettos of Handel's Operas* (New York: Garland Publishing, 1989), 2:3–10. ("The Poet to the Reader": the first sentence trans. Addison [see below], the rest trans. P.W.)

Having emphasized the absurdity of singing opera "in an unknown Tongue," Joseph Addison, and now Sir Richard Steele (his coeditor on *The Spectator*), turned their attention to some of the absurdities in the staging of opera as observed in *Rinaldo*. So famous were their articles that as late as 1789 Charles Burney, though ready to "laugh at them as heartily as anyone," felt compelled to remind readers of his *General History of Music* that Steele had been an investor in one of the theaters that suffered from *Rinaldo*'s success, and that Addison was "still bleeding for [the] fate" of his libretto *Rosamond*, which had failed miserably at the Drury Lane Theatre four years earlier. Whether or not motivated by rancor or self-interest, the articles remain classics in the long history of operatic satire.

Tuesday, March 6, 1711

Spectatum admissi, risum teneatis? . . .
[Admitted to the sight, would you not laugh?—Horace, *Ars Poetica*, 5.]

An Opera may be allowed to be extravagantly lavish in its Decorations, as its only Design is to gratify the Senses, and keep up an indolent Attention in the Audience. Common Sense however requires, that there should be nothing in the Scenes and Machines, which may appear Childish and Absurd. How would the Wits of King *Charles's* Time have laughed, to have seen *Nicolini* exposed to a Tempest in Robes of Ermin, and sailing in an open Boat upon a Sea of Paste-Board? What a Field of Raillery would they have been let into, had they been entertain'd with painted Dragons spitting Wild-Fire, enchanted Chariots drawn by *Flanders* mares, and real Cascades in artificial Land-skips? A little Skill in Criticism would inform us, that Shadows and Realities ought not to be mix'd together in the same Piece; and that Scenes, which are designed as the Representations of Nature, should be filled with Resemblances, and not with the Things themselves. If one would represent a wide Champian Country [a wide country-

Perſons Repreſented.

M E N.

Goffredo, Godfrey *Duke of* Bul-
loigne, *Genèral of the* Eu-
ropèan *Forces in the great*
Expedition againſt the Sara-
cens.
}
Signora Fran-
cifca Vanini
Bofchi.

Euſtacio, *His Brother.*
}
Signor Valen-
tino Urbani.

Rinaldo, *A celebrated* Chriſtian
Hero of the Houſe of Eſte.
}
Signor Cava-
lier Nicoli-
no Grimaldi.

Argantes, *King of* Jeruſa-
lem,
}
Signor Gio-
feppe Bofchi.

The Magician.
}
Signor Giu-
feppe Caffani

The Herald.   *Mr.* Laurence.

W O M E N.

Armida, *A Queen of the* Ama-
zons *and a famous* Enchantreſs,
come to the Aſſiſtance of Argantes.
}
Signora Eliza-
betta Pilotta
Schiavonetti.

Almirena, *Daughter to Duke*
Godfrey.
}
Mademoiſelle
Ifabella Gi-
rardeau.

Mermaids, Spirits, Furies, Officers,
Guards, *and* Attendants.

RINALDO.

side] filled with Herds and Flocks, it would be ridiculous to draw the Country only upon the Scenes, and to crowd several Parts of the Stage with Sheep and Oxen. This is joining together Inconsistencies, and making the Decoration partly Real, and partly Imaginary. I would recommend what I have here said to the Directors, as well as to the Admirers, of our Modern Opera.

As I was walking in the Streets about a Fortnight ago, I saw an ordinary Fellow carrying a Cage full of little Birds upon his Shoulder; and as I was wondering with myself what Use he would put them to, he was met very luckily by an Acquaintance, who had the same Curiosity. Upon his asking what he had upon his Shoulder, he told him that he had been buying Sparrows for the Opera. Sparrows for the Opera, says his Friend, licking his Lips, what are they to be roasted? No, no, says the other, they are to enter towards the end of the first Act, and to fly about the Stage.

This strange Dialogue awakened my Curiosity so far, that I immediately bought the Opera [libretto], by which means I perceived that the Sparrows were to act the part of Singing Birds in a delightful Grove; though upon a nearer Enquiry I found the Sparrows put the same Trick upon the Audience, that Sir *Martin Mar-all* practised upon his Mistress [in a Dryden comedy]; for, though they flew in Sight, the Musick proceeded from a Consort of Flagellets and Bird-calls, which was planted behind the Scenes. At the same time I made this Discovery, I found by the discourse of the Actors, that there were great Designs on foot for the Improvement of the Opera; that it had been proposed to break down a part of the Wall, and to surprize the Audience with a Party of an hundred Horse, and that there was actually a Project of bringing the *New-River* into the House, to be employed in Jetteaus and Water-works. This Project, as I have since heard, is post-poned till the Summer-Season; when it is thought the Coolness that proceeds from Fountains and Cascades will be more acceptable and refreshing to People of Quality. In the mean time, to find out a more agreeable Entertainment for the Winter-Season, the Opera of *Rinaldo* is filled with Thunder and Lightning, Illuminations, and Fireworks; which the Audience may look upon without catching Cold, and indeed without much Danger of being burnt; for there are several Engines filled with Water, and ready to play at a Minute's Warning, in case any such Accident should happen. However, as I have a very great Friendship for the Owner of this Theatre, I hope that he has been wise enough to *insure* his House before he would let this Opera be acted in it.

It is no Wonder, that those Scenes should be very surprising, which were contrived by two Poets of different Nations, and raised by two Magicians of different Sexes. *Armida* (as we are told in the Argument) was an *Amazonian* Enchantress, and poor Signior Cassani (as we learn from the *Persons represented*) a Christian Conjuror (*Mago Christiano*). I must confess I am very much puzzled to find how an *Amazon* should be versed in the Black Art, or how a good Christian, for such is the Part of the Magician, should deal with the Devil. . . .

To consider the Poet after the Conjurors, I shall give you a Taste of the *Italian* from the first Lines of the Preface: *Eccoti, benigno Lettore, un Parto di poche*

Sere, che se ben nato di Notte, non è però aborto di Tenebre, ma si farà conoscere Figlio d'Apollo con qualche Raggio di Parnasso. Behold. *gentle Reader, the Birth of a few Evenings, which, tho' it be the Offspring of the Night, is not the Abortive of Darkness, but will make itself known to be the Son of* Apollo, *with a certain Ray of* Parnassus. He afterwards proceeds to call Minheer *Hendel* the *Orpheus* of our Age, and to acquaint us, in the same Sublimity of Stile, that he composed this Opera in a Fortnight. Such are the Wits, to whose Tastes we so ambitiously conform our selves. . . .

But to return to the Sparrows: there have been so many Flights of them let loose in this Opera, that it is feared the House will never get rid of them; and that in other Plays they may make their Entrance in very wrong and improper Scenes, so as to be seen flying in a Lady's Bed-Chamber, or perching upon a King's Throne; besides the Inconveniencies which the Heads of the Audience may sometimes suffer from them. . . .

Before I dismiss this Paper, I must inform my Reader, that I hear there is a Treaty on foot with [the Queen's gardeners] *London* and *Wise* (who will be appointed Gardiners of the Play-House) to furnish the Opera of *Rinaldo* and *Armida* with an Orange-Grove: and that the next time it is Acted, the Singing Birds will be personated by Tom-Tits: The Undertakers being resolved to spare neither Pains nor Mony, for the Gratification of the Audience.

C [Addison]

Friday, March 16, 1711

. . . I am very glad the following Epistle obliges me to mention Mr. *Powell* [the puppeteer] . . . ; for indeed there cannot be too great Encouragement given to his Skill in Motions [puppet shows], provided he is under proper Restrictions.

"*SIR*,

The Opera at the *Hay-Market*, and that under the little *Piazza* in *Covent-Garden*, being at present the Two leading Diversions of the Town; and Mr. *Powell* professing in his Advertisements to set up *Whittington and his Cat* against *Rinaldo and Armida*, my Curiosity led me the Beginning of last Week to view both these Performances, and make my Observations upon them.

"First therefore, I cannot but observe that Mr. *Powell* wisely forbearing to give his Company a Bill of Fare [a program] before-hand, every Scene is new and unexpected; whereas it is certain, that the Undertakers of the *Hay-Market*, having raised too great an Expectation in their printed Opera [libretto], very much disappoint their Audience on the Stage.

"The King of *Jerusalem* is obliged to come from the City on foot, instead of being drawn in a triumphant Chariot by white Horses, as my Opera-Book had promised me; and thus while I expected *Armida's* Dragons should rush forward towards *Argantes*, I found the Hero was obliged to go to *Armida*, and hand her out of her Coach. We had also but a very short Allowance of Thunder and Lightning; tho' I cannot in this Place omit doing Justice to the Boy who had the Direction of the Two painted Dragons, and made them spit Fire and Smoke: he flash'd out his Rosin [candle] in such just Proportions and in such due Time, that I could not forbear conceiving Hopes of his being one Day a most excellent Player. I saw indeed but Two things wanting to render his whole Action compleat, I mean the keeping his Head a little lower, and hiding his Candle.

"I observe that Mr. *Powell* and the Undertakers had both the same Thought, and I think, much about the same time, of introducing Animals on their several Stages, tho' indeed with very different Success. The Sparrows and Chaffinches at the *Hay-Market* fly as yet very irregularly over the Stage; and instead of perching on the Trees and performing their Parts, these young Actors either get into the Galleries or put out the Candles; whereas Mr. *Powell* has so well discipilin'd his Pig, that in the first scene he and Punch dance a Minuet together. I am informed however, that Mr. *Powell* resolves to excell his Adversaries in their own Way; and introduce Larks in his next Opera of *Susanna* or *Innocence betrayed*, which will be exhibited next Week with a Pair of new Elders. . . .

"As for the Mechanism and Scenary, every thing indeed was uniform and of a Piece, and the Scenes were managed very dexterously; which calls on me to take Notice, that at the *Hay-Market* the Undertakers forgetting to change their Side-Scenes, we were presented with a Prospect of the Ocean in the midst of a delightful Grove; and tho' the Gentlemen on the Stage had very much contributed to the Beauty of the Grove by walking up and down between the Trees, I must own I was not a little astonish'd to see a well-dress'd young Fellow in a full-bottom'd Wigg, appear in the Midst of the Sea, and without any visible Concern taking Snuff.

"I shall only observe one thing further, in which both Dramas agree, which is, that by the Squeak of their Voices the Heroes of each are Eunuchs; and as the Wit in both Pieces are equal, I must prefer the Performance of Mr. *Powell*, because it is in our own Language.

I am, &c."[1]
R [Steele]

The Spectator, ed. Donald F. Bond (Oxford: Clarendon Press, 1965), 1:22–27, 63–65.

---

[1]*ADVERTISEMENT. On the first of April will be performed at the Play-house in the Hay-market an Opera call'd* The Cruelty of Atreus. N.B. *The Scene wherein* Thyestes *eats his own Children, is to be performed by the famous Mr.* Psalmanazar, *lately arrived from* Formosa: *The whole Supper being set to Kettle-drums.*

13

PIER JACOPO MARTELLO ON OPERA (1715)

Literary criticism in Italy around 1700 was very much preoccupied with the dominance of French culture in Europe and the consequent waning of Italian prestige. Gone were the days when Italian literature was held up everywhere as a model to be imitated. Instead, Italy for a century had been in the grips of a literary decadence that soon would acquire the derogatory name of *secentismo*, "seventeenth-century-ism." Its poetry, ornate and mannered, was hardly exportable anymore. Instead, the main export item now was opera, and this, if anything, only held Italy up to further ridicule (see Saint-Évremond, p. 51ff above). It was in this atmosphere that the Arcadian Academy was founded in Rome in 1690. An institution whose goal was the purification of Italian literature in all its forms, including, very importantly, tragedy (a genre in which France had recently offered the world supreme examples), the Academy soon turned its attention to opera. The Arcadians felt (quite rightly too) that opera had usurped the Italian stage, bringing about the decline of "legitimate" theater in Italy. Some writers wished to abolish opera altogether, as a degrading, "venal" spectacle. Pier Jacopo Martello (1665–1727), who helped found an Arcadian "colony" in his native Bologna, was more reasonable: he belonged to those who merely sought to reform opera. He had in fact written several librettos himself, as well as "legitimate" tragedies; and when he came to formulate his thoughts on tragedy in a treatise entitled *Della tragedia antica e moderna* (*On Ancient and Modern Tragedy*), he included in its second edition (1715) an entire section on opera. The premise of the treatise is this: on his way to France, Martello has met a stranger who, upon further acquaintance, turns out to be none other than Aristotle himself, the founder of tragic theory, miraculously come back to life. What follows, then, is a series of dialogues, carried on mostly in Paris and environs, between Martello and this latter-day philosopher, who reinterprets the classical "rules" of tragedy, adapting them quite sensibly to eighteenth-century conditions. With a light touch, pseudo-Aristotle teaches his disciple how to write a libretto. He dismisses the notion that such a work might be considered poetry in any serious way and instead gives him a down-to-earth, mildly satirical account of all the components of Italian opera that need to be taken into consideration by the would-be librettist. Of special interest is the discussion of recitative, aria (here called *can-*

zonetta or *arietta*), and da capo form. Martello's rationalistic breakdown of opera into its components set an example for much of the writing about opera, both serious and satirical, later in the century.

You have (began the impostor) enjoyed [the French opera] *Médée*, which you will agree may be termed a tragedy in that it is a dramatic imitation of better people; yet it differs, as do your [Italian] operas, from ancient tragedy, since in the latter only a part was sung, while in this all is sung. And, on this head, we may applaud Saint-Évremond's dictum: "The Greeks made beautiful tragedies in which some parts were sung; the French make bad ones in which everything is sung." But what he says about his compatriots you might as well extend to yours because, to tell the truth, the greater part of those I have heard in Venice, Genoa, Milan, Reggio, and Bologna (though it is your city) are of that sort.

You do well (I answered) to say "the greater part," and there I agree with you. But surely you will not include [among the bad tragedies] those of the severe Moniglia or the elegant Lemene [and other Arcadian poets].

I consent (he replied). Nevertheless I am sorry indeed that those otherwise distinguished and spiritual poets should have so ill employed their talent in a sort of composition that can never survive or keep their names alive; for if their dramas are ever sung again on the stage, they will be deformed anew each time, owing to the unbridled passion for novel ariettas; and if they are not sung again, why, then, behold them sunk in a deep and fatal lethargy, and already buried!

To this I answered: You are quite right in deploring the fate of those worthy minds that have got entangled in this kind of drama. And I, who have produced some myself, have had reason to curse the time I spent writing them. I have seen the most brilliant, lovely things—the things a poet is proudest of— turn out insipidly when set to music, detested by our emasculated vocalists and by the ladies who, to our shame, are called "virtuous" [*virtuose*]; while on the other hand the poem's most unfortunate passages . . . I have seen relished, welcomed, and acclaimed not only by the audience but by the singers. . . . And often what pleased me in reading has displeased me when sung, despite the promptings of reason and sentiment.

Here my companion smiled and said: That was bound to happen, because a mediocre poem that spreads easy sentiments and affections in fluent, intelligible recitatives and lilting, natural ariettas gives the composer greater freedom to roam at will and give vent to his inspiration; which, the less it is cramped by concentrated sentiment, the nimbler it will be and the readier to stimulate by way of the ear the spirits of the listener, thus with sweet harmony delighting him and moving him to applause. This type of entertainment, then, is such that it can lift people's spirits above all cares and absorb them in restful forgetfulness, making them content; and coming away from the music and the spectacle, they feel stronger and fitter for all human endeavors. Therefore, both physically and morally, this is as useful to the State as are satyr plays, comedies, and tragedies. But we must take it as a fundamental truth that in this charming entertainment music must not be denied pride of place: for she is its soul, and to her must defer all who are called upon to collaborate, whether with poetry or with furnishings.

I will not give you a music lesson, for I might not succeed too well; or if I did, I might need to use terms obscure both in themselves and quite possibly to their inventors. I will merely say this: that if ever you hear men deplore the loss of ancient music, you must on my behalf tell those worshipers of antiquity that they are humbugs. You may judge of the music of the Hebrews and other Orientals by their instruments, which were horns, kettledrums, and trumpets. The cither too, and the harp, the lyre, and the tibia were their ears' delight, as they were all of Greece's. Having heard nothing better they must have found excellent what in fact was wretched compared with today's musical perfection, accompanied by the subtle refinement of the many well-tuned instruments that enrich and fill the modern orchestra.

Let us too, out of respect for our present surroundings, avoid comparing French and Italian music. Each has its points; each its devotees. I will only say (but confidentially) that I have seen these Frenchmen rejoice when an arietta to Italian poetry and in the Italian style has been introduced into their recitations; which, to be sure, proves little, for I have seen the Italians exult as much when a French song was inserted in their operas. But this at least is certain: German as well as English ears prefer Italian music, and those nations spend heavy sums to pay for its best practitioners; and I, a Greek, find it hard not to agree with their opinion.

Well, we are embarked. Let us see whether we can spy a safe harbor in these waters, which are new to me. I shall inquire, then, whether in order to delight, opera must have the help of words and poetry: and I will frankly declare it does not. . . . But see how insatiable we are, especially when wallowing in pleasure! Knowing that birds can whistle and instruments sound, but that man alone can reason, we insist that to the sweetness of human song be added the sweetness of words to tell us of the inner motions of the soul; so that here is one more delight come to assist our entertainment, and here, finally, we come to the poetry. But poor poetry cuts quite another figure here than she does in tragedy and comedy. In those she has the principal place, in opera the lowest. . . . We have need, then, not of poets, but rather of verse-mongers: but no, not verse-mongers either, for there must be a plot, and that calls for something more than a verse-monger. Not mere verse-mongers, then, nor true poets; I am at a loss what to call those who must serve the needs of opera. . . .

The scenery must be various and imposing. Not too many forests, for gnarled tree-trunks and leafy branches are not subjects for the theater painter; and trees usually look crude and disagreeable in the candlelight. Much architecture, from various angles, and let it display width and depth far beyond reality. Gardens with real fountains contrived ingeniously onstage. A view of the sea, with frothy waves twisting and turning. And let us not forget some Gothic shrine, or perhaps a dungeon built of rustic masonry. For these are favorite scenic subjects.

Let the castratos be chosen not only for their nimble and excellent voices but for their presence, which must be elegant, not uncouth. Let the ladies be attractive and, above all, have a pleasing posture and move gracefully. Let the costumes be bejeweled and embroidered with sham gold and silver, and cut for the most part in the royal fashion. Let the voices be of such quality and number that the composer can interweave them to their individual advantage. If we heed these injunctions we shall already be able to insure a profit for the impresarios or underwriters of the operas. . . .

Since you ask me to present you with some rules for a type of composition which, in order to be pleasing, should be devoid of rules, I will mention some to you, and they shall be based on observation and experience rather than reason; and to satisfy you I will try to combine the tasks of sponsor, composer, singer, and poet, forgetting that I am a philosopher. Well then, if ever the ridiculous notion should cross your mind of agreeing to write an opera, you must first pick the plot, examine the theater's capacity, the fame of the composer, and how many and what singers the impresario has engaged. And because the poet must look to the expense too, let him find out the impresario's intentions on that score: that is, how many scenes he intends to commission from the painter; whether he will order machines from the engineer; and what costumes his wardrobe disposes of. If the theater is too small; if the undertaker is miserly and wishes to present the public with an opera containing little in the way of glitter, properties, changes of scenery; if he lacks a good painter; if he won't hear of an architect and a machinist; if he has not engaged mostly famous voices and an able orchestra; if he is horrified at the prospect of regal, showy costumes: then do not involve yourself in the opera, or you will quite lose your reputation as a poet and, though you helped him, will have him for an enemy far more than if you had turned him down under such unfavorable circumstances. On the other hand, if the impresario is less economical, though he may not be lavish; if the theater is sufficiently capacious; if the composer belongs to the better class and is tractable, like your excellent Bononcini; if some of the singers who have been engaged are well known; if the orchestra is to be copious and expert; if an able painter is to provide a suitable number of scenes; if the costumes are at least well preserved and showy; then, even if a machinist is not wanted, you may boldly undertake to write your opera—on condition, though, that the impresario will compensate you for the lack of machines by inserting some graceful ballets between your acts; and consider yourself fortunate if you should happen upon a French dancer, though he be but one of the lesser lights in this nation of dancers.

These conditions being fulfilled, you shall take care to choose a fabulous story composed of a mixture of gods and heroes or a true history of heroes as the foundation of your plot; and let it include such events as can easily be presented in your theater and such characters as can be matched with the voices at your disposal; and having shown it to the impresario and the composer, first obtain their approval and, once you have it, immediately go to work. Custom requires that your opera be divided in three acts; for were you to partition it in five, you might make people think you meant to give them a tragedy, and you would foolishly bind yourself to rules it would be quite impossible for you to observe. . . .

At the opening of your fable, see to it that the stage is furnished with characters involved in some event of consequence arousing expectation and wonder. Forget the modest principles of tragedy and epic; and imprint it on your mind that, at the rise of the curtain, the public will grow cool if it is shown two characters discoursing gravely about their private affairs. You need an abundance, if not of characters, then of supers. A coming ashore, a moresco, an exhibition of fighters or other such thing will make your spectators stare, and they will bless the money they left at the door.

In the second act you must consider the development of both the plot and the passions. Slight misunderstandings, changes of costume, written messages, portraits (all devices so looked down on by tragedians) should be held high in the esteem of your authors of operas; thus, having dropped the strict verisimilitude of Greek, French, and, yes, Italian tragedy, you will boldly appropriate the ingenious complications of the Spaniards. I do not mean by this that you are to drop all verisimilitude from your incidents, but let this precious verisimilitude of yours not prevent you from preferring the marvelous. Let the means by which the events take place lack verisimilitude, too, if you like; but then let the events themselves be plausible, and you will provoke the astonishment and applause of your audience. Let the passions be various and opposed. If possible let hatred be opposed by love, love by hatred. Anger, too, must play a part. But the amorous passion must triumph over all: let the others merely serve to bring love to the fore, which, being common to all mankind, is seen with the greatest pleasure. True, you must cherish honesty for the good of the State; but that being preserved, the amorous affection is of the greatest utility to the citizenry, urging it into legitimate unions, whence spring the benefits of a growing population, the very soul of states.

In the third act you must consider the dénouement, or resolution, which may even be brought about by the machine, if the impresario will have one; and certainly its marvelous appearance will make it most welcome, even if the complication may possibly not have been worth troubling a Divinity to descend from heaven to untangle it. Let there be recognitions and reversals of fortune. In recognitions let us be easily deceived by a sudden costume change; by certain objects found in the cradle of a character when he was an infant, now brought onstage or described in order to identify him. But as for reversals, you had better show than narrate them; for that which strikes the senses pleases the public better.

They have come to see, not to think. Let the reversals always be from bad fortune to good, and there let the opera end by means of wedding festivities; and in this dénouement let the poet resolve, for the good of the State, that the virtuous shall be rewarded with happiness, the vicious severely punished, though not with death: for deaths are out of place in these entertainments, which are meant to cheer, not dishearten the audience.

Having disposed of the economy of the plot by measuring it off into acts, you must next think of dividing each act into scenes; and this will not be the least of your labors. First you will need to know how many principal singers you are to have, in order that you may give each one an equal share in the action; else what endless squabbling between those fearless maidens and those bold castratos! You must also consider their voices and alternate them so they will favor rather than hinder the intentions of the composer. But before you cut the cloth of the acts into scenes, I exhort you to show it all to the composer and ask him which voice, in his judgment, you should place at the beginning, middle, and end of each act. You must however stipulate (he won't object) that each act shall contain one *scena di forza,* so called because of some violent or unusual opposition of contrary passions or some untoward event unexpected by the audience. Thus laid out, the opera, I warrant, will be successful; and now you will have nothing left to do but cast your drama into verse.

It must be made up entirely of recitative and ariettas, or canzonettas, as they are called. Every scene must contain either recitative, or an arietta, or (the usual case) both one and the other. Anything in the way of narration or unimpassioned expression should be expressed in recitative verse. But whatever is motivated by passion or somehow reflects greater vehemence tends towards the canzonetta. The recitative we prefer to have short enough so that it will not put us to sleep with its tedium, and long enough so that we will understand what is happening. Its sentences and syntax must be easy, and compact rather than extended; this will make it more useful for the composer, the singer, and the listener: for the composer, because he will then be able to enliven the recitative, a dead thing in itself, with a variety of cadences; for the singer, since he will thus be able to catch his breath when he sings it and renew his vocal powers at the rests; and for the listener (unaccustomed as he is to the changes wrought by music in the ordinary sound of words) because he will have to strain less than if the meaning had to be wrested from a tangle of inverted sentences. The recitative must be contained in verses of seven and eleven syllables, alternated and mixed as seems best; and if the cadences, at least, are rhymed, that will only enhance the charm of the music. What I have said regarding the brevity of recitatives must suffer some qualification in the scenes I have termed *scene di forza:* for here the recitative must predominate at the expense of the ariettas, since it is better able to convey the pulse of the action and place it in the foreground. And here the poet may vent himself somewhat and offer a modest sample of his talent; a prudent composer will allow it; nor will the singers, experts at staging, refuse him; and the impresario will be obliged to like it.

Canzonettas are either simple or compound. We shall call them simple when they are sung by one voice only, compound when sung by two or more voices. Those sung by two voices we will call duets; those sung by more may be termed choruses. Of the simple arias, we shall call some entrances, others exits, and others intermediate. From these expressions their use can be deduced. Entrances are used when a character enters upon the stage, and these tend to be acceptable in soliloquies; and the apostrophizing [rhetorical] figure is of their very essence. But of these you shall make sparing use. The same caution is advisable for the intermediate [arias]; for they have a chilling effect when, in mid-scene, mute actors are obliged to stand about and listen while another actor sings away at his leisure. Here, therefore, we should have some accompanying action, so that the others may at least be given something to do and not stand idle; in that case these [arias] will produce an excellent effect. . . . Exit arias must close every scene, and no singer may exit without first warbling a canzonetta. Whether 'tis verisimilar does not matter. It is much too pleasant to hear a scene end with spirit and vivacity. Mind, however, that when you end a scene with an exit aria you do not begin the very next one with an entrance aria. That would rob the music of its chiaroscuro. The instrumental ritornelli would tumble over each other and instead of helping would hinder the effect. Hence it is that entrance arias usually make their best effect at the beginning of an act.

Duets are heard with pleasure in mid-scene because they afford action to more than one actor; but I should also like to see a duet at the end of the second act. Choruses at the end of the last act are inescapable, since the public enjoys hearing the combination of all the voices it applauded singly in the course of the opera; and the noise made by the singers and instruments causes everyone to rise and leave replete and elated with the music they have heard, and wishing to come back for more.

These ariettas or canzonettas must be so distributed that the singers with the highest standing are given an equal number, for the singers' professional jealousy is unbending and exact; and for that matter it is useful to the production of the drama that the best voices should be displayed equally to the audience. . . .

Be sure to keep in mind that every aria must have its refrain [*intercalare*]. Refrain is what the professionals call the first part of an aria that is repeated later by the singer; since it is here that the composer displays the full glitter of his musical art, he takes pleasure in its being repeated. The singers take pleasure in it too, as does the public; and therefore you must take care, if the first part is in eight-syllable meter, not to let it exceed three lines; and if in four-syllable, not four. And let this rule be inviolable in the other canzonettas, in accordance with the length or brevity of the verses. . . .

We must still treat of the style best suited to opera. I believe this type of composition, such as it is, calls for moderation and charm rather than gravity and magnificence: music, an art invented to delight and lift the spirits, needs to be buttressed by words and sentiments clothed in delightfulness. . . . Let me repeat, therefore, that your syntax must be easy, your sentences clear and not long, the words plain and attractive, the rhymes not insipid, the verses fluent and sweetly sonorous. In the arias I advise you to use similes involving little butterflies, little ships, a little bird, a little brook: these things all lead the imagination to I know not what pleasant realms of thought and so refresh it; and just as those objects are charming, so too are the words that conjure them up and portray them to our fancy; and the composer always soars in them with his loveliest notes; and you will have noticed that even in the worst operas singers win particular applause with such arias, to which the diminutives (so hateful to the French language and temperament) add much grace. Fix it in your mind too that the more general the sentiments in an aria, the more pleasing they will be to the public; for, finding them verisimilar or true, they store them up to make honest use of them with their ladies and to sing them as daily occasions arise between lovers for jealousy, indignation, mutual promises, absences, and the like; and this will also be most convenient for you, since poets find it much easier to deal with generalities, and can fill their poetic wardrobes with them while out walking, and later use them to dress up the recitatives of operas. . . .

The profession of writing operas (my dear Martello) is a school of morals which, better than any other, teaches poets how to conquer themselves and renounce their own wishes. Be prepared cheerfully to change tolerable arias into bad ones if a singer or songstress should wish to tag onto your recitative something that earned them applause in Milan, Venice, Genoa, or elsewhere; and if its sentiment is the very opposite of what you had at that point—what then? Let them have their way, or they will swarm all over you and pierce your ear with soprano and contralto rebukes. . . . Still, if the impresario who is to pay you for your labors (don't blush, for this is the only kind of poetry meant to be written for pay) asks you to write new words, why then write them; and offer Heaven your long-suffering patience in exchange for any sins you might have committed in the past, such as desecrating a temple. You wished to have Aristotle's *Poetics* on opera? There you have it. Are you satisfied? . . .

Music alone contains the all-important secret of separating the soul from all mortal cares for at least as long as the notes can keep it absorbed, through the skillful management of consonance, whether vocal or instrumental. And if sleep is so universally praised for its power to enthrall the senses of unhappy humanity, lifting them up and, for a few hours, making them impervious to misfortune, how much more praiseworthy must an art be which, not robbing us of life as does sleep (whence it is called the Brother of Death), allows us to live ecstatically in delicious, contented peace, our senses fully about us, yet glad and truly blissful. This art, then, brought to such exquisite perfection in Italy, deserves to be the means of Italy's favorite, most lavish spectacle, one which even the loftiest brows attend with blameless alacrity; deserves, too, that foreign nations should take delight in it, as being a thing which so justly delights Italy; deserves to have voices, instruments, poetry, painting, architecture, mechanics, mimic, and any other art pay court to it and obey it. Deserves, finally, that you exclude the operatic poems from the printed collection of your theatrical works, for you should be doing music an injustice by separating a mere accessory from it, while you should reap your punishment in being mocked by your readers.

Piero Weiss, "Pier Jacopo Martello on Opera (1715): An Annotated Translation," *The Musical Quarterly* 66 (1980): 378–403.

14

THE PRÉSIDENT DE BROSSES IN ITALY (1739)

Charles de Brosses (1709–77) was not yet *Président,* that is, chief magistrate of Burgundy's supreme court, when at the age of thirty he undertook the Grand Voyage to Italy in the company of five equally cultivated friends. The journey lasted from May 1739 to April 1740 and took the friends from Dijon to the south of France, across northern Italy, down through Tuscany to Rome and Naples, then back north by a different route. Brosses wrote letters home describing everything he saw—and heard; for he was exceptionally well prepared to describe not only the artistic and architectural wonders of Italy but its music too. These letters, fifty-eight in all, were read avidly in France, where they circulated in manuscript form. In later years Brosses revised them, adding further memories; but they were not published until long after his death, in 1799. A more complete edition appeared in 1836, winning the enthusiastic approval of Stendhal, who promptly placed Brosses at the top of his list of favorites, "after Mozart and Cimarosa." The lengthy letter on Italian opera (no. 51) from which the following extracts are taken was originally dated from Rome, 2 December 1739, but was doubtless revised and enlarged a few years later. In it, Brosses reveals himself as not only witty and well informed but also fairly accurate with the facts. One of his chief concerns, as might be expected, is to contribute his own observations to the ongoing debate on the relative merits of Italian and French opera, a theme he returns to repeatedly. He shows great enthusiasm for the most recent generation of Italian composers, among them Niccolò Jommelli (1714–74), Leonardo Vinci (c. 1696–1730), and Giovanni Battista Pergolesi (1710–36). He devotes much, and well-deserved, attention to Italy's foremost dramatic poet, Pietro Metastasio (1698–1782), whose dramas were in fact opera librettos, which, as Brosses notes, were set over and over again by every composer of the period. Of interest is Brosses's description of instrumental and vocal crescendos and diminuendos, apparently common then in Italy if not in France. He joins his contemporaries in making fun of castratos, while at the same time admiring their vocal accomplishments. And he shows his "modern" taste in his enthusiasm for the new comic opera style, both in full-length *opere buffe* and between-the-acts intermezzos. It is no accident that we note in this letter an early use of the word "baroque" (in connection with the recitative); it was when people started using it that the period which we call by that name came to an end.

The number and size of the theaters in Italy are a fair mark of that nation's taste for this sort of entertainment. Ordinary cities here have better theaters than those in Paris. In big cities like Milan, Naples, Rome, etc. they are absolutely vast and magnificent, displaying fine, noble, richly ornamented architecture.

The royal theater in Naples is of a prodigious size, with seven ranks of loges served by corridors and a deep, spacious stage, fit for large-scale constructions in perspective. In Rome, the Teatro alle Dame (built by Count Alibert, a French gentleman in the service of Queen Christina [of Sweden]) is the largest and is considered the fairest; that is where the grand tragedies [i.e., *opere serie*] are acted. Second in importance is the Teatro Argentina, square at one end and round at the other, not so big as the former, but better designed and able to accommodate almost as many people in a smaller space. The Teatro di Tordinona, similar in shape, is also very lovely. . . .

Their parterres are filled with benches like a church; one sits on them. They are none the quieter for that; the din of cabals in favor of the actors, of applause while a faction's favorite is singing (sometimes even before he begins), of echoes responding from the very highest loges, of poems dropped or shouted in praise of the singer is unceasing; an ear-splitting noise so unpleasant, so indecorous, that the first rank of loges is made uninhabitable by it. Those loges are relinquished to ladies of easy virtue, as being too close to the parterre, where none but the rabble sit, and over which the first rank is hardly elevated at all.

Persons of some standing rent loges in the second, third, and even, in a crush, the fourth rank; the higher ones are for the common people. The nobility here do not, as in France, buy a ticket at the door and sit wherever they like. The tickets sold at the door are for the parterre only, and very reasonably priced; all loge seats must be rented for the whole season. . . .

Once the theaters here opened for the season, social gatherings at the palaces of the Princess Borghese, the Bolognetti, etc. came to an end. The general meeting place is the opera, which lasts very long, from eight or nine o'clock until nearly midnight. Ladies hold their *conversazione* in their loges, where the spectators they know pay them short visits. As I said, everyone must rent a loge. . . . I enter mine as if it were my home. We train our opera glasses to seek out our acquaintances and, if we choose, exchange visits with them. The fondness these people have for the spectacle and the music is more remarkable for the constancy of their attendance than for the attention they bestow upon it. After the first performances, where the silence is moderate even in the parterre, it is not *bon-ton* to listen, except to the interesting places. The principal loges are properly furnished and lit with candelabra. At times we play, more often chat, sitting in a circle all round the loge; for that is how one sits, not as in France, where the ladies adorn the hall by sitting at the front; whence you may conclude that, in spite of the magnificence of their halls and the ornateness of each loge, the total effect is far less pleasing than with us.

I took it in my head one time, when I was almost alone in my loge at the Teatro Valle, to play chess with [my friend] Rochemont during the charming comedy [i.e., comic opera] *La libertà nociva* [by Rinaldo di Capua, c. 1710– c. 1780], which is not very popular but amuses me far more than their grand tragedies. Chess is perfect for filling the emptiness of these long recitatives, and music for breaking one's excessive concentration on chess. . . .

Italian opera is very different from French, whether in the choice of subjects, the construction of the dramas, the number and kind of actors, or the manner in which they are brought together. It is not a fixed institution [*académie*] as with us, composed of the same persons and renewed only as needed. Here an impresario who wishes to establish a winter opera obtains the governor's permission, rents a theater, assembles singers and instrumentalists from various quarters, bargains with the craftsmen and scenic designer, and often ends by bankrupting them all, as do our country theatrical producers. To be safe, the craftsmen get paid in loges, which they then rent out. Every winter, two operas are produced at each theater, sometimes three; so that here we may look forward to eight during our stay. The operas are new each year, and so are the singers. No one wishes to see an opera, a ballet, a stage set, or an actor that was seen the previous year, unless it be an excellent opera by Vinci or a very famous singer. When the celebrated [castrato] Senesino appeared in Naples last autumn, people cried: "What's this? We have seen this actor before; his singing will be old-fashioned." Senesino's voice is a little worn; but to my mind he sings with better taste than anyone I have heard.

Here is how they supply so much novelty in their dramas and voices. To begin with, a lyric poem, once written, becomes common property. Composers

"THE GENERAL MEETING PLACE IS THE OPERA." *This painting by Pietro Domenico Olivero of the opening night of the 1740–41 season at Turin's Teatro Regio bears out the Président de Brosses' observations regarding the grand architecture of Italian opera houses and the lively behavior of audiences during a performance. Every detail of this famous picture is instructive, not least the scenery (here a prolongation of the auditorium's architecture), the actors onstage, and the orchestra in the shallow pit, with the composer leading the singers from the harpsichord at the left and the local maestro the instrumentalists from that on the right. The opera being performed is Francesco Feo's Arsace. Turin, Museo Civico.*

are not rare; if one of them is looking for work, he simply takes a published poem that has already been set many times before and proceeds to write fresh music to the same words. Most often appropriated are the poems of Metastasio; there is not one of them that has not been set over and over again by the most famous composers. The method is useful and convenient; it should be adopted by us, since our operas frequently fail through the fault of the poet: you cannot write good music to bad words. . . .

In Italy they do not engrave or print music, whether vocal or instrumental. There would be too much to do: the concertos and grand symphonies pour in from all sides. As for voices, not many are needed: an Italian opera is usually composed of not more than about half-a-dozen characters, and there is none of that apparatus of choruses and feasts with song and dance which we have in our operas.

The orchestra here is more numerous and varied, but the instruments are neither rare nor expensive, whereas good voices cost a fortune, besides which they must be sent for from afar at great expense.

Those worthies, the castratos, are very pretty dandies, very self-assured; and they don't offer their services for nothing. An opera will have three or four so-prano voices and a contralto, male or female, with a tenor for the kingly roles. Bass voices are not used; they are rare and not appreciated. They are only employed in farces, where the comic role is ordinarily sung by a bass. . . .

Sometimes the voice of castratos will change at puberty, or sink in pitch from soprano to contralto with the advancing years. It is by no means rare that they should lose it altogether at puberty; so that they are left with nothing at all, a wretched bargain. They have the operation when they are about seven or eight years old; the child must ask for it himself: the law makes it a condition, to make the thing more acceptable. Most of them grow big, and as fat as capons, their hips, rump, arms, throat, and neck as round and chubby as a woman's. When you meet them at a gathering, it is astonishing, when they speak, to hear a little child's voice emerging from such a colossus. Some are very pretty: with fair ladies they are smug and conceited, and, if spiteful rumor is to be believed, much in demand for their talents, which are limitless; for they are very talented. It is even said that one of these *demivirs* presented a petition to Pope Innocent XI, asking for permission to get married on the grounds that the operation had not been entirely successful; the Pope wrote in the margin: *Che si castri meglio* [Let him get castrated more successfully].

One must grow accustomed to these castrato voices in order to appreciate them. Their timbre is as clear and piercing as that of choirboys and much louder; to me they seem to sing an octave higher than the natural voices of women. Their voices almost always have something dry and shrill about them, a far cry from the young, mellow sweetness of women's voices; but they are brilliant, light, dazzling, very loud, and very wide-ranging. The voices of Italian women are quite similar, light and flexible in the extreme; in other words, they have the same character as their music. As for roundness, don't ask for it, they don't know what it is; do not speak to them of the admirable sounds of our French music, spun out, sustained, thickened and diminished by degrees, all on the same note; they would no more be able to understand what you mean than to execute such sounds. The Italians nevertheless distinguish two kinds of voice, which they call *voce di testa* [head voice], altogether light and proper for the little charming turns they give their ornaments, and chest voice, *voce di petto*, whose sound is louder and fuller, especially in the bass. . . .

Let us come now to the difference between the construction of their poems and that of ours. The French poems are made to suit this abnormal and singular dramatic genre, which is nothing but extravagant if one considers it according to the rules of nature, but in which it is understood that verisimilitude and nature are to be sacrificed to the union of a great many different forms of entertainment and to the unceasing deception of the senses. To that end we have very properly chosen fable, enchantments, magic, which favor the marvelous, machines, the intervention of gods, the variety of feasts, dances, and spectacle. . . . Here, nothing of the kind; their operas have purely historical subjects. . . .

Italian operas are true tragedies, wholly tragic, after the manner of Corneille and Crébillon. . . . But if the Italians think they have avoided the inconveniences I have noted in our operas by their choice of subject and the elimination of anything that interrupts the principal action, they are very much mistaken. In truth, their poems (I mean those of Metastasio) are admirable and very interesting; but the arias sewn at the end of their scenes are not always sufficiently connected to the subject; those exquisite arias, which place Italian music so far above our own, have the very same effect of distracting, of letting the interest cool off while charming the ears. And so, since this defect is an innate vice of operatic poems, I still prefer the variety in ours to the uniform construction of theirs. . . .

The Italians wish to have arias of all possible kinds, offering all the different images which music can represent. They have very noisy ones, full of music and harmony, meant for brilliant voices; they have others with an agreeable melody and a delightful form, meant for refined, flexible voices; others finally are passionate, tender, truly expressive of natural sentiment, whether strong or pathetic, and these are designed for the dramatic situation and the display of the singer's acting ability. Arias of the first kind present images of a turbulent sea, an impetuous wind, an overflowing river, flashing lightning, a lion pursued by hunters, a horse hearing the battle trumpet, the terror of a silent night, etc. These figures, so well suited to music, do not fit naturally into the tragedy. They must therefore be introduced by comparisons based on the relationship that may exist between the physical images and the state of mind in which the poet has placed his character. I know that such comparisons are quite out of place coming from a man who is agitated by passion and who therefore should express himself in a lively yet natural manner; but music, which plays the leading role, decrees it must be so. A simpler manner would probably give the character but two words and no image; and this music is so beautiful, so astonishing, it paints objects with such art and truth, that one willingly forgives it even graver faults, such as keeping a character onstage to have him sing a very long aria at the very moment when danger is pressing upon him to flee. Display arias of this kind are almost always accompanied by wind instruments (oboes, trumpets, and horns), which have a splendid effect, especially in airs depicting tempests at sea; a hundred string and wind instruments together could accompany without harming the vocal part. . . .

Arias of the second kind are madrigals, lovely songs containing ingenious, delicate thoughts, or comparisons based on agreeable objects such as zephyrs, birds, murmuring brooks, country life, etc. . . . The music here consists of little minuets, musettes, or other songs of an ingratiating sort, next to which our French songs are mere drones.

As for the arias of the third class, which only express passion, Metastasio takes great care to place them at the liveliest, most interesting moments of his dramas and to connect them closely to the plot. Here the composer seeks no turns, no passages, but tries to portray the sentiment simply, whatever it may be, and in all its immediacy. These arias are much less melodious than the others, but are much more pathetic and true; and believe me, I beg you, when I say that they are quite as true and pathetic as the most dramatic scenes of Lully, not to mention how much fuller they are of music. These are the places in opera that are enjoyed most of all . . . but they cannot be heard outside the theater without losing most of their value. I put in the same category simple arias tied to the action and not built on comparisons, a type in which Vinci and his pupil Pergolesi, those natural, simple composers, succeeded admirably; similarly, ghost and vision arias, to which music lends a surprising force with its inventions. . . .

So much for the musical side of Metastasio's poems; their dramatic side deserves to be mentioned too. No poet has ever been his equal in the art of exposition. This item, which torments our second-rate poets and has often caused the greatest masters to fail, presents no difficulty to Metastasio: he has no exposition. I don't know how the devil he manages to handle the protasis so that, with hardly any narration, the spectator finds himself fully informed of all he needs to know in order to understand the drama. He ordinarily begins with a brilliant action in the first scene, and he continues to treat his subject with the same celerity up to the dénouement. He is a master at engaging the passions. He is full of surprising incidents and coups de théâtre; he has even too many, and these singular coups de théâtre are often brought about at the expense of verisimilitude. . . . His plots are usually double, but he intertwines them so tightly that they cannot proceed independently; this, however, tends to weaken the interest. . . . He has many characters whose virtue puts them above the common run, a thing one enjoys seeing at the theater; he has other, singular characters that seem bizarre, overdone, too weak, or too strong. The knots of his intrigues are small, depending as they do on misunderstandings and verging on comedy. . . . He dialogues like an angel (I will except his too frequent asides) and with an air of truth I do not often find in our poets; our tirades are too long. His scenes are true conversations; his style is flowing, lively, sententious, full of ingenious ideas, sometimes precious; let us, however, do him justice: he is less precious than any of his countrymen. He is a perfect master of spectacle and knows how to introduce naturally such attractive features as festivities, battles, triumphs, and anything that will enhance their magnificence. . . .

The Italian recitative is extremely disagreeable to anyone who is not accustomed to it. It is said one enjoys it once one is used to it; and true enough, I am beginning to do so. But the natives, apparently, have not yet reached that point, for as soon as they are familiar with an opera they stop listening to the recitative, except at the most interesting scenes. I wondered at first how it could be so baroque and at the same time so monotonous. One day I asked an Englishman, who should have had no prejudices on the subject, if he thought it possible that the recitative of our operas could be as insipid and ridiculous to the ear as these. "Just as much," he replied; "I assure you that both [the French and the Italian recitative] are vexing and unbearable in the extreme." . . . [The Italian recitative] is almost nothing more than an articulated recitation, after the manner of those actors who chant when they declaim. . . . The thoroughbass accompaniment is quite simple, merely supplying a tone during the rests, to keep the singer on pitch; the harpsichord strikes its chords in a rude way, never breaking them. This is not to say there are no recitatives with obbligato strings; these, in fact, are the finest, but they are rare. When perfectly treated, like some I have heard by Jommelli, the forcefulness of their declamation and the sublime harmonic variety of their accompaniment are, I must say, the most dramatic thing imaginable, well above the best French recitatives and the loveliest Italian arias. The performance of these accompanied recitatives is extremely difficult, especially the instrumental part, because of the willfulness of the motion, which is not governed by a measured beat.

They beat time in church to Latin music, but never at the opera, no matter how large the orchestra, how many-voiced the aria's accompaniment.

. . . Their ritornellos are ravishing; and the songs that follow them so nicely turned, so enticing or surprising, that our French airs seem but plainsong next to them; it is folly to attempt to compare them. . . .

Nearly all their arias are for solo voices; they have scarcely two or three duets in any opera and almost never a trio. The duets belong to the tender, touching genre, to the most pathetic situations in the drama; they are marvelously beautiful and extremely affecting. It is here, especially, that the voices, as well as the strings, make use of that chiaroscuro, that gradual thickening of the sound, which grows louder from note to note up to the highest degree, then returns to an extremely soft and tender shade. Much admired here are the cadenzas they make at the end of every solo aria. As for myself, I do not like them at all; not only are they too frequent, but they always say the same thing. I feel like laugh-

ing when I see a fat castrato fill his lungs like a balloon and then for ten minutes roll out twenty arpeggios in close succession from the top to the bottom of
his voice without taking a breath. . . .

If there is any dancing onstage at the opera, it is not because ballets form
part of the drama; they are not introduced by any festivity or tied to the plot.
Since every opera is in three acts, each lasting about an hour, the length [of the
acts] is the occasion for two entr'actes consisting of dances or intermezzios. These
dances are a kind of pantomime placed very ridiculously in the intermissions of
a tragedy. The dancers, both male and female, are lively, light, and rise higher
than [the celebrated French dancers] Camargo and Maltère *the bird*; they have
strong legs, also a certain pleasant gentility, and they are not wanting in precision; but they have neither arms, nor grace, nor nobility. In a word, the dance
of the Italians is far beneath ours; they say so themselves. . . .

If you are shocked to see the entr'actes of a grave tragedy filled with pan-
tomimic ballets, you would be more so to see it interrupted by intermezzos. That
is what they call their little two-act farces, in a low comedy style, approximately
like those they perform outdoors at the Place Royale.

You can well imagine how wonderfully appropriate such pieces are between
the acts of a tragedy. But forgive them, I beg you: for they are a delight, when
their music is perfect and perfectly performed. These little farces have only two
or three comic characters; the music is simple, gay, natural, its expression endlessly comical, lively, and laughable. I only wish I could let you hear a husband
mimicking his wife when she loses all her money at faro, the lamentations of a
poor devil who is about to be hanged, or a bizarre quarrel in the form of a duet,
or a reconciliation between a gallant and his mistress; there's nothing pleasan-
ter in the world. Add to this the air of reality with which all this is treated by
the composer and rendered by the actor, and the singular precision of the performance. These buffoons cry, laugh boisterously, gesticulate, perform all sorts
of dumb shows without ever missing a beat. I confess that these pieces, when
they are as good as *Il maestro di musica* by Scarlatti [? probably by Auletta], *La
serva padrona* and *Livietta e Tracollo* by my charming Pergolesi, delight me
more than anything else. . . .

The magnificence of the scenery in Italian opera is such, especially when
compared with the common stinginess of ours, that I can only give you a feeble idea of it; one must have seen it. . . . The immensity of their stages allows
them to display their ingenuity in a suitable space, which we do not have in our
puny Paris halls; you cannot imagine with what truth, over all and in every detail, they render the scene of the drama. It is truly a gallery, a forest, a field, a
farm, a chamber, a vaulted prison, etc. Instead of placing the scenery on a line
with the wings, as we do, they lay it out all across the stage; colonnades or galleries they dispose obliquely over several diagonals, which enhances the effect
of the perspective; if the place is confined, they narrow the stage and enclose it
so effectively on all sides that one imagines one is in a cave, in a tent, or under

an archway. There are two or three changes of scenery in every act; they are executed none too adroitly, with less coordination and promptness than with us;
however, once complete, they are so true to life that I must make an effort to
detect where the pieces I have seen brought on are joined together.

Frédéric d'Agay, ed., *Lettres d'Italie du Président de Brosses*, 2 vols. (Paris: Mercure de France, 1986),
2:289–316. Trans. P.W.

15

METASTASIO ON SETTING DRAMATIC RECITATIVE TO MUSIC

Attilio Regolo was Metastasio's eighteenth *dramma per musica*, a relatively
late work. Written in 1740, it was withdrawn shortly before the première, owing to the sudden death of Emperor Charles VI. Ten years passed before it finally appeared, not in Vienna but at the Saxon court theater in Dresden, and
set to new music by Johann Adolf Hasse. It was Metastasio's favorite among
all his dramas; and indeed it enjoyed a career of its own as a spoken tragedy,
remaining high in the estimate of critics down to the present. Perhaps because
of its uncompromisingly elevated tone, its lack of spectacle, and, not least, its
tragic ending, it failed to attract the swarm of composers who invariably reset
the other Metastasio dramas over and over again; *Attilio Regolo* was set to music only four times in all. It tells the story of Atilius Regulus, the legendary Roman hero in the first Punic War; twice consul, then victorious general against
the Carthaginians, he fell prisoner to them at last and was sent back to Rome
to negotiate peace on condition that, should he fail, he would surrender again
to his captors. Regulus appeared before the Roman senate with the Carthagin-
ian Hamilcar by his side. After conveying the enemy's peace terms, he delivered an impassioned speech, urging the Romans to reject the offer and fight
Carthage to the end. Then, true to his word, and disdaining pleas that he remain, he surrendered once more, was taken back to Carthage, and suffered a
horrible death. The drama covers Regulus's last day in Rome: his family's attempts to save him, his refusal to be saved, his confrontation with the senate,

his farewell to the Romans. Responding to a request by Hasse, Metastasio explained his intentions as to the staging and music of the opera in a long letter that reveals his intense commitment to the projection of the dramatic content of the libretto—and incidentally presents us with quite a different picture of the poet from that transmitted by one of his most scornful detractors, Calzabigi, a few years later (see below, p. 115ff). The first half of the letter, here omitted, goes into a detailed psychological analysis of each of the seven characters in the drama. The second half, given below, is a series of suggestions for setting certain portions of the recitative as *obbligato*, i.e. with string accompaniment, a device which at the time was ordinarily reserved for moments of crisis (usually just one in any opera), typically a monologue expressing doubt, anger, despair. In his letter to Hasse, Metastasio opts for a much expanded use of this highly dramatic technique, going into details of staging which remind us that, until relatively late in the nineteenth century, librettists were also the stage directors of opera. (Note in this connection Metastasio's reference to a scenic designer's option of making a setting deep or shallow, and the consequences of that choice for the staging.) The scenes selected by him for *obbligato* treatment are, in order: the tirade of Regolo's daughter Attilia, in which she pleads with the consul Manlio for her father's safety; the confrontation of Regolo with the senate; a monologue in which Regolo, alone, awaits the senate's decision; and the last scene, that of Regolo's farewell to the Romans. The English translations given here of lines quoted by Metastasio are from the version by John Hoole published in 1800 (see also the extract appended below).

20 October 1749

. . . We come now to some of the particulars, since you so desire. I will tell you which of the recitatives, in my opinion, may be enlivened by the instruments; but I do not mean, in so doing, to limit your freedom. Where my inclination agrees with yours, let it help you in your decision; but where you do not agree with me, do not change your mind to please me.

In the first act, then, I find two places where the instruments may help me. The first is the whole of Attilia's harangue to Manlio in the second scene, from the line:

A che vengo? Ah! sino a quando...
[Wherefore am I come?
Ah! say how long...]

After the words *a che vengo* the instruments ought to begin to make themselves heard, and, now falling silent, now accompanying, now reinforcing, lend warmth to a speech that is of itself already agitated; and I would like them not to abandon Attilia until after the line:

> La barbara or qual è? Cartago o Roma?
> [Then which of these is cruel, Rome or Carthage?]

I believe in general, but especially in the present case, that one ought to be on guard against the inconvenience of making the singer wait longer than if the bass alone were accompanying. All the warmth of the speech would cool down, and the instruments instead of enlivening the recitative would weaken it, turning it into a divided picture, obscured and overwhelmed by the frame, so that it would be better in that case if there were no frame at all.

The other place is in the seventh scene of the same act, and it happens to be one of the very few places where I would like Regolo to abandon his moderation and flare up, against his custom. It is only twelve lines long, beginning at:

> Io venissi a tradirvi, etc.
> [That to betray you I came.]

until:

> Come al nome di Roma Africa tremi.
> [How Africa trembles at the name of Rome.]

If you wish to do this, I would recommend the same economy of time I recommended earlier, so that the actor will not be obliged to wait, his warmth cooling off instead of increasing, as I intended.

And since we are at the seventh scene of the first act, I will say, to oblige you, that after Manlio's line,

> T'accheta: ei viene.
> [No more—he comes.]

a very brief *sinfonia* will, I think, be needed [for Regolo's entrance into the senate], not only to give the consul and senators time to gain their seats, but to allow Attilio to enter without haste and pause to reflect. The character of this little *sinfonia* ought to be majestic, slow, and, if consistent with the motive you have

......*Libero è sempre,*
Chi sa morir. La sua viltà confessa,
Chi l'altrui forza accusa. Regolo Sc.V.

P. Ant Novelli inv.   C. Zuliani inc.

METASTASIO'S *REGOLO*, A PAEAN TO ROMAN VIRTUE. *The hero is seen admonishing his daughter, who would have him remain in Rome and escape death at the hands of the enemy: "Free is only he who knows how to die. To accuse others of coercion is to confess one's own cowardice." In the foreground, the artist has placed symbols of Rome: the river Tiber and the twin founders, Romulus and Remus.* From Metastasio, *Opere* (Venice: Zatta, 1781). Baltimore, Special Collections, Milton S. Eisenhower Library of the Johns Hopkins University.

chosen, halting, as if to express Regolo's state of mind as he reflects that he is returning a slave to that place where formerly he had sat a consul. I should wish that Amilcare begin to speak during one of the interruptions I am asking for in the *sinfonia*'s motive and that, the instruments falling silent without cadencing, he say the two lines:

> Regolo, a che t'arresti? è forse nuovo
> Per te questo soggiorno?

> [Why, Regulus, this pause?
> Say, is this place to thee so new an object?]

and that the *sinfonia* should not conclude until after Regolo's reply:

> Penso qual ne partii, qual ne ritorno
> [I think what hence I went, and what return]

bearing in mind however that after the words *qual vi ritorno* the instruments play nothing more than a simple cadence.

In the second act there is no recitative requiring an accompaniment in my opinion, other than the scene of Regolo alone that begins:

> Tu palpiti, o mio cor!
> [Why dost thou throb, my heart?]

the seventh in the act. This ought to be recited seated, up to the words:

> ...Ah! no. De' vili
> Questo è il linguaggio...

> [O! no—such language
> Befits the dastard.]

and the rest standing. But since the architect is free to make the two scenes, the loggia and the gallery, deep or shallow, if it should happen that the change is not from shallow to deep, it will be difficult to discover Regolo seated. Therefore, if he cannot thus be discovered, then to enable him to gain his seat slowly, stopping from time to time and appearing deeply absorbed in meditation (speaking, if he likes, some words from the beginning of the scene), it will be necessary that the instruments anticipate, assist, and second him for as long as the character remains seated; all the things he says are reflections, doubts, suspended thoughts, giving rise to sudden and close modulations, to be occupied at discreet intervals by the instruments; but the moment he rises to his feet, all the rest requires resolve and energy: and here my earlier concern for economy of time is again relevant. . . .

Although in the course of the third act, not less than in the other two, there may be places I have neglected that could opportunely be accompanied by the strings, I feel that it is not an advantage to make that ornament too familiar, and in the third act in particular I should wish that no instruments be heard in recitatives until the last scene. This is anticipated by the noisy tumult of the people crying:

> Resti, Regolo resti.
> [Regulus shall stay.]

The din of these cries must be great in order to imitate reality, and to show what a respectful silence the sole presence of Regolo can impose upon a whole tumultuous people. The instruments must remain silent when the other characters speak but may always, if you like, be heard when the protagonist speaks in this last scene; they should vary their motions and modulations not in accordance with the mere words, as other composers will do thinking they do well, but according to the state of mind of the persons speaking those words, as composers do who are of your caliber. For, as you know better than I, the same words can, depending on their different context, be expressions now of joy, now of sorrow, now of anger, now of pity. My hope is that, in your hands, so long a recitative, accompanied by the instruments all the while, will not grow tiresome to the listener: in the first place because you will observe that economy of time I so strongly recommended above, but also especially because you are a perfect master of the art of distributing *pianos, fortes, rinforzandos,* detached or connected strokes, slow or hurried ostinatos, arpeggios, tremolos, tenutos, and above all those singular modulations with whose secret you alone are familiar. But if, in spite of so many artistic resources, you should be of a different opinion, I will yield to your experience and will be satisfied if the following lines are accompanied, that is the first ten, from:

> Regolo resti! ed io l'ascolto! ed io (etc.)
> [Ha! Regulus shall stay! and is my sense (etc.)]

until:

> Meritai l'odio vostro?
> [Have I deserv'd to merit thus your hatred?]

further from:

> No, possibil non è: de' miei Romani (etc.)
> [It cannot be—I know, I know too well
> The hearts of Romans (etc.)]

until:

> Esorto cittadin, padre comando;
> [As citizen I exhort you,
> And as a father let me now command;]

and finally from:

> Romani, addio: siano i congedi estremi (etc.)
> [Romans, farewell! and let our parting now (etc.)]

to the end.

Do you think I have finished annoying you? No, Sir: there is yet one fly in the ointment. I should like the last chorus to be one of those with which you have instilled in the audience the hitherto unknown wish to listen to it; and since it is the Romans' last farewell to Regolo, I would desire you to make it clear that this chorus is not, like most, a redundancy, but a very necessary part of the catastrophe. . . .

Tutte le opere di Pietro Metastasio, ed. B. Brunelli, vol. 3 (Milan: Arnoldo Mondadori, 1951), 431–35. Trans. P.W.

Regolo's farewell, which elicited from the poet Giosuè Carducci (1835–1907) the wish that it be recited every year on the Capitoline Hill to commemorate the day of Rome's founding, follows in the version by John Hoole (1727–1803), translator of Italian classics and friend of Dr. Johnson:

Reg. Romans, farewell! and let our parting now
Be worthy of us. Thanks to Heaven! I leave you,
And leave you Romans. Ah! preserve unsullied
That mighty name, and be the arbiters
Of human kind, till all the world become,
By your example, Romans. Guardian Gods!
That watch this happy land; protecting Powers
Of great Aeneas' offspring! I intrust
To you this race of heroes. Still defend
This soil, these dwellings, these paternal walls.
O! grant that valour, glory, constancy,
Justice and truth may ever here reside;
And should some evil star, with adverse beams
E'er threat the Capitol, see, mighty Gods!
See Regulus—let Regulus alone
Be made your victim, and the wrath of Heaven
Be all consum'd on my devoted head:
Let Rome unhurt—but why those tears—
—Farewell!

John Hoole, trans., *Dramas and Other Poems of the Abbé Pietro Metastasio*, vol. 3 (London: Otridge, 1800), 309–10.

16

FROM ROUSSEAU'S *CONFESSIONS*

Jean-Jacques Rousseau (1712–78), a seminal figure in the history of European thought, occupies a comparable position in the history of music, especially of opera. Himself a musician, though by no means a skilled one, he earned his living as a music copyist, disdaining to subject his books to the requirements of commercial publishing. He is remembered in music history for the articles he contributed to the great *Encyclopédie*, later revised and expanded into his *Dictionnaire de musique* (1768), for his fiery participation in the War of the

Buffoons (see pp. 106–11 below), and for his own creative efforts as a composer, most notably in *Le Devin du village*, the subject of our second selection below. His fascination with self-analysis, self-portrayal, self-revelation imbues virtually all his writings to some extent, but none so much as *Les Confessions* (1770), his autobiography. Here the events of his life are intertwined with his subjective responses, external history with internal experience. His love for Italian music was awakened during his residence in Venice, where he lived from September 1743 to August 1744, employed as secretary at the French embassy. Characteristically, his most poignant memory of this, his first exposure to Italian opera, involved the interaction of an external reality with his unconscious self.

Let us not leave Venice without a word about the famous amusements of that city, or at least the small part of them which I enjoyed during my stay. We have seen, in the account I have given of my youth, how little I partook of the pleasures of that age, or at least of what are known as such. My tastes did not change in Venice, but my work, which in any case would have hindered me, made more attractive the simple amusements which I allowed myself. The first and pleasantest was the society of worthy people, Messieurs Le Blond, de St. Cyr, Carrio, Altuna, and a Friulian gentleman whose name I greatly regret having forgotten. . . . We were also on familiar terms with two or three witty, cultivated Englishmen, who, like us, had a passion for music. All those gentlemen had wives or lady friends or mistresses, the latter almost without exception girls of talent, and at their homes we had music and dancing. We gambled there too, but not much; our lively tastes and talents, and the theater, made gambling seem insipid. It is the resource of the bored. I had brought from Paris the prejudice they have there against Italian music; but from nature I had also received that tact and sensibility against which prejudices do not endure. I soon acquired for that music the passion it inspires in those whose nature allows them to appreciate it. Listening to some barcaroles I realized that I had never heard singing before; and soon I became so infatuated with opera, that, tired of babbling, eating, and gambling in the boxes when all I wished to do was listen, I often slipped away from the company to go somewhere else. There, shut in my own box all alone, I would abandon myself to the pleasure of enjoying the spectacle comfortably and to the end, despite its length. One day at the Teatro di San Giovanni Grisostomo I fell asleep more deeply than if I had been in my own bed. The noisy and brilliant arias did not wake me up. But who can convey the delicious sensation I experienced from the sweet harmony and angelic melodies of the aria that did wake me up? What an awakening! What rapture! What ecstasy, when I opened my ears and at the same time my eyes! My first thought was that I was in Heaven. That ravishing piece, which I still remember and shall not forget for as long as I live, began thus:

> Conservami la bella
> Che sì m'accende il cor.

> [Preserve for me the fair one
> Who so enflames my heart.]

I wished to own this piece, I obtained it and kept it for a long time; but on paper it was not the same as in my memory. The notes were the same, but it was a different thing. That divine piece can never, except in my mind, be performed as it sounded the day it woke me up.

The aria is from *La finta schiava*, a *pasticcio* that played at the S. Angelo, not the S. Giovanni Grisostomo, in May 1744. While Rousseau was in Venice, the very first Neapolitan-style *opere buffe* arrived there from the south, a fact remembered in the next excerpt, which deals with the creation of *Le Devin du village* (*The Village Soothsayer*), his epoch-making *intermède* in one act. This work, which he wrote at Passy in the spring of 1752, had its première at Fontainebleau on 18 October of that year, was staged at the Opéra on 1 March 1753, and continued to be performed regularly in Paris far into the nineteenth century. Its simplicity and naïveté were arresting and unprecedented: a professional composer could not have written it. And it entered French operatic history at an exquisitely appropriate moment, almost simultaneously with the arrival in Paris of the Buffoons, who triggered the famous War. Showing how the simple lyricism of *opera buffa* could be wedded to French sensibilities, *Le Devin* helped launch the important new type of *opéra comique* that flourished in the second half of the eighteenth century. Rousseau's account of the events once more brings out the interplay of external and internal forces in his life. Some of his digressions, e.g. the anecdote of the officer who lied, may not be strictly relevant to the history of *Le Devin*; but as significant examples of Rousseau's perception of the irrational in human nature, which made him such an important precursor of the romantics, they are really inseparable from the main story. And at least one of these excursions, the account of his embarrassment at not being properly dressed at the première, speaks to a universal feeling that is very much a part of the sociology of opera.

Not far from Paris I had another resting place which I liked very much, at the home of M. Mussard, my compatriot, my relation, and my friend, who had built himself a charming retreat at Passy, where I have spent many a peaceful

LE DEVIN
DU VILLAGE,
INTERMEDE;

Par J. J. ROUSSEAU;

Représenté pour la premiere fois à Fontainebleau,
fur le Théâtre de la Cour, devant LEURS
MAJESTÉS, les 18 & 24 Oct. 1752.

Et à Paris, par l'Académie Royale de Mufique,
le premier Mars 1753.

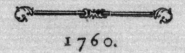

A GENEVE,
Chez PIERRE GOSSE.

1760.

AN EARLY EDITION OF ROUSSEAU'S *LE DEVIN DU VILLAGE. The title page (l.) and a decoration (r.) after King Louis XV's favorite number, "J'ai perdu mon serviteur," which he loved to sing "in the most out-of-tune voice in the kingdom."* Baltimore, Archives of the Peabody Conservatory of Music.

Que me fert d'y rêver fans ceffe?
Rien ne peut guérir mon amour,
Et tout augmente ma tristeffe.

J'ai perdu mon Serviteur,
J'ai perdu tout mon bonheur;
Colin me délaiffe.

Je veux le haïr.... je le dois....
Peut-être il m'aime encor.... Pourquoi me fuir
fans ceffe?

Il me cherchoit tant autrefois!
Le Devin du canton fait ici fa demeure:
Il fait tout; il fçaura le fort de mon amour.
Je le vois, & je veux m'éclaircir en ce jour.

moment. . . . For a long time he insisted the waters at Passy would be good for my health and exhorted me to come and take them at his house. Partly to extricate myself from the urban crush I finally surrendered and went to Passy for eight or ten days, which benefited me more because I was in the country than because I took the waters. Mussard played the violoncello and passionately adored Italian music. One night we talked about it at length before going to bed, and especially about the *opere buffe* each of us had seen in Italy and which transported us both. That night, as I could not sleep, I contemplated how one might go about giving some idea of such a drama in France. . . . In the morning, while I walked and took the waters, I composed some sort of verses very hastily and fitted them with melodies that occurred to me as I composed the verses. I scribbled it all down in a kind of vaulted chamber that was at the end of the garden, and at tea time was unable to resist showing these airs to Mussard and to Mlle Du Vernois his housekeeper, who was a really very good and amiable girl. The three pieces I had sketched were the first monologue, "J'ai perdu mon serviteur," the Soothsayer's air, "L'amour croit s'il s'inquiète," and the last duet, "À jamais, Colin, je t'engage," etc. So little did I think these worth the trouble of pursuing that, had not both of them applauded and encouraged me, I should have thrown my scraps of paper in the fire and forgotten all about them, as I have often done with things at least as good: but they so stimulated me that in six days my drama was written down, except for a few verses, and all my music sketched: so that in Paris all I had left to do was some recitative and all the filling in, and I completed everything with such speed that in three weeks my scenes were written out in a fair copy, ready to be performed. The only thing missing was the *divertissement*, which I composed much later.

Excited by the composition of this work, I was very eager to hear it, and I would have given anything to see it performed as I pleased in private, as they say Lully once had *Armide* performed for himself alone. Since it was not possible that I should have that pleasure without sharing it with the public, it was necessary, if I was to enjoy my piece, to have it approved at the Opéra. Unfortunately it was in an absolutely new style, to which ears were not yet accustomed; and besides, the failure of my [1745 opera] *Les Muses galantes* led me to expect that of *Le Devin* if I submitted it under my name. [My friend] Duclos relieved me of my quandary by undertaking to have the work tried out without divulging the identity of the author. In order not to give myself away, I did not attend this rehearsal, and the *petits violons* [i.e., the two principal violinists] who led it did not themselves find out who the author was until after the work's merit was acclaimed with an ovation. All those who heard it were charmed by it to such a degree that the next day nothing else was talked about at all the social gatherings. M. de Cury, Intendant of the Royal Entertainments, who was present at the rehearsal, asked to have the work given at court. Duclos, who knew my intentions, judged that I should be less the master of my piece at court than in Paris, and he refused it. Cury demanded it on the strength of his authority, Duclos held his ground, and their debate grew so lively that one day at the Opéra they would have left together [to duel] had they not been separated. It was decided to address me directly; I left the decision up to M. Duclos. They were obliged to go back to him. The Duke d'Aumont [first gentleman of the King's chamber] intervened. Duclos finally thought it best to yield to authority, and the piece was handed over for performance at Fontainebleau.

The part I was fondest of and where I most departed from the common path was the recitative. Mine was accented in a totally new way and went along with the delivery of the words. They dared not leave such a horrible novelty alone: they were afraid it would disgust timid ears. I consented that [my friend] Francueil and [the singer] Jelyotte should alter the recitative, but I refused to become involved in this.

When all was ready and the day fixed for the performance, it was suggested I go to Fontainebleau to attend at least the last rehearsal. I went there with Mlle [Marie] Fell, [Frédéric Melchior] Grimm, and, I believe, the Abbé Raynal, in a court carriage. The rehearsal was tolerable; I was more pleased with it than I had expected. The orchestra was numerous, made up of players from the Opéra and the King's music. Jelyotte played Colin, Mlle Fell Colette, Cuvillier the Soothsayer; the choruses were from the Opéra. I said little; Jelyotte had directed everything; I did not wish to oversee what he had done, and despite my Roman tone, I was as bashful as a schoolboy amidst all these people.

The next day, the day of the performance, I went to have breakfast at the Café du Grand Commun. It was crowded. The talk was of the previous day's rehearsal and how difficult it had been to gain admittance to it. One of those present, an officer, said he had had no trouble at all getting in; he gave a long account of it, described the author, reported what he did, what he said; but what astonished me about this rather long recital, delivered with as much assurance as simplicity, was that not one word of it was true. It was quite clear to me that the man who spoke so knowingly about that rehearsal had not been to it, since he had before his eyes, yet did not recognize, the author he claimed to have seen so much of. What was most singular about this scene was the effect it had on me. The man was of a certain age; neither his appearance nor his tone was smug or conceited; his face was that of a man of merit, his cross of St. Louis showed he was a veteran officer. He interested me despite his impudence and despite myself; as he uttered his lies, I blushed, I lowered my eyes, I sat on thorns; I sometimes sought within myself a way to believe he was in error and in good faith. Finally, trembling lest someone recognize me and confront him with it, I hastened to finish my chocolate without saying anything, and, lowering my head as I passed in front of him, I left as fast as I could, while those present commented on his report. In the street I noticed I was in a sweat, and I am sure that if anyone had recognized and named me before I left, they would have seen in me the shame and embarrassment of a culprit, all because of the feeling of pain that poor man would have suffered had his lie been exposed.

I had arrived at one of those critical moments of my life where it is difficult only to narrate, for it is impossible that the narration itself not carry within
it either censure or apology. I will nevertheless try to report how and from what
motives I conducted myself, without adding either praise or blame.

I had that day the same neglected appearance I always had: I was unshaven
and my wig unkempt. Thinking this lack of propriety an act of courage, I thus
entered the hall where soon the King, the Queen, the royal family, and all the
court were to appear. I went to take my seat in the box to which M. de Cury
guided me, which was his own. It was a spacious box overlooking the stage, across
from a smaller box higher up, where the King took his place with Mad^e de Pom-
padour. As I was surrounded by ladies and was the only man in the front of the
box, I could not doubt I had been placed there precisely so I could be seen. When
the lights came on and I saw myself in that condition in the midst of people elab-
orately dressed up, I began to feel ill at ease; I asked myself whether I was in
my proper place, whether I was suitably attired. And after some minutes of anxiety, I replied "yes" to myself, with a boldness that perhaps came from the impossibility of extricating myself, rather than from the force of my arguments. I
told myself: I am in my proper place since I am watching my piece being performed, since I have been invited here, since I composed it for this very reason,
and since, after all, no one has a greater right than I to enjoy the fruits of my
labor and of my talent. I am in my ordinary attire, no better and no worse. If I
begin again to submit to common opinion in one particular, soon I shall be sub-
mitting again in all matters. To be myself at all times I must not blush, no matter where I am, at appearing in whatever state I choose; my exterior is simple
and negligent, but not grimy, not unclean, nor is my beard, since it is given us
by nature and, depending on time and fashion, is sometimes considered an ornament. They will find me ridiculous, impertinent; well, what do I care? I must
be able to endure ridicule and blame so long as they are not deserved. After this
little soliloquy my confidence was so much restored that I should have been able
to act boldly, had I needed to. But whether because of the presence of the master or because of the natural disposition of hearts, I noticed nothing but courtesy and honesty in the curiosity directed towards me. I was so touched by this
that I began to feel anxious again about myself and the fate of my piece, afraid
that I might efface such favorable prejudices, which seemed bent only on ap-
plauding me. I had armed myself against their derision; but their gentle attitude,
which I had not expected, so intimidated me that I was trembling like a child
when the performance began.

I soon had reason to feel reassured. The piece was performed very badly as
to the acting, but it was well sung and well played as to the music. From the
very first scene, which is really naively touching, I heard a rising murmur of
surprise and approval in the boxes, something unheard of in this kind of piece.
The growing ferment soon became noticeable in the entire assembly and, to put
it in Montesquieu's terms, increased its effect by means of the effect itself. In

the scene of the two good little people['s reconciliation] the effect reached its peak. One does not clap in front of the King; that made it possible to hear everything; the piece and the author gained thereby. I heard all about me a whispering of women who seemed to me as beautiful as angels and who said to each other in low tones: that is charming, that is ravishing; there isn't a note there that does not speak to the heart. The pleasure of moving so many amiable persons moved me to tears, and I was not able to contain them at the first duet, noticing at the same time that I was not the only one crying. . . . I am sure that at that moment the voluptuousness of sex entered into it much more than authorial vanity, and surely if only men had been there, I should not have been possessed, as I constantly was, by the desire to collect with my lips the delicious tears I had caused to flow. I have seen pieces that have prompted livelier transports of admiration, but never a rapture so total, so sweet, so touching reigning over the entire spectacle, especially not at court on the day of a first performance. Those who saw it must remember it; for the effect was unique.

That same evening the Duke d'Aumont sent word that I should come to the castle the next morning at eleven o'clock, and that he would present me to the King. M. de Cury, who brought me this message, added that he thought it was about a pension, and that the King wished to announce it to me himself.

Will it be believed that the night that followed such a brilliant day was a night of anguish and perplexity for me? My first thought, after that of being presented, concerned a frequent need I have to leave the room, which had made me suffer a great deal on the very evening of the spectacle and might well torment me the next day, when I would be in the Gallery or in the King's apartments among all those great persons, awaiting the passage of His Majesty. This infirmity was the principal cause that kept me from [social] circles and prevented me from shutting myself up in a room with women. The mere thought of the state to which this need could reduce me was sufficient to provoke it in me to the point of illness, unless I enacted a scene so unthinkable that I should have preferred to die. Only those familiar with this condition can appreciate the fear of running such a risk.

I next imagined myself before the King, presented to His Majesty, who deigned to stop and talk to me. That is where correctness and presence of mind were essential, in order to respond. Would my accursed timidity, which troubles me in the presence of the most insignificant stranger, leave me in the presence of the King of France, or would it allow me to select in an instant the right things to say? Without abandoning the severe air and tone I had assumed, I wished to show myself sensible of the honor bestowed on me by so great a Monarch. It would be necessary to wrap some deep and useful truth inside an elegant, well-merited word of praise. In order to prepare a felicitous answer beforehand, I would have to guess correctly what he might say to me; and even then, I was certain that in his presence I would not recollect a word of what I had premeditated. What would become of me at that moment and under the eyes of all the court, if in my agitation I should let slip one of my usual faux pas? That danger alarmed me, frightened me, made me shudder so much that I decided not to expose myself to it at any cost.

I would lose, it was true, the pension that was somehow being offered me; but I would also be exempting myself from the obligation it would impose on me. Farewell truth, liberty, courage. How would I dare thenceforth speak of independence and disinterestedness? Once I received that pension I should be obliged to either flatter or be silent: and who could assure me that it would be paid out? How many steps would need to be taken, how many people solicited! It would cost me more trouble and much more unpleasantness to keep the pension than to do without it. I thought that, in renouncing it, I was following a line of conduct far more consonant with my principles and sacrificing appearance to reality. I told Grimm of my resolve and he did not object. To the others I pleaded reasons of health; and I left the same morning.

Jean-Jacques Rousseau, *Œuvres complètes*, vol. 1 (Paris: Gallimard, Bibliothèque de la Pléiade, 1959), 313–14, 373–80. Trans. P.W.

17

THE WAR OF THE BUFFOONS

The *buffo* style in opera was first heard outside Italy in the intermezzos brought to various European cities in the 1720s and '30s by the two or three singers required for their performance. When full-length *opere buffe* began to be exported in the late 1740s, they traveled by much the same routes with somewhat bigger companies; still, following the tried and true *pasticcio* practice, many were cut down to the size of intermezzos and patched together with music from other operas. It was just such a repertory of miscellaneous intermezzos that Parisians heard when the impresario Eustachio Bambini, on tour in northern France with his tiny, undistinguished company, was summoned to Paris by the directors of the Opéra. The Italians opened on 1 August 1752 with Pergolesi's *La serva padrona*, sharing the bill with Lully's *Acis et Galatée* performed by the regular company; the Opéra orchestra accompanied both. Not immediately successful, the Buffoons (as they were soon called) adjusted to the relative vastness of the Palais Royal and, as they added other works to their repertory, began winning enthusiastic support from a part of the public. Their most vociferous supporters, who occupied seats beneath the queen's box, were encyclopedists like Rousseau, Frédéric-Melchior Grimm (1723–1807), the Baron d'Holbach (1723–89), and other "enlightened philosophers." Their opponents, upholders of the traditional French tragic opera, sat at the opposite corner of the hall, beneath the king's box, and included critics, journalists, and musicians, most of them forgotten today. Thus was launched the War of the Buffoons (*Querelle des Bouffons*) or War of the Corners (*Guerre des coins*). It was waged, loudly, at the performances themselves and, outside the theater, in pamphlets that began pouring from the presses. Obviously, more was at stake here than the (illogical) question of which was better, Italian comic or French tragic opera. In part, it was a continuation of the old controversy that pitted Italian music against French (see pp. 52, 75 etc. above). But there were overtones: the philosophers of the Queen's corner were not only promoting a more modern, simple, "expressive" style in music; they were also attacking the establishment. And when the German Grimm published his *Little Prophet of Boehmischbroda* (*Petit prophète de Boehmischbroda*, January 1753) mocking French opera, and the Swiss Rousseau his *Letter on French Music* (*Lettre sur la musique française*, November 1753) proving to his own satisfaction that French could not be set to music, they were offending national pride. It is not surprising, therefore, that the controversy generated more heat than real substance: it was not, at bottom, about opera, and with the solitary exception of Rameau, who in a 1754 treatise took issue with some of Rousseau's formulations, the participants were all musical amateurs. The "war" ended with the final departure of the Buffoons in March 1754. The earliest of the pamphlets, given below, appeared in autumn 1752. Written by the Baron d'Holbach, it set the tone, witty and highly provocative, for the ensuing debate. The *baton* referred to in his remarks on the Opéra orchestra was wielded by a leader who beat time with it audibly, in a tradition that went back to Lully himself. The "first stroke of the bow" (*premier coup d'archet*) was also a specialty at the Opéra: overtures and some other instrumental pieces began with a very loud attack by all the strings together; Mozart was still making fun of it in a 1778 letter from Paris.

LETTER TO A LADY OF A CERTAIN AGE ON THE PRESENT STATE OF THE OPERA

Madam,

It was, there can be no doubt, a foreboding that made you decide to leave a city where the strangest extravagances were about to take place. How lucky you are not to have witnessed them! And how sad it is for me to be obliged by your command to announce to you certain calamities which, I know, will so greatly affect you! Hear, Madam, and shudder. The times you foresaw have arrived. Much to the shame of our Nation and our century, we have seen the *august* stage of the Opéra desecrated by unworthy tumblers. Yes, Madam, this so grave, so venerable spectacle, from which the immortal Lully, its founder, seemed to have excluded senseless laughter and indecent gaiety, has been abandoned to ultramontane mummers: its *dignity* has been debased by the most burlesque productions and most frolicsome music: a noisy mirth and immoderate outbursts have rent the curtain of that Temple and replaced the noble, majestic sangfroid and thoughtful, measured applause of the admirers of Campra, Mouret, Destouches. O times! O customs!

It was left for our days, days of depravity, bad taste, and vertigo, to disturb the austere countenances that had for so long been the rule at our opera house. They are laughing at the Opéra—they are laughing their heads off! Ah, Madam, the sad thought brings me close to tears.

Alas! This revolution was all too clearly foreshadowed when a sacrilegious Innovator [i.e., Rameau] dared abandon the familiar ways and bring unknown harmonies to our ears. The good citizens could not hear the orchestral pieces in *Hyppolite et Aricie*, the overtures to *Les Indes galantes* and *Les Talents lyriques* without shuddering. These elderly gentlemen in respectable wigs, whom long experience and the liveliness of their ears have for the past sixty years entitled to pass judgment unexamined and beyond appeal, interrupted the performances of [Rameau's] *Platée* with their sobs and groans; and we, Madam, if you remmber, we then paid for the desecration of the opera stage with our deep sorrow.

Heaven did not hear our wishes; and the fateful event with which *Platée*, that terrible phenomenon, threatened us has finally come to pass. The French have abandoned the music of their fathers; they rush in crowds to monstrous productions of which we have no idea; they claim to find fresh beauty in them every day. Such fanaticism was never seen before. Three miserable *intermèdes* have been fascinating the public for three months and have been more applauded at the fiftieth performance than at the first. I should never be finished if I were to describe to you all the mad things I see and all the blasphemies I hear at the performances of these *intermèdes*.

"It is," say our modern enthusiasts, "a dialogued music like no other. The melodies are simple, elegant, and expressive as none we ever heard before; they would be sufficient by themselves to impart the meaning of the words. It is the tone of nature, rendered forcefully and truthfully always, often at moments where it seems most impossible to capture. The accompaniments prick your attention, contribute to the expression, and support the voice without overwhelming it. There are refinements here which our fools never imagined their art could produce... And what do those epithets, *mummers, buffoons,* mean when applied to actors who express passions common to all mankind with the utmost delicacy, and who represent them in their most striking aspects? One who has better appreciated this extraordinary painting has said, 'It is the *thing* itself, and at the same time the melodies [*accents*] are divine!...' Is there anything more astonishing than the lengthy stubbornness with which our grandparents admired the flattest compositions... But after all, they admired them only because they knew no better... The good people came here to be amused and they were bored. They cried, yawning, 'Ah, how beautiful that is!' And we should have continued like them to mistake ennui for *dignity*, had not these Italians, so contrary to our pompous and lethargic harmony, come to open our eyes and teach us that music is susceptible of variety, character, expression, and cheerfulness; that it can be tender without being monotonous, gay without being trivial, harmonious without engendering confusion... What duets *we* have! And what duets [*they* have] in *Il giocatore* and *La serva padrona*! There is more of genius in but one of those pieces than in all our immense compilations of notes... Let us at last shake off the yoke of national prejudice and let us not be ashamed of succumbing to the melodies that have enchanted all of Europe... After the lessons we have received, it would indeed be surprising if we returned to a Gothic and barbarous music that has bored us long enough and made us the laughing stock of Europe."

Such, Madam, are the horrible things you would be obliged to hear were you here. The respectable names of Lully, Campra, Destouches, and Mouret are either no longer mentioned or are accompanied by some injurious epithet. The talk is only of Pergolesis, Orlandinis, Latillas, and a host of other unknowns who it seems to me, Madam, were never mentioned in our day.

These are the personages to whom they would have us conform, we who by rights should set the tone for all of Europe. But if the enthusiasts need to have originals, let them allow us to enjoy in peace our music, which, as all the world agrees, is most original. Let the strangers who accuse us of lightness listen, if they dare, to the productions of our composers and let them blush at their slander. Italian music has subjugated all the other nations; very well, so much the better; it will be the more honorable for us to have constantly resisted a flood that has engulfed so many barbarians.

But after afflicting you with this account of our disasters, I must not leave you in ignorance of our just causes for comfort. Amidst the general perversity, there are still some honest Israelites who have not bent their knee before the idol of the day; and if you will forgive this city for the sake of some upright persons, you will find them here. Certainly the "little violins" [*petits violons*, i.e., the two principals] have well deserved on this occasion to be called "great." Ever faithful to the ancient melody, they have not uselessly amused themselves by being zealous; they have not tried to stem the tide of fanaticism; but by clever subterfuges, by ruses known to them, they have secretly worked to ruin the endeavor to which they pretended to be contributing. They have adroitly limited the number of *intermèdes* [to be performed] to three; they have never consented that there be added ballets and other adornments, which the apostates call the *stale jokes* of our operas. If despite this they have not succeeded in wearying the public, we must allow that it was not their fault but that of the accursed *inter-mèdes*... You may believe also, Madam, that to kill those too seductive sounds they did not stint the redoubtable blows of their *baton*. One must also say to their credit that they would not have lent themselves to this novelty in the first place had they had the slightest suspicion that it would increase the receipts of the Opéra.

The saner part of our orchestra has seconded these two gallant men marvelously. The most vigorous among them have omitted nothing in order to disfigure or, if you will, *naturalize* the fatal melodies that have so turned the heads of our Frenchmen; they have employed accompaniments that were at times dragging, at times forced, nearly always against the grain, out-of-tune notes, wrong tempos, in a word all their science. To this authentic evidence of their sincere opposition to the progress of Italian melody, we cried out: "Courage, faithful orchestra! The inflexibility of your taste and the invincible stiffness of your arms are the sure guarantors of our music. Let them show up, these Pergolesis, these Orlandinis, and all these supposed Orpheuses of Italy; let them be abandoned to your care, and they shall soon expire under your indomitable fingers; and you shall continue to glitter with your 'first stroke of the bow'; and despite some traitors, who are only too evident in your midst, you shall forever remain what you have claimed to be for a long time, the most singular orchestra in the whole world."

You may rest assured, Madam, that in an affair of this importance the Commander and I have not been idle. First we cried, "Indecent! Scandalous!"; but as the applause redoubled and drowned out our voices, we dug underground passages, formed cabals, planted rumors. The Commander will answer for all women who are pretty, or claim to be. "Believe me," he said to me, "my poor Chevalier, these women want to be looked at and will never enjoy a music if men listen to it. And our fine young gentlemen who like to hum? Do you really think they will be able to bear performances in which there is not a single bad tune they can butcher?" In return, I have promised him our composers, who would have to blow on their fingers if this music caught on, and most of our singers who, except two, would be obliged to move from the opera house to the tavern. I recently met one of these; he was sad and pensive; it was not hard to guess the reason for his anxiety; we were just coming out of a performance where those cursed buffoons had been applauded with hands and feet. "What ails you, my friend?" I asked him; "you appear to be quite dejected." "Eh, Monsieur le Chevalier," he answered, "don't you see that if the public continues to be bewitched much longer by this dum-te-dum, I shall be ruined? M. Jelyotte and Mlle Fell will always get by; but you must admit that it would be hard at my age to go sing in the streets."

Truly, Madam, his state moved me to pity and I supped badly: the lad lacks only a good ear and some study to be an admirable actor; and we must not suffer the introduction among us of a music that demands qualities lacking in him and in many others who are not aware of it.

The loss this baroque music would entail of so many excellent persons reminds me of another, which will cause you some consternation at first. Jelyotte, whom even our most vehement detractors consider an inimitable singer, is leaving us; ah, Madam, in what circumstances! However, allay somewhat your fears; we have discovered in Vulcan's lair a Cyclops from whom great things are expected; and we flatter ourselves that six months' exercise will enable him to compensate for all our losses. Would that in itself not be a decisive factor in favor of our music? Studies begun during the tenderest youth and continued for years on end are barely sufficient to form an Italian singer; ours need only sol-fa a few months; indeed on occasion we have even dispensed with that, and no one is the worse for it.

And so take a little comfort, Madam; we would be inept indeed were we not able to disgust a public whose inconstancy and frivolity have been a sure resource on many another occasion of far less consequence. We will not rest till the mummers are sent back over the mountains; and I shall have the honor to inform you of our intrigues' success. Meanwhile, I am, with the deepest respect, Madam,

Your very humble and obedient servant,
* * *

Denise Launay, ed., *La Querelle des Bouffons* (Geneva: Minkoff Reprint, 1973), 121–31. Trans. P.W.

INTERLUDE: A TRAVELING COMPANY

Gasparo Gozzi (1713–86) was a Venetian man of letters and the older brother of Carlo (1720–1806), who, as author of such plays as *The Love of Three Oranges* and *Turandot*, is perhaps better known outside of Italy. Gasparo's fame rests today mainly on two gazettes which he edited, *La gazzetta veneta* (1760–61) and *L'osservatore* (1761–62). The first, especially, teems with genial observations of daily life in mid-eighteenth-century Venice, and the following account, given in its entirety below, is a fair sample. It has no more significance than any genre painting by Guardi or Longhi, but, like them, it captures the flavor of the scene, in this case a little square alongside the Grand

Canal and the people in it. (Note the traditional practice of referring to singers by the names of the operatic roles with which they have become associated.)

Saturday, 5 July 1760.—Last Tuesday, shortly before midnight, finding myself in a little square near San Moisè, I saw an opera getting ready to leave. Do not imagine this is a riddle. No: for it was really a whole opera preparing to set sail in two boats. The boats were tied to the shore, waiting to receive male and female virtuosos, ballet dancers, instrumentalists, tailors, big boxes, little boxes, suitcases, sacks, baskets, coffers, and whatever else art has invented to be transported from one place to another. A part of this baggage was already on board, a part on the waterfront or being carried by porters who came and went, picked up and put down, in a constant hustle and bustle. Little by little there arrived on the scene kings and princes, queens and princesses, troupes of dancers and players from all regions and parts; so that soon you could hear as many tongues being spoken as once were heard at the tower of Babel. As chance would have it, and to provide matter for lengthy discussions, the two boats had been impounded on account of a debt incurred by I know not whether Aeneas or Demophoon, who, having foreseen the eventuality, had got up early that morning and, taking his trunk, had gone by another route to await his colleagues onstage. But since it was not possible to set sail before the law was satisfied that the boats contained none of his property, the mooring lines remained tied and the sails furled, and there was plenty of time to chat. The masters of the boats and the sailors cursed because they were prevented from taking advantage of tide and wind; and the impresario, a smith by trade, or something of the sort, begged them to have patience, promising they should soon be freed.

There are some rough stones and marble blocks scattered about in that square which, waiting to be carved into statues, capitals, segments of columns or whatever, meanwhile do occasional duty as seats to the gondoliers and sometimes to people seeking to cool off at night. Since for the moment the company had no better sofas or couches at their disposal, some sat here, some there, some waited for persons who had not yet arrived, others just passed the time, till good fortune should grant them the freedom to sail. Here the prima donna was taking passionate leave of her lover and whispering in his ear, the while her prudent mother stayed by their side, jealous of her honor and never taking her eyes off a parrot with which she conversed, complaining to it of the night air, which was bad for her health. There a ballerina was chasing off a castrato who would not stop importuning her with his endearments, but the damsel protested she could not bear those wispy little voices, an opinion which a tenor nearby heartily praised.

"Oh, we shall have fine voices," said another, "after the dew has settled on our heads and the air has penetrated our ears; and we will cut a fine figure the

"THERE ARE SOME ROUGH STONES AND MARBLE BLOCKS SCATTERED ABOUT IN THAT SQUARE..." *(See p. 112.) Canaletto's "The Stonemason's Yard" shows us a scene very similar to that depicted by Gozzi. But the view here is of the Grand Canal in the daytime, while Gozzi's encounter with the departing opera company took place "shortly before midnight." London, National Gallery.*

first time we appear onstage sounding like snails after catching cold." "Thank Heaven for the dance," said a ballerina, "for a little fresh air doesn't cripple us, and we can dance even when we have lost our voices." "Oh, Hadrian," cried someone, "pick up your bundle and put it on board, for Sabina's dog has just pissed on it and I see Emirena's two dogs are smelling it: see, see, one of them is raising his leg." At this, the virtuoso went over and chased away the dogs just in time; but a male dancer, who had heard the virtuoso being told to pick up his bundle in such a familiar manner, took to berating the offender, saying, "I have heard a voice addressing a virtuoso in a familiar manner, and I know not, nor wish to know, whence came that voice; but I declare no well-bred person uses such language: after all, it should be remembered that musical virtuosos spend most of their lives impersonating the noblest characters of all nations and centuries and that they thereby acquire a certain nobility which must not be taken from them, nor denied them. If you add up all the hours they have spent dressed as kings and princes, holding their music sheets in their hands, learning the sayings of heroes and great men, you will realize that the rest of their lives is reduced to but a brief moment, part of which they have spent sleeping, perchance dreaming of possessing states, a scepter, and a crown. And we must remember another thing: to address them in a familiar manner is to risk doing them great harm, for it might humble them; and since they must fill their spirits with magnanimity and greatness, it is best to raise them and swell them as much as possible, so they can play their parts decorously. As for us dancers, it little matters; we are shepherds, countrymen, villagers, knife sharpeners, coopers, vintagers, and our business is to leap like deers and goats: address us as you please, a somersault will not turn out any higher or lower on that account; but let us respect our Catos and Tituses." These words were greeted with a universal guffaw. "Let us rehearse the opera," said a player. "Let us wait till we are on board," replied another, "for we shall have plenty of time." Meanwhile, gondolas were landing, bearing other female singers who, either because they had no baggage or because they had sent their best things in other boats, arrived with rough hempen sacks in the prow. While they stepped out, others shouted, "Easy! Watch out! Careful unloading those things! Look out for the china! Don't let those treasures fall in the water!" At last the entire company was assembled; and for lack of anything better to do, they began discussing the distribution of places on board the boats. It was no small matter, for everyone had a personal preference, and alliances were soon formed. But the impresario, who was informed of everything and knew his prima donna's every intrigue, for she was his secretary and he could not be separated from her since he needed her advice on all matters: the impresario decided that the dancers and instrumentalists should board one boat, the singers and other employees of the company, himself included, the other; and when someone pointed out to him that it would not be possible to rehearse the opera if the instrumentalists traveled in one boat and the singers in the other, he said that if need be they could be sent over in a ferry, or else should have to bide their time. Permission to depart finally arrived; and the devotees on shore having been bid farewell, the opera at last went its way, distributed in two boats.

Gaspare Gozzi, *La gazzetta veneta*, ed. A. Zardo (Florence: Sansoni, 1967), 194–96. Trans. P.W.

18

OPERATIC REFORM IN VIENNA: GLUCK AND CALZABIGI

Reform was very much in the air during the eighteenth century: the spirit of the Enlightenment sought to correct abuses in all the institutions of society, including the arts. Opera came in for its share of the reforming spirit. Contemporary chroniclers declared that the abuses of seventeenth-century Italian opera had been corrected by two reformers, first by the Imperial court poet Apostolo Zeno, then by his successor Pietro Metastasio: they had purged the operatic libretto of its trivialities and made it "regular," worthy even of comparison with the masterpieces of French tragedy. Modern historians take a more nuanced view of this development, being less inclined to credit the creation of *opera seria* to any one or two persons, however eminent. But there is no doubt that Metastasio's dramas, especially, were universally admired not only as librettos but as literature. It was not long, however, before critical voices were raised again, clamoring for reform: they complained of the rigidity of the new operatic conventions, which, among other things, tended to indulge a new breed of superstar singers by focusing all the musical expression in da capo arias. Italian critics like Francesco Algarotti (*Saggio sopra l'opera in musica*, 1755) turned to French opera, as others had done before: with its ballets, choruses, mythological plots, expressive recitatives, and relatively modest arias, it presented a living contrast to *opera seria* that could well serve as a model for its reform. In Vienna, where Metastasio still officiated as court poet though virtually retired from the operatic stage, there arose in the 1760s what was destined to become the best-known attempt at operatic reform. French influence was very strong there at the time, and the court theater had for some years been presenting French *opéras comiques* and ballets under the supervision of its Francophile *directeur des spectacles*, Count Giacomo Durazzo (1717–94). The musician in charge of adapting, and sometimes composing, these works was Gluck. They were joined by the choreographer-dancer Gasparo Angiolini (1731–1803) and, in 1761, by Ranieri Calzabigi (1714–95), a man of letters and adventurer recently expelled from France, where, among other occupations, he had edited the complete works of Metastasio, praising them fulsomely in a "Dissertation" that served as preface. These men collaborated for the first time in October 1761, creating a totally new form of ballet, the dance-drama *Don Juan ou Le Festin de pierre*. This was followed in October 1762 by *Or-*

feo ed Euridice, the first "reform" opera, featuring plenty of dancing, choruses, a mythological plot, expressive recitatives, and nonstandard arias. Contemporary documents are few and unsatisfactory concerning this, undoubtedly the most famous and lasting achievement of the group's reforming initiative. It was the second Gluck-Calzabigi opera, *Alceste* (1767), that prompted Calzabigi to expound his theories of reform, in a letter to Count Wenzel Anton von Kaunitz, Empress Maria Theresa's chancellor and (after Durazzo's departure from Vienna) director of theaters; in it, Calzabigi expresses his concern that *Alceste* be mounted in a manner befitting the new principles underlying this opera. The letter, though private, reads like a public statement; and its contents will indeed surface again publicly, if in condensed form, over Gluck's signature in 1769 (see the dedication of the printed score, below). In Vienna Calzabigi must have met with less than a cordial welcome from Metastasio, who now became the scapegoat of his rather strident polemic. The fifteen different singers mentioned at various points in the letter were all famous but need not be separately identified here; Calzabigi, it is clear, is citing them merely as practitioners of the bad old style or of the new. Only Gaetano Guadagni (1729–92), the famous alto castrato, deserves special notice in this context, as an eminent practitioner of the new style: he was the first Orfeo, the *musico* referred to as having been rewarded by the Empress; and even he, apparently, acted like a "rogue" in the opera *Telemaco* (1763) by Gluck. Marco Coltellini (1719–77), the librettist of *Telemaco* and of another opera mentioned here, *Ifigenia in Tauride* (Vienna, 1763), music by Tommaso Traetta (1727–79), shared Calzabigi's and Gluck's reformist orientation.

Vienna, March 6, 1767

Highness!

In transmitting to Your Highness the enclosed letter from Sig. Gluck [not extant] to which I feel I ought to draw your attention, I find it incumbent upon me to add some necessary reflections of my own to what he says about my *Alceste*.

When it is the pleasure of Her Imperial Majesty and Your Highness to order that *Alceste* be put on the stage, it is of paramount importance to choose for the opera really suitable executants. Alceste and Admetus cannot be represented by just any singers, partly by reason of the texture of this new species of drama in which all depends on the eye of the spectator and consequently on the action, but also because the music is exactly fitted to what is happening on the stage and depends much more on the expression than anything the Italians are nowadays pleased to call "song."

Only the dramas of the Abbé Metastasio, whose length—because of the large number of verses and musical arabesques—is such that they cannot, from the outset, hope to hold the attention of the spectator, enjoy the privilege of being saddles for all horses. There it is a matter not whether a character in the drama is sung by a Farinelli, Caffarelli, Guadagni or Toschi, or by a Tesi, Gabrielli or Bianchi, since the audience does not expect nor demand from the singers more than a couple of arias and a duet, without even pretending to make out all the words, having from the start abandoned all hope of taking an interest in the action; no one, after all, can listen attentively for five hours to six performers, four of whom are usually so inept that they hardly know how to enunciate, just for the pleasure of getting excited over an insipid Clelia, a cold Ersilia, an imaginary Aristea, a saucy Emira, an indecent Onoria, and a shameless Mandane, all of whom are at bottom no more than little Roman or Neapolitan courtesans who gossip about love in polite language on the stage. As for the utterly unnatural philosophizing heroes of the type of Metastasio's Horace, Themistocles, Cato, and Romulus, the like of which are not to be met in this world, about them I prefer to hold my tongue altogether.

Since these dramas could not, in performance, please the mind, they had need to entertain the senses: the eye by the sight of live horses in cardboard forests, by real battles fought on painted battlefields, by conflagrations of colored paper; the ear by using the voices as if they were violins and producing whole concertos with the human mouth alone, thus giving rise to that musical gargling which in Naples they call *trocciolette* (because it closely resembles the noise of the wheels passing over the ropes of a pulley)—and a mass of other musical whimsies comparable to those stone tidbits with which Gothic architecture decorated, or rather disfigured, its monuments and which, once so admired, are now objects of laughter and contempt to anyone who bothers to stop and look at them. And to make room for these strange embellishments the poet lent himself to the filling of his librettos with similes involving storms, tempests, lions, war horses, and nightingales which fit about as well into the mouths of passionate, desperate, or furious heroes as beauty spots, powder, makeup, and diamonds on the face, head, and neck of an ape.

Matters are entirely different in the new plan of musical drama which has been, if not invented, at least first put into practice by me in *Orfeo*, then in *Alceste*, and continued by Signor Coltellini. All is nature here, all is passion: there are no sententious reflections, no philosophy or politics, no similes, and none of those descriptions or amplifications which are only an avoidance of difficulties and are to be found in all librettos. The duration is limited to what does not tire or make the attention wander. The plots are simple, not romanticized; a few verses are enough to inform the spectators of the progress of the action which is never double, in servile, uncalled-for obedience to the silly rule concerning the *secondo uomo* and *seconda donna* when not needed. Reduced to the dimensions of Greek tragedy, they have therefore the unique advantage of exciting terror and pity in the same way as spoken tragedy. According to this plan, as Your Highness will perceive, the music has no other function than to express what arises from the words, in order not to smother them with notes or lengthen the spectacle unduly; it being ridiculous to prolong the sentence "I love you" (for instance) with a hundred notes when nature has restricted it to three (I am of the opinion that a note can never have the value of more than one syllable).

If this new plan, with the addition of pantomime in the choruses and ballets in imitation of the Greeks, should find the approval of the public and of H.I.M. (who was after all present 14 times at *Orfeo* and signified her extreme pleasure by making gifts to the composer and the *musico*), it is essential to adhere to it and not to confound it with that of Signor Metastasio, because ornaments for brunettes do not suit blondes. In the Abbé's dramas, let the Gabriellis, the Bastardellas, and suchlike pipers warble and scream their heads off in an aria about a murmuring brook so that you can't hear a word, it is no matter; but in *Orfeo*, in [Traetta's] *Ifigenia*, in *Telemaco*, and in *Alceste* we need actresses who will sing what the maestro has written and not take it upon themselves to add to the score by repeating 30 or 40 times the passages they brought in their luggage over a "farewell" or "I leave you" in their personal musical hieroglyphics of which, not to be discourteous, one might perhaps say: "Pulchrum est, sed non erat hic locus" ["It is beautiful, but this was not the place for it"].

Putting *Alceste* in the mouths of warblers like these would mean ruining the music and the poetry and failing to achieve the ultimate aim, which is to succeed and to please. So that, should an inclination for the Bastardellas, the Gabriellis, and the Apriles still persist, give them an opera by our little Arcadian shepherd Artino Corasio [i.e. Metastasio], while for *Alceste* we shall need to turn to Mingotti or Francesina, to Manzuoli or Tibaldi. For the same reason (as I have already told Sig. Gluck) we need a couple more basses to strengthen the choruses, to take the parts of the priest and the oracle, and as more effective supers in the pantomimed scenes. In this way *Alceste* will be able to succeed as a new majestic and fascinating spectacle worthy of this court and of a connoisseur like Your Highness who has happily taken an interest in it. In any other way it would be better to leave unheard this child of my poor genius and Sig. Gluck's sublime gifts, rather than let it be born a cripple, and to await more suitable circumstances. *Orfeo* went well, because there we had Guadagni whom the part fitted as if it had been written for him; otherwise its fate would have been terrible. *Telemaco*, for all its excellent poetry and its singularly divine music, went very badly indeed, because Tibaldi was no actress, Guadagni a knave, and that famous Teyber woman unsuited to the part of Circe, without enough voice to make a sorceress and do justice to music worthy of an enchantress and and enchantment.

I close with the expression of my most profound respect and remain

> Your Highness's
> most humble, devoted, and obedient servant
> De Calsabigi the elder.

Hanns Hammelmann and Michael Rose, "New Light on Calzabigi and Gluck," *Musical Times* 110 (1969): 609–10.

What follows is the most famous document of the Viennese reform, Gluck's dedication of the printed score of *Alceste* to Grand Duke Leopold of Tuscany. Its author was not Gluck, but again Calzabigi, who here refers to Metastasio only obliquely when he points to the absence of "flowery descriptions, superfluous similes, cold, sententious morals" in the libretto of *Alceste*. (Note, too, the praises of the Grand Duke's domain, Tuscany, and its capital, Florence, as the cradle of the Renaissance: Calzabigi was Tuscan.) All in all, this document deserves its place of honor as a landmark in the history of operatic reform movements: rarely have the rights of the dramatic component in opera been asserted more eloquently. At the same time, it is a declaration of the new aesthetic: "simplicity, truth, and naturalness" were the neoclassical ideals in art; and the Viennese reform operas illustrated them perfectly, though they had no effect on the further course of Italian opera.

Your Royal Highness,

When I undertook to write the music of *Alceste*, I decided to divest it wholly of all the abuses which, introduced either by the ill-considered vanity of the singers or by the excessive indulgence of the composers, have for so long disfigured Italian opera, turning the grandest and loveliest into the most ridiculous and most tedious of all spectacles. I thought I would restrict the music to its true function of serving the poetry in the expression and situations of the story, without interrupting the action or chilling it with useless, superfluous ornaments; and I considered that its effect should be the same as the effect lively colors and judicious contrasts of lights and shades have upon a correct and well-proportioned drawing, serving to animate the figures without altering their outlines. And so I decided not to stop an actor in the heat of the dialogue, forcing him to wait out a tedious instrumental introduction, nor to stop him in midword over a favorable vowel, nor to display the agility of his fine voice with a lengthy passage, nor to let the orchestra give him the time to catch his breath for a cadenza. I did not feel obliged to hurry through the second part of an aria, though it was the more impassioned and significant, in order to be able to repeat four times the words of the first part, finishing the aria where perhaps the sense was left unfinished, all so the singer might have the leisure to show the many ways in which he can vary a passage at will; in short, I have attempted to banish all the abuses against which good sense and reason have been inveighing for such a long time in vain.

I assumed that the overture ought to forewarn the spectators of the impending action and, so to speak, be its summary; that the instrumental ensemble should be commensurate with the [dramatic] interest and emotion, and not perpetuate that divisive split in the dialogue caused by aria and recitative, cutting off a period meaninglessly and interrupting in an untimely way the impetus and heat of the action.

I further believed that my weightiest task was but this, to seek for a beautiful simplicity; and I avoided making a show of complexity at the expense of clarity; I have not deemed the discovery of new things praiseworthy in itself when not called for naturally by the expression and the situation; nor has there been a hallowed rule which I have not willingly sacrificed for the sake of the [dramatic] effect.

These my principles. As good fortune would have it, my intent was marvelously seconded by the libretto, in which the celebrated Author, devising a new plan for the drama, replaced the [customary] flowery descriptions, superfluous similes, cold, sententious morals with the language of the heart, vehement passions, interesting situations, and an ever-changing spectacle. Success has justified my maxims, and the universal approval of so enlightened a city has clearly demonstrated that simplicity, truth, and naturalness are the great principles of the beautiful in all productions of art. All this notwithstanding, despite the repeated requests of the most respectable persons that I resolve to publish this work of mine, I felt what a great risk one runs in fighting prejudices that are so widely and deeply rooted, and I have felt it necessary to arm myself with the powerful patronage of Your Royal Highness, imploring the favor of prefixing to this work of mine your August Name, which so rightly gathers to itself the homage of all enlightened Europe. Only the great Protector of the fine arts, reigning over a nation that glories in having made them rise again out of their universal oppression and produced the greatest models in each of them, in a city that has always been the first to shake the yoke of vulgar prejudices in its quest for perfection, only he can undertake the reform of this noble spectacle in which all the fine arts have so great a share. When this comes to pass, to me will remain the glory of having laid the first stone, as well as this public testimonial of your high protection, under which I have the honor to declare myself, in humblest deference,

Your Royal Highness's
Most humble, devoted, grateful servant,
Cristoforo Gluck

Facsimile of the preface to the 1769 first edition of *Alceste*, in *The New Grove Dictionary of Music and Musicians*, ed. S. Sadie, 20 vols. (London: Macmillan, 1980), 7:466. Trans. P.W.

19

GLUCK IN PARIS

Gluck's conquest of Paris in the 1770s did not occur without a carefully prepared publicity campaign designed to arouse the French capital's disposition
to burst into heated debate over controversial cultural issues; and that opera
was just such an issue had been amply proved twenty years earlier by the War
of the Buffoons (see pp. 106–11 above). Now, in 1772, the opening salvo was
fired by François du Roullet, an attaché at the French embassy in Vienna, who
had fashioned a libretto for Gluck out of Racine's tragedy *Iphigénie en Aulide*;
the work was written for Paris, without any assurance it would be produced
there. Du Roullet's lengthy, sensational letter, addressed to one of the directors of the Opéra, was published in the *Mercure de France* and prompted, as
expected, instant reactions from the Parisian littérateurs, touching off a debate
that would occupy the capital for years to come. But the letter attained its purpose: Gluck came to Paris, and, after months of rehearsal, his *Iphigénie* was
performed at the Opéra on 19 April 1774. We will follow Gluck's Parisian career as it was reported on in an unusual source, the *Correspondance littéraire*.
This was a monthly letter sent from Paris in manuscript form, on condition of
confidentiality, to about a dozen royal and princely subscribers, among them
Catherine the Great and Grand Duke Leopold of Tuscany (the dedicatee of
Gluck's *Alceste*; see p. 119). Started in 1753 under the editorship of Frédéric-
Melchior Grimm, friend and colleague of the encyclopedists, it passed in 1773
into the hands of a less famous editor, Jacques-Henri Meister (1744–1826),
who guided it until the French Revolution forced him to leave Paris and suspend its publication. The articles on Gluck were probably written by Meister
himself, perhaps with the help of Germaine de Vermenoux, one of his con-
tributors. Amid the violent factionalism that swept musical circles at this time,
his was a relatively objective voice, tinged with a wit that identifies it unmistakably as Parisian.

APRIL 1774

During the past fortnight, all that Paris has been thinking of, dreaming of, is
music. It is the subject of all our disputes, of all our conversations, the soul of

all our suppers; and it would even seem ridiculous to show an interest in anything else. If you ask a political question, you receive a harmonic answer; if you
make an observation about morals, you get the ritornello of an aria; and if you
try to allude to an interesting feature of this or that play by Racine or Voltaire,
the only response is to have your attention directed to the effect produced by
the orchestra in Agamemnon's beautiful recitative. Do we still need, after all
this, to say that it is M. le chevalier Gluck's *Iphigénie* that is causing all the commotion? And a particularly animated commotion it is, because opinions are
sharply divided and all the parties are fired by the same frenzy. Three may be
discerned: that of the old French opera, which has sworn not to recognize any
gods other than Lully and Rameau; that of purely Italian music, which believes
in no melody other than that of the various Jommellis, Piccinnis, Sacchinis; finally the chevalier Gluck's own party, which claims to have discovered the music best suited to theatrical action, a music whose principles are to be drawn only
from the eternal wellspring of harmony and the intimate ties of our feelings and
sensations; a music that belongs to no one country, but whose style the genius
of the composer has succeeded in adapting to the particular cadences of our language. This last party can already boast an illustrious convert. Jean-Jacques
[Rousseau] has become the most zealous partisan of the new system; he has declared, with a self-denial rarely encountered in our sages, that he had been mistaken until now; that M. Gluck's opera upset all his notions, and that now he is
convinced that the French language is as susceptible as any other of a vigorous,
moving, and sensitive music.

The ultramontane faction cannot deny our new Orpheus a deep understanding of the secrets of harmony; but it does deny him the vocal or melodic
part. It finds the motives of his arias are nearly all either common or bizarre,
and that the better ones miss their effect for lack of development. His accompaniments, they say, are pure but monotonous; his recitatives labored and heavy.

The old pillars of French opera cry that we shall be deprived of the genre in
which we have succeeded and get nothing better in exchange. They complain
that instead of being able to sleep, as is the custom, during a scene, they are
obliged to listen to it, since nothing else is interesting, the ballets being the most
insipid thing in the world—the ballets, which ought forever to constitute the
glory and delight of such a spectacle!

However contradictory all these opinions may appear, they at least agree, it
seems to me, in showing that M. Gluck has left the beaten path and has opened
up a quite new career for artists; one does not attempt such an enterprise unless
prompted by the influence of a superior genius.

A work that excites as much activity, interest, even disagreement as does
the new opera is surely not a mediocre work; those who speak ill of it the most
are forced to admit it contains beautiful things, and the spectators least likely to
feel its quality have heard it with a kind of surprise that has seemed to stun their
criticism or ignorance.

SOPHIE ARNOULD IN THE TITLE ROLE OF GLUCK'S *IPHIGÉNIE EN AULIDE*. *Her acting and singing in Gluck's first Parisian opera were remarkable enough to be memorialized in this bust by Houdon.* Paris, Musée du Louvre.

At the first performance, which took place on Tuesday the 19th, many pieces were warmly applauded, but the work as a whole was received rather coolly, whether because the beautiful, the sublime touches us but feebly when habit or reflection have not yet taught us to recognize it, or because the dénouement, which is weak, and the final ballet, which contains nothing remarkable, chilled the spectacle. But at the second performance the opera was praised to the skies, and the author was called for half an hour but did not appear. It continues to be attended with great eagerness and will no doubt hold the stage for as long as Mlle [Sophie] Arnould will be able to sing. She acts the part of Iphigenia as it has perhaps never been acted at the Comédie Française, and she sings not only with the grace for which we have so long known her, but also with extraordinary precision, not always one of her strengths. It appears that the chevalier Gluck divined the character and range of her voice precisely and that he took from it all the notes of his melody. [Henri] Larrivée sings with no less expression, but has seized, so it seems to me, the spirit of his role with less finesse; he has more rage than passion and dignity, and that is not the haughty, superb Agamemnon's nature. [Joseph] Le Gros shouts his head off with the most beautiful voice in the world, but it is impossible to recognize Achilles in his interpretation: there is nothing more uncouth, more gross than his figure, unless it is his acting. Mlle Duplan would be a rather fine Clytemnestra if her voice were truer and more flexible; but this failing causes us to miss several felicitous aspects of her role, or at least weakens their effect.

We have not yet spoken of the words of *Iphigénie*, because no one speaks of them. The music absorbs all of the spectator's attention; none is left over for the poem. The author is M. du Roullet, a commander of Malta. He has mostly followed Racine's plot, omitting only the episode of Ériphile. It was impossible, no doubt, to follow a better model; but if at times it is permissible to take another's property, is it not an unforgivable crime to take it only to ruin it? M. du Roullet has not only cut out one of the most beautiful paintings of our ancient theater to put it in a foreign frame, he has daubed it in a strange way, sometimes preserving Racine's verses, sometimes substituting his own; giving Agamemnon lines suited only to Clytemnestra, Clytemnestra lines suited only to Agamemnon; putting in Iphigenia's mouth, when she addresses Achilles, the same things she said in the tragedy concerning her rival, etc. However, it all works out, because the action moves quite swiftly and the music develops its most touching situations with a truth and warmth of sentiment that mask the poet's negligence and awkwardness. Only the dénouement is unbearably inept and implausible. Instead of the beautiful scene indicated by Racine, we see Achilles arrive with all his soldiers, seize Iphigenia at the foot of the altar, and defy the assembled Greeks to take her from his arms. Calchas, who had just declared to the Greeks that the irrevocable will of the gods demanded the blood of Agamemnon's daughter, suddenly changes his mind and prudently assures them that Heaven is satisfied; a little flare is thrown on the altar, and that is that. This turn of events has been criticized so universally that at this very moment they are working to change it. Diana will appear in the clouds, Heaven will explain its intentions with more dignity, and Iphigenia will no longer appear to owe her life to sly Calchas's terror.

On 2 August of the same year, Gluck presented his second Paris opera, a considerably altered French version of *Orfeo ed Euridice*. Its success was overwhelming.

AUGUST 1774

The Académie Royale de Musique, after having bored us for a long time with [Mondonville's ballet] *Le Carnaval du Parnasse*, has finally given us, on Tuesday the 2nd, the first performance of *Orphée et Eurydice*, drama in three acts. M. de Moline, the author of the words, has doubtless abused the permission one might have to be mediocre when undertaking to translate a poem literally and to apply French verse to a thoroughly Italian music. But it would be ungrateful not to appreciate his work, since, be that what it may, we owe to it the pleasure of hearing the most sublime music that was ever perhaps performed in France. It is known that *Orphée* is, among all the operas of the chevalier Gluck, the one that has enjoyed the greatest success in Italy. The enthusiasm with which it has just been received in our theater, in spite of the old cabal of the Lullys and Rameaus, proves what progress this celebrated composer has caused our nation's taste to make; it proves we need no longer despair of our ears, and that by dint of patience and genius it is sometimes possible to triumph over the most respectable prejudices. As a whole, *Iphigénie* has more dignity, more pomp, and is more interesting than *Orphée*. Even disfigured, a plot by Racine is worth more than those of M. Calzabigi. Let us further admit that there are perhaps a greater number of agreeable things, of touching ideas in the music of *Iphigénie* than in that of *Orphée*; but it is true nevertheless that the beautiful pieces in the latter work are still superior to the most beautiful pieces in the former. The sorrowful and penetrating cries with which Orpheus interrupts, in a manner so true and so pathetic, the sensitive, sweet song of the nymphs weeping at Eurydice's tomb; the melodious air with which he softens the demons who bar him from the entrance to the netherworld; the superb chorus in which are expressed with so much art and truth the different gradations of their raging and relenting; the duet of Orpheus and Eurydice brought back to life, but preferring death to the indifference her spouse is obliged to affect before her; the entire scene that paints so vigorously the conflicts Orpheus feels at that terrible moment, his weakness, and the last stage of his despair; all these are so many masterpieces of harmony and of expression. I have seen several persons who are no experts in the art confess in good faith that never had music made so lively and so deep an impression upon them.

If Mlle Arnould is less successful in this new opera than in *Iphigénie*, Le Gros is infinitely more so; he sings the principal role with so much warmth, so much taste, and even so much soul, that it is difficult to recognize him, or not to regard his metamorphosis as one of the prime miracles wrought by the magic art of M. Gluck. The ballets in *Orphée* have also given more pleasure than those in *Iphigénie*; they are more connected to the subject and have a nobler, more sustained harmony. Many, however, greatly prefer the Elysian fields ballet in *Castor* [*et Pollux* by Rameau] to the one in the second act of *Orphée*, which is of the same kind. The parallel has caused them to say that the new opera is only a semi-Castor. Very well. A bad play on words is more bearable perhaps than a bad reason.

The death of Louis XV had interrupted the first run of *Iphigénie en Aulide* after only five performances. Alterations were made, especially in the ending, and on 10 January 1775 the opera was revived. Marie Antoinette, Gluck's former singing pupil in Vienna, his ardent supporter in Paris, and now the Queen of France, came to one of the performances.

JANUARY 1775

The Académie Royale de Musique has just revived *Iphigénie* by M. Gluck. Although the revival is being followed very eagerly, people are still, it seems to me, as much in disagreement over the merits of this new genre of music today as they were when it was first performed. The Sacchini and Piccinni enthusiasts find in it nothing but noise and baroque ideas lacking in taste, in genius, and even in expression. Above all, they reproach him for having written so heartrending a tragedy as *Iphigénie* in pastoral style and sometimes even in tavern style [*en style de guinguette*]. To top their blasphemies, they are not afraid of saying that what people like to call a new genre is only Lully's system warmed over, but less noble, less graceful, and less varied than what you find in the good works of that ancient composer. The chevalier Gluck's partisans claim on the contrary that he is the first to have grasped the true character of dramatic music, and that nobody has ever obtained more striking effects from simpler means, or mingled more harmony with more expression. The latter at least have on their side, apart from the eloquence of the abbé [François] Arnaud, the lovely arms of Mlle Arnould, the superb voice of Le Gros, and the impassioned acting of Larrivée. The only noticeable change that has been made in the conduct of the poem is that in the dénouement Diana appears in person atop a very beautiful cloud to adjudicate the quarrel between Achilles and Calchas. The goddess's arrival, despite the rich decorations that surround her, makes no great impression, because it is much too sudden and because the witnesses most concerned with this marvel seem for all the world not to believe it themselves, or at least not to be too interested in it. The more pompous, the more contrived such a spectacle, the less striking it is, unless it is properly integrated and true.

If the votes on M. Gluck's *Iphigénie* continue to be severely divided, they were all united the day the queen came to hear it, when the verses were applied to her in the chorus:

> Chantons, chantons notre reine,
> Et que l'Hymen qui l'enchaine
> Nous rende à jamais heureux.

> [Sing, sing our queen's praises,
> And may her marriage bonds
> Make us forever happy.]

The allusion was seized with enthusiasm. The piece had to be repeated, and all eyes turned to the Queen, who received the homage with the most amiable and interesting embarrassment. What prologues, what panegyrics can be compared to such transports of public tenderness and admiration!

On 31 December 1776 Niccolò Piccinni arrived in Paris, summoned by the partisans of Italian opera to make war on Gluck. The maneuver was by then a hallowed one in operatic history: one thinks of the Handel-Bononcini match got up by rival parties in London half a century earlier. The terrain was in any case ready, and both sides went at it with gusto. The Italophiles were led by the well-known author and academician Jean François Marmontel, who became Piccinni's tutor in French and his librettist for the opera *Roland* (1778), which enjoyed considerable success, as did several other works by the Italian composer. Personally Gluck and Piccinni remained on civilized terms throughout this latest controversy: after all, it had a great deal more to do with Paris than with music. Our excerpt describes how it began. (Grétry, neither a Gluckist nor a Piccinnist, comes in for veiled criticism; not a pupil of Piccinni, as stated, he apparently resented being cast in the shade by the whole affair.)

MAY 1777

Some great philosophers have asserted that the truth does not suit mankind, since it has been nothing to them but a source of quarrels, hatred, and divisions. Following the same principle one could far better prove that music does not suit

France, since the art has never attempted to make the slightest progress here without provoking the most violent cabals and the most ridiculous frenzies against it. We still remember all the turmoil caused among us by Rameau's new systems and by the arrival of the Buffoons from Italy. . . . How can we fittingly recount to the farthest nations the origin and progress of the great quarrel that has arisen among us between the Gluckists and the Piccinnists, a quarrel that today divides the mightiest pens of our literary world? . . . If it suffices to be the humblest of historians, the most impartial, the most faithful, then I will try.

For more than four years now M. Gluck has peacefully enjoyed the supreme honor of occupying the stage of the Académie Royale de Musique almost single-handed. A few attempts to vary somewhat the uniformity of the offerings were so unsuccessful that one may well say they only served to decorate the triumph of the new Orpheus. True, his music, announced as constituting a new genre, met with some persecution at first. It had to be so: our natural aversion to new things, except in cookery and fashion, is well known. But the chevalier Gluck's lucky star soon won out over his enemies. However powerful the eternal sect of the Lullyists and Rameauists may still be today, their cabal, stunned, gave way, or at least kept quiet. . . .

Thanks to the talents of M. Gluck and his advocates, the Opéra's management prospered. If purely Italian music still retained its partisans, they were few in number and only in private bemoaned a success too brilliant not to have set back by several years the progress of a taste they dare to qualify as the only *good taste in music.* "Do you know," they said in a whisper, "why the chevalier Gluck's operas have been so popular in France? It is because, with the exception of two or three airs that are Italian in form and some recitatives of a positively barbarous character, his music is French music, as French as any ever composed, but less natural in its melody than Lully and less pure than Rameau; it is because the chevalier Gluck has sacrificed all the resources and all the beauties of his art to theatrical effect, which was bound to please immensely a nation that will perhaps never understand melody but has the most exquisite taste for all things having to do with dramatic propriety. . . . And that is how we love music in France."

This was what people were thinking when M. Piccinni came to Paris under the protection of the ambassador of Naples. He had been preceded here long before by his amply deserved reputation. The success of his *Buona figliuola,* no matter how badly it was parodied and how mediocre had been its performance, the success of all the operas of M. Grétry, who until then gloried in being his pupil, of all the pieces composed by him that we had heard with enthusiasm at our Concerts des Amateurs and Concert Spirituel: how many reasons to be prejudiced in his favor! His arrival was announced with éclat; our most celebrated artists, our greatest virtuosos, except however M. Grétry, hastened to pay their respects to him; and the Comédie Italienne having revived *La buona figliuola,* the public shouted for the author and greeted him with repeated acclamations.

At this point the party of the Gluckists shuddered and that of the Sacchinis, Piccinnis, Traettas regained some of their courage.

It became known that . . . our august Queen wished to establish M. Piccinni in France; it became known that the Opéra had paid him a considerable sum; it also became known that M. Marmontel had arranged several of Quinault's poems to render them more susceptible of musical form and expression; that he had entrusted one of them to M. Piccinni, and that they worked together every day. How many circumstances apt to arouse the liveliest alarm! "Is it then a new revolution they are preparing for us? What tyranny! To insist on varying our pleasures! Is it possible to change one's musical system as one changes one's politics? No sooner did we become accustomed," said some, "to this new music, which at least may be listened to almost as easily as that of our fathers, than we shall have to give it up!" "No sooner," said others, "had we educated the taste of the nation than they want to plunge it back into barbarity. We had succeeded in inspiring it with an elevated taste, and see how they mean to give it a taste for tinsel, for all those frivolous ornaments which Italy herself has renounced with disgust! Is music made to gratify the ear? No: but to depict the passions in all their violence, to wrench the soul, stimulate our courage, accustom our senses to the most painful impressions, form citizens, heroes, etc., etc. Let us, gentlemen, unite all our efforts to turn away the scourge that threatens both the chevalier Gluck and the state as a whole."

As a consequence pamphlets, sarcasms, anonymous letters are flying about everywhere. . . . Discord has taken possession of all spirits, has brought turmoil into our academies, into our cafés, into all our literary societies. People who enjoyed being together avoid each other; our very dinners, which before had so happily reconciled all sorts of spirits and characters, now breathe only constraint and defiance; the most brilliant salons, once most numerous, are at present half deserted. People no longer ask, "Is he a Jansenist? Is he a Molinist? A philosopher? Religious?" They ask: "Is he a Gluckist or Piccinnist?" And everything else depends on the answer to that question.

Maurice Tourneux, ed., *Correspondance littéraire, philosophique et critique par Grimm, Diderot, Raynal, Meister, etc. . . .* , 16 vols. (Paris: Garnier Frères, 1877–82), 10:416–19, 472–73; 11:11–12, 456–61. Trans. P.W.

20

MOZART AT WORK ON *DIE ENTFÜHRUNG AUS DEM SERAIL*

In May 1781 Mozart broke with his employer, Count Hieronymus Colloredo, Prince-Archbishop of Salzburg, and took up residence in Vienna as a free lance. His first major commission there was the Singspiel *Die Entführung aus dem Serail* (*The Abduction from the Seraglio*), on which he worked that year and the next. The libretto was adapted by Gottlieb Stephanie "the Younger" from an existing libretto by C. F. Bretzner, set to music earlier that year by Johann André. Mozart kept his father in Salzburg informed of his progress; and the letters he wrote to him on this occasion are among the most exhaustive and revealing documents we have of his creativity as an opera composer. The first mention of the new opera occurs in a letter of 1 August 1781:

The day before yesterday Stephanie the Younger gave me a libretto to compose. I must confess that, bad as he may be towards other people, of which I know nothing, he is an excellent friend to me.—The libretto is quite good. The subject is Turkish and is called: *Belmonte und Konstanze*, or *Die Verführung aus dem Serail*.—The overture, the chorus in the first act, and the final chorus I will write with Turkish music. Mad:^selle Cavalieri, Mad:^selle Teyber, M:^r Fischer, M:^r Adamberger, M:^r Dauer, and M:^r Walter are to sing in it.—I am so happy to be setting the libretto, that Cavalieri's first aria, and Adamberger's, and the trio that concludes the first act are already finished. Time is short, that is true; for it is to be produced in mid-September—however—the conditions under which it is to be performed, and generally—all the other plans—cheer my spirits so, that I hasten to my writing table with the greatest anticipation, and remain sitting there with the greatest joy.

The production date was postponed. Meanwhile, Mozart sent his father some of the music, which cost the father extra postage. In his next letter Mozart proceeded to describe how he was getting on with the opera:

Vienna, 26 September 1781

Mon très cher Père!

Forgive me for making you pay more postage recently!—but I just had no essential news—and thought to please you by giving you some small idea of the opera. The opera had begun with a monologue, and I asked Mr. Stephanie to make a little arietta out of it—and that, instead of having those two chattering away after Osmin's little song, this be made into a duet.—As we have Mr. Fischer in mind for the role of Osmin and he certainly has a remarkable bass voice (in spite of the Archbishop's saying to me that he sings too low for a bass, but I assured him he'd sing higher next time—) one ought to make use of such a man, particularly as he has the local public all on his side.—But in the original libretto this Osmin has only that one little song, and nothing else to sing, except the Terzetto and finale. And so he has been given an aria in the first act, and shall have another in the 2nd too.—It was I who provided that whole aria to Mr. Stephanie;—and the greater part of the music to it was already completed before Stephanie had heard a word about the matter.—All you have of it is the beginning and the end, which ought to be very effective—Osmin's rage is made comical because it is accompanied by Turkish music.—In working out the aria, I have allowed his beautiful low notes (despite our Salzburg Midas) to sparkle.— The [passage], *Drum beym Barte des Propheten* etc. is in the same tempo to be sure, but with fast notes—and since his rage keeps growing, the allegro assai— in quite a different meter and another key—coming just as one thinks the aria has ended—ought to have the very best effect; for a man who finds himself in such a towering rage oversteps all [the bounds of] order, moderation, and resolve; he forgets himself—and so the music must forget itself too—but since the passions, violent or otherwise, ought never to be expressed so far as to excite disgust, and music, even in the most frightful situation, must never offend the ear but please it even then, that is, must always remain music, therefore I chose not a key foreign to the F (the key of the aria), but a neighboring one—not the nearest, D minor, but the next, A minor.—Now for Belmonte's aria in A major, *O wie ängstlich, o wie feurig*: you know how that is expressed—the throbbing of a heart in love is also evident—the 2 violins in octaves.—This is the favorite aria of all who have heard it—mine too—and was written entirely for Adamberger's voice. One can see the trembling—the wavering—one can see the breast heaving—which is expressed by means of a crescendo—one can hear the murmuring and sighing—which is conveyed by the first violins with mutes and a flute in unison with them.—

The Janissaries' Chorus is all one can demand of a Janissaries' Chorus— short and merry—and quite written for the Viennese.—Konstanze's aria I sacrificed somewhat to Mad:^selle Cavalieri's voluble gullet.—*Trennung war mein banges Loos und nun schwimmt mein Aug in Thränen* is what I tried to express,

Die
Entführung aus dem Serail.

Ein Singspiel
in drey Aufzügen,
nach Bretznern

frey bearbeitet, und für das k. k. Nationalhoftheater ein=
gerichtet.

In Musik gesetzt
vom
Herrn Mozart.

Aufgeführt im k. k. Nationalhoftheater.

Wien,
zu finden beym Logenmeister, 1782.

as much as an Italian *aria di bravura* will permit.—I changed *hui* [poetic for "quickly"—but also "ugh"] to *schnell* [quickly], thus: *doch wie schnell schwand meine Freude* etc.; I don't know what our German poets can be thinking of;—if they don't understand the theater where opera is concerned, at least they ought not to let their characters speak as if they were addressing pigs—*hui Sau* ["ugh, pig"].—

Now for the Terzetto, that is, the conclusion of the first act.—Pedrillo has given out that his master is an architect, in order that he may have an opportunity of meeting his Konstanze in the garden. Bassa [Selim] has taken him into his service; Osmin, the keeper, who knows nothing of this and is a rude lout and an arch-enemy of all strangers, is impertinent and won't let them into the garden. The first thing I showed you is very short—and since the text permitted it, I set it pretty well for 3 parts. But then the major suddenly begins, *pianissimo*— it must go very quickly—and the end will make a good deal of noise—which, anyhow, is all that's wanted at the end of an act—the more noise, the better— the shorter, the better—so that people won't cool off before the applause.—

Of the overture you only have 14 bars.—It's quite short—alternates constantly between *forte* and *piano;* and the Turkish music always sets in at the forte—keeps modulating through the keys—and I don't think one could fall asleep to it, even after a quite sleepless night.—Now I am sitting upon thorns— the first act was finished over 3 weeks ago—an aria in the 2nd act and the Drunk Duet (*per li Sig:^{ri}* viennesi), which consists of nothing but my Turkish tattoo, are already completed; but I can do no more, for now the whole story is being turned topsy-turvy, and that at my request.—At the beginning of the third act there's a charming quintet, or rather finale—but I would rather have this at the end of the 2nd act. To achieve this, a great change, indeed a whole new plot must be got up—and Stephanie is up to his eyes in work, and so a little patience is needed.—Everybody grumbles over Stephanie—perhaps he's only being friendly with me to my face—but he *is* arranging my libretto—and in fact just as I wish to have it—to a nicety—and more I do not ask of him God knows!—Well now, that was a long babble about the opera; but it had to be.—Please send me the march I mentioned recently. . . . Now adieu—a hearty farewell. I kiss your hands 1000 times and embrace my dear sister with all my heart (I hope her health has improved) and am ever your most obedient son W. A. Mozart.

> Among the causes of the opera's postponement was the production of three other works at the Court Theater: two by Gluck (*Iphigénie en Tauride* and *Alceste*) and *Das Irrlicht* by Ignaz Umlauf (1746–96), the Viennese singspiel composer. Mozart's irritation at the delay is evident from a letter to his father of 6 October 1781:

Now, however, I'm about to lose my patience, not being able to continue working at the opera.—I am of course composing other things in the meantime—

still—the zest is there—and what would normally take me 14 days would now take me 4.—I composed Adamberger's A major aria, Cavalieri's B-flat one, and the trio in one day—wrote them out in a day and a half.—Then again it would be of no use even if the whole opera were ready—for it would have to lie there until Gluck's two operas had been produced—and the people still have a great deal left to study.—Umlauf, too, is obliged to wait with his completed opera, which took him one year to write;—only don't think that it is good for that reason (between you and me), namely, that it took him a whole year. This opera (between you and me) I should have thought the work of 14 to 15 days, especially since the man must have memorized many operas! So all he had to do was sit down [and write]—and—surely that is what he did—you can hear it!—I must tell you that he invited me very kindly (c'est à dire, after his fashion) so he could let me hear his opera, saying, "You mustn't think it is worth your while to hear it—I'm not that good—I do the best I can." I heard he later said, "Surely Mozart has got the devil in his head, body, and fingers. He played me my opera (which is scrawled so miserably that I myself can hardly read it) as if he had composed it himself."

> Leopold Mozart's letters of this period are missing. In the following, written on 13 October 1781, Mozart was evidently responding to his father's criticism of some of the verses in the libretto:

Now as for the text of the opera.—So far as Stephanie's work on it is concerned, you are quite right.—Still, the poetry is perfectly suited to the character of stupid, coarse, nasty Osmin.—And I know very well that the style of its verse is not of the best—yet it so fittingly coincided with my musical ideas (which were already tumbling about in my head before), that it couldn't help pleasing me;—and I wager that no one will find fault with it at the performance. As for the poetry in the piece itself, I cannot despise it.—Belmonte's aria. *O wie ängstlich* etc. could hardly be better written for the music.—Except for *hui* and *Kummer ruht in meinem Schoss* [literally, "Trouble lies in my lap"] (for trouble doesn't lie), the aria isn't bad; especially the first part.—And I don't know—in an opera, the poetry should simply be the obedient daughter of the music.—Why is it Italian comic operas are so popular everywhere?—With all the rot in the librettos!—Even in Paris—I can bear witness to that. Because there the music dominates—and makes one forget everything else. So much the more, then, must an opera please in which the plot is properly worked out, but the words are written purely for the music; and not music written here and there for the sake of some miserable rhyme (which, God knows, does more harm than good to a theatrical performance), or even whole stanzas that ruin a composer's whole conception. Verse, to be sure, is indispensable to music—but rhyme for rhyme's sake the harmfulest thing. The gentlemen who go about it so pedantically will always fail, they and their music.—

Best of all if a good composer, who understands the theater and is himself able to point things out, and a sensible poet, a true phoenix, get together. Then there will be no reason to mind the applause of the ignorant. Poets almost make me think of trumpeters, with their professional antics!—If we composers always followed our rules (which, when no one knew any better, were quite good), we would produce music as incompetent as their incompetent librettos.

Die Entführung had its première on 16 July 1782. The letter Mozart wrote to his father to tell him of the opera's success is lost. The next one reads as follows:

Vienna, 20 July 1782

Mon très cher Père!

I hope you safely received my last letter in which I informed you of my opera's good reception.—It was given for the 2nd time yesterday;—can you imagine that there was an even stronger cabal yesterday than on the first evening?—The whole first act was hissed.—Still they could not prevent loud cheers of *bravo* during the arias.—And so I placed all my hopes in the closing trio—but there, misfortune caused Fischer to make a mistake—this made Dauer (the Pedrillo) go astray too—and Adamberger could hardly repair all the damage by himself— consequently the whole effect was lost, and so this time—*it was not encored.—* I was in such a rage I hardly knew myself, and so was Adamberger. I said at once that I would not allow the opera to be performed again without first hold- ing a small rehearsal for the singers.—In the 2nd act both duets were encored as at the first performance, and so was Belmonte's rondeau *Wenn der Freude Thränen fliessen.*—The Theater was perhaps even fuller than the first time.— On the previous day no reserved seats were to be had either in the noble parterre or in the 3rd tier; no more loges either. The opera has brought in 1,200 gulden in 2 days.

With this I send you the original [score] and 2 libretti.—You will find in it much that has been crossed out; this because I knew that here the score would be copied at once—therefore I gave free rein to my thoughts—and only before handing it out to be copied did I make my alterations and abridgments here and there.—And just as you receive it, so was it performed—here and there the trum- pets and kettledrums, flutes, clarinet, Turkish music are missing—because I couldn't get paper with that many staves.—They are written out on extra sheets—the copyist has probably lost them, for he couldn't find them.—The first act (while I was having it delivered I don't remember where) unfortunately fell in the muck; that is why it is so dirty.

I now have no mean task ahead of me.—By Sunday week my opera has to be set for wind band—else some other person will do it first—and have the profit of it instead of me. . . . You cannot imagine how hard it is to set such a thing for wind band—so that it will suit the wind instruments, yet lose none of the effect in the process. . . . The rest of the parts have just arrived from the copyist's. Adieu. I kiss your hands 1000 times, and I embrace my dear sister with all my heart and am ever your

most obedient son

W. A. Mozart

Wilhelm A. Bauer and Otto Erich Deutsch, eds., *Mozart: Briefe und Aufzeichnungen*, 7 vols. (Kassel: Bärenreiter, 1962–75), 3:143, 161–64, 165–66, 167–68, 212–13. Trans. P.W.

21
GRÉTRY'S *RICHARD CŒUR-DE-LION*

In the second half of the eighteenth century, the *opéra comique*, or *comédie mêlée d'ariettes* (spoken comedy interspersed with arias), branched out from humble beginnings to cover a wide range of genres: comedy, pastoral, bourgeois drama, and historical, or pseudo-historical, plays with a decidedly romantic flavor. The most famous example in the last category is *Richard Cœur-de-Lion*, a *comédie* by Michel-Jean Sedaine (1719–97) set to music by André-Ernest-Modeste Grétry (1741–1813). A great success when first performed in Paris on 21 October 1784, it continued to be produced there and in much of the rest of Europe for well over a century. Here are excerpts from a review of the first performance:

This drama, whose subject is known to everybody, is one of the most original conceptions of M. Sedaine, who has often dared, nearly always successfully, to attempt subjects and situations that seemed unlikely to work on the stage. The first two acts of *Richard* were received with the greatest applause. . . .

The music of this drama is full of beauty, agreeable negligence, and fortunate reminiscences; it everywhere breathes a spiritual and piquant naïveté. M. Grétry seems in this new composition to have forgotten his customary manner in order to transport us, through the simple and at the same time *romantic* turn of the melodies he has put in the mouth of his different characters, to the time long ago when the events of the poem took place. The romance sung by Blondel and King Richard reminds us of those sweet, touching songs one still finds in remote corners of our southern provinces, like monuments testifying that they once were the cradle of our minstrels and troubadours.

Maurice Tourneaux, ed., *Correspondance littéraire, philosophique et critique par Grimm, Diderot, Raynal, Meister, etc., . . .* 16 vols. (Paris: Garnier, 1877–82), 14:60–61. Trans. P.W.

The story "known to everybody" was that of Richard the Lion-Hearted's captivity in Austria on his way home from the Third Crusade; according to legend, his faithful minstrel Blondel, after going from castle to castle singing the first verse of a song they had composed together, finally heard the king answer with the second verse from his prison window. And so the king was saved. In Sedaine's drama, two elements have special significance: the rescue of the king in the last act, foreshadowing a vogue for "rescue operas," and the romance, a strophic song "written in a simple, touching style, and in a somewhat antique taste," according to Rousseau's definition in his *Dictionnaire de musique* (1768). In fact it was Rousseau who introduced the use of antique-sounding romances in opera, with "Dans ma cabane obscure" (in *Le Devin du village*; see pp. 99–106 above). Grétry's "Une fièvre brûlante" became just as famous (Beethoven wrote variations on it); and the tune's recurrence in fragmentary or varied form throughout the opera is an innovation of which Grétry was justly proud. In his amiable, rather chatty autobiography he gives us his own account of how *Richard* was written and first produced. There is naïveté in his prose as well as in his music: note how he grapples with the concept of a song in opera ("singing to sing"), and how he tells of giving Blondel "modern" music because as a poet he would have been "ahead of his century." In a letter to Sedaine he suggested two or three cannon shots offstage during the rescue scene, "even though gunpowder might perhaps not have been invented at that time." The time was the twelfth century; clearly, historical accuracy in opera had still a long way to go.

Never was a subject better suited to music, it has been said, than that of *Richard Cœur-de-Lion.* I share that opinion with regard to the main situation in the play, I mean that in which Blondel sings the romance

Une fièvre brûlante...,

but one must admit the subject as a whole does not call for music more than any other. I will go further: the play ought really to be declaimed; for, since the romance needs by its very nature to be sung, nothing else should be except that piece, for then it would produce an even greater effect: I remember I was tempted not to let it be preceded by any other music in the second act, solely for that reason; but reflecting that in every situation during the first act there had been singing, I gave up my first idea, never doubting besides that the spectators, through the power of illusion, would listen to the romance as if it were the only piece of music in the whole work.[1] The same reflections prompted me to write it in the old style, so it would stand out from the rest. Have I succeeded? One must think so, since I have been asked a hundred times whether I found that air in the fabliau that had supplied the story.

Sedaine, when he gave me the manuscript, said to me, "I gave this poem to a musician before; he didn't accept it, because he didn't think he could set the romance that is in it well enough. Read, decide, and don't be polite."

Though I accepted this lovely dramatic work without hesitation, I must confess the romance troubled me as much as it had my colleague: I composed it in several ways without finding what I was looking for: that is, an old style capable of pleasing modern listeners. My search, in which I chose the existing melody from among all my ideas, lasted from eleven o'clock at night till four in the morning.[2] We entrusted the role of Richard to Philippe, who had never created a role before and who, after this success, has increasingly deserved the public's approbation. At several of the rehearsals, the beauty of the situation and the actor's sensitivity, combined with his desire to do the role justice, fired his imagination to such a degree that tears would choke him as he tried to answer Blondel with

Un regard de ma belle...

On the day of the first performance, this actor, so full of ardor and zeal, was suddenly afflicted with a total loss of voice; there was no time to substitute another play: the hall was filled. He called me to his dressing room. "Let's see, sing me your romance." He uttered some sounds with difficulty. "That is certainly," said I, "the voice of a prisoner; you are producing the very effect I want; sing, and don't worry."

Clairval filled the role of Blondel to perfection. The nobility of a knight, the astuteness of a clairvoyant blind man who is setting in motion a grand intrigue: he was able to employ all those delicate nuances by turns with exquisite taste. A role never collapses when entrusted to this actor; he knows how to hold back in passages that are doubtful or too new for the public; but as it grows accustomed to them, the actor deploys all the energy his role can require. An actor-machine remains the same every day and fears only for his voice; but Clairval is not so unfortunate as to be the same at every performance; the perfection of his acting depends on the disposition of his soul, and he knows how to please the public even when he is not pleased with himself.

---

[1]Though there is much singing in *opéra comique*, there is not singing all the time. There is singing to speak and singing to sing... People must be inordinately fond of pleasure to surrender as they do to the illusions of the theater: it is as well; for a greater strictness would destroy the dramatic art.

[2]I remember ringing for some fire during the night. "You *must* be cold," said my servant;" "you have been there all this time doing nothing."

The music of *Richard,* though it has not the ancient coloring of *Aucassin et Nicolette* [1779], has the same reminiscences [of ancient times]. The overture indicates quite well, I think, that the action is not a modern one. The noble characters have a less dated tone because city customs reach the country later. The composer can thus employ different tones, which contribute to the general variety.

The air

Ô Richard! ô mon roi!

is in the modern style because it is easy to believe that the poet Blondel was ahead of his century in matters of taste and knowledge.

The trio

Quoi! de la part du gouverneur!

takes up again a form of counterpoint suitable to Sir Williams. Blondel, always careful to capture each person's tone, adopts older musical traits when he says:

La paix, la paix, mes bons amis.

These traits, which are nothing in themselves, . . . are applauded because they are true; I repeat, therefore, that nothing must be excluded from music, and that everything depends on putting a characteristic melody in its true context.

Perhaps it has not been noticed how often the melody of the romance is heard in the course of the play, either in its entirety or in part. It occurs in the following places:

ACT I

1. When Blondel is trying to attract the attention of Marguerite;
2. When she begs him to play the air often, he begins it again;

ACT II

3. The *ritornello* of the scene with Richard;
4. A verse;
5. Another verse, with refrain;
6. He plays the air noisily in order to get arrested;

ACT III

7. When he sings in the wings in order to be brought before Marguerite;
8. In the ensemble piece

Oui, Chevaliers...;

9. In the final chorus.

It would have been easy to tire the listener by repeating the same air so often; but it should be noted that the first time it is played without accompaniment; the second time varied; the third with accompaniment; the fourth and fifth

with the words; the sixth only varied, played in double stops, to indicate he wants
to make a lot of noise; the seventh he sings, without accompaniment, only half
of the refrain; the eighth, in the ensemble piece
                    Oui, Chevaliers...,
he sings his air to a different meter.

Sa voix   a   pé - né - tré mon   â   -   me, Je   la   con -
- nois,   oui,   oui   Ma - da   -   me.

Is it not as if he were saying, "His voice penetrated my soul, singing the air he
made for you"? The ninth time, finally, is in the last chorus, where this air is
sung as a trio.

No doubt it was necessary to present this air in as many different ways, if
one dared repeat it so often: nevertheless, I have never heard it said that it was
repeated too often, because the public has sensed that this air was the pivot on
which the whole play turned.

The air
                    Si l'univers entier m'oublie...,
which precedes the romance, offered something new. The veiled trumpets and
kettledrums seemed to recall sorrowfully the hero's glory; this effect was thought
to have been well conceived. The chorus that ends the second act:
                    Sais-tu! connois-tu!,...
is in the tone of the old counterpoint: the soldiers of that time returning from
the Holy Land, and the ideas we form of those religious times, suggested this
sort of music to me.

Richard first appeared in three acts, but the third act was not the one that
is now performed: the governor was asked to release Richard; he yielded to reason, and although he told Laurette that his love for her was not a factor, the
spectators believed it was and blamed the governor for not doing his duty.
Sedaine, by shortening the third act, created a fourth. . . .

This version was disliked even more than the first: nevertheless, performances continued with the same crowds in attendance, thanks to the second act.

The inhabitants of Paris were so anxious to see this work concluded in an
agreeable manner that every society was sending me a dénouement for *Richard*.
At last Sedaine adopted the siege; it reconciles everything, leaving intact the governor's conduct and presenting a fine spectacle, the only possible resource left

after the great interest aroused by the second act. It is unnecessary to discuss
the success of this play; a hundred crowded performances will hardly satisfy the
eagerness of the public.

C[itoy]en [André-Ernest-Modeste] Grétry, *Mémoires, ou Essais sur la musique*, 3 vols. (Paris: Imprimerie
de la République, An V [1797]; reprint, New York: Da Capo Press, 1971), 1:367–76. Trans. P.W.

22

THE MAKING OF *LE NOZZE DI FIGARO*

The letters of Mozart and his family, such a rich source of information about
earlier operas like *Die Entführung aus dem Serail* (see pp. 130–36 above), tell
us very little, unfortunately, about *Le nozze di Figaro*. The correspondence between the father in Salzburg and the son, now permanently settled in Vienna,
had become less frequent. A first hint of the opera to come is contained in a
letter written by Mozart to his father on 7 May 1783, less than a year after the
première of *Entführung*:

Now the Italian comic operas have begun here again and are a big success. . . .
I have looked through easily 100 librettos, in fact many more—however—I have
hardly found a single one with which I am satisfied; at least there would have
to be many changes made here and there. And if a poet were to busy himself
with that, perhaps he would find it easier to write an altogether new one. And
anyway, something new is always better.—We have here a certain abate da Ponte
as poet.—At the moment he is frightfully busy with revisions at the theater—
and he is under obligation to furnish Salieri with an entirely new libretto. That
will take him at least 2 months. After that he has promised to write a new one
for me; who knows whether he will be able to keep his word when the time
comes—or whether he will want to! You know very well that these Italian gentlemen have very polite faces!—enough, we know them!—and if he is in league
with Salieri, I shan't get anything as long as I live—and yet I should very much
like to show what I can do in the Italian opera as well.

So now the official court poet for Italian operas was Lorenzo Da Ponte (1749–1838). How he had managed to secure that position remains something of a mystery. According to Da Ponte's own memoirs (published in New York in 1807, revised in 1829–30), Emperor Joseph II had hired him sight unseen on the strength of two recommendations. His first interview with the Emperor had been simply for the purpose of thanking him: "He asked me how many dramas I had written, to which I observed frankly: 'Sire, none at all.' 'Well well,' he replied smiling, 'we shall have a virginal muse.'" It was indeed true that Da Ponte had never written a libretto before; and so it was not surprising that the first one he wrote, *Il ricco d'un giorno* (1784), set to music by Salieri, should have been a resounding failure. However, already his second one, *Il burbero di buon cuore* (1786), with music by Vicente Martín y Soler (1754–1806), made a sensation. *Le nozze di Figaro* was to be his fourth. Da Ponte is not mentioned again in all the correspondence of Mozart and his family, unless one counts the indirect reference in a letter of 11 November 1785 from Mozart's father to the composer's sister:

At last I have received a letter of November 2nd [not extant] from your brother, and it's 12 lines long. He begs my pardon, because he is rushing to finish the opera *Le Nozze di Figaro*. . . . He asks me to tell you that he has no time to answer your letter right away: that, in order to be free to compose in the morning, he has shifted all his pupils to the afternoon, etc. etc.—I know the play, it is a very elaborate piece, and the translation from the French must certainly have had to be adapted freely into an opera, if it is to have any effect as an opera. God grant that the action turn out well; I have no qualms about the music. Of course it will cost him a great deal of running around and arguing before he gets the book in the shape and form in which he means to have it: and he probably put it off and took his time about it, as is his fine habit, and now suddenly he must go at it in all earnest because Count Rosenberg is egging him on.

Count Rosenberg was the director of theaters since 1776, and we shall hear more about him presently. As for Mozart taking his time about the opera, a glance at his own catalogue of works shows what else was keeping him busy: in October he had composed the G minor piano quartet, K. 478, on November 5 and 21 he interrupted work on *Figaro* to furnish two ensemble pieces for a comic opera then playing at the court theater, and by December, having finished *Figaro*, he was back at work composing a violin sonata (K. 481), a piano concerto (K. 482), and, in January, the one-act singspiel *Der Schauspieldirektor*. *Le nozze di Figaro* had taken him about six weeks, though the orchestration and various revisions were doubtless undertaken closer to the date of the actual première, originally scheduled for 28 April 1786 but postponed to 1 May. Mozart's father, writing on the former date to his daughter, was pessimistic about the outcome:

Today, the 28th, your brother's opera, *Le Nozze di Figaro*, is being performed for the first time. It will be much if he succeeds, because I know he has amazingly powerful cabals against him. Salieri with all his followers will again take all sorts of pains to move heaven and earth. Mr. and Mrs. Duschek [friends of the Mozarts, then in Vienna] have already told me that your brother has so many cabals against him for this simple reason, that he is held in such high esteem on account of his unusual talent and ability.

Wilhelm A. Bauer and Otto Erich Deutsch, eds., *Mozart: Briefe und Aufzeichnungen,* 7 vols. (Kassel: Bärenreiter, 1962–75), 3:268, 443–44, 536. Trans. P.W.

For further particulars concerning the event we must go to the highly entertaining but also highly unreliable memoirs of Lorenzo Da Ponte, who ended his long, adventurous career in New York, where, among other things, he became the first professor of Italian at Columbia College. The librettist of *Figaro, Don Giovanni,* and *Così fan tutte,* whose fame today rests entirely on these three works, did not repay Mozart adequately when he came to write his memoirs. Nowhere do we get a glimpse of the composer as he truly was, and the disappointment is keener because of Da Ponte's known skill as a portrayer of character. Instead, Mozart here plays a secondary role in a couple of anecdotes having Da Ponte as the protagonist. In the first, he tells us the idea for the opera came from Mozart; and if Da Ponte, who took credit for most things, said so, it must have been true:

As I was chatting one day [with Mozart], he asked me whether I would find it easy to turn Beaumarchais's comedy *The Marriage of Figaro* into an opera. The proposal pleased me very much and I promised it to him. But there was a very great difficulty to overcome. The Emperor had a few days earlier forbidden the German theater company to put on that comedy, which, he said, was too freely written for a polite audience: how then to propose it to him as an opera? . . . I suggested we write the words and music in secret and await a favorable opportunity to exhibit it to the theater directors or the Emperor, a task I bravely pledged myself to undertake.

. . . And so I set about the project, and as I wrote the words he set them to music piecemeal. In six weeks' time the job was done. As Mozart's good fortune would have it, the theater was [just then] in need of scores. Seizing on the occasion, and without telling anyone, I went to offer *Figaro* to the Emperor himself. "What!" said he. "You know that Mozart, excellent in instrumental music, has written only one musical drama in all, and that was nothing special!" "I too," I replied softly, "had it not been for Your Majesty's clemency, would not have written more than one drama in Vienna." "That is true," he replied; "but I forbade the German troupe to play this *Marriage of Figaro.*" "Yes," I added;

LORENZO DA PONTE IN HIS OLD AGE. *He went to New York in 1805, settling there per-manently in 1819. The final version of his memoirs appeared there ten years later. From 1825 to his death he held the title of Professor of Italian at Columbia College, and this little-known portrait by an unidentified artist now hangs in the Casa Italiana on the university's campus.* Columbia University in the City of New York.

"but since I wrote an opera libretto and not a comedy, I have had to omit many scenes and abridge even more, and I have omitted and abridged whatever could offend the delicacy and decency of a spectacle over which Your Majesty is to preside. And as for the music, it appears to be, so far as I can judge, marvelously beautiful." "Very well: that being the case, I will trust to your taste for the music, to your prudence for the morals. Have the score sent to the copyist."

I ran immediately to Mozart, but I had not finished telling him the good news before one of the Emperor's footmen came and gave him a note ordering him to present himself at court at once with his score. He obeyed the royal command and let [the Emperor] hear several pieces; they pleased him enormously—indeed, without exaggeration, they stunned him.

> Several of the details here ring true. We have already seen that Mozart did in fact take only six weeks to compose *Figaro*. And Joseph II had indeed forbidden the Schikaneder troupe to perform Beaumarchais's comedy in 1785; a German translation was nevertheless published that year, and Mozart owned a copy. That the Emperor should have been so misinformed as to say Mozart had composed only one opera is, on the other hand, highly unlikely; more probably, he was criticizing *Entführung*: in a famous anecdote he is supposed to have told Mozart it had "too many notes." The next passage plays up the "cabals" against Mozart, and these, too, are corroborated by the Mozart correspondence; though Da Ponte's memoirs teem with conspiracies against him, suggesting he (like perhaps the Mozarts) had more than a touch of paranoia. The antagonists here are Count Rosenberg and his protégé, the Italian poet Giovanni Battista Casti (1724–1803), who, like Da Ponte, had a brief career as librettist: two of his librettos were set by Paisiello, the remaining four by Salieri.

And so we were not without a justifiable fear, both Mozart and I, lest we should suffer some fresh cabals at the hands of our two good friends.

They were not able to do much, yet they did what they could. A certain Bussani, in charge of costumes and scenery and a jack of all trades except that of an honest man, when he heard that I had woven a dance into the plot of *Figaro*, ran at once to Count [Rosenberg] and, in a tone of disapproval and astonishment, said, "Excellency, the *signor poeta* has introduced a dance in his opera." The Count immediately sent for me and, all frowns, initiated the following little dialogue....

"And so the *signor poeta* has introduced a dance in *Figaro*?"

"Yes, Your Excellency."

"Does not the *signor poeta* know the Emperor does not want any dances in his theater?"

"No, Your Excellency."

"Well, then, *signor poeta*, I am telling you so now."

"Yes, Your Excellency."

"And furthermore I am telling you it has got to be taken out, *signor poeta*."

This "*signor poeta*" was repeated in an expressive tone, implying that it signified "Mr. Jackass" or something of the sort. But my "Excellency" also had its implications.

"No, Your Excellency."

"Do you have the libretto with you?"

"Yes, Your Excellency."

"Where is the dance scene?"

"Here it is, Your Excellency."

"Here is what we do."

And with these words he took out two pages from the drama, threw them gracefully into the fire, and gave me back the libretto, saying, "You see, *signor poeta*, I can do anything." And did me the honor to dismiss me.

I went straightaway to Mozart, who, upon hearing the little tale from me, was in despair. He wanted to go to the Count, scold Bussani, appeal to the Emperor, withdraw the score: I was truly at some pains to calm him down. In the end I asked him to give me just two days and leave everything to me.

The dress rehearsal of the opera was scheduled for that very day. I went personally to announce this to the Emperor, who told me he would appear at the appointed hour. And come he did, and with him half the Viennese aristocracy. The abbé [Casti] came with him too. The first act was performed to universal applause. At the end of that act [Da Ponte is mistaken—this occurs at the end of Act III] there is a mimed action between the Count and Susanna during which the orchestra plays and the dance is performed. But since His Excellency Can-Do-Anything had removed that scene, all you saw was Count [Almaviva] and Susanna gesticulating, and, what with the orchestra silent, it looked for all the world like a puppet show. "What is this?" said the Emperor to Casti, who was sitting behind him. "One must ask the poet," replied the good abbé with a malicious little smile. I was thereupon summoned; but instead of answering his question, I presented him my manuscript, in which I had restored the missing scene. The sovereign read it and asked me why there had been no dance. My silence gave him to understand that there was some small complication beneath it all. He turned to the Count, asked him to explain the matter, and he, half stammering, said the dance had been omitted because the opera house had no dancers. "Are there any," he asked, "in the other theaters?" He was told there were. "Well, then, let Da Ponte have as many as he requires." In less than half an hour there arrived twenty-four dancers, or extras: after the second act, the scene that had been omitted was repeated, and the Emperor cried, "That's better!" . . .

Mozart's opera was performed, and, despite the "we shall hear" and "we shall see" of all the other maestros and their partisans, despite the Count, Casti, and a hundred devils, it pleased everyone and was judged by the sovereign and true connoisseurs a sublime, well-nigh divine work; and my very chaste [*castissimo*, a play on Casti] critic was the first to point out its finer points. But what were these fine points? "True, it is only a translation of the comedy by Beaumarchais; but it has some good lines and some good arias. Here, for example, are two very elegant lines:

> Non più andrai, farfallone amoroso,
> Notte e giorno d'intorno girando."

According to him, then, all the merit of the work consisted in a few good lines and, at most, some good arias.

Lorenzo Da Ponte, *Memorie e altri scritti*, ed. C. Pagnini (Milan: Longanesi, 1971), 164–65, 173–75, 176–77. Trans. P.W.

23

KIERKEGAARD'S DON GIOVANNI

Søren Kierkegaard (1813–55), the Danish philosopher whose thought influenced Scandinavian writers in the nineteenth century and the whole existentialist movement in the twentieth, was deeply affected by Mozart's *Don Giovanni* already in his student days. The figure of the opera's hero came to occupy an important place in his first major work, *Either/Or* (*Enten/Eller*, Copenhagen, 1843), where it serves to illustrate vividly, and famously, a mode of existence that finds fulfillment in the gratification of the senses. This, obviously, is not the whole story Kierkegaard has to tell, and in the "Or" part of his equation he presents a brief for the life lived ethically. But it is not for their philosophical import that the following excerpts are included here. After all, as Kierkegaard himself writes elsewhere, "A book has the remarkable characteristic that it can be interpreted as one pleases." His disquisition on Don Giovanni may therefore, if one chooses, be also viewed as a remarkable monument in the reception history of Mozart's operas, and of *Don Giovanni* in particular. In his opinion and in the estimation of many nineteenth-century writers, it stood head and shoulders above Mozart's other works. The view presented here, then, for all its remarkable insights, is essentially a product of romantic sensibilities. Mozart might not have recognized his hero; we, descendants of the romantic generation, will instead recognize some analytical attitudes that survive to this day in contemporary approaches to *Don Giovanni*.

Don Giovanni constantly hovers between being an idea, that is to say, energy, life—and being an individual. But this hovering is the musical trembling. When the sea tosses tempestuously, then the swirling billows form images of strange creatures in this wild upheaval. It is as if these creatures set the waves in motion, and yet it is the conflict of the opposing billows which creates them. So Don Giovanni is an image which constantly appears, but does not gain form and substance, an individual who is constantly being formed, but is never finished, of whose life history one can form no more definite impression than one can by listening to the tumult of the waves. When Don Giovanni is conceived in this manner, there is meaning and profound significance in everything. If I imagine a particular individual, if I see him or hear him speak, then it becomes comic to imagine that he has seduced 1,003; for as soon as he is regarded as a particular individual, the accent falls in quite another place; it stresses, in fact, those whom he has seduced and how. The naïveté of ballads and legends can successfully express such things without a hint of the comical; for reflection, that is impossible. When, on the other hand, he is interpreted in music, then I do not have a particular individual, but I have the power of nature, the demonic, which as little tires of seducing or is done with seducing as the wind is tired of blowing, the sea of billowing, or a waterfall of tumbling downward from the heights. In this respect, the number of the seduced can just as well be any other, far greater number. It is often not an easy task, when translating the text of an opera, to do it so exactly that the translation is not only singable but also harmonizes fairly well with the meaning of the text and thus with the music as well. As an example of the fact that sometimes it is altogether unimportant [to be so exact], I shall cite the number in the catalogue aria in *Don Giovanni*, without taking the matter as thoughtlessly as people generally do, thinking that such things do not matter. I, on the contrary, consider the matter aesthetically serious to a high degree, and therefore I think the number is unimportant. Yet I would commend one single characteristic of this number 1,003, that it is odd and accidental, which is not at all unimportant, since it gives the impression that the list is by no means closed, but that, on the contrary, Don Giovanni is in a hurry. One almost begins to pity Leporello, who must not only, as he himself says, stand watch outside the door, but along with that, carry on so complicated a system of book-keeping that it could well keep a registered accountant busy.

Never before in the world has sensuousness been conceived as it is in *Don Giovanni*—as a principle: for this reason the erotic is here defined by another predicate: the erotic here is *seduction*. . . . Don Giovanni is a seducer from the ground up. His love is not psychical but sensuous, and sensuous love, in accordance with its concept, is not faithful, but absolutely faithless; it loves not one but all, that is to say, it seduces them all. It exists only in the moment, but the moment, in terms of its concept, is the sum of moments, and so we have the seducer. . . . His power to deceive lies in the essential genius of sensuousness, whose incarnation he really is. Shrewd sober-mindedness is lacking in him; his life is as effervescent as the wine with which he stimulates himself; his life is dramatic like the strains which accompany his joyous feast; always he is triumphant. He requires no preparation, no plan, no time; for he is always prepared. Energy is always in him and also desire, and only when he desires is he rightly in his element. He sits feasting, joyous as a god he swings his cup—he rises with his napkin in his hand, ready for the attack. If Leporello rouses him in the middle of the night, he awakens, always certain of his victory. But this energy, this power, cannot be expressed in words, only music can give us a conception of it. It is inexpressible for reflection and thought. The cunning of an ethically determined seducer I can clearly set forth in words, and music will try in vain to solve this problem. With Don Giovanni, the converse holds true. What is this power?—No one can say. Even if I questioned Zerlina about it before she goes to the dance: "What is this power by which he captivates you?"—she would answer: "No one knows," and I would say "Well said, my child! You speak more wisely than the sages of India; *richtig, das weiss man nicht* [right, no one knows this]"; and the unfortunate thing is that I can't tell you either. . . .

By these considerations we are again brought to the main subject of this inquiry, that Don Giovanni is absolutely musical. He desires sensuously, he seduces with the demonic power of sensuousness, he seduces everyone. Speech, dialogue, are not for him, for then he would be at once a reflective individual. Thus he does not have stable existence at all, but he hurries in a perpetual vanishing, precisely like music, about which it is true that it is over as soon as it has ceased to sound, and only comes into being again, when it again sounds.

Were I to raise the question now as to how Don Giovanni looks—is he handsome, young or old, or about how old—then it is only an accommodation on my part, and anything I may say about it can only expect to find a place here in the same way that a tolerated sect finds a place in the established church. He is handsome, not very young; were I to venture a guess, I should suggest thirty-three, that being the length of a generation. The hesitation in attempting such an inquiry is due to the fact that one easily loses sight of the total in dwelling on the details, as if it were by means of his good looks, or whatever else one might mention, that Don Giovanni seduced. One sees him then, but no longer hears him, and in that way he is lost. If, as though to contribute my bit toward helping the reader to get a visual image of Don Giovanni, I were to say: "See, there he stands, see how his eyes blaze, his lips curve in a smile, so sure is he of his victory. Observe his imperial glance, which demands the things that are Caesar's; see how gracefully he moves in the dance, how proudly he stretches out

DON GIOVANNI SEEN THROUGH THE EYES OF ROMANTICISM. *Fascination with Mozart's hero was widespread among romantic writers and artists. Here, in a water color by Johann Peter Lyser, is a vision of the opening scene, under a full moon.* Staatsbibliothek zu Berlin–Preussischer Kulturbesitz, Musikabteilung mit Mendelssohn-Archiv.

his hand; who is the fortunate girl he is inviting?"—or were I to say: "There he stands in the shadow of the forest, he leans against a tree, he accompanies himself on a guitar, and look! yonder a young girl, timid as a startled fawn, disappears among the trees, but he does not hurry, he knows that she is seeking him"—or were I to say: "There he rests by the lake shore in the pale night, so beautiful that the moon pauses and lives over again its first young love, so beautiful that the young girls of the village would give much to dare to steal upon him, and taking advantage of a moment of darkness while the moon mounted heavenward, bestow a kiss upon him." If I did this, the observant reader would say: "See, now he has spoiled everything, he has himself forgotten that Don Giovanni should not be seen but heard." Therefore I don't do it, but I say: "Hear

Don Giovanni, that is to say, if you cannot get a conception of him by hearing him, then you never will. Hear the beginning of his life; as the lightning flashes forth from the murk of the thunderclouds, so he bursts forth from the depths of earnestness, swifter than the lightning's flash, more inconstant and yet as constant; hear how he rushes down into the manifold of life, how he dashes himself against its solid dam; hear those light dancing tones of the violin, hear the signal of gladness, hear the exultation of lust, hear the festive happiness of enjoyment; hear his wild flight, he is transported beyond himself, ever swifter, ever more impetuously; hear the unbridled demands of passion, hear the sighing of love, hear the whisper of temptation, hear the whirlpool of seduction, hear the stillness of the moment—hear, hear, hear Mozart's *Don Giovanni*!" . . .

That which I have so frequently emphasized in the preceding, I shall once again repeat: that Don Giovanni can only be expressed musically. I have learned this myself essentially through music, and I ought therefore to guard in every way against giving the impression that the music arrives on the scene as an import from without. . . . It is not my intention to analyze the whole opera in detail but rather the opera as a whole, not dealing with its particular parts separately, but incorporating these as far as possible in my observations, so as not to see them outside of their connection with the whole, but within it. . . .

Don Giovanni is the hero of the opera, the chief interest centers in him; not only so, but he lends interest to all the other characters. Don Giovanni's life is the life-principle within them. His passion sets the passion of all the others in motion; his passion resounds everywhere; it sounds in and sustains the earnestness of the Commandant, Elvira's anger, and Anna's hate, Ottavio's conceit, Zerlina's anxiety, Masetto's exasperation, and Leporello's confusion. As hero in the play, he gives it his name, as is generally true in the case of a hero, but he is more than a name, he is, so to speak, the common denominator. The existence of all the others is, compared with his, only a derived existence. If we now require of an opera that its unity provide the keynote, then we shall easily see that one could not imagine a more perfect subject for an opera than Don Giovanni. . . . In *Don Giovanni* the keynote is nothing other than the primitive power in the opera itself; this is Don Giovanni, but again—just because he is not character but essentially life—he is absolutely musical. Nor are the other persons in the opera characters, but essentially passions, who are posited with Don Giovanni, and thereby become musical. That is, as Don Giovanni encircles them all, so do they in turn encircle Don Giovanni; they are the external consequences his life constantly posits. It is this musical life of Don Giovanni. absolutely centralized in the opera, which enables it to create a power of illusion which as no other is able to do, so that its life transports one into the life of the play. Because the musical is omnipresent in this music, one may enjoy any snatch of it, and immediately be transported by it. One may enter in the middle of the play and instantly be in the center of it, because this center, which is Don Giovanni's life, is everywhere.

We know from experience that it is not pleasant to strain two senses at the same time, and it is often very confusing if we have to use our eyes hard when our ears are already occupied. Therefore we have a tendency to close our eyes when hearing music. This is true of all music more or less, and of *Don Giovanni* in a higher sense. As soon as the eyes are engaged, the impression becomes confused; for the dramatic unity which presents itself to the eye is always subordinate and imperfect in comparison with the musical unity which is heard at the same time. This, at least, has been my own experience. I have sat close up, I have sat farther and farther back, I have tried a corner in the theater where I could completely lose myself in the music. The better I understood it, or believed I understood it, the farther I was away from it, not from coldness, but from love, for it is better understood at a distance. This has had for my life something strangely mysterious in it. There have been times when I would have given anything for a ticket. Now I need no longer spend a single penny for one. I stand outside in the corridor; I lean up against the partition which divides me from the auditorium, and then the impression is most powerful; it is a world by itself, separated from me; I can see nothing, but I am near enough to hear, and yet so infinitely far away. . . .

This is not the place to explain what function the overture has for opera in general. Only so much can here be pointed out, that the fact that an opera requires an overture sufficiently proves the preponderance of the lyrical, and that the effect aimed at is the evocation of a mood, something which the drama cannot undertake to do, since there everything must be transparent. It is therefore proper that the overture should be the last part composed, so that the composer himself may be completely permeated with the music. The overture, therefore, generally affords an opportunity to get a deep insight into the composer and his spiritual relation to his music. If he is not successful in apprehending the central idea in it, if he is not in the most profound sympathetic contact with the keynote of the opera, then this will inevitably betray itself in the overture; it then becomes, by virtue of a loose association of ideas, an aggregate of the leading themes slung together, but with no totality which, as it essentially ought to do, contains the most profound illumination of the content of the music. Such an overture is therefore generally entirely arbitrary, that is, it can be as long or short as it will, and the cohesive element, the continuity, since it is only an association of ideas, can stretch out as long as it will. Therefore, the overture is often a dangerous temptation to minor composers; they are easily seduced into plagiarizing themselves, filching from their own pockets, something which produces much confusion. While it is clear from this that the overture should not have the same content as the opera, neither should it, naturally, contain something absolutely different. It should, in other words, have the same ideas as the opera, but in a different manner; it should contain the central idea, and grip the listener with the whole intensity of this central idea.

In this respect the ever admirable overture to *Don Giovanni* is and remains a perfect masterpiece, so that if no other proof were forthcoming for *Don Giovanni's* classicity, it would be sufficient to emphasize this one thing: the absurdity of thinking that he who had the center should not also have the periphery. This overture is no interweaving of themes, it is not a labyrinthine hodgepodge of associated ideas, it is concise, definite, strongly constructed, and, above all, it is impregnated with the essence of the whole opera. It is powerful as the thought of a god, moving as a world's life, trembling in its earnestness, quivering in its passion, crushing in its terrible wrath, inspiring in its joy of life; it is faithful in its judgment, strident in its lust, it is deliberately solemn in its imposing dignity, it is stirring, flaming, dancing in its joy. And it has not attained this by sucking the blood of the opera; on the contrary, it is related to the opera as a prophecy. In the overture the music unfolds its entire compass; with a few mighty wing-strokes it hovers over itself, as it were, hovers over the place where it will alight. It is a conflict, but a conflict in the loftier regions of the air. He who after having made a closer acquaintance with the opera, hears the overture, to him it will perhaps seem as if he had penetrated into that secret workshop where the wild forces he has learned to know in the opera move in their primitive energy, where in full fury they strive against each other. Still, the struggle is too unequal. Even before the battle, the one power is victorious; the other flees and escapes, but this flight is just its passion, its burning unrest in its brief *joie de vivre*, the quickened pulse in its passionate heat. By its flight it sets the other power in motion, and carries it along with itself. That which at first seemed so firmly fixed as to be almost immovable, must now be off, and soon the movement beomes so swift that it seems like actual combat. It is impossible to follow this farther. Here it is a matter of listening to the music, for the conflict is not a strife about words but a raging of elemental forces. I shall only note what I earlier explained, that the interest of the opera centers in Don Giovanni, not in Don Giovanni and the Commandant. This is everywhere apparent in the overture. Mozart seems purposely to have planned it so that the deep voice of the Commandant, so resonant in the beginning, gradually becomes weaker and weaker, almost loses, as it were, its majestic firmness, must hurry to keep pace with the demoniac haste which eludes him, and which almost has the power to degrade him into a race in the brevity of an instant. With this, the transition to the opera itself is more and more formed. As a consequence, one must consider the finale in close relation to the first part of the overture. In the finale, earnestness again comes to itself, while in the progress of the overture, it was as if it were beside itself. Now there is no question about running a race with passion; earnestness returns, and thereby has cut away every possibility for a new race. . . .

But if . . . the overture is to be regarded as a running start for the opera; if in the overture one comes down from these higher regions, then it may be asked where one lands best in the opera, or how does one get the opera to begin? Here Mozart has perceived the only right thing to do, to begin with Leporello. Perhaps it might seem that there was not such great merit in this, inasmuch as nearly all the adaptations of *Don Juan* begin with a monologue by Sganarelle. Yet there is a great difference, and we have again occasion to admire Mozart's mastery. He has placed the first aria in immediate conjunction with the overture. This is something which is rarely done; here it is entirely proper, and it gives us a new light on the construction of the overture. The overture is trying to settle down, to secure a footing in the theatrical effect. The Commandant and Don Giovanni we have already heard in the overture; next to them Leporello is the most important character. . . .

If anyone asks which is the most epic moment in the opera, the answer is easily and unmistakably that it is the catalogue in Leporello's second aria. . . . Leporello gives Elvira an epic survey of his master's life, and we cannot deny that it is entirely proper that Leporello should recite it, and that Elvira should listen to him, for they are both intensely interested in the matter. As we therefore hear Don Giovanni throughout the whole aria, so in some places we hear Elvira, who is now visibly present on the stage as a witness for all. . . . Leporello is the epic narrator. . . . He is altogether fascinated by the life he describes, he forgets himself in telling about Don Giovanni. Thus I have another example of what I mean when I say that Don Giovanni echoes through everything. The situation, therefore, does not lie in the conversation between Leporello and Elvira about Don Giovanni, but in the mood that sustains the whole, in Don Giovanni's invisible, spiritual presence. To explain more particularly the transition in this aria, how it begins quietly with a slow movement, but is enkindled more and more, as Don Giovanni's life increasingly resounds through it; how Leporello is more and more transported by it, carried away and rocked by these erotic breezes; how the nuances, all as dissimilar as were the women who came within Don Giovanni's range, all become audible in it—this is not the place for that.

If we ask which is the most lyric moment in the opera, the answer might be more doubtful. It can hardly be open to question, however, that the most lyric moment must be conceded to Don Giovanni, that it would be a breach of dramatic discipline were a subordinate character allowed to engage our attention in this way. Mozart has realized this. The choice is thus considerably restricted, and on closer inspection it is apparent that the only possibilities are either the banquet in the first part of the grand finale or the familiar champagne aria. As far as the banquet scene is concerned, this may indeed be regarded as a lyric moment, and the feast's intoxicating cordials, the foaming wine, the festal strains of distant music, everything combines to intensify Don Giovanni's mood, as his own festivity casts an enhanced enjoyment so powerful in its effect that even Leporello is transfigured in this opulent moment which marks the last smile of gladness, the last farewell to pleasure. . . .

It is otherwise with the champagne aria. I believe one will look in vain for a dramatic situation here, but it has the more significance as a lyric effusion. Don Giovanni is wearied by the many intercrossing intrigues; on the other hand, he is by no means spent; his soul is still as vigorous as ever; he stands in no need of convivial society, of seeing and hearing the foaming of the wine, or of fortifying himself with it; the inner vitality breaks forth in him, stronger and richer than ever. He is still interpreted ideally by Mozart as life, as power, but ideally as over against actuality. He is here, as it were, ideally intoxicated in himself. If every girl in the world surrounded him in this moment, he would not be a source of danger to them, for he is, as it were, too strong to wish to deceive them; even the manifold enjoyments of actuality are too little for him in comparison with what he enjoys in himself. Here is the clear indication of what it means to say that the essence of Don Giovanni is music. He reveals himself to us in music, he expands in a world of sound. Someone has called this the champagne aria, and this is undeniably very descriptive. But that which especially needs to be noted is that it does not stand in an accidental relationship to Don Giovanni. His life is like this, effervescent as champagne. And just as the bubbles in this wine ascend and continue to ascend, while it seethes in its own heat, harmonious in its own melody, so the lust for enjoyment sounds through the primitive seething which is his life. Therefore, that which gives this aria dramatic significance is not the situation, but the fact that the keynote of the opera here sounds and resounds in itself.

INSIGNIFICANT CONCLUSION

If now this explanation proves to be correct, then I again return to my favorite theme, that among all classic works Mozart's *Don Giovanni* ought to stand highest; then I shall again rejoice over Mozart's happiness, a happiness which is in truth enviable, both in itself, and because it makes all of those happy who only moderately understand his happiness. I, at least, feel myself indescribably happy in having even remotely understood Mozart and in having suspected his happiness. How much more, then, those who have perfectly understood him, how much more must they not feel themselves happy with the happy.

Søren Kierkegaard, *Either/Or*, trans. David F. Swenson and Lillian Marvin Swenson, with revisions and a foreword by Howard A. Johnson (Garden City, N.Y.: Anchor Books, 1959), 91–134 passim.

24

FIDELIO IN 1806

When Beethoven entrusted various manuscripts of *Fidelio* to his future biographer Schindler shortly before his death, he told him that "this child of his spirit had cost him greater birth pangs than any other and therefore was also his favorite; and that he considered [the manuscripts] particularly worthy of being preserved." The story of the opera's vicissitudes has often been told: how it failed at its première in Vienna in 1805 and again, despite revisions, in 1806; and how, after more extensive revisions, it finally triumphed in 1814. Josef August Röckel (1783–1870) was in his early twenties when, as a tenor at the Theater an der Wien, he was asked to replace F. C. Demmer, who had just sung the part of Florestan in the unsuccessful first run of *Fidelio*. In later years Röckel told of this experience several times, but nowhere in such detail as in the article below, which first appeared in a German magazine, *Die Gartenlaube*, in 1868. How far can the memory of the eighty-five-year-old singer be trusted, so many years after the events he described? Certain inaccuracies are easily noted: he states that Beethoven wished his opera to be called *Fidelio*, not *Leonore*, while the opposite is true; also, that the final version of the opera was first performed in 1823. These two passages have been omitted below. Röckel also says the 1806 *Fidelio* was performed three times, whereas it was only performed twice; but perhaps he was remembering a public rehearsal. On the other hand, his experience singing Florestan under Beethoven must have made an indelible impression on him, so that, once due allowance is made for a certain amount of Victorian hero worship and sentimentality, there is no reason to doubt the essential veracity of Röckel's narrative. It begins in December 1805, a few weeks after the failure of the first version of *Fidelio*, in which Sebastian Mayer had played Pizarro. Mayer and Röckel have been summoned to the palace of Prince Karl Lichnowsky, the great patron of Beethoven.

We were already on our way to the Prince's palace when Mayer informed me that we would find Beethoven there in the company of his close friends and that we were to give his unsuccessful opera *Leonore* another, critical reading together with the other participants in the production, in order to persuade the Master of the need for a revision. Since Beethoven placed all the blame for the opera's failure on the earlier tenor, I, in whose voice he had greater confidence, was to read the part of Florestan at sight in this solo performance. And while so doing, I, along with Mayer and the others, was to keep proposing insistently to the Master the necessary cuts and alterations, finally also the fusion of the first two acts.

I dreaded the task of sight-reading the difficult part of Florestan for the exacting and impetuous composer, although I had often heard it sung by my former teacher and present rival and had already studied it somewhat with him; I dreaded, too, the stage intrigues of the offended tenor whose successor I was to be by taking this step, and I should have liked best of all to turn back, if Mayer had not held fast to my arm and literally dragged me on. And so we entered the princely mansion and mounted the brilliantly lit staircase, where several liveried servants met us with empty tea trays. My companion, who knew the customs of the house, made a face and murmured, "Tea is over, and I fear your hesitation has left our stomachs in a very precarious situation."

We were shown into the music room, which was furnished with many-branched candelabra and heavy satin draperies, and on whose walls the splendidly colored oil paintings of the greatest masters, in their broad, glittering gold frames, testified to the elevated artistic taste and wealth of the princely family. It seemed we were being awaited, for Mayer was quite right: tea had already been served, and everyone was ready for the musical performance to begin. The Princess, an older lady, winningly amiable and indescribably gentle but pale and sickly as a result of great physical suffering (in earlier times she had had both her breasts removed), was already sitting at the piano; across from her Beethoven sat negligently in an armchair, the thick Pandora's-box score of his unsuccessful opera on his knees. To his right we saw the author of the tragedy *Coriolan*, Court Secretary Matthäus von Collin, who was chatting with the composer's closest childhood friend, Court Councilor Breuning of Bonn. My colleagues in the opera, who were already holding their parts in their hands, had taken their places in a semicircle not far from the piano—they were again Milder as Fidelio, Mademoiselle Müller as Marzelline, Weinmüller as Rocco, Caché as the gatekeeper Jaquino, and Steinkopf as the Minister. After I had been introduced to the Prince and Princess and Beethoven had acknowledged our respectful greeting, he put his score down on the music stand for the Princess—and the performance began.

The first two acts, in which I had no part, were gone through from first note to last. The clock was consulted and Beethoven was implored to let a few sections that were a little too long and only of secondary importance be omitted; he, however, defended every bar and did it with so much nobility and artistic dignity that I could have fallen to his feet. But when the main issue was broached, namely the major cuts in the exposition and consequent possibility of fusing the first two acts together, he lost control of himself and shouted, "Not a single note!" and was on the point of hurrying away with the score. But the Princess

PRINCESS MARIA CHRISTIANE LICHNOWSKY, *who in her later years played a decisive role in persuading Beethoven to revise the first version of* Fidelio.

put her hands, folded as if in prayer, on the precious score, looked up with in-describable mildness at the furious genius and, lo—his rage melted under her look, and he sat down again, resigned. The noble lady directed us to continue and played the prelude to my grand aria "In des Lebens Frühlingstagen." I there-fore asked Beethoven for the Florestan part, but my unsuccessful predecessor had not returned it despite repeated requests, and so I was told to sing from the score which the Princess was using. I was aware that this great aria meant as much to Beethoven as the whole rest of the opera, and I went at it accordingly. He asked to have it repeated over and over; the effort nearly exhausted my strength, but I sang it, for I felt only too happy when I noticed that my execution was able to reconcile the Master with his misunderstood work.

It was past midnight when the performance, prolonged by frequent repetitions, finally ended. "And the revision, the abridgment?" the Princess asked the Master with a beseeching look.

"Do not ask for it," he answered darkly; "not a note must be removed!"

"Beethoven!" cried she with a deep sigh. "Must then your great work remain unappreciated and disparaged?"

"It is sufficiently rewarded by your approval, gracious Princess," said the Master, and he slipped his slightly trembling hand out of hers.

But suddenly it was as if a stronger, more commanding spirit had possessed the delicate lady; almost kneeling and putting her arms round him, she spoke passionately: "Beethoven! No—your greatest work, and you yourself, must not fail like this! God will not have it so, who has placed the sounds of purest beauty in your soul—the spirit of your mother will not have it so, who at this moment begs and admonishes you through me—Beethoven, it must be! Give in! Do it in memory of your mother! Do it for me, for your only, your truest friend!"

The great man with the Olympian head stood long before the angelic admirer of his muse; then, as his hand brushed back a lock of hair from his face, it was as if a beautiful dream had entered his soul, and he cried, his eyes turned heavenward full of emotion, "I will do it—do it all; for you—for my mother!" And at the same time he respectfully raised up the Princess towards him and gave his hand to the Prince, as if in pledge. And we stood around them deeply moved, for we all even then felt the significance of this great moment.

Not another word was spoken after this concerning the opera—everyone was exhausted, and I confess I exchanged an understandable look of relief with Mayer when servants opened the wide double doors to the dining room and the company at last sat down to supper at the richly decked table. Perhaps not quite by coincidence I was made to sit opposite Beethoven, who, probably still dwelling in his mind on the opera, ate noticeably little, while I, assailed by the keenest hunger, swallowed the first course with a haste bordering on the comical. He pointed smiling at my empty plate: "You swallowed the food like a wolf—what was it you ate?"

"I was so hungry," I replied, "that in fact I paid no attention to what I ate."

"That is why you played the part of Florestan, the man in the dungeon of starvation, in so masterly a fashion and so naturally; we must therefore thank not your voice, nor your head, but only your stomach. Well, then, be sure always to starve yourself properly before the performance, and success will not fail us."

Everyone laughed and seemed to enjoy the fact that Beethoven was joking again more than the joke itself.

When we left the palace, Beethoven still said to me, "Your part will require the least alterations; come therefore to my dwelling in a few days to pick it up; I will copy it out for you myself."

A few days later I appeared in his antechamber; an elderly servant did not know what to do with me, since his master was just then washing. I could tell it from the noise of splashing water, which the strange genius was pouring over himself in streams, bellowing the while and moaning, which seemed in his case to be an outburst of satisfaction. I thought I could read in the old servant's unfriendly face the words, "Announce or send packing?" written in sullen, wrinkled letters; but then he suddenly asked, "Whom have I the honor to—?"

I told him my name: "Joseph Röckel."

"Why, look you," said the Viennese fellow, "I've got orders to let you in."

He then went and straightaway opened the door. I entered the abode consecrated by genius. It looked simple, almost impoverished, and a sense of order appeared never to have penetrated it. There in a corner, an open piano, heavily laden with music sheets in wild disarray. Here on a chair, a piece of the "Eroica"; single parts of the opera which presently occupied him on other chairs, some also on and under the table, which stood in the middle of the room; and amidst everything, between chamber music works, piano trios, and symphonic sketches, the mighty washstand where the master was busy rinsing his hefty torso with cold water. He received me without the slightest ceremony, and I had the opportunity to admire his well-developed muscles and strong frame. They seemed to promise the composer the life span of a Methuselah, and it must have been a violent, hostile influence that broke down this pillar of strength so early.

Beethoven greeted me affably with a cheerful smile and told me, as he got dressed, how laboriously he himself had copied out the part from the illegible score, so that I might have it promptly and in a thoroughly correct form.

A few weeks later the other members of the cast also received their parts of the revised score. We were all astonished at Beethoven's capacity for work: he completed the alterations to his great composition so quickly that we were able to perform it hardly four months after its first brief run, on 29 March 1806, again at the Theater an der Wien, but this time for a homier, "Viennese" public. [The first performances had taken place during Napoleon's occupation of Vienna and much of the public had been French.]

The composer was promised a share of the profits by the management, and I, because I had so willingly undertaken an important part that lay outside my usual repertoire, was promised a bonus. . . . We took all possible pains to ensure the work's success, and if this was not quite the case the first night, at the second and third performances [but see the introductory note] the theater was noticeably fuller; and even the critics did partial, if not total, justice to the work.

Yes, it had been better liked, but still not to the degree to which an art work so far above anything ever heard before deserved to be appreciated; this we could tell by the less-than-full house, just as Beethoven could tell it by his share of the profits; the smallness of which caused him to complain to Court Banker Braun just as I, the day after the third performance (of the revised version), went in to collect my fee. For as I happened to be waiting in the antechamber of the Baron's business office, I overheard a spirited argument the latter was having in the next room with the indignant composer. Beethoven was mistrustful and believed his share of the net profits to be greater than the amount the Court Banker, who at the same time was the manager of the Theater an der Wien, had paid him; the latter, however, observed that Beethoven was the first composer the management had ever granted a share of the profits, in recognition of his extraordinary merit; and he explained the loss at the box office by pointing to the fact that the boxes and reserved seats were indeed all occupied, but not the seats in which massive popular attendance could have resulted in receipts such as those realized at performances of Mozart's operas. He emphasized that Beethoven's music had until then gained access only to the educated classes, whereas Mozart with his operas delighted the whole populace, the masses, every time. Beethoven stormed angrily about the room and shouted, "I do not write for the 'masses'— I write for the 'educated'!"

"But they alone will not fill our theater," replied the Baron calmly; "to make a profit we need the 'masses,' and so, since you have not chosen to make any concessions to them in your music, you have only yourself to blame for the low proceeds. Had we paid Mozart a similar share of the profits on his operas, he would have been a rich man."

This unfavorable comparison with his famous predecessor appeared to cut Beethoven to the quick. Without uttering a word in response, he jumped up and shouted in a fit of rage:

"Give me back my score!"

The Baron stood hesitantly and stared, taken aback, at the enraged composer's red-hot face; he, however, repeated with fearsome passion:

"I demand my score—my score, right away!"

The Baron pulled the bell-rope; a servant entered.

"The score of yesterday's opera for this gentleman," said the former politely, and the servant promptly brought it in. "I am sorry," continued the chevalier; "however, I believe that on mature reflection—"

But Beethoven no longer heard these words; he had torn the huge volume from the servant's hands and run off, not noticing me in his haste, through the antechamber and down the stairs.

When the Baron received me a few minutes later, he could not quite master a slight tremor; he appeared to sense what a priceless treasure he had handed over. Moodily, he said:

"Beethoven was irritated and overhasty; you have some influence on him; offer everything—make him any promise in my name, to keep his work on our stage."

I excused myself and hurried after the raging master to his private retreat. But to no avail—he would hear no words of reassurance: the second version of *Fidelio* lay already in his music cabinet under lock and key.

Friedrich Kerst, ed., *Die Erinnerungen an Beethoven*, 2 vols. (Stuttgart: Julius Hoffmann, 1913), 1:112–19. Trans. P.W.

25

BERLIOZ'S ESTIMATE OF SPONTINI

Berlioz's unbounded admiration for Gaspare Spontini (1774–1851) led him to devote numerous articles to the composer and to his three principal operas, *La Vestale* (1807), *Fernand Cortez* (1809), and *Olympie* (1819). In his amusing *Les Soirées de l'orchestre* (*The Evenings of the Orchestra*, 1852), Berlioz combined four of the articles, including his previous year's lengthy obituary of Spontini, to produce a major study, the thirteenth *Soirée*, or chapter, in his book. "We are interested today in Berlioz's raptures over composers like Spontini, but we find it difficult to share them, or even always to understand them," wrote Ernest Newman in the introduction to the English version from which the following excerpt is taken. Yet one should certainly try to understand, if not share, Berlioz's raptures in this case: Spontini's influence was enormous, affecting opera composers from Weber and Schubert to Wagner, Verdi, and beyond. Berlioz is on firm ground (no "raptures" here) when, towards the end of his study, he turns to Spontini's orchestration and dramatic vocabulary.

Spontini was above all things and especially a dramatic composer whose inspiration grew with the importance of the situations and the violence of the passions he had to paint. Hence the pale coloring of his earlier scores, written to puerile and commonplace Italian libretti; the insignificance of the music he applied to the dull, petty, cold, and false genre of which the opéra comique *Julie* is so perfect a model; the ascendant movement of his thought in the two beautiful scenes of *Milton*, the one in which the blind poet laments the misfortune that deprives him for all time of the contemplation of nature's marvels, and that in which Milton dictates to his daughter his verses on the creation of Eve and her appearance amid the peaceful splendors of Eden. Hence, finally, the prodigious and sudden explosion of the genius of Spontini in *La Vestale*, that shower of ardent ideas, those tears of the heart, that stream of noble, touching, proud, threatening melodies, those warmly colored harmonies, those modulations hitherto unknown in the theater, that depth of expression (I always return to this), and that luxuriance of grand musical images so naturally presented, set down with such masterful authority, clasping the poet's thought with such strength, that it cannot be conceived that the words to which they are adapted were ever a thing apart.

There are in *Cortes*, not involuntary errors, but a few harmonic harshnesses that were intentional; in *Olympie* I can only see some magnificent audacities of that kind. But the orchestration that in *La Vestale* is so richly temperate becomes complicated in *Cortes* and is surcharged with various and useless touches in *Olympie*, to the point of occasionally making the instrumentation heavy and confused.

Spontini had a certain number of melodic ideas to cover all expressions of nobility; once the circle of ideas and sentiments to which these melodies were predestined had been completed, their source became less prolific, and that is why we do not find so much originality in the melodic style of the works, at once heroic and impassioned, that followed *La Vestale* and *Cortez*. But what are these vague reminiscences compared with the cynicism with which certain Italian masters reproduce the same cadences, the same phrases, and the same numbers in their innumerable scores? The orchestration of Spontini, the embryo and the processes of which are to be found already in *Milton* and in *Julie*, was his own invention; it derives from no forerunner. Its special coloring is due to the use of the wind instruments in a way which, if not very expert from a technical point of view, is at least skillfully opposed to the method for the strings. The function, no less important than novel, assigned by the composer to the violas, now massed, now divided like the violins into firsts and seconds, also plays a large part in this special orchestral color that is characteristic of Spontini. The frequent accentuation of the weak beats of the bar, dissonant notes resolved in another part than the one in which they have been sounded, broadly spread arpeggios of all kinds in the basses, undulating majestically beneath the orchestral mass, the moderate but exceedingly ingenious use of trombones, trumpets, horns, and kettledrums, the almost total exclusion of the shrill high notes of the piccolos, oboes, and clarinets, impart to the orchestra of Spontini's masterpieces a physiognomy of incomparable grandeur, power, energy, and often poetic melancholy.

As regards modulation, Spontini was the first to introduce boldly into dramatic music those described as *foreign* to the main key; also enharmonic modulations. But if they occur somewhat frequently in his works, they are at least always reasoned, and used with admirable art. He never modulates without plausible grounds. He does not behave like those uneasy and sterile musicians who, tired of uselessly tormenting a key without finding anything in it, change to another in order to see if they will be more fortunate in that. Some of Spontini's eccentric modulations are, on the contrary, flashes of genius. Of the first order among them is the abrupt passing from the key of E flat to that of D flat in the chorus of the soldiers in *Cortes*, "Quittons ces bords, l'Espagne nous rappelle." At this unexpected change of tonality the hearer is at once impressed in such a way that his imagination clears an immense space at a bound; he flies, so to speak, from one hemisphere to the other and, forgetting Mexico, follows in Spain the thought of mutinous soldiers. I may cite also an example in the trio of prisoners in the same opera, where at the words, "Une mort sans gloire termine nos jours," the voices pass from G minor to A flat major; and, further, the astounding exclamation of the high priest in *La Vestale*, where the voice drops abruptly from the tonality of D flat major to that of C major in the line, "Vont-ils dans le chaos replonger l'univers?"

It is Spontini again who invented the colossal crescendo of which his imitators have subsequently given us a mere microscopic diminutive. Such a one is that in the second act of *La Vestale*, when Julia, delirious and no longer struggling against her passion, feels terror blending with it and growing with the love in her distracted soul:

> Où vais-je?... ô ciel! et quel délire
> S'est emparé de mes sens?
> Un pouvoir invincible à ma perte conspire;
> Il m'entraîne... il me presse... Arrêté! il en est temps!

This progression of wailing harmonies broken by heavy and more and more violent pulsations is an astounding invention, the full value of which can only be felt in the theater, not in the concert hall. So it is again when the Mexican women, distraught by terror, run to throw themselves at Montezuma's feet:

> Quels cris retentissent!
> Tous nos enfants périssent!

I have already referred to the crescendo of the finale of *La Vestale*. Need I mention the duet between Telasco and Amazily, which begins with perhaps the most admirable recitative in existence; or the one between Amazily and Cortez, in which the martial fanfares of the Spanish army blend in so dramatic a fashion with the passionate adieus of the two lovers; or the grandiose aria of Telasco, "Ô patrie! Ô lieux pleins de charmes!" or Julia's in *La Vestale*, "Impitoyables dieux!" or the funeral march; or the aria at the tomb in the same opera; or the duet between Licinius and the high priest, a duet that Weber declared to be one of the most astounding known to him?... Need I speak of the triumphal and religious march in *Olympie*, or the chorus of Diana's dismayed priests when the statue veils itself, or the extraordinary air and situation when Statira, sobbing with indignation, reproaches the hierophant with having brought her as son-in-law the assassin of Alexander, or the choral march of Telasco's train of attendants, also in *Cortez*, "Quels sons nouveaux," the first and only one written in triple measure; or the bacchanal in *Nurmahal*; or the numberless recitatives, beautiful as the most beautiful airs, and of an accent so truthful as to make the ablest masters despair; or those slow dance movements that, with their dreamy and tender melodic inflections, at once evoke the sentiment of voluptuousness and poetize it?... I lose myself in the sinuous windings of this great temple of Expressive Music, in the thousand details of its rich architecture, in the dazzling medley of its ornaments.

The unintelligent, frivolous, or gross herd forsakes the temple today and refuses to sacrifice at the shrine; but for a few, artists and amateurs, who are perhaps more numerous than is generally believed, the goddess to whom Spontini erected this vast monument is still so beautiful that their fervor does not cool. And I, like them, prostrate myself and worship her.

Hector Berlioz, *Evenings in the Orchestra*, trans. C. E. Roche (New York: Alfred A. Knopf, 1929), 169–72.

26

E. T. A. HOFFMANN ON "MUSIC DRAMA THAT SPRINGS FROM THE HEART"

Ernst Theodor Amadeus Hoffmann (1776–1822) was a many-sided genius: musician, painter, writer, man of law. His influence on the romantic movement was immense. His works of fiction inspired operas and ballets (Offenbach's *Tales of Hoffmann*, Tchaikovsky's *Nutcracker* are examples) as well as instrumental music (Schumann's "Kreisleriana," etc.). He was a pioneering music critic as well, and in the following selection, first published separately in 1814, later incorporated in *Kreisleriana*, Part II (1815), he addressed himself to a subject close to his heart, opera. Himself an opera composer (he was composing his most successful one, *Undine*, at the time this essay was written), Hoffmann here expounds some of his basic beliefs, taking his cue from a remark attributed to the Italian composer Antonio Sacchini (1730–86). The remark obviously referred to the older style of *opera seria*, and Hoffmann is well aware of this; he does not dispute the older aesthetic but rather deplores the confused state of opera in his own time and what he views as a widespread tendency to seek easy "effects." His own idols are Gluck and Mozart (in whose honor he changed his third name, Wilhelm, to Amadeus), and they figure prominently in this essay. From Gluck he inherits the ideal of opera as "a unified whole in word, action, and music," an ideal he succeeded in adapting to new purposes and extending in his own *Undine*. From Mozart he derives the well-nigh unapproachable example of the inspired genius, whose every note arises from the necessity of the immediate dramatic context, at the same time coalescing into musically perfect forms and melodies. Opera, in Hoffmann's view, must come from the heart; to move us, the composer must himself be moved (an old maxim: "If you wish to draw tears from me, you must first feel pain yourself"—Horace, *The Art of Poetry*, 102). A work suffused in this way with the inspiration of its creator will strive for dramatic continuity and loosen the traditional forms of opera, and indeed *Undine* did just that. It is significant that, arguing for such a work, Hoffmann should have coined a new word, *Tongedicht*, here translated as "music drama." Wagner, of course, berated the later coinage *Musikdrama* and would have nothing to do with it himself. Yet Hoffmann's thought resonates in Wagner's writings; and this essay can also be viewed, therefore, as an important link in the continuum of German operatic thought that connects Gluck's "reforms" to Wagner's "art work of the future." (Note, in the third paragraph from the end, Hoffmann's reference to instrumentation as an art "enveloped in mystical darkness": the first treatises on the subject did not appear until the late 1830s.)

ON A REMARK OF SACCHINI'S, AND ON
SO-CALLED EFFECT IN MUSIC

In Gerber's *Tonkünstler-Lexikon* the following story is told about the famous Sacchini. When Sacchini was in London having lunch with Herr [Ludwig August] Lebrun [1752–90], the famous oboist, someone repeated in his presence the accusation sometimes leveled by the Germans and French against Italian composers, that they do not modulate enough. "We do modulate in church music," he said. "Because the attention is not distracted by theatrical incident, it can more easily follow artistically integrated changes of key. But in the theater one must be clear and simple; one must touch the heart but not disturb it; and one must make oneself comprehensible to less practiced ears. The composer who can write contrasting arias without changing key shows far more talent than the one who changes it every few moments."

This noteworthy remark of Sacchini's clearly sets out the whole objective of Italian operatic music at that time, and it has remained essentially the same up to the present day. The Italians did not progress to the view that in opera word, action, and music should appear as a unified whole, and that this indivisible whole should create a total impression on the listener. The music was to them more of an incidental accompaniment to the spectacle, and was only now and then allowed to emerge as an independent art creating its own effects. So it was that when the action actually moved forward, the music was kept very simple and insignificant, only the *prima donna* and the *primo uomo* in their so-called *scenas* being allowed to stand out in music of significance, or rather truth. But then no regard was paid to the dramatic context, and the aim was merely to display the singing, often merely the singer's technique, to the most brilliant effect.

In opera Sacchini rejects any forceful or upsetting elements, consigning them to the church. In the theater he will tolerate only agreeable sensations, or rather those which do not move one deeply; he wishes not to be disturbing, but merely to be gently touching. As if opera, by combining its individualized language with the universal language of music, did not by its very nature aim to exert the greatest, most profoundly stirring effect on the mind! Finally, by means of the greatest simplicity, or rather monotony, he wishes to be comprehensible even to the unpracticed ear. But it is the composer's highest, or rather his true art, that by the truth of his expression he moves everyone, and disturbs everyone, as the dramatic context dictates, and that he, like the poet, creates this dramatic context himself. All the resources that the inexhaustible abundance of music offers him are at his command, and he needs them, since they appear as essential components of this expressive truth. Then the most ingenious modulations, with their rapid changes of key at appropriate places, will be comprehensible in a higher sense to the most unpracticed ear. That is to say, the layman does not recognize the technical structure, which is not what matters anyway, but he is powerfully swept along by the dramatic momentum. In *Don Giovanni* [Act II, sc. 11] the statue of the Commendatore intones its terrible "Yes!" on the tonic E, but the composer then takes this E as the third above C and thus modulates into C major, the key taken up by Leporello. Now no musical layman will understand the technical structure of this transition, but he will tremble inwardly with Leporello; and the musician who has attained the highest level of knowledge is equally unlikely, at the moment of greatest tension, to think of the structure, since for him the scaffolding disappeared long ago, and so his response co-incides with that of the layman. . . .

The truth that opera should appear as a unified whole in word, action, and music was first propounded clearly by Gluck in his works. But what truth has not frequently been misunderstood, thus giving rise to the strangest misconceptions? What masterpieces have not spawned the most absurd products as a result of blind imitation? A weak eye sees the works of great genius like a distorted painting, since it cannot bring them into focus, and it is the disjointed impression of this painting which is then criticized and imitated. . . . One could assert that the influence of Gluck's and Mozart's works, in a purely musical sense and disregarding their texts, stemmed only from their material. Attention was directed to the material of the musical structure, and the higher meaning which this material served was not discovered. In this regard it was found, particularly in Mozart's case, that as well as numerous striking modulations, it was also his frequent use of wind instruments that seemed to heighten the astonishing effectiveness of his works; and from this sprang our chaos of overladen orchestration and bizarre, unmotivated modulation. "Effect" became the watchword of composers, and to create an effect at all costs became the sole objective of their efforts. But this very striving for effect shows that it was lacking, and could not be made to appear wherever the composer wanted it.

In a word, in order to move us, in order to stir us profoundly, the artist must be affected deeply within his own heart; and the art of composing effectively is to employ the highest possible skill to capture ideas unconsciously conceived in a state of ecstasy, and to write them down in the hieroglyphs of musical sound (notation). If a young artist asks, therefore, how he should set about composing an opera with the maximum effect, one can only give him the following reply: "Read the poem, concentrate your mind on it with all your strength, enter into the dramatic situations with all the resources of your imagination; you live in the characters of the drama, you yourself are the tyrant, the hero, the lover; you feel the pain and the joy of love, the humiliation, fear, horror, even the nameless agony of death, and the blissful ecstasy of transfiguration; you brood, you rage, you hope, you despair; your blood races through your veins, your pulse beats faster; from the fire of inspiration that inflames your breast emerge notes, melodies, chords, and the drama flows from within you translated into the magical language of music. Technical proficiency gained from studying harmony, analyzing the works of great composers, and from your own composing, will enable you to hear your inner music more and more clearly; no melody, no effect, no instrument will escape you, and so, simultaneously with the effect, you will conceive the means to achieve it, which you will then commit to the charm-book of the score, like spirits subjugated to your power." Admittedly all this is only tantamount to saying: just make sure, my dear fellow, that you are a musical genius, and then the rest will take care of itself! But it really is like that, and there is no way round it.

It must nevertheless be assumed that many suppress the true spark they carry within them, since they have no confidence in their own powers, reject any ideas springing from their own inspiration, and anxiously strive to make use of everything they see creating an effect in the works of great composers; thus they are reduced to imitating form, which can never produce spirit, since it is spirit that determines form. The eternal braying of theater directors for "Effect! Only effect!" in order to pull in the audience, as the current expression has it, and the demands of so-called fastidious connoisseurs, to whom pepper itself is no longer peppery enough, often drive musicians into a sort of hopeless desperation to outdo earlier composers in their effects wherever possible. This is how curious compositions arise in which without any motivation—that is to say without the context of the drama providing the slightest justification for it— crude changes of key and blaring chords from every conceivable wind instrument follow in rapid succession, like garish colors that never coalesce into a picture. The composer is like a man in a profound sleep who is repeatedly woken up by violent hammer blows, but then keeps going back to sleep again. Composers of this sort are absolutely amazed when, despite the pains they have put themselves to, their works utterly fail to produce the effect they had imagined. They certainly do not realize that the music that was created by their own imagination and flowed spontaneously from within them, but seemed to them too simple or too empty, would probably have been infinitely more effective. Their anxiety and lack of confidence blinded them and prevented them from properly appreciating the masterpieces they took as models; they became preoccupied by technical resources, seeing them as the means whereby effect was obtained. But as already pointed out, it is the untrammeled spirit which commands the resources and exercises total authority in those works; only the music drama that has emanated sincerely and powerfully from the heart can then enter into the listener's heart. The spirit comprehends only the language of the spirit.

To lay down rules for bringing forth effect in music may well be impossible, therefore; but a composer at odds with himself and wandering astray as though dazzled by the will-o'-the-wisps can be brought back on course by a few guiding suggestions.

The first and foremost element in music is melody, which seizes the human imagination with magical power. It cannot be said often enough that without expressive, singable melody all the adornment of instruments etc. is nothing but glossy surface . . . appealing to the mindless rabble. Singable, understood in the higher sense of the word, is an excellent adjective with which to describe true melody. It must itself be song, and must issue in a free and unforced flow directly from the human breast, which is the instrument that resounds with the most magical and mysterious sounds of nature. Melody that is not singable in this sense is nothing but a series of separate notes striving in vain to become music. It is incredible how in recent times, particularly following the example of a misunderstood composer (Cherubini), melody has actually been neglected, and as a result of the constant struggle to be original and striking a number of music dramas have appeared that are utterly unsingable. How is it that the simple airs of the earlier Italians, often accompanied only by the [thorough]bass, move and elevate the spirit so irresistibly? Does the explanation not lie entirely in their sublime, truly singing melody? Melody is in fact the undisputed, native property of that passionately musical people, and the German, though he has arrived at a higher, or rather at a true view of opera, should become familiar with their spirits in every possible way, so they will not disdain to enter his innermost being, as if by a secret, magical power, and kindle the spark of melody. An excellent example of this intimate familiarity is given by that great master of the art, Mozart, in whose breast Italian melody burned brightly. What composer wrote in a more singable style than he? Even without orchestral gloss, every one of his melodies makes a profound impression, and this explains the extraordinary effect of his compositions.

With regard to modulation, only the dramatic context can provide a justification for this; it should proceed from the various impulses aroused in the spirit. These can be gentle, strong, overpowering, gradually burgeoning, or suddenly gripping. Similarly the composer, who possesses the mysterious knowledge of harmony as a munificent gift of nature, so that technical study merely provides him with the means of consciously applying it, will move now to related, now to remote keys, now gradually, now at a stroke. The true genius does not presume to impress by artificial artistry, which becomes painful non-art; he merely follows the dictates of his inner spirit, as it translates the dramatic situations into music. Let the musical mathematicians then draw their examples from his works, and use them as practical exercises. It would lead too far to discuss the profound art of harmony here, and to show how it is rooted deeply inside us and how to those with sharper vision mysterious laws are revealed that no textbook contains. Let it suffice to point out, in order to draw attention to one particular circumstance, that abrupt changes of key are of great effect only when, despite their heterogeneity, the keys have an underlying relationship apparent to the mind of a musician. The passage mentioned earlier, from the duet in *Don Giovanni*, may also serve as an example of this. Also to be included here are enharmonic modulations, often ridiculed for being misused, but containing that underlying relationship, and frequently producing an undoubtedly powerful effect. It is as though a hidden, sympathetic bond often connected the most remotely separated keys, and as though under certain circumstances an insuperable idiosyncrasy separated even the most closely related keys. The most common and most frequent modulation of all, that from the tonic to the dominant. or vice versa, can seem at times unexpected and unusual, even unpleasant and unbearable.

It is true that a large part of the disturbing effect often produced by the inspired works of great composers comes from their instrumentation. Here too, however, it is hardly possible to venture even a single rule; for this department of the musical art is enveloped in mystical darkness. Every instrument, whatever its distinctive effect in a particular instance, is capable of a hundred others, and it is a foolish delusion to suppose, for example, that strength and power can be expressed only by them all playing together. A single note sounded by this or that instrument can produce inner turmoil. Many passages in Gluck's operas provide conspicuous examples of this, and in order to appreciate fully the variety of effect of which every instrument is capable, one need only think of the heterogeneous effects Mozart draws from the same instrument—the oboe for example. Only a few indications are possible here.

To return to the comparison between music and painting, a music drama will appear in the artist's mind like a finished canvas; and, as he contemplates it, he will spontaneously discover the correct perspective, without which no truth is possible. Instrumentation also includes the various accompanying instrumental figures, and how often one of these figures, genuinely derived from within, raises expressive truth to the highest power! How deeply affecting, for example, is the steady figure played in octaves by the second violins and violas in Mozart's aria "Non mi dir, bell'idol mio" [sung by Donna Anna in *Don Giovanni*, Act II, sc. 12]. With regard to figures, nothing can be artificially concocted or grafted on; the brilliant colors of a music drama highlight the smaller detail, and any extraneous embellishment would only destroy rather than beautify. It is the same with the choice of key, with forte and piano (which proceed from the underlying character of the work and should not be introduced just for the sake of variety), and with all the other means of expression at the musician's disposal.

One can absolutely assure the hapless composer grimly striving for effect that so long as genius resides in him, his thorough acquaintance with the works of the masters will soon give him a mysterious rapport with their spirit, and that this will arouse his latent powers, even induce a state of ecstasy, in which he awakens as from a torpid sleep into new life, and perceives the extraordinary sounds of his own inner music. Then his study of harmony and his technical exercises will give him the ability to grasp hold of the music that would otherwise rush past him; and the inspiration that gives birth to the work will powerfully seize the listener with its magical resonance, so that he will partake of the bliss enveloping the musician during those sacramental hours. This, therefore, is the genuine effect achieved by a music drama that springs from the heart.

David Charlton, ed., *E. T. A. Hoffmann's Musical Writings:* Kreisleriana, The Poet and the Composer, *Music Criticism*, trans. Martyn Clarke (Cambridge: © Cambridge University Press, 1989), 152–59. Reprinted with the permission of Cambridge University Press.

27

THE FIRST PERFORMANCE OF
IL BARBIERE DI SIVIGLIA

In 1823 there appeared in Bologna a pamphlet entitled (we translate) *Notes Concerning Maestro Rossini by a Lady, Formerly a Singer, in Response to What Was Written about Him in the Summer of 1822 by the English Journalist in Paris and That Same Year Reported in a Milan Gazette.* The author was Gel-trude Righetti-Giorgi (1793–1862), who had created the role of Rosina at the famously disastrous first performance of *Il barbiere di Siviglia* (Rome, 20 February 1816); as we shall see, the prior existence of another *Barbiere,* by Paisiello, was only one of the reasons for the failure. The "English Journalist" in Righetti-Giorgi's title takes a little explaining. The great French novelist Stendhal (pseudonym of Henri Beyle, 1783–1842) was a devotee of Italian opera, having lived in Italy for many years. On his return to France, he un-dertook to write what was to be the first full-length study of Rossini's life and music; published in 1824, his *Vie de Rossini* was an instant success. The com-poser was just thirty-two at the time; he had settled in Paris and was about to enter on the final stage of his career, which would culminate with *Guillaume Tell* five years later. Stendhal's biography, then, was timely; it was also highly entertaining. Unfortunately it is quite inaccurate and thus unsuitable for rep-resentation among these documents. Prior to that, however, in January 1822, Stendhal had contributed an anonymous article on Rossini to *The Paris Monthly Review,* an English-language periodical. It was this, translated into Italian and published in the *Gazzetta musicale* of Milan, that provoked Righetti-Giorgi's fiery outburst. Thus we have Stendhal to thank after all for this rare eyewit-ness report from Rossini's earlier, Italian career. Righetti-Giorgi transcribed the whole offending article and responded to it segment by segment. Excerpted below are the segment of Stendhal's article dealing with the first performance of *Il barbiere di Siviglia* and the singer's rebuttal. (Note: "Whistling," the Con-tinental sign of public disapproval, is here translated "booing.")

"When [Rossini] engaged to write for Rome, the impresario suggested he com-pose new music for *Il barbiere di Siviglia,* several other dramas having been turned down by the censor. The Maestro hesitated at first; then he wrote to Paisiello to obtain his permission; the latter consented, never doubting it would succeed. Rossini showed the letter to all the amateurs and also had a notice about it printed in the libretto. He composed his *Barbiere* in thirteen days and confessed that his heart was pounding at the first performance, when he took his place at the pianoforte.

"The beginning of the opera seemed tedious to the Romans, and far beneath Paisiello's. They disliked an aria sung by Rosina, 'Io sono docile,' the peevish cries of a woman getting on in years rather than the tender lament of a young woman in love. The duet between Rosina and Figaro won the first applause. The 'Calunnia' aria was judged very good; but it is very much like the 'Vendetta' aria in Mozart's *Nozze di Figaro*.

"This opera had a singular fate: at the first performance it displeased, while at the second it was received with enthusiasm. Despite this, the Roman critics found that Rossini had remained beneath all the famous composers in expressing the tender passions. The complicated trills and *volate* [flights] in which Rosina gets involved, and which are so much applauded in Paris, were almost booed in Rome. It was felt that if Cimarosa had ever composed the *Barbiere*, it would have been more comical and heartfelt; and it was the general conviction that Rossini was not the equal of Paisiello in the 'Buona sera' quintet, where Don Basilio is sent off to bed."

On this subject, Mr. British Journalist, you shall hear *me*, for whom Rossini wrote the part of Rosina in the *Barbiere di Siviglia*.

The censorship had no dealings whatever with Rossini. The poet [Jacopo] Ferretti was engaged to write a libretto for the Teatro Argentina; the principal part was to go to the tenor [Manuel] García. Ferretti presented a story about an officer who is in love with a hostess and is thwarted by a lawyer. The impresario thought the argument rather common and, abandoning Ferretti, sought out the other poet, Mr. [Cesare] Sterbini. The latter, who had previously been unsuccessful with [the libretto of Rossini's] *Torvaldo e Dorliska*, decided to tempt fate once more. The argument of the new libretto was discussed together with Rossini, and *Il barbiere di Siviglia* chosen by common consent. Rossini did not, as is generally supposed, write to Paisiello, since he believed that the same argument could be treated successfully by different artists. . . . In his Invitation to the public, Rossini declared he had intended no offense to the excellent Paisiello by undertaking an argument that had been treated by Paisiello in so masterly a fashion. This hint may have contributed to the unhappy outcome. Oh, what gossip there was that day in the streets and coffeehouses of Rome! The envious and the ill-disposed claimed Rossini had by then exhausted his earlier poetic vein; accordingly they affected the greatest surprise on hearing that the noble impresario of the Teatro Argentina had engaged him to write an opera. They were all, however, prepared to immolate him; and the better to succeed, they began by censuring him for having undertaken an argument treated by Paisiello. "See," they cried as they stood about in knots, "see how far the pride of a heedless youth can go! He is thinking of rubbing out the immortal name of Paisiello. Just wait and see, fool, wait and see!"

In such a situation one's friends are of small use, and their prudent silence can sometimes animate and excite one's enemies.

Through an unfortunate act of kindness Rossini, who greatly respected the tenor García, had allowed him to compose the airs that were to be sung beneath Rosina's windows after the *Introduzione*. And indeed García wrote them on themes from that nation's [i.e., Spain's] love songs. But García, after tuning his guitar onstage (which aroused the mirth of the indiscreet), sang his cavatinas with little spirit, and they were received with disdain. I was prepared for anything. I climbed the stair that was to take me to the balcony in order to say just these words: "Segui, o caro, deh segui così" ["Continue, my dear, oh continue thus"]. The Romans, accustomed to regaling me with applause in *L'Italiana in Algeri*, were expecting me to earn it again with a pleasant, amorous cavatina. When they heard those few words, they burst into an uproar of disapproval. There followed what was bound to follow. Figaro's cavatina, although sung in masterly fashion by [Luigi] Zamboni, and the beautiful duet between Figaro and Almaviva, sung also by Zamboni and García, were not even listened to. At last I appeared onstage, no longer at the window; and I was supported by the public's constant favor during thirty-nine previous appearances.

I was not getting on in years, Mr. Journalist: I had barely reached the age of 23. My voice was admired in Rome as the loveliest of any that had ever been heard there. Always most willing to do my duty, I had become the darling of the Romans. They therefore fell silent and prepared to listen to me. My courage returned to me; and as to how I sang the "Vipera" cavatina, let the Romans testify, as will Rossini himself. They honored me with three successive rounds of applause, and Rossini also stood up once to thank them. He, who in those days was a great admirer of my voice, turned to me from the keyboard and, jesting, said to me, "Ah, Nature!" "Thank her," I replied smiling, "for without her favor you would not now have risen from your seat." At that point the opera seemed to have come back to life; but it was not to be. Zamboni and I sang the lovely duet between Rosina and Figaro, and Envy, enraged, showed itself in all its manifestations. Booing from all sides. We reached the finale, a classical composition of which the world's foremost composers might well be proud. Laughter, shouts, and penetrating boos without respite, except for yet more din. We reached the beautiful unison melody, "Quest'avventura"; a raucous voice from the balcony yelled, "That's the funeral of Don C[esarini, the impresario, who had suddenly died four days earlier]." Nothing more was needed. It is impossible to describe the insults that were poured on Rossini, who sat undaunted at the keyboard and appeared to be saying, "Forgive them, Apollo, for they know not what they do." At the conclusion of the first act, Rossini made a show of clapping his hands—not at his opera, as was commonly believed, but at the singers who, to tell the truth, had done their best. Many took offense. This will give a fair picture of the second act's reception.

Rossini left the theater as if he had been an indifferent spectator. My soul filled with these events, I went to his house to comfort him; but he had no need of my comfort, for he was peacefully asleep.

The next day Rossini removed from his score whatever he felt was justly censurable; he then gave out that he was ill, perhaps so he would not have to appear at the keyboard. The Romans meanwhile had second thoughts and supposed that they ought at least to listen attentively to the whole opera, in order to judge it fairly. They therefore came to the theater the second night too and kept perfectly still. Mr. Journalist here begins to speak the truth. The opera was crowned with universal applause. Afterwards we all went to see the feigned sick man, whose bed was surrounded by many distinguished Roman gentlemen who had hastened there to compliment him on the excellence of his work. At the third performance the applause increased: finally Rossini's *Barbiere di Siviglia* entered the rank of those musical compositions that never grow old and are worthy to stand beside the finest *opere buffe* of Paisiello and Cimarosa.

Luigi Rognoni, *Gioacchino Rossini,* new ed. (Turin: Giulio Einaudi, 1977), 356–59. Trans. P.W.

28

DER FREISCHÜTZ: A GERMAN TRIUMPH

Der Freischütz had its first performance on 18 June 1821 at the newly erected Royal Playhouse in Berlin. Musical politics attended the birth of Weber's most famous opera. Spontini's *Olympia*, reworked specifically for Berlin and translated into German by E. T. A. Hoffmann, had had its première at the Berlin Opera shortly before, on 14 May, with much scenic splendor. Spontini was the favorite composer of King Frederick William III and had just been appointed Generalmusikdirektor over the opposition of much of the German public; indeed the Court Theater Intendant, Count Brühl, had hoped to install Weber in that position. Weber's triumph obliterated *Olympia*, and in the end both composers were the losers: Berlin remained closed to Weber for the rest of his short life, and Spontini, though he remained there until 1842, never won over the public. Heine, a witness to both operatic premières, reported gleefully on the party politics surrounding them; and Weber's son, born the following year, pictured the political situation vividly in the extract given below, from the biography of his father (published in 1864). What matters most in the

son's description is not the politics, however, but the effect on the public of
the music's unprecedented romantic qualities: the forest imagery of the overture, the horror associated with the demon Samiel, the virginal purity of the
heroine Agathe's great scena, evocative of the scents of night and rustling of
trees, the folklike spontaneity of the Bridesmaids' chorus (which in fact became a folksong for well over a century). It was indeed a triumph for German
music, but even more for romanticism. And if its novelty has faded, it pays to
remember how Berlioz idolized the work and how Pushkin characterized
young Tatyana's love letter to Eugene Onegin: it was "*Freischütz* played timidly
by beginner's fingers"—in other words, the very essence of romanticism.

Four hours before the opening of the Royal Playhouse, crowds were beleaguer-
ing its unbelievably impractical entrances. It was only thanks to the excellent
precautions taken by the police that, in the fearful crush and struggle that took
place when the doors were opened, only clothes were torn and some bruises suffered. The pit was immediately filled to suffocation by a compact mass of students, young men of science, artists, officials, artisans who eight years earlier
had borne arms and helped to chase the French invader—the youthful intelligence, the patriotic fire, the enlightened opposition to the foreigner. Under [his
wife] Caroline's box stood [Weber's pupil Julius] Benedict; the long, frail figure
of Heinrich Heine, sarcastically punning about replacing the verses of "Childe
Harold" (which occupied him at the time) with the verses of Kind ["child" in
German]; and a small, pudgy student with powerful lungs and sonorous hands.
The high society and the literary, musical, and scientific authorities of Berlin
filled the stalls and the boxes. The government officials were few, and scarcely
a uniform was visible. Little by little the orchestra filled—the musicians began
to tune their instruments—the hoarse murmur of the packed crowd, sweltering
in the overheated house, grew louder and louder. All at once came applause from
the orchestra. Weber had entered it. And now the whole house, with its thousand upon thousand hands, took up the sound, and thundered forth its echo.
Three times was Weber obliged to let fall his baton and to bow, before he could
give the signal to begin. In the midst of the storm came suddenly a solemn silence. The bewitching musical pictures of the overture were now spread forth
in all their irresistible fullness. The impression was magical. And when, after
the muted kettledrum strokes at the end, the powerful C major chord broke in,
followed by the blazing, jubilant conclusion, there was such a tempest of applause, such a universal shout of *da capo*, that the entire overture had to be repeated, and the enthusiasm was still greater if possible. The first scene, admirably
grouped and represented with life and animation, produced a great effect; but
Kilian's air and the mocking chorus, although sung with great intelligence,

seemed, from a want of appreciation of its musical audacity, to miss fire. Not so the passage in the following trio, "O lass Hoffnung dich beleben," which, partly on account of the chorus's excellent performance, partly because of its reminiscence of the overture, went immediately to the hearts of all, and drew down another storm of applause. "Nun lasset die Hörner erschallen" and the waltz, with its profoundly original dying-out at the end, had gone by. The stage grew dark, and the attention of the public during the scena of Max, "Nein, länger trag' ich nicht die Qualen," was so intense that, in spite of Stümer's artistic yet simple delivery, the beautiful *arioso* "Durch die Wälder, durch die Auen" went by virtually unnoticed. On the unexpected entrance of Samiel, a shudder ran through the agitated house, and only the gleam of light in "Jetzt ist wohl ihr Fenster offen" allayed somewhat the uncanny impression of his appearance, an impression that was even stronger upon his return in the last Allegro. Tumultuous applause crowned the conclusion of the aria. Caspar's drinking song—so contrary in conception to the usual forms—was not understood, and Blume could not manage his voice in this scene. In short, the curtain fell upon an anticlimax, the applause was lukewarm, and the long interval gave rise to animated, even tumultuous discussions. The Spontinians rubbed their hands and said with scorn, "Is this the music that will cast *La Vestale, Cortez,* and *Olympia* into the shade? What a big fuss over a simple Singspiel, or better, a melodrama!"—"What is the point of quarter-hour-long dialogues and boring narrations in an opera?"— "How monotonous, such a long act without a female voice!"—A storm of angry murmurs filled the house. During the tumult, the Master had returned to his place. The curtain rose and a salvo of applause greeted the bright, amiable figures of Agathe and Ännchen (Seidler and Eunicke), who, after the gloomy local color of the first act, seemed like redeeming rays of light. Accustomed as we are to the opera from our youth, we can hardly experience such impressions any more!—The magical duet, so new in form and treatment, and even more Ännchen's fresh arietta "Kommt ein schlanker Bursch gegangen," won the approval of the whole house. But the brightest spot of the first performance was unquestionably the great scena of Frau Seidler, "Wie nahte mir der Schlummer." At this point the opposition surrendered its arms. Surprised, carried away, wholly overcome, Weber's bitterest adversaries succumbed to the general and irresistible torrent of applause. Stalls, boxes, pit, and gallery felt the fragrance of the lovely night, heard the rustling of the trees, saw Max approaching with his cluster of flowers, and, with Agathe's rejoicing, burst forth in cheers, applause, endless calls, giving the author of this magical work their hearts, hands, and souls! From this moment the success of the opera was assured.—The following trio found the liveliest appreciation. The Wolf's Glen scene, with its adventurous accessories, its wondrous, never before attempted instrumental effects and impressive scenery, conceived so truly in accord with the Master's own peculiar genius, brought the second act to a triumphant close. "He's a devil of a fellow, that little Weber!" cried the pudgy student beneath Caroline's box, blowing into his burning hands, "but it's hard work to tell him how good he is!" If the storm of voices was heavy at the end of the first act, it was overpowering now. But how different was the nature of the tempest! The Italian party was struck dumb. Wonderful, marvelous—delicate and powerful—as new as it is beautiful—outstanding—bold, but to the point: these were some of the comments heard on all sides. But the Master had quietly gone up to Caroline's box and sat in a dark corner, holding his wife's hand as she silently wept for joy. After the entr'acte, played with life and energy by the orchestra, Agathe's prayer, close to the older cavatina in form, and Ännchen's "kreideweise Nase" with the obbligato viola and half-bantering, half-tender Allegro, sung captivatingly by Fräulein Eunicke, were very favorably received. The folksong "Wir winden dir den Jungfernkranz," so popular in the best sense of the word, so thoroughly German in its inspiration and execution, was stormily encored, although sung with trembling voice by Fräulein Reinwald. The Huntsman's chorus, although greatly applauded, did not, strange to say, win its way fully with the public until about the eighth or tenth performance. Its melody was among the few, in *Der Freischütz*, that were not sung at once at every street corner. Prince Ottokar (Rebenstein) gave the signal for the shot at the dove, and the wonderful finale—although its rather too prolonged form produced a comparative tendency to coolness in the audience—brought the opera gloriously to its close.

The curtain fell, but nobody left the house, which rang out with thunderous applause, as thousands of voices summoned the composer. At last he appeared, leading Madame Seidler and Fräulein Eunicke by the hand. Wreaths, jubilant cries, songs and verses went flying towards him.—

The success was immense, unparalleled! Critics, artists, dilettanti, and music lovers appeared intoxicated and, for the first time, at least that night, unanimous in their praise, delight, and joy. The public dispersed noisily, loudly spreading word of the new wonder.

Max Maria von Weber, *Carl Maria von Weber: The Life of an Artist*, trans. J. Palgrave Simpson (London: Chapman and Hall, 1865), 2:219–23. Revised in accordance with the original (Leipzig, 1864).

29

PARISIAN GRAND OPERA: AUBER'S *LA MUETTE DE PORTICI* AS SEEN BY WAGNER

French opera blossomed into an all-encompassing spectacle when it combined the grandeur of traditional heroic opera with the more human concerns of *opéra comique*. The grand gestures and poise of classicism were fused with the adventuresomeness and suspense of rescue opera. Local color and folk heroes now occupied the stage amid splendid scenes of nature and faithful reconstructions of historical settings. Choruses sprang into action; and the orchestra, always one of the glories of French opera, reached new heights of virtuosity and tonal brilliance. This was "grand opera," and *La Muette de Portici* (1828) by Daniel-François-Esprit Auber (1782–1871) is generally credited with initiating the new trend, closely followed by Rossini's *Guillaume Tell* (1829). A huge work in five acts, *La Muette* was an instant and lasting success both in Paris and throughout Europe. Semihistorical (it deals fancifully with the Neapolitan uprising led by Masaniello in 1647), it has a title role that is danced, not sung: for Masaniello's sister (a fictional character, like most of the others) is a mute. In other ways too, *La Muette* represents a new approach to the operatic conventions; perhaps, then, it is not too surprising to discover that one of its most ardent admirers was Richard Wagner. Interlarding his appreciation with disdainful references to Italian opera in general and Rossini in particular, Wagner does rise above his prejudices enough to give us a clear-eyed view of why *La Muette* made such a deep impression on its first appearance. He penned his article late in 1871. Auber had died on 13 May of that year, shortly after the fall of France in the Franco-Prussian War and while the short-lived Commune was in control of Paris.

REMINISCENCES OF AUBER

It has been noted as characteristic of the fate of this most interesting opera composer that his uncommonly tenacious hold on life, which at the age of eighty-nine had just borne him over his country's defeat and the hardships of the siege of Paris, should finally have broken down beneath the horrors of the Commune. In fact he narrowly missed the peculiar distinction of an atheistic burial, proposed to his survivors by the Paris Municipal Council; from that his body was happily saved, and committed to earth with all the rites of holy Church. Mr. A. Dumas *fils* then delivered a funeral oration of tender rhetorical pathos in honor of the deceased; wherein Auber, however, according to my judgment, was held up to his nation in a very false light. And just this speech—which represented Auber as a bright angel of harmony, melting away in melodic tears at the fate of his country—has once more shown me how little a Frenchman has succeeded in finding the phrase to characterize the most purely French of all his composers; at Auber's grave he deemed the occasion fully met by an empty flourish, so long as it was sentimentally high-toned enough. . . .

We Germans appear to have much better understood at once the distinctive quality of this French music, as may be seen from a comparison of our reception of the "Muette de Portici" with that of "Tell." Whoever witnessed the first appearance of the former opera upon the German stage must remember the quite astonishing impression it created; while "Tell" could never really make its way, and owes its maintenance rather to the Italianate singers than to any lively pleasure of our public in the work itself. The "Muette," on the contrary, took us all by surprise, as something entirely novel: an operatic subject of this vitality there had never been; the first real drama in five acts, with all the attributes of a tragedy, indeed even with a tragic ending. This last circumstance in itself, as I remember, made quite a sensation. Until then the plot of an opera had always been characterized by the obligation to end "happily": no composer would have dared to send people home with a sad ending as their last impression. . . .

But the "Muette" was a grand surprise from every point of view: each of the five acts presented a drastic picture of the most extraordinary animation, where arias and duets in the usual operatic sense were scarcely to be detected any more, and certainly, with the exception of a single prima-donna aria in the first act, did not strike one at all as such; in each instance it was the interconnectedness of the whole act that riveted attention and carried one away. We well may ask: How did Auber come by such an opera text? . . . What auspicious influence was at work, it is difficult to make clear to oneself: in any case it must have been something quite out of the common, something wellnigh demonic. Certain it is, that this Auber was the only man who could have written the music for it, the right, the only music, such as Rossini with his ponderous, old-fashioned Italian square structures, which drive us to despair in his "opera seria" (Semiramis, Moses, etc.), was quite incapable of producing. For the novelty in this music to the "Muette" was this unaccustomed concision and drastic compactness of the form: the recitatives shot lightning at us; a veritable tempest whirled us on from them to the chorus ensembles; and amid the chaos of fury we had sudden energetic cries to restore moderation, or fresh calls to action; then again the shouts of riot, of murderous frenzy, and between them the affecting plaint of anguish, or a whole people lisping out its prayer. Even as the subject lacked nothing of either the utmost terror or the utmost tenderness, so Auber made his music reproduce each contrast, every blend, in contours and colors of so drastic, so vivid a distinctness as we cannot remember to have ever seen before; we might almost fancy we had actual music-paintings before us, and the idea of the picturesque in music might easily have found a favorable basis here, had it not had to yield to the far more pertinent one of a highly successful theatrical plasticity. . . .

Auber's score undoubtedly presents many excellences and telling innovations, which have since become the property of all composers, and particularly of the French; to these innovations belong above all his brilliant instrumentation, the striking color, the sureness and audacity of his orchestral effects, among which we may instance his treatment of the strings (considered so daring in those days), and especially of the violins, to which as a body he allots the most venturesome of passages. If we class with these eventful innovations the master's drastic grouping of his chorus ensemble, which almost for the first time he makes a real, a seriously interesting factor in the plot, in respect of the inner structure of his music we have still to mention certain quite remarkable idiosyncracies in its harmonization and even in the voice-leading, which have been retained and carried further by himself and followers as a valuable addition to the means of appropriate dramatic characterization. In a like sense may be named the constant and subtle attention paid by the master to the progress of the play, in which he loses sight of nothing that can serve him for his orchestral preludes and postludes, thus turning into a fascinating series of suggestive musical pictures what before had consisted of mere banal commonplaces. But the extraordinary, white heat that Auber poured for this once through his music remained a peculiarity of this one work, and never could he come by it again; we must assume he stood here at the zenith of his powers, of his whole nature.

Richard Wagner, *Prose Works*, trans W. E. Ellis (London: Kegan Paul, Trench, Trübner, 1896), 5:35–43 (revised).

INTERLUDE: MADAME PASTA

Leigh Hunt (1784–1859), an elegant essayist and poet, the friend and collaborator of Byron, Keats, and Shelley, was also a sensitive literary and dramatic critic; in addition, his musical knowledge and taste made him a highly qualified critic of opera. The performance reviewed below of *Medea in Corinto*

(1813) by the respected German-Italian composer Simon Mayr (1763–1845) represented in no way a novelty to London audiences: the work had first been heard there in 1826 and would be revived again and again over the years. Nor was the star a newcomer. Giuditta Pasta (1797–1865), at that time Europe's greatest soprano, was well known in London, and the role of Medea, which she had introduced there in 1826, was one for which she was especially famous. Hunt's review, then, was less a news story than a meditation on the nature of Pasta's greatness. It allows us a glimpse into the life of a major opera house, the Haymarket Theatre, at a time when classical ideals of acting were still in full vogue. It should be noted that Hunt uses the word "attitude" in its original, technical sense: the posture of a figure in sculpture or painting. Pasta is viewed not only with admiration for her art but with affectionate concern for her figure (for what Hunt at one point discreetly calls her "superfluity of person"). In the end, short notice is taken of the other participants, three of them just as celebrated: the dancer Marie Taglioni (1804–84), the bass Luigi Lablache (1794–1858), and the tenor Giovanni Battista Rubini (1794–1854). London could afford the very best.

May 13, 1831	*King's Theatre*

Madame Pasta was received last night in the manner to be expected. Milton speaks of "raining influence." The moment she was recognized, the clapping of hands came down in a perfect *hail*-storm of approbation: and she stood bending in her graceful fashion under the shower. We looked with some anxiety to know whether our love was to be put to the test by her having grown fatter; but she is not at all so. We think she has altered in that respect for the better.

The part she appeared in was *Medea*, which is reckoned her finest. We know not how that may be, for we have seen her but in few of her characters; but that it is one of the finest things on the stage, we can bear testimony. . . .

The charm of Madame Pasta's style consists in the wonderful truth of it, invested with moral beauty; that is to say, she never minces what she feels, or goes aside of it, or affects anything as superior to it, or has any doubt about it; but is as full of faith as a child, and being child-like in her faith, she is rewarded by having as much grace in her exposition of it as a child has in its movements. We do not mean that she is as unconscious as a child. The stage itself, as well as her knowledge, would prevent that; nor would it be natural, if she were. What we mean is, that grace in her is always subordinate to the truth, and moulded by it. She knows as truly the best attitudes in which she can put herself, as she knows what passion she is to express, and she knows the one because of the other. The tree bends with the fruit. She carries so much beauty and truth in her that she must carry it in the most beautiful manner.

This is the reason why a little superfluity of person never stood in the way of the effect produced by this divine actress—at least with those who had any

GIUDITTA PASTA. *The beloved soprano portrayed by the Milanese painter Gioachino Serangeli.*
Milan, Museo Teatrale alla Scala.

perception of the morally beautiful themselves. And for the same reason, her voice, which though excellent, is not of the very finest order, does not stand in the way of what it expresses. It is the vehicle, as all voices should be, of emotion. Those who value no singer except their voice or execution be perfect, and are contented if it is, mistake the means for the end. Madame Pasta's execution can be extraordinary when she pleases; but in general she restrains it, agreeably to what nature requires. In every respect, the means with her are subordinate to the end; and hence it is that, with less means than some, there is no singer or actress upon the stage who attains her end so perfectly.

Madame Pasta's style is epic. She hits great points and leaves you to feel the rest. Her gestures are voluminous; the tender ones are full of the last soul of love, her threatening or calamitous ones, appalling; there is catastrophe in them, the certainty of doom. Thus when Jason tells her she is to look for his love no longer, and she feels the first dim movements in her soul of all that is about to happen, she walks away, *laying her hands over her eyes*, as if she did not dare to look upon the mournful and dreadful things that must happen. Afterwards, when she threatens Jason, she holds out to him a hand, trembling as if it held misery for both of them; and when she is to express a passionate resolution, by suddenly leaping to a high note, she dares, with a noble confidence, to make almost a shriek of it. It is as if a Pythian priestess were crying from her tripod. Her classical dresses and attitudes are known to everybody. They are fine, not merely because they are classical, but because the ancients, in the height and purity of their perceptions, hit upon the finest attitudes, and she and the ancients think in this matter alike. In only one point could we conceive that Euripides would have desired a finer Medea than she (supposing that he had the luck to have so good a one); and that is when she relents a while from her murderous impulses against her children and fondles them with love. We think (with submission) that Madame Pasta is somewhat *too* much absorbed in the love, and that it makes her look a little too happy. We would have had her look at them as if there were tears in her eyes.

We have not time to say more, or to speak of Taglioni, whom we must notice at a future opportunity. We can only add that the music of this opera, by Mayer, though you do not carry any passages away from it, is good and expressive; that Lablache, in [the role of] Creonte, looked like a king of the old heroic times, when kings were great stalwart fellows, a head and shoulders taller than their subjects; that his voice was worthy of such a royalty, and as easy as it was powerful; . . . and that Signor Rubini is spoiled by his execution, much about in the same manner, and with the same amount of wit, as some men are by a good set of teeth. He is always for shewing it. He is one of your greatest mistakers of the means for the end; and all the mistaken people in the house applaud him; which is a pity, for with a voice at once powerful and sweet, he ought to do better. But we are afraid he errs for want of ideas. He seems to think at present, that there are but three things in the world: to be full of demisemiquavers, to be loud, and to be soft. He thunders on one half of a bar, and languishes through the rest. He snaps a pistol at your head, and then falls to scratching it.

L. H. Houtchens and C. W. Houtchens, eds., *Leigh Hunt's Dramatic Criticism, 1808–1831* (New York: Columbia University Press, 1949), 267–69.

30

VERDI'S OWN STORY OF HOW *NABUCCO* WAS COMPOSED

Verdi, a very private man who hated all forms of publicity, did on one occasion dictate an autobiographical account of his early years to Giulio Ricordi (see p. XXX below) with a view to its inclusion in a forthcoming biography (*Anecdotal Life of Giuseppe Verdi* by A. Pougin, translated into Italian from the French and expanded by "Folchetto"). The year was 1879, Verdi was sixty-six, and the book appeared two years later. The events covered had taken place in the years 1834–42, so that between them and the interview with Ricordi lay all the composer's mature operas except the last two, *Otello* (1887) and *Falstaff* (1893). By this time, of course, Verdi was an international celebrity, and his brief narrative soon gained wide circulation, becoming part of his official biography. Yet in more recent years, faith in its accuracy has been shaken by one surprising misstatement of fact. After his successful debut with *Oberto, Conte di San Bonifacio* at La Scala in 1839, Verdi had been engaged by Bartolomeo Merelli, the powerful impresario of that theater, to write three new operas, beginning with *Un giorno di regno*, an *opera buffa*. "But now," recalls Verdi, "terrible misfortunes crowded upon me. At the beginning of April my little boy falls ill, the doctors cannot understand what is the matter, and the poor little creature goes off quickly in his mother's arms. Moreover, a few days after the little girl is taken ill too, and she too dies, and in June my young wife is taken from me by a most violent inflammation of the brain, so that on the 19th June I saw the third coffin carried out of my house. In a very little over two months, three persons so very dear to me had disappeared for ever. I was alone, alone!" Now it is entirely true that Verdi suffered this terrible tragedy, but the sequence of events was different: his daughter Virginia was the first to die, on 12 August 1838; his son Icilio Romano died the next year, on 22 October 1839, a few weeks before the première of *Oberto*; and his wife Margherita died of encephalitis on 18 June 1840. It is impossible to account for Verdi's mistaken version of these facts: he read the proofs of the new book, and besides he had given the same account to another writer ten years earlier. Does his mysterious lapse invalidate the rest of the story? Probably not. As in another reminiscence told many years after the event (see *"Fidelio* in 1806," pp. 156–62 above), one should expect a certain amount of embellishment and dramatization; but the outlines of truth are surely there, and they are worth glimpsing, in this scantly documented period of Verdi's life.

Un giorno di regno failed to please: certainly the music was partly to blame, but partly, too, the performance. With mind tormented by my domestic misfortunes, embittered by the failure of my work, I was convinced that I could find no consolation in my art and decided never to compose again. I even wrote to the engineer Pasetti, asking him to obtain from Merelli my release from the contract.

Merelli sent for me and treated me like a capricious schoolboy—he would not allow me to be discouraged by the unhappy failure of my opera, etc., etc. But I stood my ground, so that handing me back the contract Merelli said: "Listen, Verdi! I can't force you to write. My faith in you is undiminished: who knows whether, one of these days, you won't decide to take up your pen again? In that case, as long as you give me two months' notice before the beginning of the season, I promise that your opera shall be performed." I thanked him, but these words did not suffice to alter my decision and I went away.

I took rooms at Milan in the Corsia de' Servi. I had lost heart and given up thinking about music, when one winter evening on leaving the Galleria De Cristoforis I encountered Merelli, who was on his way to the theater. It was snowing heavily and, taking me by the arm, he invited me to accompany him to his office at La Scala. On the way we talked and he told me he was in difficulties over the new opera he had to present: he had entrusted it to [Otto] Nicolai [1810–49] but the latter was not satisfied with the libretto.

"Imagine!" said Merelli. "A libretto by [Temistocle] Solera! Stupendous! Magnificent! Extraordinary! Effective, grandiose dramatic situations and beautiful verses! But that pig-headed composer won't hear of it and says it's a hopeless libretto. I'm at my wits' end to know where to find another one quickly."

"I'll help you out myself," I replied. "Didn't you have prepared for me *Il proscritto*? I haven't written a note of the music: I put it at your disposal."

"Oh! that's fine—a real stroke of luck!"

Talking like this, we had reached the theater. Merelli called Bassi, the poet, stage manager, call-boy, librarian, etc., etc., and told him to look at once in the

THE SCALA THEATER IN 1852. *Home to many Verdi premières, the famous opera house is shown here as it appeared ten years after the first performance of* Nabucco, *in a painting by Angelo Inganni.* Milan, Museo Teatrale alla Scala.

archives for a copy of *Il proscritto*. The copy was there. At the same time Merelli picked up another manuscript and, showing it to me, exclaimed:

"Look! Here is Solera's libretto. Such a beautiful subject—and he turned it down! Take it—read it through!"

"What the deuce should I do with it? No, no, I have no wish to read librettos."

"Go on with you! It won't do you any harm. Read it and then bring it back to me again." And he gave me the manuscript. It was on large sheets in big letters, as was then customary. I rolled it up, said goodbye to Merelli, and went home.

On the way I felt a kind of indefinable malaise, a very deep sadness, a distress that filled my heart. I got home and with an almost violent gesture threw the manuscript on the table, standing upright in front of it. The book had opened in falling on the table; without knowing how, I gazed at the page that lay before me, and read this line:

> Va, pensiero sull'ali dorate.
> [Fly, thought, on golden wings.]

I ran through the verses that followed and was much moved, all the more because they were almost a paraphrase from the Bible, the reading of which had always delighted me.

I read one passage, then another. Then, resolute in my determination to write no more, I forced myself to close the libretto and went to bed. But it was no use—I couldn't get *Nabucco* out of my head. Unable to sleep, I got up and read the libretto, not once, but two or three times, so that by the morning I knew Solera's libretto almost by heart.

Still I was not prepared to relax my determination and that day I returned to the theater and handed the manuscript back to Merelli.

"Isn't it beautiful?" he said to me.

"Very beautiful!"

"Well then—set it to music!"

"I wouldn't dream of it. I won't hear of it."

"Set it to music! Set it to music!"

And so saying he took the libretto, thrust it into my overcoat pocket, took me by the shoulders and not only pushed me out of the room but locked the door in my face.

What was I to do?

I returned home with *Nabucco* in my pocket. One day one verse, another day another, here a note and there a phrase, little by little the opera was composed.

It was the autumn of 1841, and recalling Merelli's promise, I went to see him and announced that *Nabucco* was written and could therefore be performed in the next Carnival season.

Merelli declared himself ready to keep his word, but at the same time pointed out that it would be impossible to give the opera in the coming season, because the repertory was already settled and because three new operas by renowned composers were due for performance. To give a fourth opera by a composer who was almost a beginner was dangerous for everybody concerned, and above all dangerous for me. It would thus be better to wait for the spring season, for which he had no prior engagements. He assured me that good artists would be engaged. But I refused: either in the Carnival season or not at all. And I had good reasons for that, knowing it would be impossible to find two other artists so well suited to my opera as la Strepponi and Ronconi, whom I knew to be engaged and on whom I was much relying.

Morelli, although disposed to give me my way, was, as impresario, not altogether in the wrong—to give four new operas in a single season was very risky! But I had good artistic grounds for opposing him. In short, after assertions and denials, obstacles and half-promises, the bills of La Scala were posted—and *Nabucco* was not announced!

I was young and hot-blooded. I wrote a rude letter to Merelli, giving vent to all my resentment. I confess that as soon as I had sent it I felt a kind of remorse, and I feared that as a result I had ruined everything.

Merelli sent for me, and on seeing me angrily exclaimed: "Is this the way to write to a friend? But still, you're quite right. We'll give this *Nabucco*. You must remember, however, that I shall have heavy expenses on account of the other new operas. I shall not be able to have special scenery and costumes made for *Nabucco*, but shall have to patch up as best I can whatever we find best adapted for the purpose in the storerooms."

I agreed to everything because I was anxious for the opera to be given. New bills were issued, on which I finally read: NABUCCO!...

Towards the end of February the rehearsals began, and twelve days after the first rehearsal with pianoforte the first public performance took place, on 9th March, with Signore Strepponi and Bellinzaghi and Signori Ronconi, Miraglia, and Derivis in the cast.

Frank Walker, *The Man Verdi*, with a new introduction by Philip Gossett (Chicago: University of Chicago Press, 1982), 34–36.

31

VERDI'S OPERATIC STYLE ANALYZED BY A CONTEMPORARY

Abramo Basevi (1818–85) was the author of the first full-length study of Verdi's operas, published in Florence in 1859. After obtaining a degree in medicine, Basevi had turned to music and philosophy, composing some operas, but ultimately concentrating on music criticism, theory, and the organization of concert life in Florence. He founded two journals and wrote other books but is chiefly remembered for the work on Verdi, in which he displays considerable sophistication, a respectable historical background (for his time and place), and deep-rooted prejudices of all kinds. He is responsible for the first "periodization" of Verdi's operas, which, by 1859, included everything up to *Simon Boccanegra* and *Aroldo*. The well-known model for dividing a composer's works into periods, styles, or manners was Wilhelm von Lenz's *Beethoven et ses trois styles* (*Beethoven and his Three Styles*, St. Petersburg, 1852), which by the time Basevi wrote his book was in its third edition and continued to be influential down to our own day. Basevi divided Verdi's output into no less than four "manners," and one wonders how many more he would have discovered in the six great operas that were yet to come. After covering Verdi's first three successful operas, *Nabucco* (1842), *I Lombardi alla prima crociata* (1843), and *Ernani* (1844), Basevi presents an interesting assessment of Verdi's stature as an isolated genius in an otherwise barren landscape:

If any doubts remained in the minds of Italians regarding which composer was destined to inherit the legacy of Donizetti and Bellini in the world of music, then surely the success of *Ernani* must have dispelled them altogether. After that opera, Verdi was recognized almost unanimously in Italy as the worthy successor of the aforementioned masters. But the composer was still to write other operas before being equally acclaimed throughout Europe.

When we consider that, without Verdi, a new Lamartine might exclaim, and perhaps with more justice, that Italy is now *the land of the dead* where music is concerned, we must not only admire but be grateful to the genius from Busseto, who causes the name of Italy to resound gloriously in the arts throughout the world. The greater the marvel when one considers the swarm of composers who stood in his way on his path to eminence. From 1842 through 1857 there were not less than 641 new operas given in Italy, witness the following table showing the number produced each year:

YEAR	OPERAS	YEAR	OPERAS
1842	42	1850	27
1843	53	1851	60
1844	35	1852	60
1845	32	1853	52
1846	36	1854	44
1847	29	1855	53
1848[1]	14	1856	40
1849[2]	–	1857	64[3]

---

[1]The political events [i.e., the ill-fated war of independence in 1848–49] having transformed nearly all musical and theatrical journals, I was unable to record the new operas produced after mid-July.

[2]For the reason given in the preceding note, I leave blank the number of operas. Verdi in this year produced *Luisa Miller*.

[3]In 1858 through September there were already produced 31 new operas.

The greater part of these operas are first or second attempts by young composers, whence one may conjecture the extraordinary number of composers involved. Notwithstanding this abundance of operas and composers, Italy has never been so poor, because never before did she find herself with but one composer. The expression *but one* is not meant to imply that there are no other deserving composers; but only one, today, is able to satisfy the musical tastes of the public, not just in Italy, but throughout the world. The great Rossini, though a colossus, had nonetheless competitors who shared with him the popular favor. Verdi, instead, has up to now had no rival capable of overshadowing him. And yet, other composers have written beautiful operas, if not as fortunate. [Saverio] Mercadante [1795–1870] and [Giovanni] Pacini [1796–1867], who never laid down their pens, wrote operas that certainly are not without many virtues. Among new composers, a great many can vaunt the most brilliant successes, that is, applause and calls to the stage; but time has been the prompt, inexorable enemy of their work. [Errico] Petrella [1813–77], however, has for several years been battling with varied success on the stages of our Peninsula; and that is no small achievement.

> Basevi notes the difference in the spirit of the Italians after the failed war of independence of 1848–49. Passions have cooled. And, in line with his belief that Verdi was primarily concerned with communicating with his public, he notes the first change of "manner" in the composer:

[After 1848] there was a change in Verdi's genius, rendering him more attuned to the new period. The exaggeration that had often been condemned in Verdi's music was much toned down. As if by instinct, Verdi recognized that recent events had, if not mitigated the passions, at least held them in check; minds were not so strongly moved, and therefore there was less occasion for those violent modes that were so frequently used before. And this new universal feeling being now implanted in Verdi, the result was that his new music assumed a different aspect, so well defined and distinct as to deserve the character of a *second manner*.

It may be useful to make a brief comparison of the first and second manners, so the reader may receive some lights by which better to study the music of Verdi.

In the *first manner* the *grandiose* attitude is predominant, attesting to the influence of the last operas of Rossini. But next to the *grandiose* stands the *impassioned*, which dominates this music no less than the other. This *impassioned* is guilty of exaggeration when considered in itself, but viewed in relation to the grandiose music that surrounds it, it becomes evident that the exaggeration is needed in order to maintain a certain balance, a counterweight to the *grandiose*. It is important to note that the *grandiose* intrinsically destroys, so to speak, all individuality or personality, transforming them into the universal. So that, though the *grandiose* melody is sung by a single character, it penetrates the mind

of the spectator as if expressed by a people, a caste, a social order; for which reason the passion, to remain consonant with the *grandiose*, as if it were manifested
by not one but many persons, is greatly exaggerated. Also in Rossini's *William
Tell*, where there are some passages of impassioned music, as in the trio and in
William's aria in the third act, the passion is expressed with some exaggeration.
Without this exaggeration, the grandiose would somehow overpower the passion. Verdi shows us this exaggeration most of all in those phrases which I have
described as *impetuous* [*di slancio*]. Apart from this type of exaggeration, one
finds others in effects of sonority that were already the vogue at Verdi's first
appearance. Not long before, the trumpet had enriched itself by the addition of
keys, then valves, enabling it to sound all the notes with equal ease; soon it was
all but lording it over the orchestra. And composers vied with each other in court-
ing the instrument, writing solos for it, featuring it at several points in their operas, even making it double the voice and reinforce it. All the brass instruments,
through their family connection with the trumpet, grew in importance within
the orchestra, so much so that the poor violin, the legitimate king, came close
to being banished. And Verdi was not backward in his use of the ennobled trumpet. In this first manner, the melodies are often *largo* or *grave*, and suitable for
singing by several voices, as if to show they belong to more than one character.

In the *second manner* the *grandiose* diminishes or ceases altogether, and
each character represents only himself. Passion, being individual, has no need of
exaggeration; and the vocal line, though impassioned, proceeds more calmly. The
melodies are less *largo* and lighter, the rhythms more mobile and more uncov-
ered, the themes [*motivi*] generally more catchy and popular [*orecchiabili e vol-
gari*]. A greater need to tickle the ears has revived, in this second manner, the
parlanti [passages of syllabic recitation against an orchestral design], which Verdi
seemed to have dismissed, so little had he made use of them in his first manner. Effects of sonority are much less often used; and if so, then appropriately.

This difference between the two manners is not to be thought of as absolute,
as if the characteristics of one were never to be found in the other. Certainly
not; in the operas of the first manner one may see the *germs* of the second, just
as in the latter one finds the *remnants* of the first; other operas may also be considered as *transitional*. All Verdi's works besides display points in common,
which constitute the Verdian genre and are the expression of his talent.

With his second manner Verdi moved closer to Donizetti; the difference between them consists chiefly in this, that the former, being more impassioned,
more often attempts to agitate and stir the listener; while the latter almost always wants to delight.

Luisa Miller [1849] is the first opera that deserves to be placed at the head
of Verdi's works in the new manner.

By no means a hero worshiper, Basevi voiced strong objections to some of
Verdi's choices of subject matter. Like other critics of the day, he lambasted

Macbeth (1847) for its excursions into the supernatural. *Rigoletto* (1851) shocked him on moral grounds, but that was as nothing next to his horror at *La traviata* (1853), which, however, he correctly noted as introducing a new "manner."

Verdi was unable to resist the temptation of setting to music, and so making more attractive and acceptable, a filthy and immoral subject, universally loved because today the vice it represents is universal. . . .

    La traviata is a work that, because of the characters, the domestic affections, and the lack of spectacle, approaches comedy. Verdi embarked on a *third manner*, which in several respects comes close to the genre of French comic opera. Which musical genre, though it has not been attempted onstage in Italy, is not unknown in private halls. . . . Verdi, with his *Traviata*, transposed chamber music to the stage, and to good effect; for it suits the chosen subject very well. In this work there is greater simplicity than in others by the same author, especially in the orchestra, where the strings almost always dominate; *parlanti* occupy much of the score; there are in it several of those arias that repeat in the manner of *couplets* [i.e., in strophic form]; and finally, the principal melodies unfold for the most part in small binary and ternary [phrases], nor have they all the development required by the Italian taste. In addition, Verdi has infused much passion into this music, without, however, that exaggeration which sometimes is still found in his *second manner*; which is why Verdi, here more than in any other opera, has succeeded in expressing love with so little affectation. But the love represented by Verdi in this opera is voluptuous, sensual, wholly devoid of that angelic purity that is found in the music of Bellini. Which latter always preserves that character of innocence and that candor which fill one's soul with sweetness, even when applied to a less than honest person. The difference in the love which Bellini and Verdi depicted in their music is testimony to the different sensibilities at the respective times of the two composers. . . . If in *Norma* Bellini portrayed a guilty woman, he presents her to us so blinded by passion that she cannot see the enormity of her sin. And in any case, Norma's guilt offends us less, since the remoteness of the time and difference of customs make it harder for our conscience to identify with hers. Which is not the case with *La traviata*, where we find characters not only close to us in time and customs, but also of the same [social] condition. In this opera everything breathes lasciviousness and voluptuousness.

Simon Boccanegra was a failure in its 1856 version (it has endured in its 1881 revision). To Basevi here was yet another turning point in Verdi's career, and one that boded ill: for *Simon Boccanegra* seemed to betray a hidden sympathy with Wagner's "system." Needless to say, Basevi's conception of that "system," typical of much early criticism on Wagner, is based on misinformation and ignorance.

Great was the public's expectation for this new music by Verdi. And there circulated the most contrary opinions regarding the *manner* the celebrated master would pursue. Some imagined that, after the great success of *La traviata,* he would proceed in the same way; others thought he might follow the lines of *Giovanna de Guzman* [*Les Vêpres siciliennes*].

The great moment arrived. On the evening of 12 March 1856 the Teatro La Fenice in Venice resounded with the melodies of *Simon Boccanegra.* The opera was not a success. Attempted again in other theaters, it found a severe reception everywhere but in Naples. The fact is that in this opera Verdi, by searching for new forms to suit the dramatic expression, by attaching a greater importance to the recitative, and by paying less attention to melody, *attempted* a *fourth manner,* moving closer to German music. I would venture to say, at least judging from the Prologue, that he wished to follow—at a distance, it is true—in the footsteps of the famous Wagner, the subverter of the music of the present. It is well known that Wagner would like as far as possible to make the language of music specific, almost the shadow of poetry.

Wagner's system found, and still finds, many opponents in Germany, though it is a country that seems less averse to abstruse harmonies than Italy, and less fond of simple melodies. Wagner's *Tannhäuser* gets performed in Germany, but it does not attract crowds, except on account of the novelty of the attempt; nor can it prevent yawns except when there is a melody, a *cantabile,* or a vocal ensemble; things which, though contrary to the system, are yet to be found in the work, though in meager doses. If, then, Germany does not want that reform, all the more reason why Italy should abhor it. I will grant as a possibility that the Wagnerian reform represents *the music of the future;* but I absolutely deny that it is *the music of the present.* And if there is an art that, more than any other, should be eager to endear itself immediately, that art beyond a doubt is music, especially opera.

In the music of *Simon Boccanegra* I certainly did not find an abundance of *bel canto;* what little we do come across resembles a very old acquaintance, who, in the listener's present need, is often welcome enough. Nevertheless, the melody in this opera has the general merit of not being exaggeratedly impetuous in the Verdian way; and so it comes close to the *third manner,* which, in this particular, marks a notable progress. The instrumentation does not so much reveal industriousness as overrefinement in the harmonies, in the use of pedals, and in certain ornaments, so that the vocal part is often given a lesser role. The recitatives, so abundant in this opera, do not stand out; the themes of the *parlanti* are often unrelated to the words.

Finally, Basevi's explanation of that mysterious concept, *tinta* (coloring), which crops up so often in Verdi's own correspondence with reference to his operas. In a letter of 22 July 1848, for instance, Verdi wrote to his librettist Piave:

"Mind you, be careful to avoid monotony. In subjects that are naturally sad, if we aren't very careful we end up making it a funeral, as with *I Foscari*, for example, which has a *tinta*, a color that is too uniform from beginning to end." *I due Foscari* (1844) seems to have been notable in this regard, for Basevi mentions it too in his discussion.

Before examining [Verdi's *I masnadieri* (1847)], I should like to clear up a doubt that might occur to some with regard to my method. It might in fact be objected that, when I examine an opera analytically, many, indeed the most essential virtues and defects of the work *as a whole* may pass unobserved. But I must point out that the synthetical approach cannot be used in musical criticism, in view of the undeveloped state of opera so far. The latter can hardly be compared to a statue or a picture, where the first thing to be considered is the *whole*. In music we should in vain look for a specific idea round which to group all the separate pieces so they will make up an *entity*. Music does, however, find a support in the general conception of the drama, a center toward which the various pieces of an opera converge more or less, depending on the composer's talent [*ingegno*]; and so we obtain what is known as the general *coloring* [*colorito*] or *tinta*. However, to obtain this *coloring* is not the composer's principal end, but rather the means by which the opera's various pieces can conveniently be brought together with respect to the drama. This *coloring* is of several kinds, according to whether it is more or less well defined. In a wholly sacred subject, the *coloring* of the corresponding music, no matter how apt, will always be too vague to be uniquely suited to one oratorio rather than to another; the same thing may be said of comic subjects, etc. etc. However, the genius of composers has been able to discover more distinct colors, better suited to specific librettos. To limit our discussion to the operas of Verdi, I shall note that while in *Nabucco* the *coloring* is sacred and in no way different from that of Rossini's *Mosè*, in *I Lombardi* you will find a more definite *coloring*, admirably suited, thanks to a certain freshness, to the sacred Christian genre. This virtue alone is sufficient to place Verdi by the side of the greatest composers. *I due Foscari*, too, has a special *tinta*, but not as alive as that in *I Lombardi*, although more so than in other operas by the same master; of which there are some that have none at all. There is no doubt that the general *colorito* of an opera reveals better than anything else a composer's talent, since it shows his powers of synthesis. Once the composer has imagined how to impart the necessary *colorito* to the music through the disposition of the notes, the use of harmonies, the choice of instruments, etc., he will have created a type, a rule, a goal to which he can easily relate the separate pieces, the themes, the accompaniments, etc. The result is a *whole* that astonishes and irresistibly attracts the listener, who, filled with admiration, will be obliged to recognize the work of a great talent.

In *I masnadieri* we find not a trace of this general *tinta;* instead we seem to observe different pieces stitched together, instead of a continuous canvas containing different designs.

Abramo Basevi, *Studio sulle opere di Giuseppe Verdi* (Florence: Tofani, 1859), 57–59, 156–59, 230–32, 264–66, 114–16. Trans. P.W.

32

WAGNER ON THE EVOLUTION OF HIS STYLE

Among Wagner's writings in mid-career (see p. 201 below), *A Communication to My Friends* (1851) stands out as retrospective, a summing up, more than a program for the future. It served in fact as a preface to the publication in book form of the texts of the last of his early operas, *Der fliegende Holländer* (1843), *Tannhäuser* (1845), and *Lohengrin* (1848). Wagner himself furnished the reason for this *Communication*: he wished to explain the apparent contradiction between the style of his early works and the dramatic theories he had been propounding lately. In the following excerpt he looks back at his very first operas, *Die Feen* (1834, after a fable by Carlo Gozzi), *Das Liebesverbot* (1836, after Shakespeare's *Measure for Measure*), and at *Rienzi* (1840, after the novel by Bulwer-Lytton), the work that actually launched his career. He was from the first his own librettist, and in discussing the operas that followed (the three whose text he was now publishing in book form), he goes into some depth as he analyzes his dual role as both poet and composer of his operas. It is in the reciprocal influence of those two functions that he finds the driving force behind his unique stylistic development, one that took him from his frankly imitative youthful operas to the increasingly unconventional works of the 1840s, culminating in *Lohengrin*. And he was as yet only on the threshold of his innovations: the vast, unexplored land of his mature music dramas still lay ahead.

With *Rienzi* I still only intended to write an "opera"; I sought materials for the purpose, and, concerned only with "opera," I derived these from finished works, their form already shaped according to artistic criteria: I arranged a dramatic fable by Gozzi, a play by Shakespeare, finally a novel by Bulwer aiming solely at opera. With *Rienzi* I arranged the material more freely, according to the impression it made on me: that is, the way I perceived it through my "opera glasses"—one could hardly do otherwise in the case of a historical novel. With *Der fliegende Holländer*, whose origins in special autobiographical circumstances I have already described more particularly, I entered upon a new path, since I myself became the artificer of the material, which lay before me only in the simple, raw outlines of a folk saga. From now on, my relation to all my dramatic works was to be in the first place that of *poet*, and only in the complete execution of the poem did I again become a musician. However, I was a poet conscious beforehand of his *musical* expressive potential in the execution of his poems; I had exercised this [musical] potential to such an extent that I was totally in command of my ability to use it in realizing a poetic intention; and I could not only rely on the help of that ability when drafting my poems, but, secure in that knowledge, I could even shape them more *freely* in accordance with poetic necessity than if I had formed them expressly to be set to music. Before that, I had acquired the ability to express myself musically the way one learns a language. He who has not yet thoroughly mastered a foreign, unfamiliar language must, whenever he speaks it, take into account the peculiarities of that language; to make himself understood, he must constantly be mindful of how he expresses himself and calculate *what* he wants to say entirely with that in mind. And so in everything he utters he is quite engrossed in observing the formal rules of the language and hence cannot quite express spontaneously what he really feels, what his sentiments are, what his views; rather, he must model the way he communicates his feelings and opinions according to expressions he does not command as readily as those of his mother tongue, in which, totally unconcerned with the means of expression, he finds the right expression quite spontaneously. But I had now thoroughly mastered the language of music; I had command of it now as a true mother tongue; and so, what I wished to communicate no longer needed to be accompanied by a concern for the way it was expressed: expression was quite at my beck and call for the impulsive communication of a particular view or feeling. . . . But that which is expressed by the language of music consists solely of *feelings* and *impressions*: it expresses to the fullest the emotional content of the elemental human language, quite independently of our word-language, which has become a purely reasoning system of communication. And so, what remains inexpressible by the absolute musical language is the precise definition of the object of the feeling and impression that caused their own distinct definition: the necessary broadening and expansion of the musical language's expression consists therefore in acquiring the ability to define also that which is individual and particular with recognizable clarity, and this it acquires

only by its union with the word-language. But this union can only be successful when the musical language is linked intimately to those elements of the word-
language that are congenial and related to it in the word-language; the linking
must occur precisely at the point where in the word-language itself an indomitable urge for true, sensuous expression makes itself felt. This is determined
only by the *content* of that which is to be expressed, depending on how far it
has grown from a reasoned into a felt content. A content that can only be grasped
by reason can only be communicated by the word-language; but the more it expands into an emotional moment, the more clearly does it require an expression
that can only be accorded to it in full measure by the language of tones. From
this the content of that which the poet of words and tones must utter becomes
quite manifest: it is *the purely human, released of all convention.* . . .

I have indicated here what influence my command of the spirit of music had
on the choice of my poetic material and on the poetic form it assumed; it only
remains for me to explain what counter-influence my poetic process, thus determined, had on my musical expression and its form.—This reciprocal influence manifested itself mainly in *two* ways: in the *dramatic-musical form*
generally, and in the *melody* in particular.

If, from the moment I have indicated as a turning point in my artistic orientation, it was the *material* once and for all that determined me, that is, the
material seen through music's eye, then of necessity I was obliged, in shaping
it, to progress gradually to the total abolishment of the *operatic form* I had inherited. This operatic form had in itself never been a precise one applicable to
the whole drama, but rather only an arbitrary conglomeration of single, small
song forms that in their haphazard sequence of arias, duets, trios, etc., with choruses and so-called ensemble pieces, actually made up the essence of the operatic form. In the poetic construction of my materials such a filling out of
pre-existing forms could not possibly matter to me any more, but only the representation of the dramatic subject in a manner true to the feelings with which
it was imbued. In the whole course of the drama I saw no possible subdivisions
or sections other than the acts, in which the place, the time, or the scenery, in
which the characters in the drama change. In my scenic construction all petty
details, unavoidable for the modern playwright retelling complicated historical
events, became quite unnecessary thanks to the plastic unity of the mythological material, and the dramatic energy could be concentrated in a few, always important and decisive moments of the development. . . . As I had an ever surer
feeling for this, it no longer even occurred to me to interrupt and inhibit the
natural growth of the musical form arising necessarily from the very nature of
the scene with arbitrary external borrowings, with the violent introduction of
conventional operatic song forms. And so I absolutely did not set about de-
stroying the aria, duet, and other operatic forms out of principle or, shall we say,
as an intentional reviser of forms; but rather, the omission of those forms resulted quite spontaneously from the nature of the material, whose true repre-

sentation through the expression necessary to it was my sole concern. The unconscious knowledge of those traditional forms so influenced me still in my
Fliegender Holländer that an attentive observer will recognize how it affected
my arrangement of the scenes; only gradually, with *Tannhäuser,* then more decisively with *Lohengrin,* in other words with my growing awareness of the nature of my material and its necessary means of representation, did I free myself
wholly from that formal influence and make the form of the representation ever
more clearly dependent on the requirements and characteristics of the material
and the situation. . . .

I remember that, before I proceeded to the actual writing out of *Der fliegende
Holländer,* I drafted Senta's ballad in the second act and worked it out in both
verse and melody; in this piece I unconsciously planted the seeds for all the music in the opera: it was the poetic image of the whole drama, as it appeared before my mind's eye; and when it was time to give a title to the finished work, I
was more than tempted to call it a "dramatic ballad." During the final working
out of the composition, the thematic image expanded spontaneously as a complete texture over the entire drama; all I needed to do, without further conscious
effort, was to let the diverse thematic seeds contained in the ballad develop further and completely each in its own way, and all the main moods of this poem
appeared before me in well-defined thematic form. . . . I proceeded in a like fashion with *Tannhäuser,* and finally with *Lohengrin;* except that here I did not have
before me a previously completed musical piece like that ballad but created a picture first, in which all the thematic threads came together from the structure of
the scenes, from their organic growth; and I let that picture appear in changing
guise wherever it was necessary to the understanding of the main situation. Besides which my procedure, especially in *Lohengrin,* acquired a clearer artistic
form through the ever new transformation of the thematic material according
to the character of the situation, which resulted in a greater variety musically
than was the case, for instance, with *Der fliegende Holländer,* where the recurrence of the theme often had only the character of a pure reminiscence (a thing
that had existed in the work of other composers before me).—

I must now still describe the influence of my general poetic procedure on
the construction of my themes themselves, on *the melody.*

I remember how, in the "absolute-music" period of my youth, I often pondered how I could succeed in discovering truly original melodies that would carry
a special stamp peculiar to me. The closer I came to the period in which I de-
pended on the poetic material for my musical construction, the more this concern over the specialness of melody disappeared, until I finally lost it altogether.
In my earlier operas I was guided simply by the traditional or modern melody,
which I imitated in its essence and, precisely for that reason, attempted to make
special and personal by means of harmonic and rhythmic affectations. But I always had a greater inclination for broad, slowly unfolding melodies than for the
short, interrupted, and contrapuntally built melody of instrumental chamber

music proper: in my *Liebesverbot* I had openly lapsed into imitating the modern Italian *cantilena*. In *Rienzi* I was influenced everywhere (unless the *material* had already inspired me otherwise) by the Italian-French melody, as it had
affected me especially in the operas of Spontini. The operatic melody that has
impressed itself on the modern ear, however, lost its influence over me increasingly and finally completely as I busied myself with *Der fliegende Holländer*. If
my shedding of this external influence was due to the nature of the whole procedure which I embarked on with this work, I nevertheless did gain compensat-
ing nurture for my melody from the folk song, to which I was brought closer.
Already in that ballad I was influenced by the unconscious knowledge of the
characteristics of national folk melody; even more decisively, however, in the
spinning song and especially in the sailors' song. . . . But I was no longer concerned with *opera melodies*, only with the most appropriate expression for my
dramatic subject; in *Der fliegende Holländer*, therefore, I did touch upon folk
melody, but only where the material brought me in touch with the national folk
element. Wherever I needed to express the feelings of dramatic characters, as
they themselves expressed them in emotional language, I had to keep my distance from folk melody, or better, I could not fall back on that mode of expression; for here the speech itself had to be rendered according to its deepest
emotional import, so that *not the melodic expression in itself, but the expressed
feeling* would elicit the sympathy of the listener. And so the melody had to arise
quite spontaneously from the speech; it could not draw attention to itself as pure
melody, but only insofar as it was the most meaningful expression of a feeling
that had been clearly indicated in the speech. With this necessary conception of
the melodic element I now parted completely from the ordinary procedure of
opera composers, in that I no longer intentionally sought out the accustomed
melody, in a certain sense not even melody altogether, but instead only *allowed
it to arise* from the emotionally delivered speech. But that this occurred during
the very gradual weakening of the influence of accustomed operatic melody will
be very evident from a consideration of my music to *Der fliegende Holländer*:
in it I was still guided by the accustomed melody to such an extent that here
and there I still quite openly retained the cadenza; and let this demonstrate, to
anyone who admits that with *Der fliegende Holländer* I entered upon a new direction with regard to melody, with how little premeditation I took this new
road.—In the further development of my melody, as I pursued it just as spontaneously in *Tannhäuser* and *Lohengrin*, I did free myself more and more definitely from that influence, to the extent to which the feeling expressed by the
verse prompted me to lend it enhanced musical expression; and yet even here,
and especially in *Tannhäuser*, the prescribed form of the melody, that is, the
necessarily felt intention to communicate the speech *as melody*, is still clearly
recognizable. As I *now* realize, I was forced into that intention by the *imperfec-
tion of modern verse*, in which I was still unable to find a natural source and
condition for the *sensual* communication of the musical expression as melody.

... The rhythm of modern verse is only a *built-in* phenomenon, and this must have been felt most keenly by the composer who wished to gather the material for his melody only from that verse. Confronted with that verse, I was obliged either to renounce melodic rhythm or, when I felt a need for it from the purely musical point of view, to borrow the rhythmic component of the melody, after arbitrarily composing the melody, from "absolute" operatic melody and then graft it artificially onto the verse. . . . I had given up traditional melody completely; without nurture or justification for its rhythmic component in the verse, I now gave it, instead of a *false* rhythmic garb, a harmonic characteristic, which, having a decisive effect on the sense of hearing, made it the most appropriate expression of the feeling presented by the verse. I further enhanced the individuality of this expression with an ever more descriptive accompaniment of the *orchestra*, whose role it was to make palpable the harmonic motivation of the melody; and this procedure, basically directed to *dramatic melody* alone, I have most decisively observed in *Lohengrin*, where I thus pursued the course I had embarked on in *Der fliegende Holländer* to its necessary conclusion. . . .

Richard Wagner, *Drei Operndichtungen nebst einer Mittheilung an seine Freunde* (Leipzig: Breitkopf und Härtel, 1852), 143–62. Trans. P.W.

33

WAGNER'S THEORY OF DRAMA

It was in the period following his participation in the Dresden uprising (May 1849) and subsequent flight to Switzerland that Wagner wrote his first books of operatic theory: *Art and Revolution* (1849), *The Art Work of the Future* (1850), and *Opera and Drama* (1852). His composing was at a standstill; his latest opera, *Lohengrin*, completed in 1848, was performed in his absence in 1850. But already in Dresden he had begun work on what was to become the major undertaking of his life, the vast *Ring of the Nibelung* cycle; so far he had only written the text of the last of the four dramas, *Götterdämmerung* (initially *Siegfrieds Tod*, later much revised), and twenty-six years were to pass before he would complete the whole cycle. But this, and the other three great works that lay ahead—*Tristan und Isolde* (1859), *Die Meistersinger* (1867), *Parsifal* (1882)—were no longer to be cast in the mold of traditional opera.

Wagner was now at the crossroads, and it was precisely during this pause in his creativity, between the completion of the first draft of the *Götterdämmerung* text and the resumption of work on the remaining texts of the *Ring* in the early 1850s, that he developed the premises on which he was to base his later dramatic works. His operas until then had been controversial but in the end successful. With his theoretical writings, and with the dramatic works that followed, Wagner broke new ground, provoking a storm of critical reaction that would accompany him for the rest of his days, spilling over well beyond the operatic world into virtually all fields of intellectual endeavor, both in Germany and abroad. Provocative his writings were (and still are today, though not always for the same reasons), especially the writings of this period, when he was still smarting from the frustrations of his impulsive, ill-fated revolutionary adventure and identifying his intended reforms of opera with the social upheaval he felt they required for their realization. Opera was to be done away with and so was the spoken drama. All the arts indeed were to renounce their independence in favor of an ideal collective, or comprehensive, or common work of art, the art work of the future. Wagner's meticulous requirements for the theater building that would house this work of art remained in his thoughts through the years and came finally to fruition with the crowning achievement of his career, the establishment of his own festival theater at Bayreuth. All Wagner's arguments hinge on his exalted conception of art as the salvation of humanity, the only goal worth striving for. And indeed it has been rightly said that nothing else mattered to him. "Truth" and "nature" are repeatedly invoked against the falseness of social (hence artistic) convention. But "art," "artist," "artistic" are the words that recur with incantatory frequency. The prose is turgid, the thought at times impenetrable, but there is no mistaking the passion of this operatic reformer whose ultimate mission was to redeem mankind. The selection that follows is the fourth chapter from *The Art Work of the Future*. It is presented uncut: abridgment here would amount to distortion.

IV. BASIC CHARACTERISTICS OF
THE ART WORK OF THE FUTURE

If we examine the relation of modern art—insofar as it is truly *art*—to public life, we will at once realize how totally unsuited it is to influence that public life in terms of its noblest aspiration. The reason is that, as a merely cultural product, it has not really sprung from life and so, as a hothouse plant, cannot possibly take root in the natural soil and natural climate of the present age. Art has become the private property of an artist class; the pleasure it provides is reserved to those who *understand* it, and understanding it requires a special study remote from real life, the study of *art scholarship*. This study, and the understanding accruing from it, everybody nowadays thinks he has acquired when he has got the money with which to pay for the proffered artistic pleasures: but whether the majority of today's art lovers are able to understand the artist at his best is a question the artist, if asked, can only answer with a deep sigh. But should he consider the vastly greater mass of those whom our unfavorable social conditions exclude in every way from an understanding or simply the enjoyment of modern art, then today's artist would have to realize that all his artistic striving is basically a selfish, complacent striving wholly for its own sake, that his art is, in terms of public life, nothing but a luxury, a redundant, self-gratifying pastime. The gap, observed daily and bitterly lamented, between the so-called educated and uneducated is so tremendous, a mediation between them so unthinkable, a reconciliation so impossible, that, with a little honesty, modern art, based as it is on that education, should in deepest shame admit it owes its existence to a life element that in turn owes *its* existence to the deep ignorance of the real mass of humanity. The only thing modern art, in its present circumstances, should accomplish, and attempts to in honest hearts, namely *the diffusion of culture*, it cannot, for the simple reason that art, in order to affect life, must blossom from a *natural* culture, that is, one that has grown from below; it can never pour culture down from *above*. In the best of cases our cultured art resembles a man who tries to communicate with people in a foreign tongue they do not understand: everything he says, and especially his cleverest remarks, can only lead to the most laughable confusion and misunderstandings.—

Let us first describe what modern art should do, *theoretically*, to free itself from the isolation of its incomprehensibility and to stride forward to a general appreciation in public life: how this liberation can only occur through the *practical* agency of public life will then become self-evident.

Fine art, as we have seen, can only attain creative success when it undertakes its works in alliance with *artistic*, not merely *practical*, man.

Artistic man can derive full satisfaction only from the union of all the arts into a *common* work of art: every *singling out* of his artistic capacity makes him *unfree*, not wholly what he can be; whereas in the *common* work of art he is *free* and wholly what he can be.

The *true aspiration* of art is therefore the *all-inclusive*: whoever is animated by a true *artistic impulse* develops it to the fullest not for the glorification of *his particular capacity* but rather for that of *mankind in art altogether*.

The highest common work of art is the *drama*: it is present in its *fullest realization* only when in it are present *all the other arts in their fullest realization*.

FIRST EDITION OF WAGNER'S *ART WORK OF THE FUTURE*.

True drama is thinkable only as the consequence of the *common urge of all the arts* to communicate in the most direct way with a *common public*: every individual art can manifest itself and make itself fully understood to the common public only in conjunction with the drama's other arts, for the intention of each individual art is realized fully only with the reciprocal understanding and collaboration of all the arts.—

Architecture can have no higher aim than to create, for the benefit of a community of human beings artistically portraying themselves, the spatial environment needed for the manifestation of the human work of art. The only edifice answering a true need is that which corresponds to a human purpose: the highest purpose of man is art, the highest artistic purpose, drama. In the usual utilitarian building, the architect need only satisfy the basest purposes of man: in it, beauty is luxury. In the luxurious building he must satisfy an unnecessary and unnatural need: his creation therefore is arbitrary, unproductive, unlovely. However, in erecting the former building, designed to answer a common purpose in all its parts—a *theater*, in other words—the master builder will act solely as an *artist* and according to the dictates of the *work of art*. In a comprehensive theater building, the measure and reason for the smallest particular are given by the requirements of art alone. These requirements are two: *giving* and *receiving*, which interact and interconnect fully. The *stage* must first of all satisfy all spatial conditions for the performance of a collective dramatic action; secondly, however, it must satisfy these conditions with the aim of conveying this dramatic action to the eyes and ears of the audience in perceptively understandable form. In the disposition of the *auditorium*, the necessary guidelines are given by the need for the optical and acoustical perception of the work of art, a need that can be satisfied, apart from functional considerations, only by the beauty of the arrangements; for the expectation of the common audience is the expectation of the *work of art*, and all that meets the eye ought to contribute to its comprehension.[1] Thus, through looking and hearing, the audience is completely transported onto the stage; the actor is an artist solely through his assimilation into the public. Everything that breathes and moves onstage breathes and moves because of the expressive need to communicate, to be seen and heard in that space, which, to an extent, appears to the actor onstage to contain all of humanity; but the audience, that representative of public life, for its part loses its

---

[1] The task of the theater building of the future cannot by any means be considered accomplished by our modern theater buildings: in these, traditional assumptions and rules are in force, having nothing in common with the demands of pure art. Where speculation for the sake of profit on the one hand and a craving for luxury on the other are the decisive factors, the absolute interests of art must necessarily be severely compromised; thus no master builder alive will, for example, succeed in raising into an aesthetic principle the separate levels and compartments of our auditoriums, by which our public gets divided into the most diverse social classes and categories of citizenship. If one thinks of the spaces in the collective theater of the future, it is easy to see that there is undreamt-of scope here for the imagination.

sense of presence in the auditorium; it only lives and breathes in the work of art, which it feels is life itself, and the stage the world.

Such are the wonders that blossom from the architect's construction, to such magic can he give a basis and foundation in reality, provided he makes the intentions of the highest art of mankind his own and brings to life the requirements for its existence from his personal artistic resources. How cold, inert, and dead, on the other hand, his construction seems when he renounces any aim higher than that of luxury, disregards the needs of art, which everywhere in the theater would suggest to him the most appropriate appointments and ideas, and instead acts solely according to the speculating whim of his self-aggrandizing willfulness, piling the masses and ornaments tier upon tier, row after row, lending palpable substance to the pride of an arrogant plutocrat today, to that of a latter-day Jehovah tomorrow!—

But even the most beautiful form, the most sumptuous stone walls are not sufficient of themselves to fully satisfy the spatial requirements for the presentation of the dramatic work of art. The stage, whose task it is to present the picture of life to the spectator, must also, for a full understanding of life, be able to represent the living image of nature, for only there can man as artist act wholly as such. The walls of the stage, which stare coldly and impassively down at the artist and out at the public, must adorn themselves with the fresh colors of nature, with the warm lights of the sky, to be worthy of participating in the human work of art. Plastic *architecture* here finds its limits, its lack of freedom, and, in need of love, throws itself into the arms of the art of painting, which can redeem it in the loveliest way by merging it with nature.

Here *landscape painting* steps in, summoned by a common need which only it can satisfy. What the painter wishes to absorb visually from nature with a fortunate eye, what he wishes, as artistic man, to present to the full community for their artistic enjoyment, he here adds as his rich portion to the unified work of all arts. Through him the stage attains to full artistic truth: his draftsmanship, his color, his warm, animating application of light force nature to serve the highest artistic purpose. What until now the landscape painter, moved by the urge to communicate what he has seen and grasped, was forced to confine within the narrow frame of a picture—what he hung up on the egoist's secluded chamber wall or consigned to the contextless, unrelated, distorting pell-mell of a picture warehouse—*that* he will now produce to fill the wide frame of the tragic stage, making the whole space of the stage testify to his power to recreate nature. What until now he could only indicate with his brush and with a refined blending of colors, only approaching life-like imitation [*Täuschung*], he will here bring completely to life through the artistic use of all the optical, all the artistic lighting means at his disposal. He will not be offended by the apparent crudeness of his artistic tools, the apparent grotesqueness of his procedure in engaging in so-called scene painting, for he will consider that, in relation to the finished work of art, even the finest brush is but the humblest means, and that the artist can only feel *proud* when he is *free*, that is, when his work of art is complete and alive and *he himself* and all his tools are assimilated in it. The completed work of art that confronts him from the *stage* will bring him a far greater satisfaction in this framework and in full public view than that which he created earlier with more refined tools; truly he will not regret giving up the plain canvas once at his disposal in favor of the stage's space used on behalf of this work of art: for though, in the worst of cases, his work will appear the same no matter from within what frame it is viewed, if only it presents its subject in an understandable manner, his art work will at any rate make a livelier impresssion within *this* frame and will elicit a greater, more widespread understanding than the earlier landscape picture.

The organ for all understanding of nature is man: the landscape painter not only needed to communicate this understanding to man, but first indeed needed to make it clear through the representation of man within his painting of nature. Now that he places his work of art within the frame of the tragic stage, he will extend the man to whom he wishes to address himself into common, fully public mankind and have the satisfaction, his understanding thus extended, of gaining it as a sharer in his own joy; at the same time, he will fully bring about this public understanding by subordinating his work to a common, most exalted and universally comprehensible artistic purpose and having this purpose unerringly revealed to the common understanding by real, living man in all the warmth of his being. Most comprehensible of all is the dramatic action, just because it is artistically complete only when all the resources of art are enlisted in support of the drama, and real life is brought into full view in the most faithful and comprehensible manner. Every art communicates *understandably* only insofar as the kernel within it, which can enliven and justify the work of art only when related to or derived from man, matures into the *drama*. An artistic creation will be universally comprehensible, fully grasped and justified, to the extent to which it is assimilated into the drama, suffused by the drama's light.[2]

Now *man as artist* steps on the architect's and painter's stage, just as natural man enters the theater of nature. What the *sculptor* and *historical painter*

---

[2] It cannot be a matter of indifference to the modern landscape painter to realize how few really understand his work nowadays and with what dull-witted, idiotic contentment the philistine world that pays him gawks at his nature pictures; how the so-called "pleasant spot" can satisfy the idle, thoughtless viewing pleasure of these same people who feel *no* need, just as our modern content-less musical products stimulate their hearing pleasure to the point of mindless rapture—a disgusting reward for the *artist's* contribution, yet fully consonant with the intentions of the *industrialist*. There is a sorry relationship between the "lovely spot" and the "pretty music" of our time; what ties them together is assuredly not meaningful thought, but rather that sloppy, sordid thing called *Gemütlichkeit*, which selfishly turns away from the sight of human misery all around in order to hire itself a private little heaven in the blue haze of common nature: everything is heard and seen with pleasure by these cozy people, except *real, undistorted man*, who awaits them, admonishing, at the end of their dreams. *But it is just he whom we now must place in the foreground!*

labored to make in *stone* and on *canvas* they now make of *themselves*, their own figure, the limbs of their body, the traits of their countenance, bringing it to conscious, artistic life. The same purpose that guided the sculptor in grasping and reproducing the human figure now leads the *actor* in the handling and conduct of his own real body. The same eye that permitted the historical painter, with his drawing and colors, to find beauty, charm, and character in the arrangement of costumes and grouping of figures, now arranges the abundance of *real human presence*. Sculptors and painters removed the *buskin* and *mask* of Greek tragedy, on which and behind which real man still moved according to a certain religious convention. The two plastic arts were right to annihilate this last distortion of purely artistic man, and thus they created in stone and on canvas the tragic actor of the future. As they envisioned him in his undistorted truth, so they will now let him reveal himself in reality, his form, nearly as they described it, now an animated portrayal.

Thus the illusion of plastic art beomes the reality of drama; the plastic artist reaches out his hand to the *dancer* and *mime* in order to merge with him, to be dancer and mime himself.—So far as lies in his power he will have to communicate to the eye the inner man, his feeling and will. The full length and breadth of the scenic space is his, for the plastic conveying of his form and movements as an individual or in association with his fellow performers. But where his ability ends, where the full deployment of his will and feeling drives him to reveal the inner man through *speech*, there the word will express his clearly conscious purpose: he becomes a *poet*, and in order to be a poet, a *musician*. As dancer, musician, and poet, however, he is one and the same, nothing other than an *acting, artistic man who to the fullest extent of his capacity projects himself into the highest power of receptivity.*

In him, the direct actor, the three sister arts unite with compounded effect, where the utmost capacity of each attains to its highest development. Working together, each gains the ability to be and to accomplish precisely what each aspires to be and to accomplish, according to its very essence. Because each, at the point where its capacities cease, can be assimilated into the other at the point where *its* capacities begin, each maintains itself pure, free, and independent in its own identity. The *mimetic dancer* loses his limitations as soon as he can sing and speak; the productions of *music* gain universal significance through the agency of the mime and the poetic word, in the same measure, indeed, as music itself is assimilated in the motions of the mime and the word of the poet. But the *poet* in truth only becomes a man through his passage into the flesh and blood of the *actor*; for though he indicates to each of the artistic manifestations the intention that binds them together, guiding them to a common goal, nonetheless that intention is transformed from will to reality only when *the poetic will is dissolved in the reality of the performance*.

Not a *single one* of the richly developed capacities of the individual arts will remain unused in the collective art work of the future; it is there, in fact, that those capacities will attain to their full validity. Thus especially music, which has developed in so singular and many-faceted a way in its instrumental branch, will be able to unfold its richest potentiality in this art work, indeed, will in turn incite the mimetic art of dance to altogether new discoveries, no less than it will lend new breath in undreamt-of abundance to the art of poetry. In its isolation, music has fashioned for itself an organ capable of the most immeasurable expression: the *orchestra*. The tone language of Beethoven, introduced by the orchestra into the drama, constitutes a totally new phenomenon for the dramatic work of art. If architecture and, especially, scenic landscape painting succeed in placing the acting dramatic artist in the environment of physical nature and provide him with an always rich and suggestive background from the endless store of natural manifestations, then in the orchestra, that living body of immensely various harmony, the individual actor is given an inexhaustible wellspring of, as it were, artistic-human natural elements by way of support. The orchestra is, so to say, the ground of endless general feeling, out of which the individual feeling of the single actor can grow to its utmost extent: it replaces somewhat the stark, immovable floor of the actual stage with a soft, gently flowing, yielding, impressionable, ethereal surface, whose immeasurable bottom is the sea of feeling itself. The orchestra resembles the *earth*, which lent Antaeus new, immortal life force as soon as he touched it with his feet. By its very essence quite the opposite of the natural scene surrounding the actor, and therefore quite properly located outside the scenic frame in the sunken foreground, it however constitutes at the same time the perfect complement of the actor's scenic surroundings, for it extends the inexhaustible *physical* element of nature by means of the no less inexhaustible artistic, *human* element of feeling. Together, they envelop the actor as if with the atmospheric ring of the natural and human element; in it he moves securely and to the fullest, like the heavenly bodies; and from it at the same time he is enabled to radiate on all sides his feelings and views extended to the furthest point, reaching, like the rays of a heavenly body, to the remotest distance.

Thus, complementing one another in their alternating round, the united sister arts will show themselves and make their mark by turns: all together, in pairs, or singly, according to the needs of the dramatic action, which alone provides the measure and the intention. Now plastic mimicry will listen intently to the dispassionate brooding of thought; now the impetus of thought's resolve will rush to express itself with the immediacy of gesture; now music, alone, will express the flood of feeling, the shudder of emotion; then again, all three in common embrace will lift the drama's intent to the level of direct, potent deed. For there is one thing all the arts here united must strive for in order to become free in action, and that is indeed the *drama*: therefore they should all be concerned with the realization of the drama's intention. If they are aware of this intention and direct all their will only towards its accomplishment, they will gain the strength to prune away everywhere the selfish shoots of their individual essences from their several stems, so that the tree may grow, not shapelessly in every direction, but to the proud peak of its branches, twigs, and leaves, to its crown.

The nature of man, like that of each of the arts, is in itself overabundant and many-sided: yet the *soul* of each individual is but *one thing*, his essential drive, his most irresistible urge. Once this one thing is recognized by him as his basic essence, he is able, for the indispensable attainment of the one thing, to resist all weaker, subordinate desires, all feeble cravings whose fulfillment might prevent his quest. Only the incompetent, the weak man is unaware of the most urgent, most vehement desire within his soul; with him, every moment is dominated by random, externally stimulated cravings which, precisely because they are only cravings, can never be quelled; and so, tossed back and forth willfully from one to the other, he never attains real enjoyment. But should this man, who feels no need, have the strength obstinately to pursue the satisfaction of random cravings, the consequence then will be those hideous, unnatural apparitions in life and art, which, whether as excesses of mad, egoistic frenzy, as the murderous lust of despots, or as lewd modern operatic music, fill us with such unspeakable horror. But if the individual recognizes within himself a strong desire, an urge that forces back all other yearnings, in short the necessary inner drive that constitutes his soul, his essence, and if he bends all his energies to satisfy it, he will then raise his power and his personal capacities to their utmost strength and height.

The individual man whose body, heart, and intellect enjoy perfect health can feel no higher need than that common to all his kind; for, as a *true* need, it can only be one that is capable of being satisfied in the community alone. But the most necessary and strongest need of the fully artistic man is that of communicating himself, in all his essence, to the fullest community, and this he can only accomplish with the necessary common intelligibility in the *drama*. In the drama he broadens his own particular being by representing not himself but an individual personality that is universally human. He must completely step outside himself in order to so thoroughly grasp in all its essence a personality foreign to his as to be able to portray it; he will succeed in this only if he studies exactly, perceives vividly this one individual in his relation, interpenetration, and fulfillment with other individuals, and so must study these other individuals too; he will thus be able to absorb sympathetically that relation, interpenetration, and fulfillment within himself; and so the complete representative artist is the individual man broadened into *the very essence of the species* in the full abundance of his own particular being. The space in which this wonderful process takes place is the *theatrical stage*; the artistic collective work that gives it birth is the *drama*. To bring his own particular essence to the highest fulfillment of its potential in this *one* exalted art work, the individual artist, indeed, the individual art itself must suppress all willful, egoistic inclination towards untimely expansion, doing a disservice to the whole; thus will the collaboration be stronger in attaining the highest common objective, which cannot be realized without the individual, nor without the occasional imposition of limits on the individual.

That objective, the drama's, is however at the same time the only truly artistic objective that can possibly be *realized*: anything foreign to it is of necessity lost in a sea of uncertainty, unintelligibility, loss of freedom. That objective, however, is not to be attained by *one art all for itself*,[3] but by *all in common*, and that is why the *most comprehensive* art work is at the same time the only true, free, i.e. universally *intelligible* art work.

Richard Wagner, *Das Kunstwerk der Zukunft* (Leipzig: Wigand, 1850), 183–204. Trans. P.W.

---

[3]The modern *playwright* will feel the most reluctance to admit that drama is not the exclusive property of even *his* art, the *art of poetry*; more particularly, he will not bring himself to share it with the composer, or, as he would put it, to let the play become an opera. Quite right, too: so long as opera exists, the play should continue to exist, and that applies to pantomime as well; but so long as disagreement on this point is thinkable, the drama of the future must remain unthinkable. However, if the poet's doubts lie deeper and if he is committed to the proposition that it is inconceivable that *song* should take the place of spoken dialogue in each and every case, then one must retort that in two respects he has not yet grasped the character of the art work of the future. In the first place he does not appreciate that in this art work music will be given a place quite different from the one it occupies in modern opera: that only where music is *most capable* will it expand to its fullest, while where dramatic speech, for example, is the *most necessary*, music will subordinate itself to it; that in fact music, without falling silent, has the peculiar capacity of adhering so imperceptibly to speech's thoughts that it leaves speech nearly free while yet supporting it. This granted, then in the second place the poet must realize that thoughts and situations where even the softest and most discreet musical support would yet seem obtrusive and troublesome can only be derived from the spirit of our modern plays, which will find absolutely no breathing space in the art work of the future. The man who will represent himself in the drama of the future will no longer have anything to do with the prosy intrigues, the obligatory, modish hodgepodge which our modern poets must tangle and untangle in the most complicated way in their plays. His speech and action, dictated by nature, are: "Yes!" and "No!" All else is evil; i.e., modern, superfluous.

34

DIVERGENT REACTIONS TO
BORIS GODUNOV

Musorgsky's masterpiece received its first performance on 27 January/8 February 1874 in St. Petersburg. It was a great popular success and was repeated four times that season before sold-out houses. The critics were another story. After all, Musorgsky had been one of the *kuchka*, the St. Petersburg "Five," whose aggressive theories regarding the future of Russian music had raised the hackles of conservatives. In the eyes of these critics Musorgsky stood condemned *a priori*: *Boris* could only be the product of repugnant aesthetic doctrines, realism chief among them. And yet César Cui, a fellow member of the "Five," found fault with the opera precisely for its failures to adhere to *kuchkist* doctrine. From the very first, then, *Boris* met with conflicting reactions, and that was only the beginning of its tortuous reception history. Hermann Laroche, professor of music history at the Moscow Conservatory and friend of Tchaikovsky, shared with Eduard Hanslick, the Viennese critic whose writings he translated, the latter's elegant self-assurance in the face of music he could not understand. Though he had regarded with benevolence three scenes from *Boris* performed the year before, he found much to disapprove of when he reviewed the opera as a whole at its première.

The success of a new staged work is rarely as great as it seems at its first performance, but the success of Mr. Musorgsky's *Boris* can hardly be called transitory. The writer of these lines is far from an enthusiast of the composer, but he unhesitatingly recognizes that Mr. Musorgsky is capable of pleasing and even of captivating many. He has talent; but even if he had no talent at all, he would still possess many other qualifications for success. He is utterly a man of the times, and yet he is still a Russian. Out of the many varieties of the "authentically Russian," he personifies precisely that type in which there is more liberal instinct than there is knowledge, skill, or intellectual development. Such personalities are well known to the experienced observer of Russian life: a man who has taught himself "little by little, somehow and any which way" [a line from Pushkin's *Eugene Onegin*, describing the education of the hero], who feels the constriction of his surroundings and is unconsciously struggling toward the light, toward broad open spaces—such a man is an agreeable phenomenon, fully understandable and for the most part honorable. . . . He is not only a musician, he is also a poet. Like Richard Wagner, he creates his own libretto and combines in himself competencies that are usually separated out in persons with no understanding of each other at all. In both spheres, Mr. Musorgsky commands our attention by the abundance of his progressive spirit and by the paucity of his development. . . .

I forgot to mention that I do not understand liberals of Mr. Musorgsky's sort. Such liberals look at the soaring poetic line of [Pushkin's] *Boris* as old-fashioned rhetorical rubbish that it's time to do away with. In the opinion of the liberals, the real-life Boris, the real Pretender, the real Marina did not speak anywhere near as eloquently as Pushkin forced them to speak. The realism with which Mr. Musorgsky is permeated has compelled him to perform a merciless operation on Pushkin's poetry. Our present-day poet has in places completely destroyed the verses of the poet of bygone days; in places he has chopped these verses up into little pieces and mixed them in with pieces invented by him; he has torn big strips out of the living flesh of Pushkin's poetry, and patched the gaping wounds with plasters from his own home apothecary. I could cite many examples of this domestic cure to which Pushkin was subject at the hands of doctoring realism. . . . [There follows an example of Musorgsky's "vulgar prosifying" from the Fountain scene.] This is far from being Pushkin, but we can console ourselves with the fact that it is life itself.

One way or another, in language and in verse, Mr. Musorgsky is undoubtedly a realist. What that means for me is that he cultivates liberal instincts and aspires to liberate himself from any sort of shackles, among which must be numbered a high style and classical versification. Mr. Musorgsky's liberal spirit is not limited to external effects, however; the new poet looks on history itself through the eyes of progress. . . .

I have just spoken of Mr. Musorgsky's declamation; this side of vocal music is one of the favorite hobbyhorses of that liberalism which aspires to reform our art. Mr. Musorgsky's recitative is the apex of liberalism: there is no conventional form, no melodic, harmonic or rhythmic law that might constrain or stop him in his goal of transmitting the accents of simple speech by means of musical accents. But it is not this orientation alone that sustains him: it is clear that he also has talent. In his manner of illustrating the rise and fall of the human voice, its stops, hesitations and rapid patter, one is aware of an indisputable keenness of observation; one sees a person capable of noticing how people speak and the moment and the individual accent of a personality. . . . This is the brightest side of realistic opera, but precisely here the education of the realist gives itself away in the most unambiguous fashion. The musical gusts in which Mr. Musorgsky lives cast him in two diffent directions at once, and he swings between the two without finding a point of support in any firm system. On the one hand, he would like the long and short, the low and high notes to correspond literally to the prosody of the words. On the other hand, he draws on the melodic turns of Russian folk songs, whose style bursts forth in the recitative passages of *Boris* at times in small, at other times in large segments. There is no declamation freer and more irregular than that found in folk songs; this circumstance results from a verse line that is not strictly regular with respect to number of syllables, so that the same musical rhythms fall on verse lines with different distributions of accent. And this is so even when the songs' refrains are repeated in couplet form. That is why one sometimes encounters in Mr. Musorgsky's romances such curious declamation. . . . But despite these deviations and hesitations, the new opera reveals, in patches, both talent for recitative and sensitivity to Russian folk singing. . . .

It is most regrettable that our musical realist is gifted with great ability. It would be a thousand times more pleasant if his method of composition were practiced only by untalented dullards, if feebleness of education were never masked by an inborn flair. . . . All his compositions are worked out on the piano: take away his piano today, and tomorrow he will cease to be a musician. *Boris Godunov* is, first and foremost, an improvisation for the piano. It is remarkable with what love the author cleaned up, smoothed out and dressed up the piano-vocal score of his opera before releasing it for publication, not to mention the subtlest markings of intensity, legato and staccato, the pedal, etc.; not to mention the virtuoso passages of the second scene of the Prologue, with the portrayal of the bells; not to mention, finally, how Mr. Musorgsky, as a subtle and sensitive pianist, ofttimes carefully marks what to play with the right hand, what with the left—his entire opera, despite all its harmonic blunders, is laid out from a pianistic perspective very sonorously and elegantly: chord sequences are wild and scandalous, but a given individual chord is distributed in such a way that it is comfortable to reach and sounds distinctly, effectively. In places it seems as if the author were reckoning primarily on piano "salon performances." . . . The choice of tonalities, the modulations and voice leading of this strange composer are so pianistic that they can only be explained as an incessant noodling about on the keys with an abundant use of the right pedal.

At the opposite end of the critical spectrum stood Musorgsky's close friend Vladimir Stasov, spokesman, champion, and theorist for the Five. The following excerpts are taken from a biographical essay he published in 1881, shortly after Musorgsky's death. Here some of the aspects of the opera that Laroche had castigated as defects (e.g., the libretto, the "realistic" vocal settings) are singled out for special praise, and it is easy to guess the identity of at least one of the "worst music critics" alluded to below.

Musorgsky followed the text of Pushkin's drama closely in only a few places. For all its many beautiful features, that dramatic text could not be transmitted completely nor in its entirety, since it is comprised for the most part of scenes that are excessively short and too compressed (a misapplied imitation of Shakespeare). Musorgsky composed most of the text himself. Later, people (especially the worst music critics) reproached him severely for this, not understanding that there was nothing else he could have done. Musorgsky had at his disposal neither Pushkin himself nor even some mediocre versifier; and even if he had, doubtless he would have had a terrible time with him (as happened earlier with Glinka and Dargomyzhsky, who were also obliged to insert quite a few of their own verses into librettos adapted from Pushkin). It is worth noting that Musorgsky, although not a poet by profession, wrote for *Boris Godunov*—as for many of his previously composed romances—a good number of talented and poetic verses, full of power, conciseness, precision, expressiveness, and rich imagery. At the same time, true to the system he had tested in *The Marriage*, Musorgsky composed music directly to prose, in this instance to Pushkin's prose in one place and to his own in another. And the music did not suffer in the least because of it; on the contrary, the music sometimes won. Generally speaking, our profound art critics did not notice that Musorgsky, of all those composers who set their own texts, wrote verse and prose far better than the others (including, of course, Berlioz with his pompous verses and prose, and Wagner with his insufferably pretentious and befogged rhetoric). . . .

The opera *Boris Godunov*, which achieved its full and final form after the reworkings and additions of 1870–71 [actually 1871–72], is one of the most powerful works not only of Russian but of all European art. The common people are portrayed here in forms of truth and realism such as no one had ever attempted before (in Dargomyzhsky's *Stone Guest* the people do not appear on stage at all). . . . The monks Varlaam and Misail, the innkeeper, the Tsarevich's nurse, the border police, the holy fool, and popular masses of peasant men and women in the first and last acts—all these are types quite unprecedented in opera, both in Russia and throughout Europe. Compared with them, even the best popular choruses of Meyerbeer (to say nothing of Glinka or Wagner) are idealized, impersonal, conventionalized, and not national in spirit. The closeness to reality that we find in Musorgsky's music one can find only in the best folk scenes of [the prose writers and playwrights] Gogol and Ostrovsky. In those scenes Musorgsky is indisputably their equal. A grasp of history, a profound rendering of the innumerable nuances of the people's spirit, of their mood, intelligence and stupidity, strength and weakness, tragic quality and humor—all this is unparalleled in Musorgsky. The people, as submissive and stupid as sheep, electing Boris to the throne under the policeman's cudgel, and then, as soon as the policeman has moved away, fully ready to turn their humor against themselves (Act I); a crowd of people gathered from all parts of Russia, inflicting savage reprisals on their domestic and foreign enemies, on their cruel superiors, and on Catholic Jesuits, but first viciously playing with their victim and mocking him; the vicious and greedy Varlaam with the police officers at the Inn; the humble monk Pimen, a chronicler and pious soul, a genuinely epic Russian personality—what profound, authentic historical pictures these are! And what deeply truthful Russian speech one hears from all these Mityukhs, Fomkas, Epifans, holy fool Ivanyches and Afimyas, innkeepers, bands of little rascals and dozens of other nameless persons! What Russian voice intonations! With good reason did the historian Kostomarov, who had studied well the Russian people's Time of Troubles, exclaim in ecstasy to the author after seeing and hearing *Boris Godunov* on the stage: "This is like a page from history!" . . . No other results were possible from a person, and from an artist, as truly "of the people" as Musorgsky was. . . .

I cannot analyze here all the perfections of this opera, but I firmly believe that as the artistic and historical intelligence of our society grows, the more frequently and deeply will people study this masterpiece, one of the greatest pearls of Russian nationalist art. If the Germans study the operas of Wagner, which seem to them truly national and great, so painstakingly and with such love and attention to detail, then the same should be expected for Musorgsky's opera in the future—for it is an opera not seemingly but authentically, equivalently national, historical, and infinitely truthful in its every turn of speech, phrase, and word.

Caryl Emerson and Robert William Oldani, *Modest Musorgsky and* Boris Godunov: *Myths, Realities, Reconsiderations* (Cambridge: Cambridge University Press, 1994), 145–47, 134–36.

35

TCHAIKOVSKY ON *EUGENE ONEGIN*

Tchaikovsky's comments on his operatic masterpiece are scattered quite widely over the many letters he wrote during the period of its gestation and early performances. The recipients included his brothers Anatoly and Modest, various friends and colleagues, and most importantly, his patroness Nadezhda von Meck. Out of an English-language compilation, a sort of montage of excerpts from his vast correspondence (see the source cited at the end), it has been possible to carve a mini-montage of Tchaikovsky's thoughts on *Eugene Onegin*, which, thus assembled, present a surprisingly consistent authorial voice, despite the variety of recipients to whom they were originally addressed. (The bracketed page references at the end of each excerpt are to the English-language source, which in turn refers the reader to the Russian originals.) The opening excerpt is from a letter to his brother Modest, reporting on a visit to the singer Elizaveta Lavrovskaya on 13 May 1877.

The conversation turned to subjects for an opera. Her stupid husband churned out indescribable rubbish and suggested the most impossible subjects. Lizaveta Adreyevna was silent and smiled good-naturedly, then suddenly said, "But what about *Eugene Onegin?*" This suggestion was so incredible that I said nothing. Then later, when I was dining alone at the inn, I remembered about *Onegin*, thought it over, began to find Lavrovskaya's idea possible, then was carried away by the idea, and by the end of the meal had decided upon it. I immediately ran to find a copy of Pushkin. I eventually tracked one down, went home, reread it with delight and spent a completely sleepless night, the result of which was a scenario for a delightful opera with the libretto by Pushkin. Next day I went to visit Shilovsky. [65]

> His friend Konstantin Shilovsky, an actor and poet, had been suggesting to Tchaikovsky various unacceptable operatic subjects.

I spent two days at Kostya Shilovsky's. I went to see him to ask him to *deal with* the scenario of the new opera. I intend to write a delightful work which perfectly suits my musical personality. Everyone to whom I have mentioned it has first been astonished and then in *raptures*. [65]

> The astonishment caused by Tchaikovsky's announcement, and the composer's own incredulous reaction to the initial suggestion that he write an opera on *Eugene Onegin*, need to be understood in their historical context. Pushkin's verse novel, published in parts in 1825–32, in its final form in 1837, was by then (and still is) a treasured piece of Russia's cultural heritage. Setting it to music, though the music came to Tchaikovsky in a surge of inspiration, posed aesthetic questions the composer was well aware of, and they never ceased to occupy his thoughts.

You won't believe what a frenzy I have got myself into over this subject. How glad I am to be spared Ethiopian princesses, Pharaohs, poisonings, and all kinds of stilted mannerisms. What a wealth of poetry there is in *Onegin*. I am not deluding myself; I know that there will not be much theatricality or action in this opera. But the general level of poetry, the humanity, the simplicity of subject matter, combined with the *brilliant* text, compensate handsomely for these shortcomings. [66]

[Shilovsky] is now writing the libretto for the opera in accordance with my instructions. As soon as the examinations are over [Tchaikovsky was on the faculty of the Moscow Conservatory] I am going to see him and will immediately get down to composing the opera. And it is essential that I should write this *opera* because I feel an irresistible urge to do so and must not let the opportunity slip. [68]

It will not, of course, have any strong, dramatic action but on the other hand the social side will be interesting and on top of that how much poetry there is in it all! Take the scene of Tatyana with her nurse—what is that alone worth? [68]

I cannot understand, Nadezhda Filaretovna [i.e., Mme von Meck], how anyone with your strong and lively interest in music can fail to appreciate Pushkin, the genius of whose gifts very often breaks out of the narrower paths of verse into the infinite scope of music. That is not an empty phrase. Regardless of the substance of what he expounds in verse form, there is *something* in the verse itself, in the succession of sounds, which penetrates to the depths of one's soul. That something is music. [69]

Now that my first ardor has passed and I can look at the work more objectively it seems to me that [the opera] is doomed to failure and public neglect. The story is very ingenuous, there is nothing in it which is good theater, the music lacks sparkle and brilliant effects. But I think that a *select* few may, when they listen to this music, be moved by the same feelings as stirred me when I wrote it. I am not trying to say that my music is so good that it is inaccessible to the *contemptible* masses. I cannot understand at all how anyone could write intentionally either for the masses or for the elect; my view is that one should compose in direct response to one's own inclination and with no thought of pleasing this or that section of humanity. I did, in fact, write *Onegin* without pursuing any extraneous purposes at all. But the way it worked out, *Onegin* will not be *interesting* in the theater; so those for whom *dramatic* action is the first requirement in opera will not be satisfied. However, those who are capable of finding in the opera the musical re-creation of ordinary, simple emotions, common to all humanity and far removed from the tragic, the theatrical, may (I hope) be pleased with it. In short, the opera has been composed sincerely, and it is in the sincerity that I place all my hopes. [71–72]

I have finished orchestrating the first act of *Onegin*. I was very keen to do it. To see it produced *actually in the Conservatory* is my fondest dream. It is designed for modest resources and a small stage. . . . If it is carefully produced, I think that this opera ought, with its guileless plot, its marvelous text, and its simple human feelings and situations, to create a poetic effect. [75]

Answering a letter from Yevgeny Albrecht, dean of the Moscow Conservatory, Tchaikovsky explained why he was insisting on the première taking place there, rather than at the Moscow Imperial Opera. Of the pupils he mentions, Mariya Klimentova would in fact create the role of Tatyana and Gilev that of Onegin. Among the members of the faculty named, Rubinstein is Nikolay Grigoryevich, founder and director of the Moscow Conservatory and brother of Anton, who will make his appearance in a later excerpt.

If I have to wait for a *real* Tatyana, a *real* Onegin, an *ideal* Lensky and so on then, of course, the opera will never be staged. Whatever Klimentova might be like, she is still better for me than Raab, Velinskaya, Menshikova, and so on [from the Imperial Opera] because she will be rehearsed by Galvani, you, Samarin, and Rubinstein. Gilev is also better for me than Melnikov, and Silberstein than Dodonov because they are pupils, young people still not in the rut of that disgusting banality which is what I fear for my opera above all else. I will *never* offer this opera to the theater management before it is performed at the Conservatory. I wrote it for the Conservatory because I do not need in this work a large theater with its *dull routine, its conventionality, its undistinguished producers, its nonsensical staging (even if it is opulent), its flapping robots instead of a conductor etc. etc.* This is what I want for *Onegin*: (1) singers of middle rank, but well-drilled and sound; (2) singers who can also act *simply* but *well*; (3) a production which is not opulent but adheres strictly to the period; the costumes must be exactly of the period in which the opera takes place (the twenties); (4) the choruses must not be a flock of sheep, as they are in the Imperial Opera, but people, who take part in the action of the opera; (5) the conductor must not be a machine, nor even a musician à la Nápravník: he only cares about getting a C# and not a C but I want someone who will be a true guide to the orchestra. In short, for this production I need neither Kister, nor Kavelin, nor Nápravník, nor Merten, nor Kondratyev, nor Dmitriyev, but I do need *Huber, Albrecht, Samarin, and Rubinstein,* i.e. true artists and, moreover, my friends. Not for all the world will I give *Onegin* to the managements in Petersburg or Moscow and if it is destined not to be put on at the Conservatory then it will not be put on anywhere. I am prepared to wait as long as you like. So far as Klimentova's unsuitability is concerned, an *entirely* suitable singer will never be found. If we are to wait for this *ideal* Tatyana we shall have to wait for ever more. [87]

The following, to Mme von Meck, was written from Milan, where Tchaikovsky had attended a performance of a new opera, Marchetti's *Ruy Blas.*

The performance of this opera provoked melancholy thoughts. There is a young queen in it with whom everyone is in love. The singer who took this role was very conscientious; she did all she could. But how little did she resemble a graceful, royal lady with the power to captivate every man she met! And the hero, Ruy Blas! Again, his singing was not at all bad. But instead of a young man, a handsome and elegant hero, we had nothing but a flunkey! No illusion at all. I thought about my own opera. Where am I going to find a Tatyana as Pushkin imagined her and as I have tried to portray her in music? Where is there a singer who even remotely resembles the ideal Onegin, that cold dandy, *comme il faut* to the marrow of his bones? Where will we find a Lensky, a youth of eighteen, with a thick crop of curls and the impetuous, quirkish ways of a young poet *à la* Schiller? How Pushkin's charming picture is vulgarized when it is transferred to the stage with its sacred routine of senseless traditions, and with its veterans like Alexandrova, Komissarshevsky, and *tutti quanti* who quite shamelessly assume the roles of sixteen-year-old girls and beardless youths! The moral of which is: it is much nicer to write instrumental music because there are fewer disappointments. [91]

I have finished the piano arrangement. Now all I have to do is put in the markings and make a clean copy of the libretto. Then the opera will be complete in all respects. But what will be its fate? . . . It seems to me that this opera is more likely to be successful in private houses and perhaps even on concert platforms than on large stages; for this reason the fact that it will be published long before going into the repertoire of the large theaters is not unfavorable. The success of the opera must begin from below and not from above, i.e. it is not the *theater* which will make it known to the public but, on the contrary, if the public gradually gets to know it, it may come to like it and then the *theater* will put the opera on to satisfy a public demand. Perhaps I am on the wrong track but I think that with a really efficient, careful production it could even work on the stage. But for such a production all the stilted, ingrained, formal conventions would have to go and I *would have to have the right* to demand everything that I considered necessary for the proper staging of the opera. This is why I will not take the first step towards having it produced in a State theater and will wait until they humbly ask me for it. Then I shall say: with pleasure, but if you want it you must do it like this and like this, not like that. [102]

I have played through almost the whole of *Eugene Onegin*! The composer was also the only listener. I'm ashamed to admit it, but all right, I'll tell it to you as a secret. The music brought tears of delight to the listener's eyes and he said all manner of nice things to the composer. Oh, if only everybody else who hears this music in the future could be as moved by it as was the composer! [126–27]

I played through the whole of *Onegin* to my [sister's family]. Their impressions were extremely favorable. I am ashamed to admit it but I cannot deny that I enjoyed it as much as they did and there were moments when I had to stop from excitement and my voice refused to sing because my throat was full of tears. But then the more I think of performing the opera the more I am convinced that it is *impossible,* i.e. a performance that would correspond to my dreams and intentions. I am at a loss to know what to do about *Tatyana* and *Lensky* in particular. Consequently, I am inclined to think that, apart from the Conservatory performance, which I regard as a student exercise and a try-out, my opera will never see the stage. [134]

My retirement from my professorial duties and the appearance of *Onegin* have created something of a sensation in the musical world here [in St. Petersburg]. People are talking about me a lot and have concocted all sorts of fantasies. Everybody is convinced I am trying to get a chair in Petersburg. Oh, how far from the truth they are! Of the musical people here I have seen only [Karl] Davydov [director of the St. Petersburg Conservatory], where we spent the whole evening getting to know *Onegin*, which, apparently, he likes. . . . My goodness! What bliss it is to be free and not to have to correct sixty harmony and orchestration exercises every day! [141]

I arrived in Moscow just before the rehearsal started. It was being done with costumes and full stage lights but there were no lights in the auditorium. So I was able to sit in a dark corner and listen to my opera without being pestered. I enjoyed it very much. The performance was very satisfactory on the whole. The chorus and orchestra did their bit beautifully. The soloists, of course, left a very great deal to be desired. Gilev was very conscientious as Onegin but his voice is so feeble, so dry and charmless. Klimentova as Tatyana comes nearer to my ideal and this is largely because, despite her marked lack of ability as an actress, she sings with warmth and sincerity. Lensky was sung by some Medvedev fellow, a Jew, with not at all a bad voice but still a complete novice and his Russian pronunciation is poor. Of the secondary roles, Triquet and Prince Gremin were well done. The staging was extremely good and in my view some of the scenes (particularly the dance in the country) were beyond criticism in this respect. The same might be said of the costumes. These few hours spent in a dark corner of the theater were the only ones that I enjoyed in the whole of my stay in Moscow. During the intervals I met all of my colleagues. I was very glad to see that they were all, without exception, remarkably enthusiastic about the music for *Onegin*. Nikolay Grigoryevich, who is very sparing with his praise, told me that he was *in love* with the music. After the first act Taneyev wanted to tell me how much he liked it but broke into sobs instead. It's hard to put into words how touched I was. In fact everybody without exception was so enthusiastic and sincere in telling me how they liked *Onegin* that I was surprised and gratified. [171–72]

> The first performance took place on 17/29 March 1879. Among the travelers from St. Petersburg was Anton Rubinstein, who had founded the St. Petersburg Conservatory and had been Tchaikovsky's teacher there during its inaugural seasons.

My brothers and a few other people including Anton Rubinstein and Alexandra Panayeva, the object of Anatoly's affections, arrived on Sunday morning (the day of the performance). I was in a very agitated state of mind all day, in particular because I had had to agree to Nikolay Grigoryevich's insistent request that I should appear on the stage if there were any curtain calls. My worries rose to a pitch of extremity during the performance and got to the point where they were an excruciating torment. Before it began Nikolay Grigoryevich called me on to the stage. When I got there I saw, to my horror, the whole Conservatory assembled and Nikolay Grigoryevich at the head of the professors with a wreath which he presented to me to the accompaniment of loud applause from every-body present. I had to say a few words in reply to his speech. The Lord alone knows what an effort it cost me! I was given a lot of curtain calls at the inter-vals. I did not, incidentally, observe that the audience was exactly in raptures. I conclude from this that it was me the public was calling onto the stage and not the performers; the performance was interrupted by vigorous applause only twice; after Tatyana's couplets and Gremin's aria. It was noticeable that they did not like Onegin and Lensky. They gave Klimentova a very warm reception. And there was vigorous applause for the chorus after the two choral numbers in the first act. After the performance there was a supper at The Hermitage and An-ton Rubinstein was there. I really don't know whether he liked *Onegin* or not. At any rate he didn't say a word to me. There were speeches and I for my part was compelled to get up and say a few words. Making speeches at dinners and suppers is one of the most disagreeable things I have to do. Towards the end everybody livened up and Anton Rubinstein spoke once or twice. [172]

> Four years later he again had occasion to pay homage to Pushkin, in a letter to Mme von Meck:

You say that in *Eugene Onegin* my musical patterns are better than the canvas to which they are applied. But I would argue that if my music for *Eugene One-gin* has any qualities of warmth and poetry then it is because my emotions were stirred by the charm of the subject. I also think, incidentally, that you are wrong to see only verbal beauty in Pushkin's text. Tatyana is not merely a young lady from the provinces who has fallen in love with a dandy from the capital. She is a girl full of pure, feminine beauty, still untouched by contact with the realities of life; she has a dreamy nature, vaguely seeking her ideal, and passionate in her pursuit of it. Seeing nothing which answers to her ideal she is not satisfied but neither is she disturbed. But all it needed was for a person to turn up whose ap-pearance marked him off from the dreary provincial milieu and she imagined that he was her ideal; passion took an overpowering grip of her. The power of a young girl's love is portrayed brilliantly, superbly by Pushkin, and from my ear-liest years I have always been deeply moved by the profoundly poetic quality of Tatyana's character after Onegin appears. So, if I burnt with the fire of inspira-tion when I wrote the letter scene, it was Pushkin who kindled the fire, and I can tell you frankly, with no false modesty, and I am well aware of what I am saying, that if my music contains only a fraction of the beauty which I found in the subject itself then I will be very proud and well pleased. I can also see very much more than you do in the duel scene. Surely there is something profoundly dramatic and touching in the death of a richly gifted young man because of a fateful clash with society's view of *honor*. Surely there are dramatic elements in the bored lion of the capital taking the life of a young man for whom, in truth, he has much affection, out of *boredom*, out of a trivial irritation, without really thinking about it, because of a fateful coincidence of circumstances! All right, perhaps this is all very simple, even mundane, but the simple and the mundane do not exclude either poetry or drama. [254–55]

> *Onegin*'s reception outside Russia came only gradually. One of the first foreign cities to request it was Hamburg, where it opened, in German, on 19 January 1892. Although at the last moment he decided not to conduct it, Tchaikovsky was clearly impressed by the rising young musician who conducted it in his stead.

There was *only one* rehearsal of *Eugene Onegin* in Hamburg which I conducted before the performance today. They have learned the work extremely well and the production is not bad, but there are changes in the *recitatives* because of the German text and I couldn't help getting lost and muddling it. Despite all their attempts to persuade me I have withdrawn from conducting it because I am frightened of ruining the whole thing. By the way, the conductor here isn't just some middling character: he's a positive *genius*, and dying to conduct the first performance. I heard him conduct *the most astounding* performance of *Tannhäuser*. The singers, the orchestra, the producers, the conductor (they call him Mahler) are all in love with *Eugene Onegin*. [390]

Alexandra Orlova, ed., *Tchaikovsky: A Self-Portrait*, trans. R. M. Davison (Oxford: Oxford University Press, 1990), pages as indicated in the text above.

36

NIETZSCHE *VS*. WAGNER

The literature on Wagner that appeared during the composer's life and for some time afterwards is for the most part passionately for or against him, and it rarely sticks to opera: after all, Wagner didn't. And so he was championed or condemned not only as a composer but also as an essayist and, later, as the highly visible promoter of the Bayreuth Festival. His new theater was inaugurated in 1876 with the first performance of the complete *Ring of the Nibelung*, an event that attracted world-wide attention and brought, in addition

to opera-goers and newspaper critics, a cross-section of the artistic and political elite of the day. One who came but did not stay till the end was Friedrich
Nietzsche (1844–1900), then a young professor of classical philology at the
University of Basel and a rising author and philosopher. With him, Wagner
was an obsession. He worshiped him and knew him personally; indeed, their
friendship had been a very close one for the past seven years, despite their
age difference (Wagner was some thirty years older). Nietzsche had lent his
talent to the cause with *Wagner in Bayreuth*, a pamphlet written to coincide
with the opening of the festival; but already then his blind faith in the Master
was beginning to falter. The mundanity of the festival and of its performances
finished the job: "My mistake," he wrote later, "was that I came to Bayreuth
with an ideal and was thus doomed to experience the bitterest disappointment.
The preponderance of ugliness, grotesqueness, and strong pepper thoroughly
repelled me." The rift was gradual but irreversible, and even Wagner's death
in 1883 failed to end Nietzsche's disenchantment. His continuing involvement
is evident in the writings that followed: in *Thus Spake Zarathustra* (1885) the
allusions to Wagner are covert, in *Beyond Good and Evil* (1886) explicit. Then
came the explosion: *The Case of Wagner* (1888), excerpted below, was closely
followed by *Nietzsche contra Wagner* (1889). The writing in these is brilliant,
witty, vitriolic, the expression of Nietzsche's bitterness over his fallen idol. At
the same time, however, it is prophetic, for it voices opposition to Wagner's
fundamental aesthetic and moral principles in a manner that foreshadows the
reaction of the early twentieth century to the ideals of romanticism in general.
Nietzsche's famous panegyric of Bizet's *Carmen*, with which *The Case of Wagner* begins, is much more than a rhetorical ploy. In the first place, of course,
it is a genuine appreciation of what came very soon to be recognized as a
masterpiece; but then, too, it is a ringing affirmation of the human element in
art, and so a rejection of the surrender of self in a mystical conception of art
as a quasi-religion, having Bayreuth for its temple.

1

Yesterday—would you believe it?—I heard Bizet's masterpiece for the *twentieth* time. Once more I held out with gentle reverence; once again I did not run
away. This triumph over my impatience surprises me. How such a work completes one! Through it one becomes a "masterpiece" oneself.—And indeed, each
time I heard *Carmen* it seemed to me that I was more of a philosopher, a better philosopher than I normally think I am: so forbearing, so happy, so Indian,
so *settled*... To sit for five hours: the first step to holiness!—May I be allowed
to say that Bizet's orchestral sound is almost the only one that I can endure
now? That *other* orchestral sound, all the rage at present, the Wagnerian, is brutal, artificial, and "innocent" at the same time and addresses all the three senses

BRÜNNHILDE AT THE FIRST BAYREUTH FESTIVAL. *Amalie Materna in the costume partly designed by Wagner for the first production of the entire* Ring *cycle in 1876.*

of the modern soul at once.—How detrimental to me is this Wagnerian orchestral sound! I call it "scirocco." A disagreeable sweat breaks out all over me. Gone is *my* fine weather.

This music seems to me perfect. It comes forward lightly, gracefully, stylishly. It is lovable, it does not *sweat*. "All that is good is easy, everything divine runs with light feet": this is the first principle of my aesthetics. This music is wicked, refined, fatalistic: at the same time it is popular—it has the refinement of a race, not of an individual. It is rich. It is precise. It builds, organizes, concludes: thus it is the opposite of the octopus in music, of the "endless melody." Have more painful tragic accents been heard on the stage before? And how are they obtained? Without grimaces! Without counterfeiting! Without the *lie* of the grand style!—Finally: this music assumes the listener is intelligent, even a musician. Also in *this* respect it is the opposite of Wagner who, apart from everything else, was in any case the most *ill-mannered* genius on earth (Wagner takes us for ———, he repeats a single thing so often that we become desperate—that we ultimately believe it).

And once more: I become a better man when this Bizet speaks to me. Also a better musician, a better *listener*. Is it in any way possible to listen better? I even dig *under* this music, I hear its very cause. I seem to assist at its birth, I tremble before the dangers that accompany any bold enterprise, I am enraptured over happy accidents for which Bizet is not responsible.—And strange to say, at bottom I do not give it a thought, or am not *aware* how much thought I really do give it. For quite other ideas are running through my head the while... Has anyone ever observed that music *emancipates* the spirit? gives wings to thought? and that the more one becomes a musician the more one is also a philosopher? The grey sky of abstraction as if crossed by flashes of lightning; light strong enough to reveal the filigree of all things; the large problems within reach; the world surveyed as if from a mountain top.—I have just defined the philosophical pathos.—And unexpectedly, *answers* drop in my lap, a small hailstorm of ice and wisdom, of problems solved... Where am I?—Bizet makes me productive. Everything that is good makes me productive. I have gratitude for nothing else, nor have I any other *proof* of what is good.

2

This work also saves; Wagner is not the only "Saviour." With it one bids farewell to the *damp* north and to all the fog of the Wagnerian ideal. Already the plot delivers us from it. From Mérimée it still has the logic in the passion, the direct line, the *inexorable* necessity; above all, it has all that belongs to the warm regions, the dryness of the air, the *limpidezza* of the air. Here in every respect the climate is altered. Here another kind of sensuality, another kind of sensibility, another kind of high spirits speak to us. This music is spirited; but not with the high spirits of the French or the Germans. Its high spirits are African; fate hangs over them, their happiness is short, sudden, without reprieve. I envy Bizet for having had the courage of this sensibility, which until now in the cultured music of Europe had found no means of expression—of this southern, browner, more sunburnt sensibility... How beneficent to us are the golden afternoons of its happiness! We look out: have we ever seen the sea so *smooth*?—And how this Moorish dance speaks to us and makes us calm! How, for once, even our insatiability learns to be sated in its lascivious melancholy!—Finally love, love translated back into *nature*! *Not* the love of an "exalted maid"! No Senta-sentimentality! [Senta redeems the Flying Dutchman in Wagner's opera.] Instead, love as fate, as *fatality*, cynical, innocent, cruel—and precisely for this reason, *nature*! The love whose means is war, whose very essence is the *mortal hatred* between the sexes!—I know no case in which the tragic irony that constitutes the kernel of love is expressed with such severity, or in so terrible a formula, as in the last cry of Don José with which the work ends:

> Yes, it is I who have killed her,
> I—my adored Carmen!

—Such a conception of love (the only one worthy of a philosopher) is rare: it distinguishes one work of art from among a thousand others. For as a rule, artists are no better than the rest of the world, they are even worse—they *misunderstand* love. Even Wagner misunderstood it. They imagine that they are selfless in it because they appear to be seeking the advantage of another creature often to their own disadvantage. But in return they want to *possess* the other creature... Even God is no exception to this rule. He is very far from thinking, "What does it matter to thee whether I love thee or not?"—He becomes terrible if he is not loved in return. *L'amour*—and with this maxim one may carry one's point with gods and men—*est de tous les sentiments le plus égoïste, et, par conséquent, lorsqu'il est blessé, le moins généreux* (B. Constant) [Love is, of all sentiments, the most egoistical and consequently, when hurt, the least generous].

3

Perhaps you are beginning to see how very much this music *improves* me?—*Il faut méditerraniser la musique* [we must Mediterraneanize music]: I have reasons for this principle (see *Beyond Good and Evil*, p.220). The return to nature, health, high spirits, youth, *virtue*!—And yet I was one of the most corrupt Wagnerians... I was able to take Wagner seriously... Ah, that old magician! what tricks has he not played on us! The first thing his art offers us is a magnifying glass: we look through it and no longer trust our own eyes—everything grows bigger, *even Wagner grows bigger*... What a clever rattlesnake! All its life it rattled on about "resignation," "loyalty," and "purity," then retired from the *corrupt* world with a paean to chastity! And we believed it...

—But you will not listen to me? You even prefer the Wagner *problem* to that of Bizet? But neither do I underrate it, it has its charm. The problem of salvation is even a venerable problem. Wagner pondered over nothing so deeply as over salvation: his opera is the opera of salvation. Someone always wants to be saved in his operas: now a little man, now a young lady—this is *his* problem.—

And how lavishly he varies his *leitmotif*! What rare, what sensuous modulations! Who, if not Wagner, has taught us that innocence prefers to save interesting sinners (the case in *Tannhäuser*)? Or that even the wandering Jew gets saved and *settles down* once he marries (the case in *The Flying Dutchman*)? Or that corrupted old females prefer to be saved by chaste young men (the case of Kundry [in *Parsifal*])? Or that beautiful girls most love to be saved by a knight who is a Wagnerian (the case in *Die Meistersinger*)? Or that even married women like to be saved by a knight (the case of Isolde)? Or that the venerable Almighty, after having compromised himself morally in every possible way, is at last delivered by a free spirit and an immoralist (the case in the *Ring*)? Admire, more especially, this last piece of wisdom! Do you understand it? I—take good care not to understand it...

. . .

4

—I will still relate the story of the *Ring*. This is its proper place. It, too, is a story of salvation: except that this time it is Wagner who is saved.—Half his lifetime Wagner believed in the *revolution* as only a Frenchman could have believed in it. He sought it in the runic inscriptions of myth, he thought he had found a typical revolutionary in Siegfried.—"Whence arises all the evil in the world?" Wagner asked himself. From "ancient contracts," he replied, as all revolutionary ideologists have done. In plain words: from customs, laws, morals, institutions, from all those things on which the ancient world, the ancient society rests. "How can one rid the world of this evil? How can one be done with the ancient society?" Only by declaring war on the "contracts" (on tradition, on morality). *This Siegfried does.* He starts early, very early: his birth is already a declaration of war against morality—he is the result of adultery, of incest... *Not* the saga, but Wagner himself is the inventor of this radical feature; on this point he *corrected* the saga... Siegfried continues as he began; he follows only his first impulse, he flings all tradition, all respect, all *fear* to the winds. Whatever displeases him he strikes down. He tilts irreverently at old godheads. His principal undertaking, however, is *to emancipate woman*—"to save Brünnhilde"... Siegfried *and* Brünnhilde; the sacrament of free love; the dawn of the golden age; the twilight of the gods of the old morality—*evil is done away with*... For a long while Wagner's ship sailed happily along this course. No doubt about it, along it Wagner sought his highest goal.—What happened? An accident. The ship dashed into a reef; Wagner ran aground. The reef was Schopenhauer's philosophy; Wagner had stuck fast on a *contrary* view of the world. What had he set to music? Optimism? Wagner was ashamed. It was moreover an optimism for which Schopenhauer had devised a bad epithet—*unscrupulous* optimism. He was more than ever ashamed. He reflected for some time; his position seemed desperate... At last, a way out dawned on him: what if he were to interpret the reef on which he had been wrecked as the goal, the hidden intention, the actual purpose of his journey? To be wrecked *here*, this was also a goal. *Bene navigavi, cum naufragium feci* [I was sailing correctly when I was shipwrecked]... And he translated the *Ring* into Schopenhauerese. Everything goes wrong, everything goes to rack and ruin, the new world is just as bad as the old: *nothingness*, the Indian Circe beckons... Brünnhilde, who according to the old plan was to have taken her leave with a song in honor of free love, consoling the world with the hope of a socialist Utopia in which "all will be well," now gets something else to do. She must first study Schopenhauer; she must first versify the fourth book of *The World as Will and Idea*. *Wagner was saved*... Joking apart, this *was* a salvation. The benefit Wagner owes Schopenhauer is incalculable. It was the *philosopher of decadence* who allowed the *artist of decadence* to find himself.——

5

... I place this point of view first and foremost: Wagner's art is diseased. The problems he sets on the stage—all of them problems of hysteria—the convulsiveness of his emotions, his over-excited sensibility, his taste which demands ever sharper spices, his instability, which he dressed up to look like principles, last but not least his choice of heroes and heroines, considered as physiological types (—a gallery of the diseased!—): all this taken together presents a morbid picture that leaves one in no doubt. *Wagner est une névrose* [Wagner is a neurosis]. . . .

11

... Another spirit prevails on the stage since Wagner rules there: the most difficult things are expected, blame is severe, praise very scarce,—the good and the excellent have become the rule. Taste is no longer necessary; nor even a good voice. Wagner is sung only with ruined voices: this has a "dramatic" effect. Even talent is out of the question. *Espressivo* at all costs, which is what the Wagnerian ideal, the ideal of decadence, requires, is hardly compatible with talent. For this, all that is required is *virtue*—that is, training, automatism, "self-denial." Neither taste, nor voice, nor talent: Wagner's stage requires but one thing: *Teutons*!... Definition of the Teuton: obedient and long-legged. . .

There is a deep significance in the fact that the rise of Wagner should have coincided with the rise of the "Reich": both events are proof of one and the same thing—obedience and long-leggedness.—Never was there greater obedience, never better commanding. Wagnerian conductors in particular are worthy of an age that posterity will one day call, with timid awe, *the classical age of war*. Wagner understood how to command; in this respect, too, he was a great teacher. . . .

EPILOGUE

. . . Modern man represents biologically a *contradiction of values*, he sits between two stools, he says yes and no in the same breath. No wonder that it is
precisely in our age that falseness itself became flesh, became even genius! That
Wagner "dwelt among us"! Not without reason did I call Wagner the Cagliostro
[i.e., the impostor] of modernism... But all of us, whether we know it, will it, or
not, have within our bodies values, words, formulas, morals that are *antagonistic* in their origin—physiologically we are *false*... A *diagnosis of the modern
soul*—where to begin? With a determined incision into this agglomeration of
contradictory instincts, with the suppression of its antagonistic values, with vivi-
section of its most *instructive* case.—To the philosopher the case of Wagner is
a *stroke of luck*. This essay, as anyone may see, was inspired by gratitude.

Friedrich Nietzsche, *The Complete Works*, vol. 8, *The Case of Wagner* . . . , trans. A. M. Ludovici (Edinburgh: Foulis, 1911), 1–11, 13, 34–35, 51. Revised on the basis of Giorgio Colli and Mazzino Montinari,
eds., *Nietzsche Werke: Kritische Gesamtausgabe*, VI/3, *Der Fall Wagner* . . . (Berlin: de Gruyter, 1969),
7–11, 13–15, 16, 32–33, 46–47.

37

VERDI'S *OTELLO*

After the triumph of *Aida* (1871), Verdi seemed to have retired from the operatic stage. The story of how he was gradually lured back by his publisher
Giulio Ricordi (1840–1912) has often been told. The earliest attempts to get
him interested in a new project date from June 1879, when Ricordi paid him
a visit with Boito, who showed him the outline of a libretto he had derived
from Shakespeare's *Othello*. And although the composer and poet were soon
exchanging ideas regarding details of the versification, Verdi did not finally
commit himself to writing the opera until 1884, by which time he had probably composed most of Act I and in any case hammered out with Boito much
of the shape of the libretto as a whole. The following excerpts from their correspondence show them at work on the words for the Act III finale. Otello,
overcome by jealousy as a result of Iago's poisonous insinuations and by now
helplessly out of control, insults Desdemona and violently throws her to the
ground during a solemn state reception. The action will be set in the form of

a grand *concertato*. And almost everything that is proposed in Boito's opening letter and in Verdi's response to it will be incorporated in the final version
of the libretto.

Wednesday [Milan, 24 August 1881]

Dear Maestro,

You must have been thinking that, in addition to my hat, sponge, and brush,
I had forgotten the grand [third-act] finale of *Otello*. Not so. I was pondering
this finale, pondering it; and since it is a rather large morsel, I was not able to
assimilate it into the *bloodstream of the form*, if I may put it that way, and had
no little trouble obtaining the result which by now you already know, and which
is the consequence, I think, of all our conversations at S. Agata.

The ensemble has, as we planned, its lyric and its dramatic elements *fused
together*; that is, it's a lyric, melodious piece beneath which there winds a dramatic dialogue. The principal figure of the lyric side is Desdemona, the principal figure of the dramatic side Iago. Thus Iago, after being momentarily
overwhelmed by an event beyond his control (the letter recalling Otello to
Venice), ties all the threads of the tragedy together again instantly, with match-
less speed and energy, and makes the *catastrophe* his own once more; in fact he
makes use of the unforeseen event to precipitate the final disaster. All this was
in Shakespeare's mind, all this appears clearly in our work. Iago goes from Otello
to Rodrigo, the two instruments left to him for his misdeed, then has the last
word and the last gesture in the act.

Please see whether the two parts, the lyric and the dramatic, seem to you
well fused. See, too, whether the length of each is measured properly. I haven't
stinted with the verses because I remembered your admonishment: *"Say whatever needs to be said, and let everything be explained."* In so saying, you sensed
that the dialogue beneath the lyric piece had to be well developed if it was to
be tragic, and you perceived very well, and I acted accordingly. Indeed, should
you feel that the dialogue between Iago and Rodrigo is somewhat truncated
and not very clear, here are four lines which, if need be, will round it off and
complete it:

IAGO.
A notte folta io la sua traccia vigilo
E il varco e l'ora scruto, il resto a te.
Sarò tua scolta. A caccia, a caccia! Cingiti
L'arco.

RODR.

Sí. T'ho venduto onore e fè.

IAGO.

In deepest night I'll watch his every move,
The path, the time. The rest is up to you.
I'll be your sentry. Up, to the chase! Gird on
Your bow.

RODR.

Yes, I've sold you honor and faith.]

A point needs to be made. The dialogues between Iago and Otello, Iago and Rodrigo follow each other; the former comes first, the latter next. During the Iago-
Otello dialogue, what is Rodrigo doing? Nothing. Yet his voice could contribute
an additional *real part* to the beginning of the vocal ensemble, be a fifth part,
until it is time for his dialogue with Iago. In that case I offer you four lyric verses
that Rodrigo could sing with the others while Otello speaks with Iago and while
the ensemble piece is getting under way:

RODR.

(Per me s'oscura il mondo,
S'annuvola il destin,
L'angelo casto e biondo
Fugge dal mio cammin.)

RODR.

My world grows dark,
My fate overcast,
The chaste blond angel
Abandons my path.]

To this one might say: Since we have concerned ourselves with Rodrigo's
attitude during the Iago-Otello dialogue, why are we not concerned with Otello's
attitude during the Iago-Rodrigo dialogue? No. Otello's pose is predetermined,
mandated by the drama. We have seen him slumped by the table after the words,
"A terra! e piangi!" ["To the ground! And weep!"], and thus slumped he must
continue, not getting up even when talking to Iago for the duration of the whole

COSTUME DESIGN FOR IAGO AT THE PREMIÈRE OF *OTELLO*. *The designer Alfredo Edel has here portrayed Victor Maurel, who created the part in 1887*. Milan, Archivio Storico Ricordi. Used by permission.

ensemble piece. He need neither *speak* nor *sing* while Iago speaks to Rodrigo.
Silent, he looms larger and more terrible, more real. He will only get up to
scream, "Fuggite!" ["Flee from me!"], and then he will collapse to the ground.
That's the right way. So far we are in perfect agreement, I hope. But perhaps
you will point out that Desdemona (being, as I said, the *principal figure in the
lyric side of the piece*) ought to have four more lines than the others. The more
so as her first four lines are not suited for melodic treatment. In that case here
are the four lines that conclude Desdemona's stanza; but to read them, I see, and
also to write them, one needs to turn the page: (!)

DESDEMONA

. . . .

. . . .

. . . .

. . . .

. . . .

. . . .

. . . .

. . . .

Sole sereno e vivido
Che allieti il cielo e il mare,
Tergi le stille amare
Che sparge il mio dolor!

[Bright sun serene,
Joy of the sea and sky,
Dry the bitter tears
Shed by my grief!]

We had agreed that the lyric part of the piece was to be in one meter and
the dialogued part (including the Chorus) in a different meter. That is what I
have done. The *dialogue* is in eleven-syllable lines, which can be split or not, as
you wish; if split, they resolve into pairs of five-syllable lines from top to bottom. You can therefore use one or the other of the two procedures; and I needed
to do it that way, because an eleven-syllable meter, an uninterrupted eleven-
syllable meter prolonged beneath a lyric movement, would perhaps have been
too heavy, a five-syllable meter too light. I didn't like mixing the two meters
visibly [on the page], preferring the device you see; besides, I think the result is
effective.

Now I think I have nothing left to tell you, except to thank you again for the lovely day at S. Agata, which will forever remain in my memory and which increased, dear Maestro, the affection I feel for you.

. . . Please do not spare me, but make me work: when I work for you I am happy.

Yours affectionately,
A. Boito

[Milan, 27 August 1881]

Dear Boito,

I am in Milan and your two letters were forwarded to me from Busseto.— The Finale is good, very very good. What a difference from the first [draft] to this one!

I will add the four lines for Rodrigo.

Maybe the other four for Desdemona won't be necessary.

It's so true that Otello silent is larger and more terrible that I would not let him talk at all during the whole ensemble. It seems to me Iago alone could say, and more briefly, all that needs to be said for the spectator's comprehension without having Otello reply.

IAG.

T'affretta! Il tempo vola! All'opra ergi tua mira! all'opra sola! Io penso a Cassio... L'infame anima ria gli svellerò. Lo giuro. Tu avrai le sue novelle a mezzanotte.

[IAGO

Make haste! Time flies! Set your sights on the task! The task alone! I will take care of Cassio... I will eradicate his infamous wicked soul! I swear it. You shall have his news at midnight.]

(With the verses adjusted, of course.)

After the ensemble and after the words, "Tutti fuggite Otello!" ["All flee Otello!"] it seems to me Otello doesn't speak and scream enough. He is silent during four lines, and it seems to me (speaking from a theatrical point of view) that after [Iago's "Lo assale una malia] Che d'ogni senso il priva" ["(He is subject to fits) that deprive him of all reason"], Otello should yell one or two lines... "Fuggite. Io detesto *voi, me,* il mondo intero..." ["Flee. I detest *you, myself,* the whole world..."].

And it also seems to me one might do without some lines when Otello and Iago are left alone.

[OTELLO]
Fuggirmi io sol non so... Ah l'idra! Signor
Vederli insieme avvinti. Ah maledetto
Pensiero... Sangue Sangue...
       un grido e   Il fazzoletto.
       sviene

[IAGO]
Il mio velen lavora

[VOICES]
·Viva l'eroe di Cipro

[IAGO]
Chi può vietar che questa fronte io prema
Col mio tallone

[VOICES]
       Gloria
Al Leon di Venezia

[IAGO]
       Ecco il Leone!

[OTELLO
Only I cannot flee from myself... Ah, the hydra! Lord,
To see them entwined together. Ah cursed
Thought... Blood Blood...
       a cry and   The handkerchief.
       he faints

IAGO
My poison works

VOICES
Long live the hero of Cyprus

IAGO

Who can prevent me from pressing this forehead
With my heel

VOICES

Glory
To the lion of Venice

IAGO

Here is the lion!]

A choked cry on the word *fazzoletto* seems more terrible to me than a cry on a common exclamation, *Oh Satana*—The words *Svenuto... Immobil... muto...* [*Fainted... Motionless... mute*] stop the action somewhat. One thinks, one reflects, but here it is important to end quickly. Give me your opinion.

I'm not done!! The Chorus does little or nothing. Couldn't some way be found to make it move a little? For ex.: after the words *In Cipro elegge un successor....* [*Elects a successor in Cyprus....*] *Cassio!* Chorus: four lines, maybe not of revolt but of protest... *No No: Noi vogliamo Otello* [*No no: we want Otello*].

I know very well that you will answer at once: "Dear Maestro, don't you know that nobody dared to breathe after a decree of the Most Serene [Venetian Republic]? And that sometimes the mere presence of a notable was enough to disperse and quell an uprising?

I would dare to reply that the action takes place in Cyprus; that the Most Serene [officials] were far away; and maybe for this reason the Cypriots were bolder than the Venetians.

If you happen to come to Milan I hope to see you. I don't know, but I believe you have all the poetry of the third act.

In haste addio addio.

G. Verdi
Hotel Milan

Carteggio Verdi-Boito, ed. M. Medici and M. Conati, with M. Casati (Parma: Istituto di Studi Verdiani, 1978), 58–62. Trans. P.W.

At about the time of the above exchange, Verdi was also corresponding with a friend in Naples, the artist Domenico Morelli (1826–1901), about a picture the composer had proposed he should paint of Iago standing over the inert figure of Otello. The painting was never realized, but the letters the two friends exchanged reveal how the character of Iago was slowly taking shape in Verdi's mind at this very early stage in the composition of the opera.

[Naples, September 1881]

Dear Verdi,

. . . Iago: easier said than done! How to paint him? Now I think I've found him in a type of figure, a certain face, the proportion of his limbs (underdeveloped, I would say); the next moment I feel that this is not our author's character; and I must forget the figure I have been toying with for such a long time and find another.

If Shakespeare had not made him a soldier, or at least hadn't had him say he had been to the wars, I would feel freer to stamp his hypocrisy on his figure and face. But then there is this: the *true* dramatic action of a person contemplating a suffering man with (apparent) solicitude. The more he is a hypocrite, the more his wickedness becomes hidden and invisible; and you know how hard that is in a painting, where everything is visible!

I know very well that when one conceives something correctly, one can paint anything, but there are limits to how justly one can express a given subject conceived by someone else, leave alone when it is our *friend* [Shakespeare], with whom you can't win or even tie. Depart from the model? I wouldn't dare.

Imagine how happy I should be if I could send you a sketch done in *gunpowder*. But now I find another difficulty: I had conceived this scene as taking place in a chamber of the palace, because in Michel's translation it says: *Un appartement dans le château.* And I thought it only right that very sensitive and secret matters be discussed in a secluded place. Absolutely marvelous for my painting! I should have made a picture full of floor, and on the floor I should have laid out Otello. It's terrible to look down from above at a man lying on the floor. On a street pavement he might at first sight seem murdered, fallen, drunk; not in a chamber. Especially not on the floor of a patrician chamber with a colorful carpet, Otello not in Turkish dress, which would be a mistake; let him by all means have an Oriental look, but let him be dressed in the Venetian manner. And he'll look fine in light colors (Moors always choose light, gaudy colors for their clothes, never black). Dressed in black will be Iago, who stands bent over him, in the act of assisting him, chagrined.

But...but...you understand only too well what I am saying. Well, then, I discovered in the English original that the scene is laid *before the castle*, and in the Hugo translation *devant le château.*

What is to be done? In the theater it doesn't matter; the public is used to consider certain changes as necessary to the performance. But in painting the same changes might well be called crude errors. And, quite apart from critics, theaters, and exhibitions, I don't have the courage to fly in the face of William and Mr. Walkley, who first printed the tragedy. Who knows whether in the manuscript the place of the action is indicated specifically? What is your opinion? Yours,

Morelli

S. Agata, 24 September 1881

Dear Morelli,

What is your opinion? I quote from your last letter... My opinion is that if my name were Domenico Morelli and I wished to paint a scene from *Otello*, and more specifically the one in which Otello faints, I shouldn't worry at all over the direction *"Before the castle."* In the libretto Boito has written for me that scene takes place *indoors*, and I am very satisfied with it. *Indoors* or *outdoors* makes little difference. Furthermore, in such matters we needn't be too particular, because in Shakespeare's time recognition of the setting was left up to chance!—Iago dressed in black, black like his soul: nothing could be better. But I don't understand why you would want to dress Otello in the Venetian style! I know very well that this general in the service of the Most Serene [Republic] under the name of Otello was actually one Giacomo Moro, a Venetian [perhaps one Cristoforo Moro, yet the historical basis for the story of Othello is by no means certain]. But since Mr. William wanted a *Moor*, let him, Mr. William, worry about it. Otello dressed as a Turk might not be right; but why not dressed as an Ethiopian without the usual turban? As for Iago's characteristics, the matter is more serious. You would like a body small in stature, with (you say) relatively underdeveloped limbs, and, if I understood correctly, one of those sly, malignant, so to say *pointed* figures. If that is how you conceive him, paint him that way. But if I were an actor and had to play Iago, I should wish to have a rather slender and tall body, thin lips, small eyes close to the nose like monkeys, a high, backward-sloping forehead, and a head well-rounded behind; an absent-minded manner, nonchalant, indifferent to everything, disbelieving, witty, speaking well and ill lightly, with an air of having his thoughts on matters quite different from those he is speaking about; so that, if someone were to take him to task, *"What you are saying, proposing, is an abomination,"* he might answer, *"Really?... I didn't think... Forget about it!..."* That type of person can deceive anybody, up to a point even his wife. A small, malignant figure arouses everybody's suspicion and deceives no one!—*Amen.* You may laugh, as I do, over this whole long chat!... But whether Iago is tall or short, Otello Turkish or Venetian, paint him as you like; it will in any case be good. Only don't spend too much time thinking about it. Go, go, go... hurry... Greetings, also from my wife. Yours affectionately,

[G. Verdi]

Gaetano Cesari and Alessandro Luzio, eds., *I copialettere di Giuseppe Verdi* (Milan: Commissione Esecutiva per le Onoranze a Giuseppe Verdi nel primo centenario della nascita, 1913), 695–96, 317–18. Trans. P.W.

How much thought went into the psychological makeup of the characters in *Otello* is evidenced also by the remarkable introduction to the production book for the opera, published by Ricordi not long after the first performance (1887). The introduction, signed by Boito, is given below in its entirety. It goes without saying that his analysis of the opera's characters reflects Verdi's views as well: the composer approved the publication. (It should be noted that, after paraphrasing Hamlet's speech to the players, Boito misdates the play: c. 1604 would be closer to the mark. Also, in *Othello*'s list of characters, Iago is not identified as a "scoundrel," merely as Othello's "ancient" [ensign].)

CHARACTERS

All theatrical artists, even the very best, ought to have imprinted in their memories the following words, written three centuries ago, which still today are the most perfect and most modern acting lesson ever conceived.

Here is the lesson:

> Repeat this speech as I spoke it, in your natural voice. But if you scream it as many of our actors do, I would as soon have the town crier speak my lines. Do not saw the air with your arms, be sober in your gestures and speech. Even at the very height of the whirlwind of passion you must preserve your composure and be masters of yourselves.
>
> Oh, how it offends me to hear a big fellow tear a passion to tatters and deafen the audience! I would have such a fellow whipped for overdoing everything and out-Heroding Herod.
>
> You must study to make the action suit the word, the word the action. Never falsify nature. Anything overdone departs from the aims of the theater. The theater must be the mirror of nature.
>
> I have seen players, and heard them praised, who had neither the accent nor the gait of Christians or men. They so strutted and bellowed that I thought (not to offend God) that they were an artificial and monstrous imitation of humanity.

These words are by Shakespeare (*Hamlet,* Scene IX [actually, Act III, scene ii]), and three centuries have gone by, not a year more or a year less, since the day they were first spoken in 1588. We have thought it useful to remind theatrical artists of these words before outlining—in bold strokes and very generally, so as to be understood by those who shall read us—the main traits of the characters in *Otello.*

We shall begin with the character who lends his name to the tragedy.

OTELLO

Moor. General of the Venetian Republic. He is past forty. Strong, forthright figure of a soldier. Simple in his bearing and gestures. His command is imperious, his judgment calm: the scene following the first-act duel suffices to reveal those qualities in his nature. That action shows him in all his glory, in all his strength, in all his splendor. His opening words thunder in the storm, they thunder victory; his last words sigh in the kiss, they sigh love. First one sees the hero, later the lover, and one should make evident how great is the hero in order that one may understand how worthy he is of love and of how great a passion he is capable. Later, from that prodigious love, will be born the terrible jealousy brought about by Iago's cunning. Reason and justice guide Otello's actions up to the moment when Iago (who appears to be honest and is so believed) succeeds in dominating him. From that moment (the actor must put all his effort in this), from that moment the whole man is transformed, and it is precisely at Iago's infamous words, in the second act, that this transformation takes place: *And were you to hold my whole soul in your hands, you would not learn it from me!* and Otello cries out and Iago at once adds, *My lord, beware of jealousy.*

Jealousy! The word has been spoken. First Iago has wounded the heart of the Moor, then he has twisted his knife in the wound. Otello's torments have begun. The man is transformed. He was wise and now he raves, he was strong and now grows weak, he was just and upright and now becomes criminal, he was healthy and happy and now he moans and faints like a poisoned man or one struck down by epilepsy. And Iago's words are true poison, injected into the Moor's blood. The fatal progress of that moral poisoning must be expressed in all its horror. Step by step, Otello passes through the most hideous torments of the human heart: doubt, fury, deathly prostration. Otello is the grand victim of the tragedy, he is Iago's grand victim. If the personification of an abstract idea were not a cold, false, puerile, and hackneyed device in the theater, one might maintain that Otello is Jealousy, Iago Envy.

IAGO

Iago is Envy. Iago is a scoundrel. Iago is a critic. Shakespeare, in his list of characters, describes him thus: *Iago, a scoundrel,* not a word more. Iago on the square in Cyprus defines himself thus: *I am nothing if not critical.* He is a spiteful, malevolent critic, he sees the evil in humans, in himself: *I am a scoundrel because I am human;* he sees the evil in nature, in God. He practices evil for evil's sake. He is an artist in fraud. The cause of his hatred of Otello is not very weighty, considering the revenge he exacts for it. Otello has made Cassio captain instead of him. But that cause is enough for him; if it were greater, his wickedness would be less. This cause is all he needs in order to hate the Moor and envy Cassio and act as he does.—Iago is the true author of the drama; he creates its threads, gathers them, combines them, interweaves them.

The grossest error, the most vulgar error an artist might commit in attempting to interpret this part would be to represent him as a mixture of man and demon! To give him a Mephistophelean sneer, a Satanic leer. Such an artist would show he had not understood Shakespeare, or the work under discussion.

Every word Iago speaks is human, wickedly human, but human. He must be young and handsome; Shakespeare makes him twenty-eight years old. Cinzio Giraldi, the author of the novella from which Shakespeare derived his masterpiece, says of Iago: *An ensign of very pleasant aspect, but of the most rascally nature that ever was in man.*

He must be handsome and appear to be jovial and plainspoken and almost genial; he is believed to be honest by everyone but his wife, who knows him well. If there were not something thoroughly engaging about his pleasant appearance and apparent honesty, he could never become as powerful as he is in deceit.

One of his skills is the ability he has to change his aspect depending on the persons with whom he finds himself, in order the better to deceive or dominate them.

Free and easy with Cassio; with Roderigo, ironical; with Otello he appears genial, considerate, devotedly submissive; with Emilia brutal and threatening; obsequious with Desdemona and Ludovico. This is the bottom, this the outward appearance, these are the various aspects of this man.

DESDEMONA

The ladies who will interpret this role are advised not to widen their eyes, not to agitate their bodies and arms, not to take giant steps, not to seek so-called *effects*. If the artist is intelligent and respects art, she will find her effects without seeking them, if not she will seek them without finding them. Face, look, speech: these are the three sources of expression in the actor's art. Except in unusual cases where horror borders on the extreme, an uncontorted face, unglaring eyes, unemphatic speech must be able to express all shades of sorrow and joy. A deep feeling of love, purity, nobility, gentleness, naïveté, resignation must appear in this most chaste and harmonious figure of Desdemona. The simpler and milder her movements, the greater the compassion she will awaken in her audience; the graces of youth and beauty will complete the impression.

EMILIA

Iago's wife. Devoted to Desdemona. She abhors her wicked husband and fears him and suffers his violence and domination; she knows his perverted mind. But in the end she reveals his infamy with all the strength and courage of an oppressed being who rebels.

CASSIO

Captain of the Venetian Republic. Handsome, very young, gay, brilliant, elegant conqueror of women of easy virtue, he is a bit infatuated with his volatile liaisons, a bit vain, but he is a valiant soldier who can defend himself vigorously, his sword in hand. Good fencer, jealous guardian of his honor.

RODERIGO
He is a young Venetian gentleman, rich and elegant, and hopelessly, platonically in love with Desdemona unbeknownst to her. He is an idealist, naïf, a dreamer who allows himself to be let down and dominated by Iago. Iago uses him as a docile, passive tool to realize his scheme.

LODOVICO
Senator of the Venetian Republic. Ambassador to Cyprus. A grave man, even if still young in years. A personage worthy of the high offices to which he has been called. Highly authoritative in his appearance and speech.

MONTANO
Otello's predecessor as governor of Cyprus. A warrior, faithful to his duty, good swordsman, strong soldier, severe commander.

ARRIGO BOITO

Giulio Ricordi, *Disposizione scenica per l'opera OTELLO* . . . (Milan: R. Stabilimento Musicale Ricordi, [1887]), 3–6. Trans. P.W.

INTERLUDE: VERDI AND WAGNER IN VIENNA

Performers, whether vocal or instrumental, love to remember the extraordinary, and sometimes funny, events they experienced in the course of their professional careers. Some publish their memoirs, which usually consist of little else than a series of anecdotes about the famous people they have known. Occasionally, one comes across tidbits that are not to be found anywhere else; the following, from the memoirs of Joseph Sulzer (1850–1926), is a case in point. A son of Salomon Sulzer, the famous Jewish cantor admired by Schubert and Liszt, Joseph was a cellist in the Vienna Philharmonic, its principal from 1880, as well as a member of the Hellmesberger Quartet. As is well known, the Vienna Philharmonic has a double existence: in addition to its activity as a concert orchestra, it plays in the pit of the Vienna Opera during the opera season. Thus Sulzer was in a position to know and witness the activities of virtually all the famous musicians of his time, since sooner or later they all came to Vienna—if they were not already there.

In June 1875 there occurred two sensational performances at the Court Opera; the theater was filled down to the very last seat. This, in the wake of the great stock market crash when all artistic enterprises suffered, was an unusual event, and it was due to the drawing power of Giuseppe Verdi, who on June 11 conducted his Manzoni Requiem and a week later his *Aida*. . . . [The Requiem] was enthusiastically received, and Verdi and his choice singers were fêted with prolonged, frenzied applause and countless curtain calls. . . .

The performance of *Aida* was received with, if possible, even greater enthusiasm. From time to time the public's fanatical applause, strengthened in the hall's upper regions by the stamping of feet, made us think we were in the lower regions of the Inferno, and Verdi's comment on the tumult was, "Bravo! Not even we Italians can make more ado about nothing!"

The rehearsals under Verdi were extremely interesting. He made use of his mother tongue, was of course fully understood by the Italian singers, half understood by our native Bigno, but not at all understood by Signor Hablawetz, which caused several amusing misunderstandings. Verdi's youthful impetuousness was shown by the following incident. In a passage in Act IV, the backstage music was out of step with the orchestra, a situation caused by the backstage conductor's inability to see Verdi's beat very clearly, since the opening made for that purpose in the scenery was not big enough. Without a moment's hesitation Verdi climbed up from the pit onto the stage, widened the aforesaid opening with his penknife, and the contact between the two orchestras was immediately restored.

Verdi's outward appearance is well known from his numerous portraits. But none of those pictures can convey the expression in his big, dark eyes, which had such a pleasant effect on everyone and led one to guess at the rich qualities of heart and mind that were his.

In 1875, not only could the opera boast a sensational success with the presence of Verdi, but the Musikvereinsaal too could boast one, for there, on March 1 and 15, some great musical performances took place under the direction of Richard Wagner. It is surely unnecessary to say that the attendance at these highly interesting events was enormous and that the great master was cheered and acclaimed. At these performances Wagner's "Kaisermarsch" and excerpts from *Tristan und Isolde* and *Der Ring des Nibelungen* were heard for the first time in Vienna. . . .

The court opera distinguished itself that same season with brilliant and exceptional presentations, the most interesting being the performance of Wagner's

Lohengrin under the master's personal direction. The memory of that exemplary performance and the rehearsal that preceded it is precious to me, since I was so lucky as to experience the powerful impact of that immortal man's fascinating personality at close quarters for many hours and to see the wonderful effects of his incredibly brilliant leadership.

Wagner did not by any means handle the conductor's baton like a professional conductor. At times the master conducted with rhythm and precision, but then there were other moments when, fatigued or absorbed, he conducted nonchalantly or—not at all. A fatal confusion would have ensued, had not a *deus ex machina* in the person of [the great conductor] Hans Richter intervened at such moments and saved the situation. For Richter, foreseeing such a calamity, had honored the master by assuming the duties of the timpanist and, unbeknownst to Wagner, conducting from that position with his drumsticks.

Unusually instructive and highly interesting were Wagner's professional witticisms during the rehearsal of *Lohengrin*. Among other things, he asked the cymbalist not to play "tschinn" in bar 54 of the Prelude, but rather "tschi—i—i—n" (let them ring).

Joseph Sulzer, *Ernstes und Heiteres aus den Erinnerungen eines Wiener Philharmonikers* (Vienna: J. Eisenstein & Co., 1910), 24–27. Trans. P.W.

38

VERISMO

Verismo was the Italian version of realism, the literary movement espoused by such novelists as the brothers Goncourt and Émile Zola in France. 1870 had marked the end of an era for both countries: the Italians, having gained Rome as their capital, were now faced with the prosaic task of running a new nation beset with internal problems; and the French were painfully engaged in a similar endeavor after their disastrous defeat by the Prussians. In Italy as in France, the age of romantic dreaming and heroics was over. Literature was experimenting with sterner tasks: following the lead of the natural sciences, the realists sought to record their unadorned observations of human society, eliminating themselves from the picture altogether and letting the "objective" representation of facts speak for itself. The portrayal of social inequities, of the suffering of the working classes and the poor, had an explicit reformist motivation for the French writers. To Italians like Giovanni Verga (1840–1922), the most important exponent of *verismo*, the "scientific" observation of reality was an end in itself; the task of literature was simply to portray society as it was, impersonally, impassively. Literature could not change it. The poor and the uneducated presented a richer ground for observation, that was all: their language was simpler, their behavior more truly expressive of their inner emotional life. Verga turned to his native Sicily as the locale for the works of his maturity. His "Cavalleria rusticana," the short story presented below in its entirety in a masterly translation by D. H. Lawrence, appeared in 1880; its title, "Rustic Chivalry," refers to the honor code broken in the story, and to the inevitable expiation. Verga later transformed the story into a one-act play, expanding and altering it considerably. The main change occurred in the character of Santuzza (the Santa of the story), who now became a more important, more pathetic figure; the part was created by the great Eleonora Duse, and the première (Turin, 1884) was a great success. Even more successful was the one-act opera by Mascagni based on Verga's play; first performed in Rome on 17 May 1890, it has never left the stage since. With it, *verismo* briefly entered operatic history. Leoncavallo's *I pagliacci* (1892), written in direct imitation of Mascagni's work and usually paired with it in performance, is the other durable veristic opera. Though not a lasting phenomenon, *verismo* represented a startling departure in the subject matter of opera.

CAVALLERIA RUSTICANA

Turiddu Macca, son of old Mother Nunzia, when he came home from being a soldier, went swaggering about the village square every Sunday, showing himself off in his *bersagliere's* uniform with the red fez cap, till you'd have thought it was the fortune-teller himself come to set up his stall with the cage of canaries. The girls going to Mass with their noses meekly inside their kerchiefs stole such looks at him, and the youngsters buzzed round him like flies. And he'd brought home a pipe with the king on horseback on the bowl, simply life-like, and when he struck a match on his trousers behind, he lifted his leg up as if he was going to give you a kick.

But for all that, Lola, Farmer Angelo's daughter, never showed a sign of herself, neither at Mass nor on her balcony; for the simple reason that she'd gone and got herself engaged to a fellow from Licodia, a carter who took contracts, and had four handsome Sortino mules of his own in his stable.

When Turiddu first got to hear of it, oh, the devil! he raved and swore!—
he'd rip his guts out for him, he'd rip 'em out for him, that Licodia fellow!—
But he never did a thing, except go and sing every slighting song he could think
of under the beauty's window.

"Has Mother Nunzia's Turiddu got nothing else to do but sing songs like a
forlorn sparrow, every mortal night?" said the neighbours.

However, he ran into Lola at last, as she was coming back from her little
pilgrimage to Our Lady of Peril; and she, when she saw him, never turned a
hair, as if it was nothing to do with *her*.

"It's rare to set eyes on you!" he said to her.

"Hello, Turiddu! They told me you'd come back on the first of this month."

"They told me more than that!" he replied. "Is it right as you're marrying
Alfio, as contracts for carting?"

"God willing, I am," replied Lola, twisting the corners of her kerchief at her
chin.

"There's a lot o' God willing about it! You suit your own fancy! And it was
God willing as I should come home from as far as I did, to hear this nice bit of
news, was it, Lola?"

The poor man tried to keep a good face, but his voice had gone husky; and
he walked on at the heels of the girl, the tassel of his fez cap swinging melancholy to and fro, on his shoulders. And to tell the truth, she was sorry to see
him with such a long face; but she hadn't the heart to cheer him up with false
promises.

"Look here, Turiddu," she said at last to him, "let me go on and join the
others. What do you think folks'll say if they see me with you?"

"You're right!" replied Turiddu. "Now you're going to marry that chap Alfio, as has got four mules of his own in his stable, it'd never do to set folks talking! Not like my poor old mother, as had to sell our bay mule and the bit of
vineyard, while I was away soldiering.—Ah well, the time's gone by when Bertha
sat a-spinning!—And you've forgotten how we used to talk together at the window in the yard, and how you gave me that handkerchief before I went away—
God knows how many tears I cried in it, going that far off, I'd almost forgotten
even the name of where I came from.—Well, good-bye, then, Lola. *It showered
a while, and then left off, and all was over between us!*"

And so Miss Lola married the carter; and the Sunday after, there she sat on
her balcony, with her hands spread on her stomach to show all the great gold
rings her husband had given her. Turiddu kept going back and forth, back and
forth up the narrow street, his pipe in his mouth and his hands in his pockets,
to show he didn't care, and ogling all the girls. But it gnawed him inside himself to think that Lola's husband should have all that gold, and that she pretended not to notice him, when he passed.

"I'll show that bitch summat, afore I've done!" he muttered to himself.

Across from Alfio's house lived Farmer Cola, the wine-grower, who was as rich as a pig, so they said, and who had a daughter on his hands. Turiddu so managed it that he got Farmer Cola to take him on, helping in the vines, and then he started hanging round the house, saying nice things to the girl.

"Why don't you go and say all those sweet nothings to Mrs. Lola, over the road?" Santa replied to him.

"Mrs. Lola thinks she's somebody. Mrs. Lola's married my Lord Tom-noddy, she has!"

"And I'm not good enough for a Lord Tom-noddy, am I?"

"Your're worth twenty Lolas. And I know somebody as wouldn't look at Mrs. Lola, nor at the saint she's named after, if you was by. Mrs. Lola's not fit to bring you your shoes, she's not."

"Ah là! it's sour grapes, as the fox said when he couldn't reach—"

"No, he didn't! He said: 'Ah, but *you're* sweet, my little gooseberry!'"

"Eh! Keep your hands to yourself, Turiddu!"

"Are you afraid I shall eat you?"

"I'm neither afraid of you nor your Maker."

"Eh! your mother was a Licodia woman, we know it! You've got a temper right enough. Oh! I could eat you with my eyes!"

"Eat me with your eyes, then; we shall make no crumbs! But while you're at it, lift me that bundle of kindling."

"I'd lift the whole house up for you, that I would."

She, to hide her blushes, threw a stick at him which she'd got in her hand, and for a wonder missed him.

"Let's look sharp! We shall bind no kindling with nothing but talk."

"If I was rich, I should look for a wife like you, Miss Santa."

"Eh well! I shan't marry my Lord Tom-noddy, like Mrs. Lola, but I shan't come empty-handed neither, when the Lord sends me the right man."

"Oh ay! we know you're rich enough, we know that."

"If you know it, then hurry up; my Dad'll be here directly, and I don't want him to catch me in the yard."

Her father began by making a wry face, but the girl pretended not to notice. The tassel of the *bersagliere's* cap had touched her heart, swinging in front of her eyes all the time. When her father put Turiddu out of the door, she opened the window to him, and stood there chattering to him all the evening, till the whole neighbourhood was talking about nothing else.

"I'm crazy about you," Turiddu said. "I can neither eat nor sleep."

"You say so—"

"I wish I was Victor Emmanuel's son, so I could marry you."

"You say so—"

"Oh, Madonna, I could eat you like bread!"

"You say so—"

"Ah, I tell you it's true!"

"Eh, mother, mother!"

Night after night Lola listened, hidden behind a pot of sweet basil in her window, and going hot and cold by turns. One day she called to him:

"So that's how it is, Turiddu! Old friends don't speak to one another any more!"

"Why!" sighed the youth. "It's a lucky chap as can get a word with you."

"If you want to speak to me, you know where I live," replied Lola.

Turiddu went so often to speak to her, that Santa was bound to notice it, and she slammed the window in his face. The neighbours nodded to one another, with a smile, when the *bersagliere* went by. Lola's husband was away, going round from fair to fair, with his mules.

"I mean to go to confession on Sunday. I dreamed of black grapes last night," said Lola.

"Oh, not yet, not yet!" Turiddu pleaded.

"Yes. Now it's getting near Easter, my husband will want to know why I've not been to confession."

"Ah!" murmured Farmer Cola's Santa, waiting on her knees for her turn in front of the confessional, where Lola was having a great washing of her sins: "It's not Rome I'd send you to for a penance, it isn't, my word it isn't!"

Master Alfio came home with his mules, and a good load of cash, and brought a fine new dress as a present to his wife, for the festival.

"You do well to bring her presents," his neighbour Santa said to him. "She's been adorning your house for you, while you've been away."

Master Alfio was one of those carters who go swaggering with their cap over their ear; so when he heard his wife spoken of in that way, he went white as if he'd been stabbed.

"By God, though!" he exclaimed. "If you've seen more than there was to see, I won't leave you your eyes to cry with, neither you nor the rest of your folks."

"I'm not the crying sort," replied Santa. "I didn't cry even when I saw with my own eyes Mother Nunzia's Turiddu creeping into your wife's house at night."

"All right!" replied Alfio. "I'm much obliged!"

Now that the cat had come back, Turiddu no longer hung round the little street in the daytime, but whiled away his chagrin at the inn, with his friends; and on the Saturday evening before Easter they had a dish of sausages on the table. When Master Alfio came in, Turiddu knew in an instant, from the way he fixed his eyes on him, what he'd come for, and he put his fork down on his plate.

"Did you want me for anything, Alfio?" he said.

"Nothing particular, Turiddu. It's quite a while since I've seen you, and I thought I'd have a word with you—you know what about."

At first Turiddu had offered him his glass, but Alfio put it aside with his hand. Then Turiddu rose, and said:

"Right you are, Alfio!"

The carter threw his arms round his neck.

"Shall you come to the cactus grove at Canziria tomorrow morning, and we can talk about that bit of business of ours, boy?"

"Wait for me on the high-road at sunrise, and we'll go together."

With these words, they exchanged the kiss of challenge; and Turiddu nipped the carter's ear between his teeth, thus promising solemnly not to fail him.

His friends had all quietly abandoned the sausages, and they walked with Turiddu home. Mother Nunzia, poor thing, sat up waiting for him till late every evening.

"Mother," Turiddu said to her, "you remember when I went for a soldier, you thought I should never come back? Now kiss me like you did then, because I'm going off in the morning, a long way."

Before daybreak he took his clasp-knife, which he had hidden under the hay when he was taken off as a conscript to the army, and then he set out for the cactus grove at Canziria.

"Oh Jesu-Maria! where are you going in such a fury?" whimpered Lola in dismay, as her husband was getting ready to go out.

"I'm not going far," replied Master Alfio. "And better for you if I never came back."

Lola, in her night-dress, kneeled praying at the foot of the bed, pressing to her lips the rosary which Fra Bernardino had brought from the Holy Land, and repeating all the *Ave Marias* there were to repeat.

"You see, Alfio," Turiddu began, after he had walked for some distance along the road beside his silent companion, who had his cap pulled down over his eyes, "as true as God's above, I know I'm in the wrong, and I would let myself be killed. But my old mother got up before I started out, pretending she had to see to the fowls, and I could tell she knew. So as sure as God's above, I'm going to kill you like a dog, so the poor woman shan't have to cry her eyes out."

"All right, then," replied Alfio, pulling off his sleeved waistcoat. "Now we shall strike hard, both of us."

They were both good fighters with the knife. Alfio struck the first thrust, and Turiddu was quick enough to catch it on his arm. When he gave it back, he gave a good one, aiming at the groin.

"Ah! Turiddu. Do you really mean to kill me?"

"Yes, I told you! Since I saw my old woman with the fowls, I can't get her out of my eyes."

"Then open your eyes, then!" Alfio shouted at him; "I'll give you more than you asked for."

And as the carter stood on guard, doubled up so as to keep his left hand over his wound, which hurt him, his elbow almost brushing the ground, suddenly he seized a handful of dust and threw it full in the enemy's eyes.

"Ah!" screamed Turiddu, blinded. "I'm done!"

He tried to save himself by jumping desperately backwards, but Alfio caught him up with another stab in the stomach, and a third in the throat. "—and three! That's for the house which you adorned for me! And now your mother can mind her fowls—"

Turiddu reeled about for a moment or two here and there among the cactuses, then fell like a stone. The blood gurgled frothing from his throat, and he couldn't even gasp: Oh, Mother!

Giovanni Verga, *Cavalleria Rusticana and Other Stories*, trans. D. H. Lawrence (New York: The Dial Press, 1928), 37–50.

39

FOUR MEN AT WORK ON *LA BOHÈME*

Just as there are four principals—Rodolfo, Marcello, Schaunard, Colline—in Puccini's *La bohème*, so there were four principals in its creation: the professional librettist Luigi Illica (1857–1919), the playwright and man of letters Giuseppe Giacosa (1847–1906), the publisher Giulio Ricordi (1840–1912), so prominent in the genesis of Verdi's *Otello* (see p. 230f above), and of course the composer himself, Giacomo Puccini (1858–1924). Ricordi served as a sort of court of appeals during the sometimes heated squabbles concerning the ultimate shape this opera, based on Henry Murger's *Scènes de la vie de bohème* (1851), was to assume. Illica undertook the drafting of the scenario, with important interventions by Puccini. Giacosa took care of the versification and the smaller details, putting on the final touches, though in one of the letters below he is heard complaining that none of his touches ever seemed to be final. Between the first mention of the opera in 1893 (in connection with a dispute that arose between Puccini and Leoncavallo, who was also at work on the same subject) and its first performance under Toscanini in Turin on 1 February 1896, the correspondence between the two librettists, the publisher, and the composer flowed thick and fast. In it, the opera is seen taking shape amid bursts of inspiration, drastic changes of direction, fits of anger, and heartfelt reconciliations, as befitted the creators of a work in which the main characters behaved in much the same way. The only detached participant here was Ricordi; but then, he could afford to be above the fray: though a composer himself, he was a shrewd businessman, hence a realist, and besides he was older than the rest. In our selection from the fifty or so pages this exchange occupies in the published source, we begin with a bitter complaint addressed by Illica to Ricordi:

[Milan, February 1894]

Dear Signor Giulio,

Puccini has gone off and I meanwhile, from my bed where I'm nailed down by a stubborn influenza, am writing you . . . about—what else? *La bohème.*

And so Puccini doesn't like at all the solution we found Sunday evening. He wants to begin [the last act] the way it is fixed in his head, with Mimì in bed, Rodolfo at his table writing, and the stub of a candle lighting the scene.

That is, no separation between Rodolfo and Mimì!

Well then, in that case there's really no *Bohème* left at all, and what's more, no Mimì by Murger!

What we have is a meeting in a garret between a journalist-poet and a little seamstress. They love each other, quarrel, then the little seamstress dies...

The case is pitiful, but it isn't *La bohème*! The love element is moving (and romantic), but Murger's Mimì is more complex! One should also have some pity for the librettists!

Now I say that it's already wrong that the separation between Rodolfo and Mimì should not occur in full view of the public; imagine if there is not to be any separation at all! Because the essence of Murger's book is precisely that great freedom in love (supreme characteristic of *La bohème*) practiced by all the characters. Think how much greater and more moving Mimì can be when—though she could go on living with a lover who furnishes her with silk and velvet—feeling that her phthisis is killing her she goes to die in the desolate, cold mansard, just so she can die in the arms of Rodolfo. It seems inconceivable to me that Puccini should not understand the greatness [of this situation]!

Yet this is Murger's Mimì!

And note (to me it seems almost inspired) how novel it would be to begin the last act exactly the way the first began. Only now it isn't winter but autumn. From the wide window one doesn't see all the roofs of Paris covered with snow, but Rodolfo gathers a leaf brought in by the wind and his thoughts return to Mimì.

One could begin with Rodolfo alone—and meanwhile apprise the public of the separation—that very necessary separation!! (Up to now we haven't had a solo for the tenor!)

In the whole drama our bohemians do nothing but eat well and drink even better: here we might show them to the public engaged in sharing a herring four ways and finding in it a hundred different flavors.

In the end, if we want to, there's the possibility of completing the libretto and healing the great wound it suffered when the "courtyard" scene was cut.

But at this point, it seems to me you should take our side rather than Puccini's.

Believe me, the newspapers will be exceedingly severe. They will say there was no need of two of us to write a libretto—or rather—extract an incomplete libretto from a book.

This way, instead, while leaving Giacosa the greatest latitude and freedom, everything will be repaired; what is more, this last act will be powerfully moving and poetic.

And so—as we agreed on Sunday—we too shall be able to breathe a little. For if we were to remove the "courtyard" and replace it with "nothing," it would be too little.

Forgive all this chitchat, but Puccini can be frightening... Unfortunately (it must be confessed!) you usually side with him!

But the truth must out, and the culprits are always Giacosa and yours truly.

A "courtyard" scene had indeed been cut, and much of what Illica suggested here—the separation of the two lovers, the opening of Act IV resembling the opening of Act I, even the shared herring—found its way into the final version. Some five months later, it was Puccini's turn to complain to Ricordi. The subjects here are the "Latin Quarter" and "Barrière d'Enfer" acts, the latter of which proved to be, despite Puccini's misgivings, a rich source of musical inspiration to him. It is interesting to note that it was the composer who shaped the Musetta episode in the "Latin Quarter" act.

Milan, 21 July 1894

My dear signor Giulio,

I shall be in your study Tuesday morning at 10. Illica's irritation surprises me and I find it odd. When he came here we agreed perfectly . . . and he deplored that I wasn't composing *La bohème* and said he would always be ready to support me in every way. Now that I have come back to him, he amuses himself by giving himself airs, and then if he says I put it aside, whose fault was it? Had the work been as it should have been, that is, logical, compact, interesting, and well balanced, that would have been enough. But it was nothing of the sort so far. Must I blindly accept the gospel according to Illica? I'll take no enemas, thank you, I'm too experienced for that. Now I begin to see *La bohème*, but only with the "Latin Quarter" the way I described it during my last conference with Illica, with Musetta's scene, which *I* thought up: and the death I will have the way I conceived it, and then I'm sure I shall produce an original and vital work. As for the "Barrière," I remain of the same opinion, namely, that I don't much like it. I see in it an act where there's little music: only the comedy flows, but it's not much. I should have wished for some further melodramatic elements; we shouldn't forget that we have plenty of comedy in the other acts. In this one I wanted a scenario that would let me range freely in a somewhat more lyrical vein... Enough, let Signor Illica calm down and we'll do the job; but I occasionally want to speak my piece too, and not be ordered about.

Meanwhile, my cordial greetings, and see you on Tuesday.

Scarcely two weeks later, Puccini seemed utterly at peace with his librettist:

Torre del Lago, 3 August 1894

Dear Illica,

How glad I am of the news you give me! I saw you were fired with enthusiasm and never doubted it would be a masterpiece!

I'm working. I hope to get some material in a fortnight. Can you send me the "[Latin] Quarter" by then? Musetta I shall treat in a *pastoral* way as you suggest. Excellent the Alcidoro, etc. Good too Schaunard's toast, and I'm also very pleased with the Musetta business; that way I have a *complete* character, also musically.

I have full confidence in you and believe this libretto will turn out a masterpiece of humor and emotion. The definition of love you added to the opening scene is wonderful and novel: "L'amore è un caminetto che sciupa troppo" ["Love is a chimney that uses too much fuel"], etc. Keep it up.

In the next letter, to Ricordi, Puccini shows exactly what he conceived Giacosa's role to be in the collaboration:

Torre del Lago, 7 September 1894

My dear signor Giulio,

You will have seen Illica. Now I'm waiting for the cuts and the revision by Giacosa (absolutely necessary, also for the sake of the work's unity, and then, when duly pondered, the libretto acquires etc. etc). Now the original work is there! Very much so! The last act is splendid. The "[Latin] Quarter" too, but very difficult; I had that acrobat removed, and it will be necessary to prune other things. It would be good if you too were to look it over, to purge it of some bizarre things that are really not needed. For ex.: The horse is the king of the animals, rivers are wines made of water, and many more that Illica dotes on as if they were his children (if he had any). What needs to be shortened a great deal is act 2, the "Barrière" [which became act 3]: all that stuff at the beginning is useless, and we have agreed to tighten it, as well as all the rest, and the final quartet: but this is the weak act. That is my opinion, I could be wrong! so much the better for me. But what I think has succeeded very well indeed is the last: the death and all that happens before it are *truly moving*.

At this time Ricordi was in Paris with Verdi and Boito, getting ready the pre-mière of *Otello* in French at the Opéra. His response to Puccini's letter is there-fore also interesting for its information on the older composer, his rehearsal methods, and his personal interest in Puccini.

Paris, 29 September 1894

My dear, good Puccini,

You can't believe how pleased I was to receive here a letter from you; we are working like slaves!!... I haven't the time to breathe!... Suffice it to say that yesterday I had not the time to have lunch and didn't eat till half past 6 in the evening... Verdi, who will be 81 years old in a few days, has grown younger since last spring! Yesterday he had the gumption to order, be present at, and di-rect the following rehearsals: 12 o'clock: detailed study, choruses—from 1 to 2: conductor of the orchestra—from 2 to 2:30: rehearsal of the ballet—from 2:30 to 5:30: piano rehearsal with soloists, acts 3 and 4!! I must say! . . .

By the way, on Tuesday 9 October Verdi will be 81 years old: if you wish to telegraph him a word of good wishes, I'm sure he will greatly appreciate it, since, despite his many occupations, he has twice already spoken to me about you, what are you doing, etc. etc.

And now that I've given you my news, let us speak about us.

I see you first want Giacosa's revision!... Alas!... It will greatly draw out the proceedings, and I don't know when you will hold in your hands enough mate-rial to work on without having to resort to mosaic work. But I immediately wrote to Milan, urging great haste. If you like you can also write directly to Tito [Ri-cordi, Giulio's son], since if Giacosa should be in Milan, so much the better, we would save time. The more I think about it, the more I like *Bohème*!

To be sure, in my modest opinion, the 2nd [now 3rd] "Latin Quarter" act is an arduous enterprise, because it's hard to give the whole scene a sprightly form, keep things flowing, not leave any holes through which cold air might blow, creating voids. But Puccini has sturdy shoulders, strong lungs!! After all, is he, or is he not, the Doge [his nickname among the collaborators on the opera]? No verses in French: let Giacosa translate them in such a way that, if necessary, also the French meter can be adapted to the music. Let me hear from you again. And the Rodolfo-Mimì duet? finished?... Are you satisfied?... And the hunt?... Paris?... very beautiful! But I can't wait to leave.

P.S. And the Great Kaiser-Leon-Cavallo is he doing it, or isn't he? I mean *La bohème* of course.

"The hunt" was a reference to Puccini's well-known passion for that sport. Leoncavallo's *Bohème*, published by Ricordi's rival Sonzogno, had its première one year after Puccini's; and though it survived for a while side by side with the latter, it eventually disappeared from the stage. It is time now to hear from the fourth collaborator, Giacosa:

Milan, 25 June 1895

Dear Giulio,

I have completed, and I think very satisfactorily, the "Barrière" act. You tell me you want the 4th and final act by Saturday. How can I, with my house upside down because of the move? I must leave the apartment vacant by the 30th of this month: you can imagine there's not a piece of furniture left in place today.

I must confess to you that I'm exhausted by this continuous redoing, retouching, adding, correcting, cutting, sticking back together, expanding here in order to shrink there. Were it not for my great friendship towards you and my affection for Puccini, I should by now have freed myself, for better or for worse. That blessed libretto—why, I have rewritten it for you *three times*, and some pieces four or five times. How can I keep going at such a pace? You have, out of kindness, assigned me an increase of 200 lire, but I beg you to reflect that, after I handed in the completed last act, I was obliged to go back to work at a highly detailed, arid task, spending three or four, and often even five hours a day at it. In the time devoted to this patchwork I could easily have written four articles for the "Nuova antologia," for which I get paid 300 lire per printed sheet. It's not a fortune! But still you ought to realize how absolute and urgent is my need to attend to other tasks as well, in order to make a living!

I swear to you that I'll never again be caught writing librettos. Meanwhile, as I say, the "Barrière" act is completed. I'll bring it to you this evening. See to it that Puccini is there too. As for the last act, I'll try to satisfy you, but I don't have a home. I would work at the Society [of Authors], but there I get disturbed every minute. Then, too, I need to be at home packing and supervising the workers. But I won't be leaving Milan till the end of July. Sunday I'll put my things in storage, pack off my family, and go settle down in some quiet hotel all by myself. And there, not having the family around, which after all are always a cause of distraction, there in a few days I will be done. But will it be done? Or will we need to start all over again?

Till this evening.

The time eventually came for putting the new opera in rehearsal. About a month before the première we find Puccini in Turin, and his letters to Illica are mostly very short, reflecting the hectic pace of those final weeks.

Turin, 6 January 1896

Dear Illica,

I found Toscanini very obliging indeed. I've received your kind letter: the article is fine, but we need to talk. For the moment your presence is not needed, we're only at the beginning. I'm waiting for [the tenor] Gorga in order to make some decisions. Yesterday (in the morning) I thought it a good idea to go see Signor Giulio and tell him everything! The baritone is vile!... The others (except Colline, whom I haven't yet heard) are all right. Write to me soon.

Turin, 10 January 1896

Dear Illica,

This Marcello simply will not do. He understands nothing and won't succeed even with as many rehearsals as they have at Bayreuth. La Ferrari excellent, excellent the Musetta, excellent Pini-Corsi and Polonini. The tenor has arrived but he is always sick. I'll hear him again tomorrow and I'll report to you. As for Colline, still no word. They tell me the part will be taken by a bass from *Götterdämmerung*, but I think he has a hard, unsuitable voice.

To sum up, we're behind and incomplete. I'll wait, then blow my top.

Illica now joined Puccini in Turin and from there reported to Ricordi, who responded:

Milan, 23 January 1896

My dear Illica,

I thank you for your letters, which portray the situation with your usual humor. It seems to me there is a lack of understanding as to the patience you need to produce an opera like *La bohème*. As I telegraphed to you, Verdi and Boito, with the undersigned as assistant, held 23 detailed staging rehearsals with the soloists, asking them (*patiently* and *courteously*) to do segments of scenes over and over again, always *without singing*! For throats are not made of tempered steel, and once the vocal cords are tired, we're done for!

I shall come on Sunday, as I promised, so that on Monday we can have two good rehearsals: impossible for me to come sooner, given my business engagements. And so we'll dine together on Sunday, with the Doge.

The first performance (on 1 February) was a popular success. The reviews were mixed, and it is interesting to note how little Ricordi was affected by this. His response to Illica's report on the press was mailed from Rome, where the next staging of *La bohème* was already in progress.

Rome, 12 February 1896

My dear Illica,

. . . I'm not the least upset about what you tell me concerning the reviews of *La bohème*: it only reinforces my conviction that it is a novel, bold work of art, and therefore subject to discussion and even lack of understanding, I mean by the intellectuals, who can never be truly dispassionate, whereas the public enjoys it and is moved!

Eugenio Gara, ed., *Carteggi pucciniani* (Milan: Ricordi, 1958), 99–100, 104–105, 107, 110, 111–12, 114–15, 137–38, 138–39, 140. Trans. P.W.

40

PELLÉAS ET MÉLISANDE

Maurice Maeterlinck's play *Pelléas et Mélisande* was first performed on 17 May 1893 by a recently formed company called La Maison de l'Œuvre, which set itself the task of presenting avant-garde drama to the Parisian public. The company's stage manager was Camille Mauclair, a young critic and poet who took an active part in promoting the play in the weeks before its première. In the following letter to a theater critic for the paper *Gil Blas*, Mauclair described the visual characteristics of this first production. They must have impressed Debussy, who had read *Pelléas* (it had been published a year earlier) and can hardly have failed to appreciate its vaporous realization onstage when he attended the first performance. It was Mauclair, later that year, who obtained Maeterlinck's permission for Debussy to set the play to music.

Dear Lacour,

Here, succinctly, are some ways of regarding the scenic apparatus I was telling you about apropos *Pelléas*. Its basic principle is this: instead of the drama being set within *real* scenery and props, it is to be surrounded by a sort of symphony of lines and colors that harmonize with the play and its general feeling. I take this as my starting point: that the furnishings, details, trompe l'oeil, painted mirrors, etc. with which scenery is generally encumbered are not only ugly and incomplete, unstable by nature and bric-à-brac, but utterly useless as well, since here the plot no longer unfolds in a salon among fashionable people of our day. An all-encompassing drama—and by that I mean a work with wide significance and not subject to the times, but generally rich and passionate in human sentiment—a drama like Ibsen's *The Lady from the Sea* or *Ghosts*, like all of Shakespeare, and finally like Maeterlinck's *L'Intruse* or *Pelléas*, such a drama can only be weighted down by a production à la Sardou [the author of *Tosca*] or furnishings, which nobody notices and which themselves never matter. The scenery mustn't distract the public's attention to the drama; yet it must be there, in order not to leave the stage empty. Well then, what must we do? We must discover the meaning of the work and set it plastically within an appropriate frame.

Here then, briefly, you have what seems logical to me, not to mention that it is infinitely more practical and manageable than the usual aria of furnishings which always seem like temporary camps when the scene changes from one act to the next. Then, too, the multitude of scene changes in Shakespeare, for example, makes all ornamental trappings impossible. What, do you think anyone has ever noticed the scenery in *Hamlet*? It takes place three quarters of the time in the dark and only the rest of the time, that's all, in the light. The 2nd act of [Daudet's] *L'Arlésienne*, where the sun plays the leading role, is ridiculous onstage, because everything is there except the sun. And we'll never go see the furniture in *The Lady from the Sea*—where the sea is the backdrop! You need a mundane play for that to be of interest; where you have a drama, utmost simplicity works best.

For *Pelléas*, therefore, I have designed, and had my friend the painter Vogler establish, a scene with borders and frames (supporting, sliding), very movable, of large, vague foliage. A simple mechanism permits one to modify the proscenium according to the stage directions (*Pelléas* is all in half-light with changes of locale—night, park, grotto, fountain, or palace rooms). The scenery is harmonized in very dark blue, bluish gray, dark orange, moss green, sea green; and the actors' costumes, which I have also designed, after old Flemish engravings in fairy tales of no specific period, the costumes harmonize with the scenery in a scheme ranging from black, brown, gray, mauve, hyacinth, moonlit green all the way to the creamy brown of Mélisande's costume. All of it discreet, the material supple crepe in a gamut of subdued nuances, the whole play being in very frail and fading nuances (the action can be placed in a vague 11th century).

Here, then, is a symphony of old-tapestry tones in harmony with the play: that is what I have tried to do, thus avoiding the needless embarrassment of following the multitude of little, short scenes in the Maeterlinck with artificial foliage or horrible gilded panels. Do you grasp the idea through this gibberish of mine? I think with this you will be able to write an article, present the thing as a curiosity of the dramatic art, the more so as, you know, this is the décor of

PELLÉAS ET MÉLISANDE. *Lithograph by Maurice Denis for the program at the first perfor-mances of Maeterlinck's play in 1893. Mélisande is seen against a flat background showing the lovers embracing as Golaud advances with his sword.*

the future. I really feel people don't care a hang for the latest-style furniture and real chickens onstage: we will move on to a more intelligent practice!

You will, won't you my dear Lacour, find something to talk about in this long letter? I think I've included 2 or 3 sentences expressive enough so that, if you reread them, you'll be able to supply all that I have left out.

> A cordial handshake.
> Camille Mauclair

Write the article within 8 days! It's coming up, you know...

François Lesure, "La longue attente de *Pelléas* (1895–1898)," *Cahiers Debussy* 15 (1991): 3–4. Trans. P.W.

Maeterlinck was at the height of his fame, and the new play (it was his fifth) did not disappoint. The story of Debussy's meeting with the author and the vicissitudes of their relationship as the play was transformed into an opera are familiar. After many delays in the course of its composition, Debussy's *Pelléas* had its première at the Opéra-Comique on 30 April 1902. An interview with the composer earlier that month appeared in the April number of the *Revue d'histoire et de critique musicale*. It seems quite accurate in reporting Debussy's feelings and attitudes. A certain belligerence is noticeable, typical of the symbolist milieu to which Debussy (and also Mauclair) belonged: if the romantics had rebelled against classicism, the symbolists in turn were rebelling against the romantics. Simplicity appeared now as the new ideal, and it is no surprise, towards the end of the interview, to find the spirit of Mozart being invoked by Debussy.

ON THE EVE OF "PELLÉAS ET MÉLISANDE"

In visiting M. Claude Debussy, the composer of *Pelléas et Mélisande*, I had no intention of asking him indiscreet questions about his opera. Such "revelations" before a première usually reveal nothing, for the author would rather that the critic at the next day's performance still have something to do and not surrender before the great battle.

It is nevertheless interesting to know what M. Debussy means by that so simple yet complex word, "music," which for each composer becomes "his music," even when it has no very distinct personality.

M. Claude Debussy, whom I urged or allowed to talk, flatters himself that he has no musical system; he does not even understand how one could have one. He even maintains that those who pretend they do don't apply it while composing, and that theories are born only after the works have been created.

The clearest thing about M. Debussy's negative system is that the young author admits having been very Wagnerian and has completely stopped being so. He accuses Wagner's art of falseness because it does not seem possible to him to have symphonic music in the theater. One mustn't forget one has to do with people who are alive and haven't the time to wait out symphonic episodes. So long as the symphony unfolds, all movement ceases; it is impossible to reconcile the dramatic movement with the symphonic movement. To back up this idea, M. Debussy proves with numerous examples that Wagner's heroes run out of things to say at certain times only because they must allow the symphony to develop.

M. Debussy, to prevent such inconveniences, has been led to seek out a declamation that adapts itself not to a musical movement, but to a musical word. He thus explains this turn of phrase, which might seem obscure:

Every sentence has its rhythm; now, in music it is important to respect the words without underlining them unreasonably. When we say, "Close the door" or "It's a lovely evening," all the words have an equal value contributing to the formation of the sentence. He won't allow music to affect a sonorous syllable any more than does ordinary conversation. He thus banishes from his conception music that is "useless," the 135 measures it takes to explain a state of mind that remains as unexplained afterwards as it was before. Only the character himself should explain his state of mind and not have recourse to a symphonic digression.

The composer of *Pelléas et Mélisande* has thus wished to react against the influence of Wagner, which he deems injurious and false; it encumbers and harms music, according to him, and above all it proves nothing. His dream is to attain a simpler formula based on humanity; he has wished to create a language that does not renounce the means the symphony can supply but at the same time is not enfeoffed by it, and that, above all, avoids development, that long-winded, boring thing. In Wagner (for that's M. Debussy's *Delenda Carthago* ["Carthage must be destroyed"]), the most useless things get tangled in a long commentary. Now, the action should keep going, even rush on, and it is important to keep up with it, or else one creates an anti-human work. Thus M. Debussy's music is intimately bound to the action. It ignores arias, disdains recitatives; it is a musical atmosphere that is at one with the moral or physical atmosphere.

From the technical point of view, it is based not only on a natural rhythm but also on a theory of accent; thus the accent of sorrow or of joy is expressed simultaneously from the lyrical and from the musical side. It is produced at the same time, without the several measures that, elsewhere, create the effect.

Evidently this concern for truth in the dramatic and musical action may also be found in the orchestral material of M. Debussy. Moreover, he wishes to declare that there is no orchestral score simpler than *Pelléas*. The modern school, with the pretext of conveying impressions or emotions, has resorted to bizarre instruments; the bass drum and triangle are still today the indispensable instruments to produce some emotion. He thinks that's useless. By going back to Mozart's orchestra one can attain emotional effects that are just as considerable and above all more sincere.

That is M. Debussy's most ardent concern; he is considered complicated, yet he knows of no musician more enamored of simplicity than he is; no one has so great a need for clarity. Musical notation is another matter: that can be complicated, as long as the effect is simple. The means in art are nobody's business; and more especially in music, arduous notation is purely a matter of reading, nothing else.

As for the singers, he does not, like Wagner, have contempt for them; he makes them absolutely living things in his work. They are no longer instruments as at Bayreuth, nor mechanical puppets as in Meyerbeer. When a character has something natural to say, the musical phrase is natural; he becomes lyrical only when it is necessary. M. Debussy repudiates non-stop lyricism, because we are not lyrical in life, only at certain decisive moments.

How did the young musician have the idea of setting Maeterlinck's drama to music? One fine evening after buying the book, he began reading it and saw there a fine subject for a musical drama. He didn't get in touch with Maeterlinck until he had matured his subject. It was important to find out if the author would consent to let his work be set to music. It might be added that Maeterlinck was very astonished that the subject should please a musician. Since, as he himself admits, he doesn't understand anything about music, he was not curious to become acquainted with the score. And over the last year he has had differences with the musician, with the result that the musical drama will only be revealed to him on the day of the dress rehearsal: much like those princesses of the Orient who did not remove their opaque veil until the day when a hero came to seek their hand in marriage.

As for M. Debussy, he awaits the public's verdict: he has written, says he, a simple thing, in order to interest everyone in his work; its secrets will be very easy to penetrate. I have tried to reproduce as faithfully as possible the young musician's ideas. Let us await the performance.

Claude Debussy, *Monsieur Croche et autres écrits*, ed. François Lesure (Paris: Gallimard, 1971), 265–68. Trans. P.W.

The première attracted extraordinary interest, even if it was not a complete success. Opinions, as might be expected with such an unusual work, were divided, but the opera remained in the theater's repertory for the next twelve years, achieving well over one hundred performances. Meanwhile it traveled abroad, reaching England in 1909. The critic Edwin Evans, about to give a lecture on it before the London première, asked Debussy for some guidelines and received the following response:

80, Avenue du Bois de Boulogne 18.IV/09

Dear Sir,

On reflection, I find it rather difficult to discuss *Pelléas* and to point to its salient characteristics, so please excuse what follows:

First of all you will do well to eliminate from the discussion the matter of whether there is or is not melody in *Pelléas*... It must be clearly understood that melody—or *Lied*—is one thing and "operatic expression" another! It is much too illogical to think that a *fixed* melodic line can be made to hold the innumerable nuances through which a character passes. That is not only a mistake of taste but a mistake of "quantity."

If in *Pelléas* symphonic development does not, on the whole, find much of a place, it is a reaction against that pernicious neo-Wagnerian aesthetic which claims to render simultaneously the feelings expressed by the character and the inner thoughts which motivate him... In my opinion these are two contradictory operations, from the operatic point of view, and bringing them together can only lead to a mutual enfeeblement. Perhaps it is better that music should by simple means—a chord? a curve?—try to render successive atmospheres and moods as they occur, and not force itself to laboriously follow a symphonic plot which is preconceived and *always arbitrary*, and to which one will inevitably be tempted to sacrifice the emotional plot; but one will have succeeded in writing a fine symphonic development...! Again, that has no place in lyric drama; what is more, it is too cheap a way of avoiding a difficulty. That is why there is no "guiding thread" in *Pelléas* and why the characters are not subjected to the slavery of the "leitmotif," as a blind man is the slave of his poodle or of his clarinet!—Notice that the motif which accompanies Mélisande is never altered; it comes back in the 5th act unchanged in every respect, because in fact Mélisande always remains the same and dies without anyone—only old Arkel, perhaps?—ever having understood her.

Emphasis must be laid on the simplicity in *Pelléas*—I spent twelve years removing anything *parasitic* that might have crept into it.—At no time did I try to use it to revolutionize anything whatever... but it has become customary to drag music into "places of ill repute" or to turn it into a game that no one can understand without a rigorous course of instruction.

I have tried to prove that when people sing they can remain human and natural, without ever having to look like fools or enigmas! That upset the "professionals" at first and also the plain public, which, accustomed as it was to being moved by means as false as they were bombastic, did not understand that it was not being asked for anything beyond a little goodwill.—It is not in the least important to penetrate the secret of the means that have been employed. Such curiosity is as reprehensible as it is ridiculous and, to be frank, completely useless.

...That is all, my dear Sir, that I can find to tell you... The rest belongs to anecdote, on which I am not very well informed.

Please accept, along with my kind wishes, my thanks for your valuable help. With my best regards to Mrs. Evans,

Yours sincerely,

Claude Debussy

Roger Nichols and Richard Langham Smith, *Claude Debussy: Pelléas et Mélisande* (Cambridge: Cambridge University Press, 1989), 185–86.

41

STRAUSS AND HOFMANNSTHAL WORK ON *DER ROSENKAVALIER*

To appreciate the full import of the following selections from the correspondence of Richard Strauss (1864–1949) with the Austrian poet Hugo von Hofmannsthal (1874–1929), one ought to be familiar with *Der Rosenkavalier*, more specifically with Act II, which is here seen in the making. While space does not permit a detailed synopsis of the opera, the following may do for an understanding of these letters. The comedy is set in mid-eighteenth-century Vienna. Sophie, the young daughter of the newly rich Faninal, has been promised in marriage to Baron Ochs auf Lerchenau, an older nobleman whom she has never seen. The official marriage proposal is conveyed to her by the young Count Octavian Rofrano (nicknamed Quinquin) in a glittering ceremony in which he presents her with a silver rose. Ochs arrives soon afterwards and shows himself to be a vulgar brute. Sophie is horrified. She and Octavian fall in love. Octavian fights a duel with the Baron, wounding him slightly in the arm. The Baron makes a scene, but his cheerfulness is restored by a note inviting him to an amorous rendezvous with a chambermaid (actually Octavian in disguise); the note is brought by Valzacchi and Annina, two Italians who live by their wits. The rendez-vous will occur later, in Act III, when Lerchenau will be utterly foiled and the young lovers happily united. The Marschallin, an older noblewoman and Octavian's first love, does not appear in Act II; her personality lends a deeper humanity to this otherwise lighthearted comedy of manners. *Der Rosenkavalier*, first performed on 26 January 1911 at the Dresden Opera, became the greatest success of Strauss's operatic career, and Hofmannsthal's share in it cannot be overestimated. Yet what emerges from the following exchange is Strauss's own surprising inventiveness. The entire action of Act II, after the presentation of the rose, is his; and it is to Hofmannsthal's credit that he sensed the rightness of the other's suggestions, carrying them out almost completely. One should note, in Strauss's letter of 13 August, the reference to Verdi's *Falstaff*, an opera he much admired, which in fact provided the model for the Baron's scene after the duel. Finally, Hofmannsthal's reference to Wagner's "erotic screaming" (letter of 2 September) completes the picture: the two men were definitely working towards a new, more classical style.

Mürren, 9 July 1909

Dear Herr von Hofmannsthal,

Three days of snow, rain, and fog have made me come to a decision today which I don't want to keep from you any longer. Please don't get angry, but think over calmly all I'm going to say to you. Even on my first reading of Act II I felt that there was something wrong with it, that it lacked the right dramatic climaxes. Now today I know approximately what's wrong. The first act with its contemplative ending is excellent as an exposition. But Act II lacks the necessary clash and climax: these can't possibly all be left to Act III. Act III must overtrump the climax of Act II, but the audience can't wait as long as that: if Act II falls flat the opera is lost. Even a good third act can't save it then.

Now let me tell you how I picture the second act. If you can think of something better still, *tant mieux.*

Well, then, up to the Baron's entrance everything is fine. But from there onwards it's got to be changed.

The Baron's two scenes with Sophie are wrongly disposed. Everything of importance in these two scenes must go straight into the first scene, when the Baron must at once become so distasteful to Sophie that she resolves never to marry him. Octavian must remain a witness to the *whole* scene, quietly getting more and more furious as the Baron, not in the least embarrassed by his presence but on the contrary treating him as a young buck and bragging to him about his successes with women, performs his capers with Sophie. Then the Baron's exit, to sign the marriage contract, and his parting words to Octavian, advising him to "thaw Sophie out a bit." Then the declaration of love between Octavian and Sophie, together with the highly dramatic effect of the couple surprised by the two Italians.

But from here onwards: attracted by the shouting of the Italians, the Baron himself enters, and the Italians tell him everything. The Baron, at first amused rather than angry, to Octavian: "Well, my lad, it didn't take you long to learn from me." The argument between Octavian and the Baron becomes increasingly heated; they fight a duel and Octavian wounds the Baron in the arm. At the Baron's scream: "He has murdered me" everybody rushes in. Grand tableau. Scandal: "The Rose Bearer has wounded the bridegroom!" Faninal horrified. The Baron's servants bandage their master. Sophie declares she will never marry the Baron. Here Faninal's part could be a little stronger: he shows Octavian the door, informs Sophie that the marriage contract has been signed, sealed, and delivered, and that he'll send her to a convent if she won't have the Baron. Exit Octavian, furious; to the Baron: "We shall meet again." Sophie is carried off in a faint. The Baron remains alone, this time still the victor. Short monologue, partly cursing Octavian, partly bemoaning his wound, and partly rejoicing in the luck of the Lerchenau's. The Italians creep in and hand him Mariandel's invitation to a *tête-à-tête*. This can be left as an effective suprise for the audience. No leading up to it. The end of the act remains as before, except that one might work in the point that the Baron does not tip them. The later scene, which you have sent me, is not necessary.

The arrangement between Octavian and the Italians can be brought up briefly at the beginning of Act III, just before Valzacchi hands the lady's maid over to the Baron. As the Baron catches sight of Mariandel he exclaims again: "The resemblance!" and this pretty theme can then recur repeatedly during the scenes between the Marschallin and the Baron. The Baron in *tête-à-tête* with his right arm bandaged is also a comical situation.

What do you think of it? Don't be too anxious about motivating the Italians' change of sides. Perhaps you'll even find an opportunity to work in the little scene of Octavian outbidding the Baron with the Italians, somewhere during the confusion of the scandal ensemble with its choruses. The audience *does not need it*. They'll tumble to it all right. The more mischievous Octavian is the better. At all events the clash must come in Act II: the fade-out ending will then be most effective. At present it isn't effective because the climax preceding it is too weak. Have I made myself clear? Do please think it over. If you like I could come to Aussee to consult with you. As it now stands I can't possibly use the second act. It is not well planned and is flat. Believe me: my instinct does not deceive me. The song: "Mit dir, mit dir keine Nacht mir zu lang" ["With you, no night will be too long for me"] can be introduced in the first, and only, scene between the Baron and Sophie. It'll then be most effective just before the curtain, as a reminiscence. I can also see a lot of comedy in the third act when the Baron, caressing Mariandel, is time and again reminded of that scoundrel of a Rose Bearer and works himself into a rage. That, as I see it, should be great fun. He thus fluctuates between amorousness and fury over the resemblance with those cursed features. A good comedy theme, I think.

Well now, I hope you won't be angry with me. But I feel that, as it now stands, I can't do anything with the second act. It's too much on one level. I must have a great dramatic construction if I want to keep myself interested for so long in a particular setting. Alternatively, Octavian might declare immediately after the duel that he too is willing to marry Sophie. Octavian could be a Baron and Lerchenau a Count; Faninal, a comical title-hunting character, wavers between the Baron and the Count, and eventually prefers the Count.

It's only an idea.

It is certainly right that in Act II Octavian should be defeated and Lerchenau, though winged, emerge victorious, until, in the third act, he is utterly and completely licked.

A possible good way of introducing the Marschallin into Act III would be if she had already, by way of gossip, learned of the events at Faninal's house. As you see, a wealth of themes: all that's wanted is the poet who could draw it all together and clothe it in graceful words, and that's you. Please don't let me down!

Shall I come to Aussee? Or do you get my point? Have I expressed myself clearly enough? No ill feelings. I've started on the draft of Act II and shall compose it, for the time being, as far as Lerchenau's entrance.

With best regards, yours
Richard Strauss

Rodaun, 10 July [1909]

My dear Doctor,

You will not seriously believe that I could leave you in the lurch at such a juncture, or that I might create difficulties.

What you ask me to do is essential from your point of view, it contradicts neither the spirit of the chief characters nor the overall conception of the comedy. I will therefore make the alterations, and that as soon as possible. Only it may take me a little while to assimilate these ideas into my imagination since they are not my own, to feel and see once more the whole piece as a living organic conception.

In what is now to be the single scene between the Baron and Sophie (Lerchenau's entrance down to his exit with the notary) you must give me scope to establish the situation (as in *Meistersinger*) or else my characters will lack all substance; I don't mean I want more space for this, but not less than the scene now takes roughly down to the bottom of page 14 of my MS. Then I shall bring in the essential dramatic points from the final scene as it stands (his brazen impudence with her and the decidedly angry rebuff)—and so on according to your suggestions. . . .

Yours sincerely,
Hofmannsthal

Mürren, 10 July 1909

Dear Herr von Hofmannsthal,

While I'm criticizing, and since you've now got over the first shock of my letter of yesterday, I will risk continuing to speak my mind. I keep thinking about the second act, and I'm more and more confirmed in my belief that, generally speaking, yesterday's letter has hit the mark in so far as the architecture and development of the act are concerned. No doubt it also happens to you, as it frequently does to me, that one is dissatisfied with something, but does not fully realize it until someone else puts his finger on the sore spot. You yourself felt that all was not right with Act II when you so emphatically urged me to consider Act III. But, as I said, Act III can't do the job by itself. The second act must be the success and the third must consolidate and reinforce it. I therefore implore you once again to condense the two duets in Act II between Octavian and Sophie, but even more so between the Baron and Sophie, into one scene each, or at least to transfer all the essentials of the second scene in each case into the first scene, so that of the second scene between Octavian and Sophie only the climax remains. In other words: throughout the whole scene between the Baron and Sophie (with Octavian as a progressively more and more infuriated listener) the psychological atmosphere must become so menacing, and Sophie's revulsion against the Baron so strong, that the moment the Baron leaves to append his signature (Sophie need not sign at all or else she can have signed beforehand) she bursts out: "Save me from that monster" and falls into Octavian's arms. Now a short, passionate duet ending with their kiss and their discovery by the Italians. Please don't be angry with me for thus putting the spurs on your Pegasus, but this opera must be first-rate and, as I've said, the second act isn't up to what I expect of you or to what you're capable of.

One other thing: since you've got to rewrite so drastically, will you please also revise once more the whole dialogue between the Baron and Sophie. Compared with the rest, I find it a little unimaginative and colorless, and I can't help feeling that your taste and talent could produce something much more witty and polished here. This dialogue is not up to Act I.

I hope I shall soon have good news from you and remain, with kindest regards, yours most sincerely,

Richard Strauss

Garmisch, 20 July 1909

Dear Herr von Hofmannsthal,

Do not, I implore you, let my criticism discourage you. I can only judge from my own experience, but nothing does me so much good, nothing stimulates and fructifies my ambition and creative energy so much as adverse criticism from one to whose judgment I attach some importance. My criticism is intended to spur you on, not to discourage you. I want to draw the best out of you. . . .

In the proposed scene between the Baron and Sophie I feel sure that, during your revision, you'll hit on something even better, more comical and more striking. I know how it is: one feels annoyed when somebody else doesn't like a thing, but it goes on rankling all the time until one's hit on something better. Additions to Act I now all duly to hand. It's just that I always forget to acknowledge receipt straight away. So don't worry.

> With best regards, yours
> Richard Strauss

Don't forget that the audience should also laugh! *Laugh,* not just smile or grin!

I still miss in our work a genuinely comical situation: everything is merely amusing, but not *comic!*

> Aussee, 3 August [1909]

My dear Doctor,

I hope the second act gives you pleasure now, pleasure which you owe in the first place to yourself. From this one occasion I have learnt something fundamental about dramatic work for music which I shall not forget.

I have recast the wooing scene, too, to make it really funny with the Baron's irrepressible and pretty brazen sallies which culminate in that impertinent little song, with Faninal's (and the duenna's) grotesque enthusiasm and with Octavian's rising fury. I hope at the same time that I have so managed the scene which leads up to the duel that, given *reasonably* downright acting on the part of the basso buffo, it may raise a laugh or two rather than mere smiles. Actually I do not by any means deny that there is a great deal of difference between what is merely gay and what is broadly comic; only I tell myself that a general atmosphere of gaiety with animated, well-contrasted characters and without long-winded machinery or dull stretches must, *in the long run,* prove superior even in the eyes of the public to anything approaching the more obvious operetta. (See *Meistersinger* or *Figaro,* which contain little to make one laugh and much to smile at.)

If, what is more, we have a first act which is leisurely and full of sentiment, a second which is now very lively, and a third which will produce, in the police interrogation scene, the height of forthright *quid pro quo* and confusion, then we are, I think, out of the wood. Given time I hope to make *a great deal* of this third act, both of its funny and of its emotional sections. . . .

> With best wishes and regards, yours,
> Hofmannsthal

Garmisch, 13 August 1909

Dear Herr von Hofmannsthal,

In Verdi's *Falstaff* there is an amusing monologue at the beginning of the last act; it starts with the words, "Mondo ladro" ["Wretched world"]. I picture the scene of the Baron, after Faninal's exit, similarly: the Baron on the sofa, the surgeon attending to him, the mute servants lined up behind the couch, and the Baron talking in snatches, partly to himself and partly to the others, in turn boastful and sorry for himself, always interrupted by orchestral interludes

Groaning with pain
cursing Quinquin
appraising his bride.

The plan is good, but it needs working out a little—some 8 lines or so.

But now something rather more important! From page 19 onwards, the scene between Sophie and Octavian doesn't quite suit me yet. What I need here is something much more passionate—after that preceding scene, and before the fatal scene when the Baron surprises the two.

As it now reads it is too tame, too mannered and timid, and too lyrical. For the time being I shan't be able to place the little duet since I've used up most of the lyricism at the beginning of Act II.

Couldn't you let me have this scene anew?

Sophie much more horrified and desperate, almost throwing herself at Octavian's neck; from page 21 onwards intensifications towards a climax and no more gentleness.

Can it be done? If not, I shall have to try and manage with what I've got. But I picture at this point something entirely different from the atmosphere of lovingly-gentle silence. First, Sophie's passionate outburst: "Dear cousin, save me, rid me of that monster; I'd sooner go to a convent than marry this boor," turning gradually into a full declaration of love up to the culminating point when the Italians start yelling.

With best regards, yours
Richard Strauss

Aussee, 2 September [1909]

My dear Doctor,

Perhaps the enclosed words for the duet between Octavian and Sophie immediately after the duenna's exit will suit you now; I hope they may. Sophie's appeal: "blieb' er nur bei mir!" ["stay with me!"] (to be repeated ad lib.) might, so I imagine, provide the requisite occasion for swelling and poignant as well as tender music. What I would wish to avoid at all cost is to see these two young creatures, who have nothing of the Valkyries or Tristan about them, bursting into a Wagnerian kind of erotic screaming. If it isn't quite right yet, please let me have a line at once; we shall get it straight.

Yours sincerely,
Hofmannsthal

Garmisch, 18 Sept. 1909

Many thanks for your letter: am impatiently awaiting the Baron's monologue, the more so as the final conclusion of Act II is now all composed and, I believe, has turned out a first-class hit. "I am satisfied with myself." I am feeling well and fit, and wish you likewise all the best for the successful conclusion of the comedy. Let me have your address just in case: I shan't worry you without weighty reason, especially as I shall embark on the orchestration of the first two acts in Berlin on 1st October. A tedious task! With best regards, yours very sincerely,

Richard Strauss

A Working Friendship: The Correspondence between Richard Strauss and Hugo von Hofmannsthal, trans. H. Hammelmann and E. Osers (New York: Random House, 1961), 36–41, 43, 45–46, 47–49, 51.

42

DUKE BLUEBEARD'S CASTLE

Bartók wrote his only opera in 1911. It is a setting of a previously written play, and as such illustrates an early twentieth-century penchant for what the German musicologist Carl Dahlhaus has called "literature opera": *Pelléas et Mélisande, Salome, Wozzeck* are other notable examples. The poet in the present instance was Béla Balász. Three years younger than Bartók, Balász belonged to the same coterie of young intellectuals and artists then rising to prominence in Budapest, all keenly aware of contemporary artistic developments in western Europe, yet all seeking to attain a higher level of artistic expression through a fusion of modernism with quintessential elements of their own Hungarian heritage. Ballász wrote the one-act play in 1908–10 and published it in 1910, with a dedication to Bartók and Kodály. Bartók began setting it to music in February of the next year, at first without the poet's knowledge, then with his enthusiastic endorsement, and finished it that September. In 1912 he entered the opera in two competitions, but it failed in both. It failed as a play, too, in 1913, when Ballász put it on with another one, Bartók playing some of his new piano pieces during the interval. The opera finally received its première on 24 May 1918 at the Royal Opera House in Budapest. The following is an explanation of *Bluebeard* written by Balász at some point after 1913, with a view to a spoken performance in Vienna that never materialized. The affinities here to the symbolist movement in general and to Maeterlinck in particular are unmistakable, as is the poet's striving for a specifically Magyar mode of expression.

Is it permissible to "explain" verse? Let us suppose that, perhaps, not all its parts are entirely clear; isn't it just then that the essence—music—does its work in sleeping shadows? All explanations are Roentgen pictures: they break up the shape, the form. Prefaces are all in vain. True poetry is: *seduction!*

But if the poetry is available to us only in translation, then there is some need of explanation. Because just where the work's sense and meaning do not come to light in logical, clearly formulated matters—no doubt this happens with all true poetry—these dual essences are comprehensible only in the linguistic shape and the text's musical irradiation of the words' music. This, however, is lost in translation.

In such a case it is perhaps not superfluous to say a few words about what the original poetry actually wanted to say, since it was Béla Bartók's wonderful music that gave musical form to the spirit of the original Hungarian verse, and the translated text cannot always bring this out convincingly. So we need to say a little about the original poetry *to be able to explain the music.*

I did not write the Hungarian original of *Duke Bluebeard's Castle* as a libretto, but simply as poetry, as one is used to writing verse in general. It appeared separately, and was also accorded a dramatic scene, even before Bartók had set it to music. I created this ballad of mine in the language and rhythms of old Hungarian Székely folk ballads. In character these folk ballads closely resemble old Scottish folk ballads, but they are, perhaps, more acerbic, more simple, their melodic quality more mysterious, more naive, and more songlike. Thus, there is no "literature" or rhetoric within them: they are constructed from dark, weighty, uncarved blocks of words. In this manner I wrote my Hungarian language *Bluebeard* ballad, and Bartók's music also conforms to this.

I called my *Bluebeard* a ballad for the stage because the stage here occupies not only the necessary space for the unfolding of the dialogue. The stage itself takes part in the dialogue. In the Hungarian dramatis personae I identified the play's three participants: Bluebeard, Judith, and the castle.

My ballad is the "ballad of inner life." Bluebeard's castle is not a real castle of stone. The castle is his soul. It is lonely, dark, and secretive: the castle of closed doors.

It is precisely this tragic obscurity, this suffering withdrawal into seclusion, that attracted the woman with strange power, even though she had heard frightful rumors about murdered women. Into this castle, into his own soul, Bluebeard admits his beloved. And the castle (the stage) shudders, weeps, and bleeds. When the woman walks in it, she walks in a living being.

And the woman wants to throw open all the doors. Her love and compassion lead her to this. She would like to bring light, and warmth, into the dark, close castle. "Your poor castle won't be dark. There will be windows. There will be balconies!"—she speaks in this manner, and thinks only of the castle, of it alone!

When the castle's doors open forth, laboriously and painfully at first, she, however, has no fear of the dangerous and, until then, hidden secrets that spring forth from the depths of the rooms; after all, more light enters the poor, dark castle. But she sees traces of blood everywhere. Where will they lead? Do they not mark the path of her own fate?

She opens the doors one after the other, each with increasing restlessness and impatience. She searches for the cause of the traces of blood. She demands: From whence does the blood come? And when, through the fifth door, a flood of light and warmth engulfs the castle, and Bluebeard—liberated, redeemed, luminous, grateful in his happiness—wants to enfold the woman in his arms, already the daylight is no longer visible to the woman who brought it to him. She sees only the bloody shadows.

Nevertheless, she searches further; she wants to throw open the last door, too. "What do you want, then?"—Bluebeard asks her. "Look, my castle now gleams. Your blessed hands did this." "I don't want you to have any doors closed to me"—answers the woman. She left everything behind, and came to him, because she loves him. Not a single door should be locked before her if he wants his home to become her home. She says this, and inquires about the women whom the man loved before her.

Her every flattery useless, the man does not give her the seventh key. "You are my castle's radiant splendor. Kiss me, kiss me, ask me nothing."

The woman then cries out in the man's face: "I know, Bluebeard, I know what the seventh door conceals. All your former wives are there! Slaughtered, frozen in blood. Ah, the rumors were true, the horrible rumors!"

The man now hands her the key. "Open it, Judith. You shall see them. There are all my former wives." And when the woman looks inside, she staggers back in alarm: not as if she had seen the dead women, no! The women are alive! From behind the seventh door the wives—who had been loved at one time by the

man—rise to their feet, dreamlike, from the deep recesses of slumbering memory. And wreathed with diadems and halos, they are more beautiful than all
women presently living. Oh, how plain, how miserable Judith feels when Bluebeard sings in dreaming ecstasy of his past loves.

But she doesn't shudder in horror until he begins to beautify her, to adorn
her with jewels. "Ah, Bluebeard, you are not dreaming, I am your poor, living
wife." But the man covers her with glittering ornaments, and Judith gradually
grows numb with death. The man's dream kills her, the very dream she herself
has conjured up in him. And the dreaming man remains alone once more, his
castle again locked and dark.

This is the meaning of the Hungarian ballad about Duke Bluebeard's castle.

Carl S. Leafstedt, Inside Bluebeard's Castle: *Music and Drama in Béla Bartók's Opera* (New York: Oxford
University Press, 1999), 201–3.

43

BUSONI AND THE REINSTATEMENT OF DISBELIEF

"There is no doubt that no one ever spoke singing" wrote Peri, the first composer of opera (see p. 15), and so all the early operas were steeped in mythol-
ogy: where you have the supernatural anything is possible, even song instead
of speech. Yet skepticism never really died. "Is it to be imagin'd that . . . orders in time of battle are given, singing; and that men are melodiously killed
with swords and darts?" asked Saint-Évremond sarcastically (p. 53). Italians accepted the basic operatic convention even with the advent of realistic subject
matter, as in *opera buffa*. The French and Germans were more reluctant: the
dialogue in *opéra comique* and *singspiel* was spoken, not sung. Then romanticism brought back the supernatural, "yet so as to transfer from our inward
nature a human interest and a semblance of truth sufficient to procure for these
shadows of the imagination that willing suspension of disbelief for the moment, which constitutes poetic faith" (Coleridge, *Biographia Literaria*, chap.
14). Busoni came at a time when romanticism was exhausted and opera

in crisis. The limits of Wagnerism, he wrote, were reached by Wagner himself and could not be extended further. Italian *verismo* strained his credulity (or poetic faith). In the second edition (1916) of his *Sketch of a New Aesthetic of Music*, the future composer of the operas *Arlecchino*, *Turandot*, and *Doktor Faust* devoted some remarkable pages to the future of opera. Advocating disbelief on the part of the spectator and detachment on the part of the artist (in direct opposition to Horace's injunction, "If you wish to draw tears from me, you must first feel pain yourself," *Ars poetica*, 102), Busoni proposed a return without personal involvement to the supernatural, the unrealistic. A visionary and perhaps a genius, Busoni exerted considerable influence on some 20th-century composers, especially on his pupil Kurt Weill, and anticipated some of Bertolt Brecht's views on opera, including his disdain for the bourgeois hedonism of its audiences and their craving for emotional "experience" in the theater (see pp. 289ff below).

Most of the newer theater music suffers from the mistake of trying to repeat the events happening onstage, instead of pursuing its own particular mission, which is to express the state of mind of the characters as the events unfold. If the stage represents the illusion of a storm, the fact is amply taken in by the eye. Yet almost all composers go to the trouble of describing the storm in tones, which is not only an unnecessary and weaker repetition, but a missed opportunity to fulfill their mission. Either the person onstage is psychologically affected by the storm, or, because of thoughts that engage him more strongly, he remains untouched. The storm is visible and audible without the help of music; but what meanwhile transpires in the mind of a person is invisible and inaudible, and this is what music ought to make comprehensible.

Then again, there are "visible" states of mind onstage which music may well ignore. Let us take the theatrical situation of a merry group of people singing as they walk off into the night and disappear from sight, while in the foreground a silent, embittered duel is being fought.[1] Here the music will need to keep present the merry company that is lost to sight by continuing their song: what the two in front are doing and feeling is easily perceived without further explanation, and the music must not, dramatically speaking, have a part in it, must not interrupt the tragic silence.

I consider conditionally justified the practice of older opera, in which, after a dramatically agitated scene, the resulting mood was summed up and vented in a closed number (the aria).—Words and gestures communicated the dramatic course of the action, musically seconded in a more or less meager recitative; a

---

[1]From Offenbach's *Les Contes d'Hoffmann*.

resting place having been reached, the music took over again. This is less su-
perficial than we are made to believe nowadays. But again it was the stiffened
form of the aria itself that led to its falsity of expression and decline.

Sung words onstage will always remain a convention and a hindrance to all
truthful effect; in order to emerge from this conflict decently, an action in which
the characters are to sing must from the very beginning be rooted in the unbe-
lievable, the unreal, the improbable, so that one impossibility may rest upon another, making both of them probable and acceptable.

Already for this reason and because at the very outset it ignores this principle, I consider the so-called Italian *verismo* untenable for the musical stage.

When addressing the question of opera's future, it is necessary to be clear
about this further question: "At what points is music onstage indispensable?"
The precise answer informs us, "With dances, with marches, with songs and—
with the introduction of the supernatural into the action."

There results accordingly a future possibility in the idea of supernatural material. And more: in the idea of absolute "play," of the entertaining masquerade, of the stage as manifest and preannounced dissimulation, in the idea of the
joke and of unreality as opposites of the seriousness and reality of life. Then it
becomes appropriate for characters to sing when declaring their love and vent-
ing their hatred, and to die melodiously in a duel, to hold high notes during pathetic explosions; it is then quite right for them to behave on purpose differently
than they do in life, rather than (as in our theaters and particularly in opera)
doing everything wrong unintentionally.

Opera ought to take possession of the supernatural or unnatural as the only
area of appearances and feelings that is by nature its own and so create a make-
believe world that reflects life in either a magic or a distorting mirror, which
will consciously provide that which is not to be found in real life. The magic
mirror for serious opera, the distorting mirror for comic. And let dancing and
masquerade and hocus-pocus be liberally worked in, so that the spectator may
be aware every moment of the charming lie and not surrender to it as to an
experience.

Just as the artist, if he wishes to move, must not himself be moved if he is
not at that very moment to relinquish his mastery over his medium, so must
the spectator, wishing to taste the theatrical effect, never mistake it for reality,
if artistic enjoyment is not to descend to human empathy. Let the actor "play"—
not experience. Let the spectator remain disbelieving and therefore unencum-
bered in his intellectual receptivity and his epicurism.

Relying on such premises, one might well look forward to a future for opera.
But the first and strongest obstacle, I fear, will come to us from the public.

It is in my opinion quite criminally disposed with regard to the theater, and
one can assume that the majority want the stage to provide them with an overpowering human experience because such a thing is missing in their everyday
mediocre lives; and also because they lack the courage to face conflicts for which

they yearn. And the stage grants them these conflicts without the accompanying dangers and unpleasant consequences, without compromising them and, most
important, without any effort on their part. For there is one thing the public
doesn't know and doesn't wish to know: that in order to be receptive to a work
of art, the receiver must do half the work.

Ferruccio Busoni, *Entwurf einer neuen Ästhetik der Tonkunst*, 2nd ed. (Leipzig: Insel-Verlag, [1916]), 16–20.
Trans. P.W. (In mem. O.W.)

44

IN DEFENSE OF *KÁT'A KABANOVÁ*

Although Leoš Janáček's sixth opera, *Kát'a Kabanová* (Brno, 1921), had some
success in Czechoslovakia during the '20s and '30s, and three German productions in the pre-Nazi era, it had to wait until after World War II before it
began to be heard in the West. After Munich and Zurich, London heard it for
the first time in April 1951. It had for the most part an unfavorable reception,
both public and critical. The spirited defense of the opera given below appeared that autumn in *The Music Review*. In the course of rebutting some of
the critics' objections, its author, Charles Stuart, succeeds in providing an excellent analytical introduction to what many consider one of the operatic masterpieces of the twentieth century.

Katya Kabanova, the first Janáček opera to be produced in England, had so cold,
patronizing or frankly hostile a reception from most of the papers when put on
at Sadler's Wells last spring that we are not likely, so far as I can see, to hear
much more of it. Let us take an affectionate valedictory glance, before it is quite
forgotten, at a score exceptional alike for its structure and the intensity of its
poetry.

We were told by *The Times* the morning after that *Katya* lacks thematic organization. This is not a reproach. It is a compliment. "Organization" is a base
word with no business in this context. We organize sales drives, crypto peace

movements, jumble sales and the like. What *Katya* boasts is not thematic organization but thematic life. Its tunes and harmonic formulae, analogously with the body's organs and networks, are so many channels or centers of aesthetic vitality; of spirit, in short.

What foxes case-hardened ears and *routinier* imaginations is that Janáček's thematic method has nothing in common with Richard Wagner's. Debussy used to complain, not justly but with grains of truth, that the typical Wagner character every time he puts his beard round the prompt wing thrusts his leitmotiv under your nose like a visiting card. Janáček's method is subtler, and needs to be, because his working-scale is smaller. Katya herself has not one visiting card, in Debussy's sense, but (on a rough count) thirteen or fourteen. Actually, of course, there are thirteen or fourteen Katyas, Janáček's heroine being not a fixed quantity or static concept but a creature who, under inner stress, is subject to constant psychic change. Instead of staring at a lithograph we are turning the pages of a book. Generally speaking, each group of Katya themes, having served a given dramatic episode, is discarded for good. Sentimental flashbacks (at this time of day rather a facile dodge) are discouraged. What was valid enough thematically on page two is superseded by page twenty.

Does this make for incoherence? Mr. [Ernest] Newman, in *The Sunday Times*, rather thought it did. Janáček, he complained, is incapable of sticking to one musical idea for more than two or three minutes at a time. Whether a composer changes tack every two minutes, every three minutes or every half-minute is of no consequence whatever. What matters is that his changes of tack shall intelligently complement each other, adding up to a plotted and valid musical course. This, in effect, is what happens throughout *Katya*. In every bar Janáček knows what he's about and where he's going. Each of his six scenes is compactly ordered in a formal sense. Whoever doesn't acknowledge this is either musically illiterate or unacquainted with the score.

In speaking of Katya's thirteen or fourteen personal themes I hope I do not give the impression of a sequence of stick-on labels or *pro-tem* signature tunes. Themes are things a composer discusses. A stick-on label is its own beginning and end. Instead of discussing it we look the other way. Janáček's thematic discussions are rather hard to spot. As I see it, that is *prima facie* evidence of their quality. Consider the serene music for solo flute with accompaniment of detached chords which we hear when Katya comes on in the opening scene. Although it took me a long time to realize it, the above material in modified forms is present in the orchestra for quite seventy bars before Katya's actual appearance. Her music goes before, prefiguring her while she approaches, filling the young Boris with mystical unease. . . .

The effect, once you have grasped what Janáček is about, is most moving; but I am quite sure it passes clean over most heads (as it did over mine) even at a second or third hearing. It would be shortsighted to complain about this. An opera is not up to much which yields all its treasures at first knock.

As the foregoing examples suggest, Janáček does not so much put his themes through the symphonic hoops and over the symphonic hurdles as state them in variant forms, a device which reduces discussion to essentials. The first scene of act two is haunted by a hypnotic, twirling sequence of alternate major thirds and perfect fourths which, as I hear them, symbolize the amorous obsession which is assailing and tragically mastering Katya. The subject occurs under three guises. . . .

I do not pretend that each of these variants corresponds with some distinctive streak in Katya's psychology or in the dramatic substance of the scene. Janáček's purpose here is to convey obsession without overreaching himself and incurring musical monotony. Vertically the intervals are always the same: it is the horizontal lines that change—just sufficiently to bring new and revivifying tints from familiar harmonic substance. About "thematic transformation" of this kind there is nothing showy, nothing pedantic, nothing pre-endorsed by the textbooks: all we need say is that it is quintessentially musical and of powerful indirect service to the libretto.

That Katya is given a chain rather than a central group of themes does not preclude occasional anticipations, advance hints and recurrences. Towards the end of her unforgettable monologue in the second scene of act one, Katya sings (in Norman Tucker's translation), "It is so dreadful a sin to love another man. Who can help me? What will the end be?" At the same time the orchestra enounces a subject which we are to hear restated under different aspects in the love scene of the subsequent act. It is customary for opera composers to introduce their love-themes-in-chief with a great clearing of decks and throats; on such occasions they shush, reiterate and underline. Janáček, on the other hand, seems almost to hope we shall not notice what's happening. He smuggles in his love theme shyly, almost furtively. . . .

Allusions and quotations of this kind are so restrained and half-lit that to find them one must go through the score with a small-tooth comb. In the small-tooth comb I am an unrepentant believer. To rejoice intelligently in the whole one must rejoice furiously in the smallest part. Those aesthetes (there are such) who decry the analysis of works they purport to love are mere quacks. In this aspect *Katya* is sound as a bell. It lives up to both small-tooth comb and microscope.

Not that Janáček is subdued and subtle all the time. Occasionally there are massive strokes. When Katya's husband packs his bag at the end of the first act, we are given a stretch of tingling "departure music" which presently becomes loaded and brassy with menace. Husband and wife have reached the end of their way. The orchestra is telling us that what is on the surface a conventional parting is in effect a final sundering, shot with agony and sorrow. Now much the same musical material is used, with astonishing imaginative mastery, after the final catastrophe, when Katya's body is carried up on to the Volga quay from which she has thrown herself in despair and mental dissolution. There is the same tingling, the same whip-crack in the orchestra, but this time the parting is a more momentous parting, the journey more dread. The pounding bass which has hitherto leapt a bodeful fourth suddenly hammers out a clinching fifth, which brings the curtain down to a tragic shout of B flat minor.

As an example of the recurring motive I should have thought this as obvious as anything in *Walküre* or *Aida*. Yet at Sadler's Wells even this object lesson seems, in the case of most hearers, to have gone in at one ear and out at the other. The surprising thing is how much we all of us overlook on first contact with a masterpiece. Tunes and structural features which later are as unmistakable as the Skylon [a Festival of Britain landmark in 1951] simply aren't there at all on first hearing, a phenomenon which accounts for the hilarious comicality of so much "spot" criticism, my own included.

But the difficulty of initially coming to grips is no excuse. In the case of *Katya* the willing mind and the reasonably practised ear gather enough of individuality and high beauty at a first hearing to look with reasonable confidence for more. For my own part, although I missed so much on the night of the Wells première, I found myself mentally on my toes even during the opening scene between Boris and Vanya which, although an otherwise enthusiastic colleague finds it "conventional," has a highly original musical text. The first real landmark was Katya's monologue in the second scene, to which reference has already been made: it was instantly evident that this is not only a main pillar of the score but also one of the most challenging pages of musical portraiture in operatic literature.

There are touches in the love music which sound naive, almost neo-Weberian, to begin with; much less so, I think, when related to their context and above all to Katya's personality. Sweetness is mitigated by strength. A harmonic idiom which, for the romantic aspects of the story, draws on Tchaikovsky and early Strauss, not to mention Dvořák and Smetana, makes skillful use for other expressional purposes of modalism and the whole-tone scale, the latter in a vein which recalls not so much Debussy as certain of Sibelius' moods. Here and there we get a superb harshness. One detail always makes me catch my breath even in the piano score. I refer to the stuttering, brassy figure . . . which sounds against a soft pattern of choral voices "off" during Katya's final sorrowing. The effect is tearing and peremptory. Death's finger seems to beckon. The terror and beauty of this detail are in themselves sufficient to establish Janáček's technical *bona fides*. A man who can conceive a master-stroke of this kind could not possibly be the muddle-headed, short-winded amateur we read about in certain critical quarters. On this point, for the rest, the score as a whole is conclusive: it is controlled craftsmanship (as well as finer things) all the way.

Is *Katya*, then, the entire and perfect chrysolite? Far from it. Janáček's special talent, as shown in this work, at any rate, is for music which runs neck and neck with *inner* conflict. Physical action, of which we have samples in the confession and suicide scenes, makes him restive. What's the point, he seems to ask impatiently, of all this running about when the only thing that truly matters is what goes on in men's minds and hearts? Still, running about there has to be; the theatre cannot well get on without it. In *Katya* the physical happenings are confused, untidy, almost ludicrous. There's nothing much the producer can do about this, I imagine: the defects of act three arise because Janáček found the external world and its goings on rather a bore. For real music-drama in Janáček's sense we must turn once more to Katya's monologues (she has a second big *scena* before committing suicide). Nothing happens outwardly, but once you are attuned to the music everything is pure theatre, with each gesture, every square inch of paint, every watt of lamplight playing its part.

There has been some lament that in *Katya* there's not a single aria. Nor is there for that matter in the whole of *Pelléas*, most of *Wozzeck* and a vast acreage of Strauss and Wagner. On this point Janáček has refused to compromise, for compromise would have been ruinous. *Katya* is a shortish work divided into six scenes: chopping and changing between melodic recitative on the one hand and arias and formal ensembles on the other would have left the characters with no room to turn round. Janáček's solution is a continuous orchestral commentary which indisputably bears the main musical burden, plus a vocal line designed to convey the words lucidly in recitative patterns which, though shapely and interesting enough in their own terms, never distract the ear from the orchestral exposition. The vocal line, in other words, never approaches autonomy. On the other hand, it never approaches the utilitarian gabble which disfigures so many pages of *Elektra*, for example. A minor characteristic, especially in Katya's part, is the superimposing of vocal phrases in common time, or in irregular groupings (fives, for example) upon triple measures in the orchestra. Evidently it is necessary to understand the Czech text before we can relish such niceties to the full, but even in English they are not to be despised.

The romantic tints and surgings of Janáček's orchestra sometimes push him willy-nilly towards great lyrical outbursts of precisely the sort he has on principle foresworn. A case in point is the crucial entry of Boris in the last scene. This is attended by a great orchestral stoking-up which in Tchaikovsky, for example, would have denoted a ten- or twenty-page duet for the lovers. Instead of anchoring himself melodiously in G flat, Janáček lets the voice parts subside and peter out. The result is undeniably anticlimactic. Here is a fascinating glimpse of the technical dilemmas in which a composer may involve himself when striking out on a path of his own. But the vocal writing of *Katya* is for the most part satisfying enough. With those who wish to revive the *da capo aria* in contemporary terms I am in lively sympathy: but there are right contexts and wrong contexts for this purpose, and *Katya* is emphatically among the wrong ones.

To conclude. Every technical objection levelled at *Katya* by the Sadler's Wells critics can be comfortably refuted by anybody who spends half a day with the score. That the work can ever mean much to the big aria-hunting public is exceedingly doubtful. What one must lament, however, is that it should have been torpedoed by the so-called specialists: another case of *trahison des clercs* [treason of the educated classes] in music.

Charles Stuart, "*Katya Kabanova* Reconsidered," *The Music Review,* 12 (1951): 289–95.

45

ALBAN BERG ON *WOZZECK*

Berg began work on *Wozzeck* in 1914, shortly after having witnessed a stage performance of the masterpiece by Georg Büchner (1813–37). Called up in the Austrian army at the outbreak of World War I, he was forced to interrupt work for three years, during which he had a taste of military life at first hand, though only on the home front. Completion of the opera proceeded slowly, and the full score was not finished until April 1922. The première took place at the Berlin Staatsoper under Erich Kleiber on 14 December 1925. Surrounded by controversy because perceived by many as a dangerous example of "atonality" and because of political intrigues against Kleiber, *Wozzeck* nevertheless was a great public success from the start, and there were critics even then who recognized it as a milestone in the history of opera. One view of it that became fashionable among critics was that, by concentrating on traditional musical forms, Berg had intended to reform opera ("reform" again!), leading it into a post-Wagnerian era. When in 1927 Berg was asked by the League of Composers in New York to contribute an article on *Wozzeck* to their magazine, he addressed himself to this issue.

A WORD ABOUT *WOZZECK*

I find it hard to answer the request to write something about my opera *Wozzeck,* for it is ten years since I started to compose it. Since then so much has been written about it that I can say nothing, especially of a general nature, that has not already been said, and, should I nevertheless do so, I would have to plagiarize my own critics, which of course is not expected, particularly of me.

There is one inducement, however, and that is to correct an error, arising as soon as the opera became known, which has spread widely since. I never entertained the idea of reforming the artistic structure of the opera through *Wozzeck.* Neither when I started nor when I completed this work did I consider it a model for further operatic efforts, whoever the composer might be. I never assumed or expected that *Wozzeck* should in this sense become the basis of a school.

I wanted to compose good music; to develop musically the contents of Büchner's immortal drama; to translate his poetic language into music; but other than that, when I decided to write an opera, my only intention, as related to the technique of composition, was to give the theater what belongs to the theater. In other words, the music was to be so formed as to consciously fulfill its duty, at each moment, of serving the action. Even more, the music should be prepared to furnish whatever the action needed for transformation into the reality on the stage. It was the function of the composer to solve the problems of an ideal stage director. And at the same time, this intention must not prejudice the development of the music as an entity that was absolute, that was purely musical. There was to be no interference by externals with its individual existence.

That these purposes should be accomplished by a use of musical forms more or less ancient (considered by critics as one of the most important of my ostensible reforms of the opera) was a natural consequence. For the libretto it was necessary to make a selection from the twenty-six loosely constructed, partly fragmentary scenes by Büchner. Repetitions not lending themselves to musical variations had to be avoided. Finally, the scenes must be brought together, arranged and grouped in acts. The problem therefore became, utterly apart from my will, more musical than literary, one to be solved by the laws of musical structure rather than by the rules of dramaturgy.

It was impossible to take the fifteen scenes I selected and shape them in different manners so that each would retain its musical coherence and individuality and at the same time follow the customary method of development which is appropriate to the literary content. An absolute music, no matter how rich structurally, no matter how aptly it might fit the dramatic events would, after a number of scenes so composed, inevitably create musical monotony. The effect would become positively boring with a series of a dozen or so formally composed entr'actes which offered nothing but this type of illustrative music. Boredom, of course, is the last thing one should experience in the theater.

I obeyed the necessity of giving each scene and each accompanying piece of entr'acte music, whether prelude, postlude, connecting link or interlude, an unmistakable aspect, a rounded off and finished character. It was therefore imperative to use everything warranted to create individualizing characteristics on the one hand, and coherence on the other; thus the much discussed utilization of old and new musical forms and their application in an absolute music.

In one sense, the use of these forms in the opera, especially to such an extent, was unusual, even new. But certainly, as conscious intention, it is not at all to my credit as I have already demonstrated, and consequently I can and must reject the claim that I am a reformer of the opera through such innovations. However, I do not wish to depreciate my work through these explanations. Others who do not know it so well can do it much better. I therefore would like to suggest something which I consider my particular accomplishment.

No matter how cognizant any particular individual may be of the musical forms contained in the framework of this opera, of the precision and logic with which everything is worked out and the skill maintained in every detail, from the moment the curtain parts until it closes for the last time, there is no one in the audience who pays any attention to the various fugues, inventions, suites, sonata movements, variations and passacaglias... No one who heeds anything but the social problems of this opera which by far transcend the personal destiny of Wozzeck. This I believe to be my achievement.

Alban Berg, "A Word about Wozzeck," *Modern Music* 5, no. 1 (November-December 1927): 22–24.

In 1930 Berg wrote a two-part essay, in effect a set of instructions intended for distribution with the performance materials of *Wozzeck*. The title in German was "Praktische Anweisungen zur Einstudierung des *Wozzeck*" ("Practical Directions for the Preparation of *Wozzeck*"). The first part, "The Music," while in effect indispensable reading for all concerned with the production of the opera, makes little sense without a copy of the score, to which it constantly refers. It has therefore been omitted here. The second part, given below, while still requiring a close acquaintance with the opera, may be read and appreciated independently, even though the stage designer and director (for whom this section is primarily intended) are occasionally referred to specific places in the score. It may be noted that Berg is at some pains to indicate ways in which directors may exercise a limited amount of creativity within the parameters of the printed stage directions. It is as if he had sensed what would become a dominant trend for the rest of the century.

PRODUCTION AND STAGING

Not only is a precise knowledge of the Büchner drama assumed, but also of the music, at least so far as its character and its language, its dramatic style, are concerned. In spite of this unconditional requirement, the designer will be left sufficient scope for applying his own manner and style to his task. And this is so even if a realistic representation prevails throughout, as I think necessary, so that an immediate and unambiguous recognition and overall view of the place in which each scene is set is assured.

Knowledge of the music and of the diversity that has been sought in every respect, and which is also found in the musical language of the individual scenes, will lead in itself to a similar diversity (in every respect) in the stage design. This diversity will manifest itself as much in the distinctions between the street scenes (in the town and before the door of Marie's house), or between the large open space in which the tavern garden scene of Act II is placed and the narrow corner of the low dive of III/3. What possibilities for contrast, for example, between the latter scene and the landscapes in Acts I and III, especially that of the "open field," in which the sky, with its phenomena, spans the whole stage!

The scenic representation of these natural phenomena (the sunset that, to Wozzeck, is so uncanny) must likewise unfold with the utmost clarity imaginable (for the spectator as well), as, for instance, in the scenes at the pond, where the moon that is first seen near the horizon (III/2) again breaks through the clouds, but now higher in the sky (III/4). The water in the pond should also be recognizable as such. At one of the performances it was found to be very effective—and in complete correspondence with the music—to have the water in the pond begin to move gently at bar 275, to have this movement of the waves reach a climax at bars 285–86, and then to let it slowly subside, all movement ceasing completely at bar 302.

An exception to the demand for the greatest possible realism may perhaps be made in the low tavern scene (III/3). This scene, placed between the two scenes at the pond, may be given an immaterial, ghostly effect, for which it would suffice to have a mere suggestion of the place. This would permit the change of scene preceding and following to be managed within the unusually short period of time indicated. It should not be necessary to say so, but changes of scene here, as everywhere in the work, must be managed strictly within the time allowed by the continuous and uninterrupted music between the scenes. Now as ever, I must stress the importance of a precise observance of the stage directions regarding the curtain and changes of scene. And to this I must add that by "curtain" I literally mean only the principal curtain at the close of each act, whereas I have thought of the conclusions of the scenes within the acts in a less restrictive sense, as marked by drop curtains, gauze screens, blackouts (?), etc. In any case, at the exact place where the direction "Change of Scene" appears the stage must become invisible (also inaudible!), and only where the direction "Curtain rises" is given is it to be visible again. (It has been proved to be practical to direct the manipulation of the curtain from the orchestra rather than from the stage, where, because of the physical activity in scene-shifting the orchestra is often not heard and the required connection between the curtain and the music therefore almost impossible to realize.)

It is also important to observe the hour represented in the individual scenes. These changing times of the day and night must be clearly recognizable. For example, the twilight in the 5th scene of Act I must be substantially differentiated in its lighting from the other scenes that are played in the same setting, II/3 and III/5. It is likewise well to differentiate between the gradually fading evening light of I/3 and the morning sunlight in the same setting of II/1, as well as the night-time candle light of III/1.

NB: The night scene (II/5) in the barracks becomes brighter at bar 761, since the returning Drum Major enters with a light and puts it down somewhere. When he disappears with it at bar 808 the gloom of the beginning of the scene is restored.

The work of the stage manager also demands an intimate knowledge of the music. The general meaning of a stage direction in Büchner is often only made explicit through the music. Marie's murder, for example, occurs at the moment that Wozzeck—once only—"plunges the knife into her throat" (bar 103). Everything that follows (bars 104–106) refers musically only to Marie and to her death. Any further carnage must therefore be avoided!

Likewise, in the next to last scene (III/4) Marie's corpse should dominate the scene only in bars 239–49, in correspondence with the course of the music, which is devoted entirely to Wozzeck except for these bars. The corpse must therefore remain almost invisible (perhaps in the shadow of the willows) the whole time.

On the other hand there are other scenes in which the fantasy of the producer is given much greater leeway. For example, in the scene in the Doctor's study it would not be unsuitable to have the action made more lively by a medical examination, temperature-taking, etc. in keeping with and parallel to the dialogue. Similar liberties may be taken in the two tavern scenes, in which, however, the seemingly harmless fun of the first (II/4) and the uncanny, almost demonic exuberance of the second (III/3) should be well differentiated.

But even in such scenes, which from the point of view of stage direction are more freely composed, the demands made by the musical characterization of certain roles must be taken into consideration. For example, with the appearance of the Idiot (Act II, bar 643) it gradually becomes quiet and at bar 651 every distraction through noisy and otherwise importunate activity on the part of the other guests at the inn should be avoided. A similar instance is found in the dialogue between the Captain and the Doctor at the forest path near the pond (III/4). Both of them, standing the whole while more or less aside, should perform this dialogue in a quasi-muted manner, for the main thing here is the music and the visual aspect of the scene.

Finally, and most important of all: the preparation of the scenes in which Marie's child appears (preferably played by a little girl, since girls are much more gifted than boys at that age), and above all the preparation of the final scene (with the important ensemble of the other children) cannot begin too early! These scenes must be absolutely secure by the time the general rehearsals on-stage begin, and by that time they should also have been completely rehearsed onstage and with the orchestra. Otherwise the scenes with the children will not only slow up rehearsals in the final period before the opening night, but it will no longer be possible to get these scenes ready through extra rehearsals. Such extra rehearsals, which usually can only be given with coach and piano, are no substitute for the contact between the orchestra and the children.

Alban Berg, "The Preparation and Staging of Wozzeck," trans. George Perle, *The Musical Times* 109 (1968): 518–21. Reprinted by the kind permission of Mr. George Perle.

46

BRECHT ON "EPIC OPERA"

Kurt Weill's and Bertolt Brecht's opera *Aufstieg und Fall der Stadt Mahagonny* (*Rise and Fall of the City of Mahagonny*) had its first performance on 9 March 1930 in Leipzig. As Brecht's footnote 3 below testifies, the event provoked riotous behavior in the audience, and protests on moral and political grounds accompanied the opera as it appeared in other cities—in stark contrast to the reception given to the same authors' *Die Dreigroschenoper* (*The Threepenny Opera*), which, since its première three years earlier, was quickly becoming the biggest theatrical success of Weimar Germany. Social criticism already marked the earlier work. In *Mahagonny* it became the main message and, for Brecht, the only reason for any opera to exist. With the publication of his *Remarks* on the work in 1930, Brecht made the need for theatrical reform (or "innovation") contingent on the reform of society as a whole. By now he was (and would remain for the rest of his life) a committed Marxist, and his comments on contemporary efforts to break with operatic convention are abrasive precisely because these efforts did not presuppose a simultaneous restructuring of society (see his references to Strauss's *Elektra*, Krenek's *Jonny spielt auf*, Stravinsky's *Oedipus Rex* by innuendo, and finally on *Gebrauchsmusik*). Kurt Weill had no such agenda, and the articles he published that year on *Mahagonny* differ substantially from Brecht's. As a result of their differences, the two dissolved their partnership in December 1931, during rehearsals for the opera's Berlin première. Brecht's essay is thus bound up with very specific historical circumstances. Yet there resonate through it themes that would inform all his later work and would have repercussions on much of the best theater—and opera—of the later twentieth century. (The cosigner of Brecht's article, Suhrkamp, was his publisher.)

REMARKS ON THE OPERA *RISE AND FALL OF THE CITY OF MAHAGONNY*

OPERA YES—BUT WITH INNOVATIONS!

For some time now there has been much talk about modernizing opera. Opera, it is felt, should be given a *contemporary* content, and its form should be *technified* [*technifiziert*] without altering its culinary character. Since opera is held dear by its public precisely because it is reactionary, one should be thinking about the influx of new social classes with new appetites, and indeed that is being done: one is intent on *democratizing* opera, naturally without altering the character of democracy, which consists in giving the "people" new rights, but not the possibility of realizing them. In the end, it is all the same to the waiter whom it is he is serving: serve he must! And so, innovations that will lead to modernizing opera are demanded or defended by the most progressive people; a discussion of principle regarding opera (its function) is not demanded and would not be defended.

This modesty in the demands of the most progressive people has commercial grounds of which they themselves are only partly aware. Such big establishments as opera, theater, the press etc. put across their conception incognito, so to say. While they have long been using the intellectual product (in this case music, poetry, criticism, etc.) of the intellectual workers who still share their profits—economically speaking, therefore, sharers in power, socially speaking proletarianoids—only to nourish their public organizations, and so evaluate this product their own way, steering it into their own channels, the intellectual workers themselves still harbor the illusion that this whole operation merely involves the use of their intellectual work and is therefore a secondary matter having no influence on their work but, on the contrary, providing them with influence. This confusion in the minds of musicians, writers, and critics concerning their situation has huge consequences, which are far too little noticed. For, thinking they own an establishment that in fact owns them, they defend an establishment over which they no longer exert any control, which no longer, as they still believe, is a means for those who produce, but has become a means directed against those who produce, that is against their own productivity (when the lat-

THAT WAY TO MAHAGONNY. *Drawing by Caspar Neher, the stage and costume designer for the Brecht-Weill opera.* Photo courtesy of the Weill-Lenya Research Center, New York.

ter pursues its own or new tendencies that are not consonant with or are opposed to those of the establishment). Their productivity takes on the aspect of catering. A value system arises that is based on commercialism. And this has as a general consequence that every work of art is judged in accordance with its suitability to the establishment, and never the establishment in accordance with its suitability to the work of art. They say: this or that work is good; and what they mean is: good for the establishment. But that establishment is determined by the existing society and accepts only that which keeps it in the society. Any innovation that doesn't threaten the social function of the establishment, namely, evening entertainment, might come under consideration. Not to be considered are innovations that might put pressure on its functional marketability, that would shift the establishment's place in society, bringing it closer to institutions of learning or publishing organizations. Society absorbs from the establishment what it requires in order to reproduce itself. And so the only "innovation" that will succeed is one leading to the modernization, but not the transformation, of existing society—regardless of whether this form of society is good or bad.

The most progressive people don't think of changing the establishment, because they believe they have an establishment that serves what they freely conceive, in other words, that changes automatically with each of their conceptions. But they do not conceive freely: the establishment fulfills its function with or without them, the theaters play every evening, the newspapers appear so many times a day; and they absorb whatever they need; and they simply need a given quantity of material.[1] . . .

OPERA YES—

The opera we have is the culinary opera. It was a source of enjoyment long before it became merchandise. It serves enjoyment even when it demands or dispenses education, for then it demands or dispenses the education of taste. It approaches all subjects hedonistically. It "experiences" and serves as an "experience."

Why is *Mahagonny* an opera? Its basic approach is that of opera, namely culinary. Does *Mahagonny* approach its subject hedonistically? It does. Is *Mahagonny* an experience? It is an experience. For: *Mahagonny* is a joke.

The opera Mahagonny *does conscious justice to the irrational element in the operatic genre.* The irrationality of opera consists in this, that here rational elements are used, concreteness and reality are striven for, while at the same time everything is undone by the music. A dying man is real. If at the same time he sings, the sphere of the irrational has been attained. (If the *listener* were to sing upon seeing him, that would not be the case.) The more unclear and unreal reality becomes because of the music, the more the whole event becomes enjoyable: for the result is a third, very complex thing, itself very real, with potentially very real effects, but totally remote from its object, from the reality it makes use of. The degree of enjoyment is directly dependent on the degree of unreality. . . .

This kind of approach is purely hedonistic.

So far as the content of this opera is concerned—*its content is enjoyment.* A joke, then, not just in its form, but also as object. Pleasure should at least be an object of investigation, if investigation is to be an object of pleasure. It appears here in its current historical guise: as merchandise.[2]

We won't deny that this content must have a provocative effect at first. When for example in the thirteenth segment the glutton eats himself to death, he does so because hunger is rampant. Although we never even hinted that oth-

---

[1]But those who produce act wholly on the instructions of the enterprise, economically and commercially; it monopolizes their activity, and the products of writers, composers, and critics increasingly take on the appearance of raw material: the end product is manufactured by the enterprise.

[2]Romanticism, too, is merchandise here. It appears purely as content, not as form.

ers were starving while he ate, nevertheless the effect was provocative. For although not everyone who has food dies from eating, there are nonetheless many who die of hunger because he dies from eating. His enjoyment is provocative because it is so fraught with implications.[3] As a source of enjoyment opera today has a provocative effect in such situations. Not of course on the few who listen. In its provocative element we see reality reinstated. *Mahagonny* might not be in the best of tastes, it might even (with a bad conscience) seek recognition because of that lack—it is culinary through and through.

Mahagonny is nothing if not an opera.

—BUT WITH INNOVATIONS!

Opera needed to be brought up to the technical standards of modern theater. The modern theater is epic theater. The following table shows some changes in emphasis from the dramatic to the epic theater.[4]

DRAMATIC THEATER FORM	EPIC THEATER FORM
action	narration
involves spectator in a staged action	makes the spectator an onlooker, but
consumes his active participation	awakens his participation
enables him to feel	forces him to make decisions
experience	global view
the spectator is transported somewhere	he is confronted with something
suggestion	argument
his feelings are preserved	he is driven to recognize
the spectator is in the midst, he empathizes	the spectator stands opposite, he studies
mankind as a known quantity	mankind the object of inquiry
unchangeable mankind	changeable and changing mankind
expectation as to the outcome	expectation as to the unfolding action
concatenation of scenes	each scene independent

---

[3] "A worthy gentleman with a beefy face had pulled out a bunch of keys and was fighting piercingly against the epic theater. His wife did not desert him in the hour of decision. The lady had stuck two fingers in her mouth, shut her eyes tightly, puffed out her cheeks. She outwhistled the cash-register keys."

(A. Polgar on the first performance of the opera *Mahagonny* in Leipzig.)

[4] The table does not show absolute opposites but merely shifts in emphasis. Thus, in the course of communicating, preference might be given to emotionally suggestive or rationally persuasive means.

development	montage
linear events	curves
evolutionary necessity	skips
mankind as fixed point	mankind as process
thought determines being	societal being determines thought
feeling	reason[5]

The penetration of the methods of epic theater in opera leads principally to a radical **separation of the elements.** The great struggle for primacy among word, music, and production (in which the persistent question is, which is the prime mover—music the mover of the stage production, or the stage production the mover of the music, etc.) can simply be set aside by means of the radical separation of the elements. So long as "Gesamtkunstwerk" means that everything is one big wash, so long, in other words, as the arts are to be "fused," each single one of the elements needs to be equally degraded, having been reduced to being a mere cue to the other. The process of fusion engages the spectator, who also gets fused, thus representing a passive (suffering) part of the "Gesamtkunstwerk." This sort of magic must of course be fought against. Anything that attempts to present hypnotic effects, produce unworthy intoxication, or cloud the proceedings must be given up.

Music, word, and stage needed to become more independent.

a) MUSIC

For music the following shift in emphasis has taken place:

DRAMATIC OPERA	EPIC OPERA
music serves	music communicates
music intensifies the text	displays the text
music declares the text	takes the text for granted
music illustrates	takes a position
music depicts the psychological situation	provides the context

Music is the most important contribution to the theme.[6]

---

[5]On change of emphasis within a theatrical production, see my essay "Dialogue on the Art of Theater."

[6]The huge number of laborers in opera orchestras allows nothing but associative music (one wave of sound producing another); therefore a reduction of the orchestral establishment to at most 30 specialists is necessary. The singer becomes a reporter whose private feelings must remain private.

b) TEXT

The joke gave rise to the opportunity to work up something didactic, direct, so that it would not be merely irrational. It assumed the form of the depiction of morals. The portrayers of morals are the acting characters. The text was not to be sentimental or moral, but rather was to depict sentimentality and morality. As important as the spoken words were now (in the captions [displayed on posters]) the written ones. By reading, the public gains easily the most comfortable relationship to the work.[7]

c) STAGE

The exhibition of independent images within a theatrical performance represents a novelty. [The designer Caspar] Neher's projections stand side by side with the events onstage, so that the real glutton is sitting in front of the glutton in the drawing. The scene repeats in flowing form what is held fast in the picture. Neher's projections are just as independent an element of the opera as are Weill's music and the text. They are its visual material.

   These innovations naturally assume also a new attitude on the part of the public that frequents opera houses.

THE CONSEQUENCES OF THE INNOVATIONS:

IS OPERA HARMED?

Doubtless certain wishes of the public that were satisfied without question by the old opera are no longer taken into consideration by the new one. What is the public's attitude at the opera, and can it change?

   Pouring out of the subway station, eager to become as wax in the hands of the magicians, grownups, relentless men proven in the struggle for existence, hasten to the box office. Together with their hats they leave at the cloakroom their usual behavior, their attitude "in life"; having left the cloakroom they settle in their seats with the attitude of kings. Should we resent them for it? To find this ridiculous it isn't necessary to prefer a royal attitude to that of cheesemongers. The attitude of these people at the opera is not worthy of them. Can they possibly change? Can one persuade them to bring out their cigars?

   The ground is paved for a change in that, technically speaking, the "content" has become an independent component to which text, music, and stage

---

[7]On the significance of the "captions" see "Remarks on the Threepenny Opera" and footnote 1 to the "Threepenny Film."

"are related"; in that illusion has been given up in favor of something one may discuss; and in that the spectator, instead of having to experience, may so to say vote; instead of identifying, may confront. The change transcends by far any question of form and begins to grasp the essential, social function of the theater.

The old opera excludes any discussion of content. Should it happen that, at the enacting of any given chain of events, the spectator should take a stand on those events, the old opera would have lost the battle, and the spectator would have got "out of it." Naturally, the old opera also contained elements that were not purely culinary—we must differentiate the period of its rise from that of its decline. *Zauberflöte, Figaro, Fidelio* contained ideological, activist elements. Yet the ideological, shall we say the daring element was so conditioned by the culinary that the *meaning* of those operas died away, fading into sheer pleasure. Though the essential meaning died away, it does not follow that the opera no longer had any meaning; it had another one, that of opera. The content was subsumed by the opera. Today's Wagnerians content themselves with the recollection that the original Wagnerians established, and therefore were aware of, a meaning. Those who still depend on Wagner for their productions stubbornly maintain an ideological attitude. (An ideology that, quite useless besides, still sells as a source of pleasure!) (*Elektra, Jonny spielt auf.*) An entire, richly developed technique, which made this attitude possible, is being preserved; with the attitude of an ideological adherent, the petty bourgeois lives his leisurely everyday life. Only from this point of view, the point of view of a dying meaning (mind you: this meaning *could* die), can the continuing innovations that affect opera be understood—as desperate attempts to lend this art a belated meaning, a "new" meaning, so that in the end it is the musical element itself that becomes this meaning; where, then, the flow of musical forms acquires a meaning *qua* flow, and certain proportions, shifts, etc. from being a means have successfully become a goal—progress that is the consequence of nothing and has nothing as a consequence, that does not arise from any new need but only satisfies old needs with new attractions, that in other words has a purely conservative purpose. New material elements are adopted that were previously unknown "in this setting," since, when "this setting" was adopted, they were unknown elsewhere too. (Locomotives, engine rooms, airplanes, bathrooms, etc., serve as distractions. The better composers deny content altogether and present it, or better remove it, in Latin.) This is progress that only demonstrates that something has been left behind. It is made without the basic function's being changed, or better, in order that it should not be changed. And *Gebrauchsmusik?*

At the very moment when art for art's sake was attained in its barest form in concert music (as a reaction against the emotional force of impressionistic music), there emerged, borne by the foam, so to say, the concept of *Gebrauchsmusik*, in which music used, as it were, the layman. The layman was used the way a woman is "used." Innovation after innovation: the tired listener began to enjoy playing. The battle against listener's sloth turned into the battle for listener's activity and then into performer's activity. The orchestral cellist, head of a numerous family, no longer played for ideological reasons, but out of sheer joy. The culinary element was safe!

One has to ask: why this marching in place? Why this stubborn holding onto the hedonism, the intoxication? Why this scant interest for one's own concerns beyond one's four walls? Why no discussion?

Answer: Nothing can be expected from discussion. A discussion concerning the present form of society, even one concerning its least important components, would at once and irresistibly lead to an absolute threat to this form of society as a whole.

We have seen that opera is sold as an evening's entertainment, on account of which all attempts to change it come up against clearly defined limits. So we see: this entertainment must be splendid and devoted to illusion. Why?

In today's society the old opera cannot be, so to say, "wished away." Its illusions have important functions in society. The intoxication is indispensable; nothing can take its place.[8] Nowhere if not at the opera does a human have a chance to remain human! His rational faculties have long since been lowered to such things as fearful mistrust, cheating others, self-centered calculation.

The old opera subsists not only because it is old but principally because the conditions it serves are still the old ones. Yet not quite. And therein lie the prospects for the new opera. Today it is already possible to ask whether opera is not yet in a condition where further innovations will no longer lead to the renovation of the genre but to its destruction.[9]

No matter how culinary *Mahagonny* may be—as culinary as is fitting for an opera—still it already has a social function; for it puts the culinary element up for discussion, it confronts the society that makes such operas necessary; it still sits grandly, so to say, on the old branch, but at least it is beginning to saw it off (absentmindedly or out of a bad conscience)... And that's what the innovations have done with their singing.

True innovations strike at the root.

---

[8]Life, as it is imposed on us, is too hard for us, it brings us too much pain, too many disappointments, insoluble tasks. In order to bear it, we cannot do without palliatives. Of these there are perhaps three kinds: powerful distractions that allow us to minimize our suffering, substitute pleasures that reduce it, intoxicants that make us insensitive to it. Something of this sort is indispensable. Substitute pleasures such as those supplied by art are illusions with respect to reality, therefore not less effective, thanks to the role played by the imagination in our psychic life (Freud, *Civilization and its Discontents*, p. 22 [German ed.]). Under certain conditions, these intoxicants are responsible for the needless loss of great stores of energy that could be used for the betterment of the human lot (ibid., p. 28).

[9]In the opera *Mahagonny* they are those innovations that enable the theater to display representations of morals (to reveal pleasure as well as the pleasure seeker as merchandise) and those innovations by means of which the spectator is made morally aware.

FOR INNOVATIONS—AGAINST RENOVATION

The opera *Mahagonny* was written [actually begun] three years ago, in 1927. In subsequent works ever greater attempts were made to emphasize the didactic at the cost of the culinary. That is, to develop a didactic object out of a medium of enjoyment and to restructure certain institutes from places of pleasure into organs of publication.

Brecht. Suhrkamp.

[Bertolt] Brecht, *Versuche 1–12: Heft 1–4* (Berlin: Suhrkamp, 1959), 101–7. ©Stefan Brecht. Trans. P.W.

47

SHOSTAKOVICH AND THE *LADY MACBETH OF MTSENSK* DEBACLE

Shostakovich's second opera, *Lady Macbeth of the Mtsensk District*, completed in 1932 and first performed on 22 January 1934 in Leningrad, was an instant, tumultuous success. Already prominent in the first Soviet-educated generation of composers, Shostakovich with this opera became its undisputed leader, recognized as such both in the Soviet Union and abroad, where the work enjoyed several performances. Its American première took place (in concert form) in Cleveland on 31 January 1935 under Artur Rodzinski, who repeated it the following week at the Metropolitan Opera. It was evidently in preparation for these performances that the League of Composers published the following article in its quarterly journal. The footnote at the very beginning reflected Shostakovich's true intentions at the time with regard to his future operas. It will be seen presently why nothing came of them.

MY OPERA, LADY MACBETH OF MTZENSK [*]

I began to write the opera *Lady Macbeth of Mtzensk* at the end of 1930 and completed it in December of 1932. Why did I select just this novel by Nikolai Leskov for its subject?

First, because very little of our heritage in Russian classic literature had been utilized in the development of Soviet opera. Second—and this was most important—because Leskov's narrative is imbued with rich dramatic and social content. There is, perhaps, no other creation in all Russian literature which so vividly portrays the position of women in old, pre-revolutionary Russia.

But I have given *Lady Macbeth of Mtzensk* a different treatment from that of Leskov. As will be seen from the title itself the novelist approached his subject ironically. The name indicates an insignificant territory, a small district; and the characters are little people, with passions and interests not comparable to those in Shakespeare's play. Moreover Leskov, an outstanding representative of pre-revolutionary literature, gives us no illuminating interpretation of the incidents which are developed in his story. As a Soviet composer, I determined to preserve the strength of Leskov's novel, and yet, approaching it critically, to interpret its events from our modern point of view.

Accordingly, the subject itself has been somewhat altered. In Leskov's novel Ekaterina Lvovna Izmailova, the heroine, commits three murders before she is sentenced to hard labor in Siberia. She kills her father-in-law, her husband and her nephew. As I proposed to justify the action of Ekaterina Lvovna and create an impression of a definite personality, deserving of sympathy, I omitted the third murder, undertaken solely to make herself the heir of her slain husband.

Now to arouse sympathy for Ekaterina was no simple matter. She has committed a number of crimes against accepted moral or ethical laws. Leskov presents her simply as a cruel woman who "wallows in fat" and murders innocent people. But I have conceived Ekaterina as a woman clever, gifted and interesting. Set by fate in gloomy, miserable surroundings, belonging to a merchant class which is hard, greedy and "small," her life is sorrowful and pitiable. She does not love her husband, she has no happiness, no recreation. There now appears Sergei, a clerk hired by her husband, Zinovy Borisovich. She falls in love with this young man, an unworthy and negative creature, and in her love she finds joy and the purpose of her existence. In order to marry Sergei she commits her series of crimes. When Timofeevich, her father-in-law, catches Sergei after a meeting with her and orders him to be lashed, she is inspired by a desire for revenge. She poisons her father-in-law for the sufferings inflicted upon her

---

[*]This opera, soon to be seen and heard in America, is the first of a projected cycle of four in which the composer, Shostakovitch, plans to trace the condition of women in Russia. Lady Macbeth is of 1840, the second will be set in the Czarist period of about 1860, the third in the 1917 revolution, and the fourth will present woman in Russia today.

lover. Sergei now urges her to marry him and, together with Ekaterina, he stran-
gles her husband. Thus in her love for Sergei Ekaterina sacrifices all of herself.
On the discovery of the crimes they are sentenced together to Siberia at hard
labor. When she finds that he no longer loves her and has turned to the prosti-
tute Sonetka, she drowns her rival and herself. Without Sergei's love, life has
lost its only interest.

It is unnecessary for me to relate the action further. For I have justified it
chiefly by the musical material. It is my belief that in opera music should play
the principal and the deciding role.

I have tried to make the music of the opera as simple and expressive as possible. I do not agree with the theories, at one time current among us, that in the
modern opera the vocal line must be absent, or that it should be no more than
speech in which the intonations are to be accented. Opera is above all a vocal
production and singers should occupy themselves with their real duty—that is,
to sing, and not to speak, recite or intone. Thus I have built all the vocal parts
on a broad cantilena taking into account all the possibilities of that richest of instruments, the human voice.

The musical development progresses constantly and on a symphonic form;
in this respect I have abandoned the old operatic formula of construction on individual parts. The musical stream flows unbroken and is interrupted solely by
the ending of each act; it resumes its course in the following one, not piece-wise,
but by developing further on a grand symphonic scale. This must be taken into
consideration during the production of the opera, as in each act, except the fourth,
there are several scenes and these scenes are separated not by mechanical pauses
but by musical entr'actes during which the change of scenery takes place. The
entr'actes between the second and third, fourth and fifth, sixth and seventh and
between the seventh and eighth scenes are merely the continuation and further
development of preceding musical ideas and play a great part in the characterization of what takes place on the stage.

And now a few words in regard to the principal personages and their musical characterization. The most important is, of course, Ekaterina, a dramatic soprano. Her musical language is shaped completely by my idea that she must by
every means evoke sympathy. In her music there are a tender and warm lyricism, a sincere, profound sorrow in suffering, and also joy in moments of happiness. The musical language given to Ekaterina Lvovna has been designed for
the one purpose of justifying this "criminal." To quote the famous words of Do-
broliubov about Leskov's character, she is "a ray of light in a kingdom of gloom."

The suffering folk of that epoch are presented in the fourth act—at hard labor. There is no darker picture of the old days than that of the halting place of
convicts, of broken people moving under guard through the far off expanses of
the former Russian empire, to penal servitude. How unforgettable is the picture
drawn by Dostoievsky in his "Memoirs of the House of the Dead": the little girl
who gave him, a convict at hard labor, a kopeck, and the peasants in the villages

СУМБУР ВМЕСТО МУЗЫКИ

Об опере «Леди Макбет Мценского уезда»

"MUDDLE INSTEAD OF MUSIC." The Pravda *article that shut down Shostakovich's* Lady Macbeth *and struck terror in the hearts of all artists liable to come under suspicion of* "formalism."

who sacrificed their bread to the "unfortunates." Such reactions I intended to arouse for the prisoners in the fourth act of my opera.

All the remaining members of the cast—Boris Timofeevich, Zinovy Borisovich, Sergei, etc.—are but expressions of the dismal and hopeless existence of the merchant class of that period. Izmailov's clerks are potentially the same future merchants as the Izmailovs, they cheat and short-change so that in time they themselves may open their own little shops and become real merchants. These characters I have endowed with negative traits.

Sergei, the clerk, is the evil genius who turns up in Ekaterina Lvovna's hard life. He is a "small" scoundrel whose aim in life is to attain security and, as he says, "to satiate himself with woman's sweet flesh." Because of him Ekaterina murders her father-in-law and her husband. When she is no longer a rich merchant's wife, but a common convict, without a moment's thought he throws her aside and finds a new woman. He has picked up a little "culture," reads books and expresses himself in high-sounding language; his outlook upon the world is servile and mean.

Thus for Sergei the music is insincere, showy, theatrical; his sufferings are affected; through his handsome, gallant exterior peers the future "kulak." He is a Don Juan, not in the sense of the famous legend, but a cruel, cunning criminal. Even in Siberia at hard labor he still remains a "small," coarse person.

Boris Timofeevich, Ekaterina's father-in-law, is a solid and powerful old man, who stops at nothing to gain his desires. His son Zinovy Borisovich, Ekaterina's husband, is a pitiable wretch, the "frog who longed to be an ox." When he tries to speak authoritatively as the master in his home, the music exposes him and we see a weak, pathetic specimen of the merchant class.

A final word in regard to the general musical character of the opera. As previously stated, it is written from first to last note upon a symphonic form; the orchestra must therefore never be reduced to a mere accompaniment. On the other hand it must not be elevated to such a position that it will distract from and stifle the action of the stage.

Modern Music 12, no. 1 (November-December 1934): 23–28.

By 1936 *Lady Macbeth* had been performed about two hundred times in Leningrad and Moscow alone. At one point, three separate productions were playing simultaneously in Moscow. Then on 26 January 1936, Stalin, Molotov, and their entourage went to see the opera. Shostakovich, alerted, attended the performance expecting the leaders would want to compliment him afterwards, as they had done with a minor composer (Dzerzhinsky) earlier that month. Instead, Stalin and his entourage left before the end of the performance. Troubled, Shostakovich nevertheless did not expect what happened next: on 28 January, *Pravda*, the official government newspaper, came out with an unsigned editorial (given below) blasting the opera and carrying unspecified, and therefore terrifying, threats to the composer and all other "leftists" and "formalists," not just in music but in all the arts, and even in the sciences. And lest it should be thought this was simply a newspaper editorial, it was followed up with a powerful barrage of public browbeating, including meetings of the Moscow and Leningrad Unions of Composers, at which Shostakovich and his opera, and the trends they exemplified were excoriated. "Meyerholdism" in the editorial is a reference to Vsevolod Meyerhold, the Moscow theatrical director and mentor of the composer, who eventually fell victim to the Stalinist purges and was shot in 1940. Shostakovich, officially reinstated after his Fifth

Symphony was performed in 1937, suffered renewed public degradation in 1948, and was finally rehabilitated after Stalin's death in 1953. However, the events of 1936 left an indelible mark on the composer and in one respect proved fateful: for Shostakovich never wrote another opera.

MUDDLE INSTEAD OF MUSIC
About the Opera "Lady Macbeth of the Mtsensk District"

With the general cultural development of our country there grew also the necessity for good music. At no time and in no other place has the composer had a more appreciative audience. The people expect good songs, but also good instrumental works, and good operas.

Certain theaters are presenting to the new culturally mature Soviet public Shostakovich's opera *Lady Macbeth* as an innovation and an achievement. Musical criticism, always ready to serve, has praised the opera to the skies and given it resounding glory. The young composer, instead of hearing serious business-like criticism, which could have helped him in his future work, hears only enthusiastic compliments.

From the first minute, the listener is shocked by deliberate dissonance, by a confused stream of sounds. Snatches of melody, the beginnings of a musical phrase, are drowned, emerge again, and disappear in a grinding and squealing roar. To follow this "music" is most difficult; to remember it, impossible.

Thus it goes practically throughout the entire opera. The singing on the stage is replaced by shrieks. If the composer chances to come on the path of a clear and simple melody, then immediately, as though frightened at this misfortune, he throws himself back into a wilderness of musical chaos—in places becoming cacophony. The expression which the listener demands is supplanted by wild rhythm. Passion is here supposed to be expressed by musical noise. All this is not due to lack of talent, or to lack of ability to depict simple and strong emotions in music. Here is music turned deliberately inside out in order that nothing will be reminiscent of classical opera, or have anything in common with symphonic music or with simple and popular musical language accessible to all. This music is built on the basis of rejecting opera—the same basis on which leftist art rejects in the theater simplicity, realism, clarity of image, and the unaffected spoken word—which carries into the theater and into music the most negative features of "Meyerholdism" infinitely multiplied. Here we have leftist confusion instead of natural, human music. The power of good music to infect the masses has been sacrificed to a petty-bourgeois, formalist attempt to create originality through cheap clowning. It is a game of clever ingenuity that may end very badly.

The danger of this trend to Soviet music is clear. Leftist distortion in opera stems from the same source as the leftist distortion in painting, poetry, teaching, and science. Petty-bourgeois "innovations" lead to a break with real art, real science, and real literature.

The author of *Lady Macbeth* was forced to borrow from jazz its nervous, convulsive, and spasmodic music in order to lend "passion" to his characters. While our music critics swear by the name of socialist realism, the stage serves us, in Shostakovich's creation, the coarsest kind of naturalism. He reveals the merchants and the people monotonously and bestially. The predatory merchant woman who scrambles into possession of wealth through murder is pictured as some kind of "victim" of bourgeois society. The story of Leskov has been given a significance it does not possess.

And all this is coarse, primitive, and vulgar. The music quacks, grunts, and growls, and suffocates itself, in order to express the amatory scenes as naturalistically as possible. And "love" is smeared all over the opera in the most vulgar manner. The merchant's double bed occupies the central position on the stage. On it all "problems" are solved. In the same coarse, naturalistic style is shown the death from poisoning and the flogging—both practically on stage.

The composer apparently never considered the problem of what the Soviet audience expects and looks for in music. As though deliberately, he scribbles down his music, confusing all the sounds in such a way that his music would reach only the effete formalists who had lost their wholesome taste. He ignored the demand of Soviet culture that all coarseness and wildness be abolished from every corner of Soviet life. Some critics call this glorification of merchants' lust a satire. But there is no question of satire here. The author has tried, with all the musical and dramatic means at his command, to arouse the sympathy of the spectators for the coarse and vulgar leanings and behavior of the merchant woman Katerina Ismailova.

Lady Macbeth is having great success with bourgeois audiences abroad. Is it not because the opera is absolutely unpolitical and confusing that they praise it? Is it not explained by the fact that it tickles the perverted tastes of the bourgeoisie with its fidgety, screaming, neurotic music?

Our theaters have expended a great deal of labor on giving Shostakovich's opera a thorough presentation. The actors have shown exceptional talent in dominating the noise, the screaming, and the roar of the orchestra. With their dramatic action they tried to reinforce the weakness of melodic content. Unfortunately, this served only to bring out the opera's vulgar features more vividly. The talented acting earns gratitude; the wasted effort, regrets.

Victor Ilyich Seroff with Nadejda Galli-Shohat, *Dmitri Shostakovich: The Life and Background of a Soviet Composer* (New York: Alfred A. Knopf, 1943), 204–7.

INTERLUDE: AN ITALIAN CLAQUE

The claque (a French word) was born at the Paris Opéra in the nineteenth century, but it has flourished elsewhere too. Paid applauders, or claqueurs, have helped the careers of many a deserving and undeserving opera singer and composer. In Italy they acquired some national traits, very finely portrayed in the following account of his short-lived participation in this activity by Eugenio Montale, the Italian poet and essayist. The piece first appeared in the Milan daily *Corriere della sera* in 1950.

At the opera the other evening, the claque leader must have fallen asleep. (The opera, beautiful but unpopular, encouraged sleep and made it hard to time the *benes* and the *bravos*.) That's the only way I can explain to myself how it happened that a bass aria composed of two matching stanzas was interrupted by tempestuous applause at the end of the first stanza, that is to say, at a point where no musical clause, no vocal effect could justify the sudden clapping. What had happened? The claque leader, waking up, had given his signal at the wrong time, that's all. There was some hushing, and the aria continued; but now the game was up, and when effect made its appearance as the bass at last descended into the "cellar," the listless applause that issued forth from a place that was by now topographically suspect persuaded no one.

We should be very indulgent towards claqueurs. I don't believe they make a lot of money; and where the public displays unjustified coldness towards the champions of operatic art, they perform a task that is perfectly understandable. An opera, a musical drama without applause does not warm the heart, is not even a show. To do without seeing Radames and Ramfis take a curtain call after the synchronous bellow of "Immenso Ftà," not to want to scrutinize close up their bathrobes, their turbans, is to renounce half the pleasure *Aida* can offer; not to grunt approval of Sparafucile's deep gargle as he moves away from Rigoletto after offering him his foul services represents at least a want of charity, of human solidarity. That modest, grating sound is not a hard sound to produce, but it is more than a sound, it is the symbol of the life of a diver. Whoever has lived in rented rooms, in fourth-class hotels and pensions, has heard thousands of such non-Dostoyevskyan "voices from underground."

Last evening's applause took me back in time. It used to be that claqueurs were recruited from among barbers. They were not applauders by profession but out of sheer enthusiasm; and if that enthusiasm produced some loose change, so much the better. I myself, when I decided to make a study of bel canto, was initiated by my barber's "circle." Barber Pecchioli, the claque leader of my city, was a connoisseur and rarely gave the signal with a snap of his fingers. In the better-known pieces, in the more obviously effective arias, he let his followers and the paying public take over. He only intervened in difficult cases: in some *pianissimo*, in some rare *diminuendo*, in the riskier vocal plunges. Then he murmured a "bravo" so spontaneously that no one could suspect there was a price, a tariff attached to it.

Personally, I must say I wasn't one of his favorite clients before I put my vocal destiny in his hands. A rare client, one of those that go to the barber only for a haircut and refuse the shampoo, the lotions, and the expensive massage, I could not awaken his sympathy. Nevertheless, on one occasion he decided to have recourse to my temporary aid, and on that evening I found myself among the troops of his claque. . . .

In those days the music of the future was represented almost exclusively by Wagner, by then endured by most people. But a music like that of Signor Rebillo, all dissonance and screeching, had never been heard before. Was Rebillo a genius or a madman? To judge by the titles of his compositions—I remember a *Dying Water Lily*, presented as a "musical still life"—I should conclude that he was at least a precursor. But at that time I would have known even less than I do now.

And so it happened that on the evening of the concert I too entered the theater with a complimentary pass and with the intention of doing my duty; but when the dying Water Lily had breathed its last and I was about to begin clapping, a chorus of hisses and protests arose from every row of seats and every corner in the galleries, and the faint cry of "Viva Rebillo!" was submerged by an almost unanimous yell of "Basta! Out with the author! Out the door!" that even reached the climactic note of "Death to Berillo!"—where the musician's name appeared garbled in a most poetic way. Was there an active counterclaque? Or did Signor Rebillo have many enemies in the city? I never found out. Caught up in the turmoil and far from Pecchioli, I hastened to align myself with the majority and like a coward joined those who were yelling "Down with him! Out the door!" The evening ended amidst hissing and laughter, and I left without being spotted by my "leader."

Eugenio Montale, *Farfalla di Dinard* (Milan: Leonardo, 1994), 56–58. Trans. P.W.

48

PETER GRIMES IN POSTWAR LONDON

The Second World War had ended in Europe just a few weeks before Benjamin Britten's first full-length opera, *Peter Grimes*, had its première, on 7 June 1945, at Sadler's Wells in London. Its success was instantaneous and lasting. The distinguished American literary critic Edmund Wilson was on assignment from *The New Yorker* at the time, visiting some of the war zones in newly-liberated Europe. In London, the devastation from the bombing was to be seen everywhere, as was the psychological aftermath of the war effort. It was therefore a not wholly unrelated experience that awaited him when, in July, a girl he knew ("G.") took him to see *Peter Grimes*, that summer's theatrical sensation.

I was a little taken aback one evening for which I had had vague other plans to find out that I was going with G. to a new opera by Benjamin Britten which was being done at Sadler's Wells. She had bought the tickets herself and said nothing about it in advance. The only thing I had heard by Britten had been a *Requiem* that had not much impressed me, and I did not feel particularly eager to sit through an English opera called *Peter Grimes*, based on an episode from Crabbe. G. did try, with her usual lack of emphasis, to get me to read the libretto, of which she had procured a copy, but she did not explain that this work had been something of a sensation in London, where the critics, who, like me, had not at first expected anything extraordinary, had been roused from their neat routine to the point of hearing it several times and writing two or three articles about it. But she knew that I ought to hear it, and it is one of my debts to G. that she made me go to *Peter Grimes*, which I should unquestionably otherwise have missed.

For, almost from the moment when the curtain went up on the bare room in the provincial Moot Hall—which no overture had introduced—where the fisherman Peter Grimes was being examined at a coroner's inquest in connection with the death of his apprentice, I felt the power of a musical gift and a dramatic imagination that woke my interest and commanded my attention. There have been relatively few composers of the first rank who had a natural gift for the theater: Mozart, Musorgsky, Verdi, Wagner, the Bizet of *Carmen*. To be confronted, without preparation, with an unmistakable new talent of this kind is an astonishing, even an electrifying, experience. The difficulty of describing *Peter Grimes* to someone who has not heard it is the difficulty of convincing people whose expectations are likely to be limited by having listened to too much modern music that was synthetic, arid, effortful and inadequate, that a new master has really arrived; of conveying to them the special qualities of a full-grown original artist. In my own case, I am particularly handicapped by lack of technical knowledge and training, so that I can only give an account of the opera's spell without being able to analyze it intelligently. The best I can do, then, is to report my impression—subject to expert correction—that Britten's score shows no signs of any of the dominant influences—Wagner, Debussy, Stravinsky, Schoenberg or Prokofiev—but has been phrased in an idiom that is personal and built with a definiteness and solidity that are as English as Gilbert and Sullivan (one can find, for an English opera, no other comparison in the immediate past). And the result of this is very different from anything we have been used to. The ordinary composer of opera finds his conventions there with the stage; but, when you are watching *Peter Grimes*, you are almost completely unaware of anything that is artificial, anything "operatic." The composer here seems quite free from the self-consciousness of contemporary musicians. You do not feel you are watching an experiment; you are living a work of art. The opera seizes upon you, possesses you, keeps you riveted to your seat during the action and keyed up during the intermissions, and drops you, purged and exhausted, at the end.

The orchestra, in *Peter Grimes*, plays a mainly subordinate role, and the first effect on the hearer, during the opening scene in the Moot Hall, is of a drastic simplification of opera to something essential and naked, which immediately wakes one up. There is no Wagnerian web of motifs that tells you about the characters: the characters express themselves directly, either conversing or soliloquizing in song, while the orchestra, for the most part, but comments. The music is a close continuity, though articulated rather than fluid, of vivid utterances on the part of the personages and—except in the more elaborate interludes—sharp and terse descriptive strokes, in which from time to time take shape arias, duets, trios and choruses. These—almost never regular in pattern and never losing the effect of naturalness—have their full or fragmentary developments, and give way to the next urgent pulse of the blood-stream that runs though the whole piece. In the same way the words of the libretto, by the poet Montague Slater, which are admirably suited to the music and which the music exactly fits, shift sometimes into the imagery of poetry but never depart far from the colloquial and are sometimes—with no loss of dignity—left perfectly bald and flat. But we soon come to recognize in the music the extraordinary flexibility, the subtlety and the variety, which are combined with a stout British craftsmanship that has a sure hand with mortise and tenon and that knows how to plant and mass a chorus, and with a compelling theatrical sense, an instinct for tempo and point. And—what is most uncommon with opera—we find ourselves touched and stirred at listening to an eloquence of voices that does not merely charm or impress us as the performance of well-trained singers but that seems sometimes to reach us directly with the emotions of actual people. Nor do these voices find their expression exclusively through the singers' roles: one of the most effective devices of *Peter Grimes* is the use of the orchestral interludes that take place between the scenes while the curtain is down. Thus at the end of the first scene in the Moot Hall, where you have just been seeing Peter Grimes consoled by Ellen Orford, the schoolteacher, the only being in the town who cares for him, the orchestra develops a theme which seems to well up out of Ellen's heart, and then rises and falls with a plangency that, sustained through the long passage with marvellous art, conveys, as if her spirit were speaking, her sympathy and pain for Peter. And at the end of the scene that follows, when a storm has been heard coming up as Balstrode, the retired captain, has been trying to remonstrate with Peter over his plan to take another apprentice and prove to the town that he is not a monster, the winds and the waves break loose the moment the curtain falls, fiendishly yelping and slapping in a way that represents with realism—Britten was born on the Suffolk coast—the worrying raving crescendo of an equinoctial gale but that howls at the same time with the fierceness of Peter's rebellious pride and of the latent sadistic impulse of which he is half unconscious but to which the new situation will eventually give free rein. The sea's restive and pressing movement has been all through the scene that preceded; and in the next, in the local tavern to which the people have resorted for warmth and cheer, the hurricane wildly intrudes whenever the door is opened and at last, with the entrance of Grimes, rushes into the room to stay. This long act, which is brought to its climax by the silence that greets Peter's appearance and that concentrates the hostility of the town, and by the arrival of the orphan whom, the carrier refusing, Ellen has herself gone to fetch and for whose welfare she hopes to make herself responsible—this act has an intensity and an impetus that carries one through, without a moment's letdown, from the opening to the end. Nor is what follows much less effective. The whole drama is a stretching of tension between the inquest and the inevitable crisis when Grimes will, if not deliberately kill, at least cause the death of, the second apprentice; and I do not remember ever to have seen, at any performance of opera, an audience so steadily intent, so petrified and held in suspense, as the audience of *Peter Grimes*. This is due partly to the dramatic skill of Britten, but it is due also to his having succeeded in harmonizing, through *Peter Grimes*, the harsh helpless emotions of wartime. This opera could have been written in no other age, and it is one of the very few works of art that have seemed to me, so far, to have spoken for the blind anguish, the hateful rancors and the will to destruction of these horrible years. Its grip on its London audience is clearly of the same special kind as the grip of the recent productions of *Richard III* and *The Duchess of Malfi*. Like them, it is the chronicle of an impulse to persecute and to kill which has become an obsessive compulsion, which drags the malefactor on—under a fatality which he does not understand, from which he can never get free, and which never leaves him even the lucidity for repentance or reparation—through a series of uncontrollable cruelties which will lead, in the long run, to his being annihilated himself. At first you think that Peter Grimes is Germany. He is always under the impression, poor fellow, that what he really wants for himself is to marry Ellen Orford and to live in a nice little cottage with children and fruit in the garden "and whitened doorstep and a woman's care." Above all, he wants to prove to his neighbors that he is not the scoundrel they think him, that he really means no harm to his apprentices and that he will make a good family man. But he cannot help flying into a fury when the boy does not respond to his will, and when he gets angry, he beats him; and his townsmen become more and more indignant. At last, shouting, "Peter Grimes!," they go on the march against him, determined to capture him and make him pay, just at the moment when he has paused and relented, and when their approach will precipitate, in his dash to escape, his pushing the boy so that he falls over the cliff, which is finally to settle his fate. (A comparison of the text of the opera with the story as told by Crabbe in *The Borough* shows that Britten and Montague Slater—though they have used here and there a few lines from Crabbe—have put Peter in a different situation and invented for him a new significance. The outlaw fisherman in Crabbe is married, though his wife does not figure in the story, and he has no connection with Ellen Orford, who is the heroine of a separate episode. The mainspring of the original version is Peter's rebellion against his father: he is in Crabbe completely antisocial and has no hankering for middle-class decency.) But, by the time you are done with the opera—or by the time it is done with you—you have decided that Peter Grimes is the whole of bombing, machine-gunning, mining, torpedoing, ambushing humanity, which talks about a guaranteed standard of living yet does nothing but wreck its own works, degrade or pervert its own moral life and reduce itself to starvation. You feel, during the final scenes, that the indignant shouting trampling mob which comes to punish Peter Grimes is just as sadistic as he. And when Balstrode gets to him first and sends him out to sink himself in his boat, you feel that you are in the same boat as Grimes.

Edmund Wilson, *Europe without Baedeker: Sketches among the Ruins of Italy, Greece and England, together with Notes from a European Diary: 1963–1964* (New York: The Noonday Press, 1966), 186–91.

49

STRAVINSKY, AUDEN, AND
THE RAKE'S PROGRESS

After viewing Hogarth's eight paintings of "The Rake's Progress" (1733) at the Chicago Art Institute in May 1947, Stravinsky decided they would form the subject of an English-language opera he had been meaning to compose. He was living in Hollywood at the time, and he asked his neighbor Aldous Huxley to recommend a librettist. Huxley recommended W. H. Auden; the result was one of the most successful operas of the later twentieth century. The first contacts between the composer and the librettist (who would soon be joined by Chester Kallman as collaborator) are recorded below. Note, in the first letter, Stravinsky's original intention of avoiding recitative and using spoken dialogue instead; he later changed his mind and employed "secco" recitative, complete with harpsichord.

October 6, 1947

Dear Mr. Auden:

Mr. [Ralph] Hawkes wrote me of his interview with you and your enthusiasm to write the libretto to my projected opera and to start working right away. But how to go about it—you in New York, I here until spring? Corresponding on such [an] intricate matter, of course, [is] quite arduous, but what is there to be done?

At any rate, I believe, the first thing is that you prepare a general outline of *The Rake's Progress*. I think at the moment of two acts, maybe five scenes (five [*sic*] for the first and two for the second act). I also plan to incorporate a Choreographic Divertissement in the first act's finale. Chamber music orchestration of which [the] dimension [is] not yet established. Mr. Hawkes suggested about ten characters, but I believe seven soloists a good number.

After the outline is completed, I suggest you prepare a free verse preliminary for the characters (arias, duets, trios, etc.), also for small chorus. Bear in mind that I will compose *not* a musical drama, but just an opera with definitely separated numbers connected by spoken (not sung) words of the text, because I want to avoid the customary operatic recitative. Please, do feel absolutely free in your creative work on the chosen theme. Of course there is a sort of limitation as to form in view of Hogarth's style and period. Yet make it as contemporary as I treated Pergolesi in my *Pulcinella*. As the end of any work is of importance, I think that the hero's end in an asylum scratching a fiddle would make a meritorious conclusion to his stormy life. Don't you think so?

Am grateful to Aldous Huxley who suggested you to me as a prospective collaborateur. Not so long ago I heard with delight your brilliant commentary verses in an English travelogue film. The more I am glad that you can undertake this work. Looking forward to your reaction to all the above said.

Sincerely
[Igor Stravinsky]

October 12, 1947

Dear Mr. Stravinsky,

Thank you very much for your letter of October 6th, which arrived this morning.

As you say, it is a terrible nuisance being thousands of miles apart, but we must do the best we can.

As (a) you have thought about the *Rake's Progress* for some time, and (b) it is the librettist's job to satisfy the composer, not the other way round, I should be most grateful if you could let me have any ideas you may have formed about characters, plot, etc.

I think the Asylum finale sounds excellent, but, for instance, if he is to play the fiddle then, do you want the fiddle to run through the story?

You speak of a "free verse preliminary." Do you want the arias and ensembles to be finally written in free verse or only as a basis for discussing the actual form they should take? If they were spoken, the eighteenth-century style would of course demand rhyme, but I know how different this is when the words are set.

I have an idea, which may be ridiculous, that between the two acts, there should be a choric parabasis as in Aristophanes.

I need hardly say that the chance of working with you is the greatest honor of my life. . . .

Yours very sincerely, Wystan Auden

P.S. I hope you can read my writing. Unfortunately I do not know how to type.

The ensuing correspondence, during the period of actual work on the project, is spotty, since the two met quite frequently, the first time in Hollywood, later in New York, to discuss matters in greater detail than was possible by mail.

Still, at least two details were worked out at some length by correspondence: an extra stanza for the Roaring Boys and Whores in Act I, scene 2, and some verses for Baba the Turk in what became the trio in Act II, scene 2.

November 17, 1948

Dear Auden,

I need to repeat the music of the attached verse. Be an Angel and compose four new lines of same length and rhythm to fit with the already existing music. It will be up to you to decide (for the sense) which one of the two groups of your verses is to be sung . . . first. . . . Please, please, answer as soon as possible.

Cordially
[Igor Stravisnky]

[Enclosed:]   ROARING BOYS and WHORES
                While food has flavor and limbs are shapely
                And hearts beat bravely to fiddle or drum
                Our proper employment is reckless enjoyment
                For too soon the noiseless night will come.

November 23, 1948

Dear Igor Stravinsky,

I got back from Washington yesterday afternoon to find your letter. I enclose another verse which should, I think, come first. It is difficult in this metre to get an *exact* rhythmic identity—e.g., *Who cares what* is slightly different from *For too soon*, but they are, I hope, near enough. In case you can't read my pencil on the score, here is the verse in printed caps:

> SOON DAWN WILL GLITTER OUTSIDE THE SHUTTER
> AND SMALL BIRDS TWITTER; BUT WHAT OF THAT?
> SO LONG AS WE'RE ABLE AND WINE'S ON THE TABLE
> WHO CARES WHAT THE TROUBLING DAY IS AT?

I'm very excited about what I hear of the music from Robert Craft. Very mozartian, he says.

Yours ever, Wystan Auden

November 27, 1948

Dear Auden,

Many, many, many thanks—That is exactly what I need. Don't worry about a slightly different rhythm which occurs from time to time—the music smooths it down.

Looking forward to show you (in February) the first act, which I hope will be completed before going East (end of January).

All best. Cordially
[Igor Stravinsky]

October 18, 1949

Dear Wystan,

I have not heard from you for a long time but I suppose, and I hope, that you are in New York now, because I need your help badly and urgently.

I have just driven my music to the Trio (Act II, Scene II) and my composing is stalled because any music I might compose for Anne and Rake will be drowned under Baba's comic interference and the audience's laughs (I am positive about this).

My first move has been to reunite Anne's and Tom's verses by staggering their lines until the very end when I let them sing twice together (please check with the enclosed pattern). [But] my efforts to hold the audience's attention focused on a single action are [in] vain, as long as Baba keeps interfering by inserting her parlando monologue while Anne and Rake sing. I cannot figure any other way out but for you *to compose verses for Baba's grumbling.* The verses that I want you to compose should match those of Anne and Rake, and might stagger with them most of the time, except when you would find it possible to melt them with the words of Anne or Rake, without, of course, drowning any of them.

Be an angel and send me this overhauled trio as soon as possible. It will then be a genuine trio and not a duo with a third person's intervention. My suggestion would be to reduce Baba's words to not more, and even rather less, than either Anne's or Rake's.

Give me some news concerning [yourself] and your plans. I shall be in New York on March 20, and it is not impossible for me to be there before. I hope you will not leave as early as you did this year, because it is important to both of us to go through everything regarding Act III.

As ever, affectionately yours,
[Igor]

October 24, 1949

Dear Igor,

Many thanks for your letter. In order to distinguish Baba in character and emotion from the two lovers, it seems to me that her rhythm should be more irregular and her tempo of utterance faster. In writing her part, therefore, I have given any line of Baba's twice the number of accents as compared with the equivalent line of Anne or Tom's.

[Enclosed:] Why this delay? Away, or the crowd will... [she sees Anne] O!
        And why, if I may be allowed to inquire, does my husband desire
        To converse with this person? Who is it, pray,
        He prefers to his Baba on their wedding day?
        A family friend? An ancient flame?
        A bride has surely the prior claim
        On the bridal night! I'm quite perplexed
        And more, I confess, than a little vexed.

If you find I have given her too many lines, cuts are easy to make, e.g.

v. 1 can become: Why this delay... Away... O. Who is it pray
                      He prefers to his Baba on their wedding day.

v. 2   An ancient flame? I'm quite perplexed
                      And more, I confess, than a little vexed.

v. 3   Here there is a succession of short phrases, which
                      can be used or not ad lib.

I hope you had a good summer and am longing to hear the new scenes. I had a wonderful time in Italy and managed to get a lot of work done. . . .

Much love to you and Vera and come east soon.

Wystan

November 15, 1949

Dear Wystan,

Pardon me for being so late in thanking you for your brilliant versified version of Baba's interfering recitative. I am delighted, and I have already composed the trio.

STRAVINSKY CONDUCTING THE PREMIÈRE OF *THE RAKE'S PROGRESS*. *A news photo of the composer at La Fenice theater, Venice, on the night of 11 September 1951. From L'Illustrazione Italiana, Oct. 1951.*

In Baba's first two interferences I dropped only the alternate words as per your advice. I kept the whole of her babbling in the third one.

And you sent it to me so quickly! Thanks so much.

I am composing now the end of that scene, which is a chaconne; even when the crowd greets Baba, the chaconne continues, thus ending the whole scene.

After that I shall carry on without respite until I finish the third scene, before next March, as I want not to miss you in New York.

Bob Craft just writes me that you have booked passage for March 13. This shortens my deadline by a fortnight. Nevertheless I hope I will finish the second act and be able to show it to you. Please keep the dates of March 11 and 12 free for me as we have so many things to decide together concerning Act III.

Will be glad to hear from you soon.

As ever, cordially yours,
[Igor]

Stravinsky: Selected Correspondence, ed. and with commentaries by Robert Craft, vol. 1 (New York: Alfred A. Knopf, 1982), 299–300, 306–8, 309–11.

The first performance took place at La Fenice, Venice, on 11 September 1951 with Stravinsky conducting. Auden wrote an article on the opera for the festival magazine *La Biennale di Venezia* (October 1951). It was translated and printed in Italian. What follows is a retranslation into English, since Auden's original is lost.

HOW THE LIBRETTO OF THE OPERA "THE RAKE'S PROGRESS" WAS BORN

BY W. H. AUDEN

I came rather late to an interest in operatic music; then, thanks above all to the enthusiasm and erudition of my friend and collaborator Chester Kallman and to the opportunities provided by the Metropolitan Opera House in New York to hear perfect performances, I became a real opera fan.

Stravinsky's invitation to me in the autumn of 1947 to write a libretto for him on the subject of "The Rake's Progress" therefore struck me not only as an unexpected honor, but also as the divine answer to a prayer, because for some years I had been nurturing a desire to try my hand as a librettist.

The theme of Hogarth's sequence—the story, that is, of a young man who allows himself to be destroyed by the temptations which his good fortune offers him—was a favorite one in eighteenth-century England; even Dr Johnson wrote verses on the subject:

> Long-expected one and twenty
> Ling'ring year at last is flown.
> Pomp and Pleasure, Pride and Plenty
> Great Sir John, are all your own . . .

> Call the Bettys, Kates, and Jennys
> Ev'ry name that laughs at Care,
> Lavish of your Grandsire's guineas,
> Show the Spirit of an heir . . .

But the twin of this story was just as popular, namely the tale of the "Virtuous Apprentice," the youth who, although deprived of financial and social advantages, ended up, by the use of his prudence and intelligence, marrying the master's daughter and becoming a rich gentleman.

As a subject for an opera, the "Rake's Progress" has one great advantage: it is a myth; it represents, that is, a situation in which all men, at least potentially, find themselves, in so far as they are human beings. The traditional feeling that an *opera seria* should not be based on a contemporary subject is, in my opinion, correct for the following reason. All of us have learned to talk, but few of us have been able to learn to sing. Opera, like the classical ballet, is therefore in essence the act of a virtuoso, and a triumphant victory over fate. This means that the paradox implicit in all the arts, by which all the emotions and situations which in real life would be painful become in art a source of pleasure, is quite explicit in the art of opera. In fact, while the singer may be playing the role of a deserted bride who is about to kill herself, the audience knows and cannot forget that she is actually doing what she loves most in life. If the tragic situation were contemporary—were, that is, a situation which some people really and unfortunately are in and others luckily are not—this paradox would disturb the audience. On the other hand, the story Hogarth depicts will not do for a libretto as it stands: in the first place and above all, because Hogarth's rake has a passive character which simply yields to temptation. A passive hero is impossible in opera because music is supremely an assertion of volition and a passionate assertion. In spite of all my admiration of *La Bohème*, for example, I can never make any sense of the gap between the irresolution with which the characters act and the resolution with which they sing. In the second place, all the temptations which Hogarth's character yields to, wine, women and cards, etc. [*some text is apparently lacking in the original Italian here*] are all those which have no importance in visual art, but which, on the contrary, are very significant in a dramatic plot.

In composing our libretto, Mr. Kallman and I have retained the essential elements of Hogarth's version, such as the unforeseen inheritance, the squandering of it, the marriage to an ugly old woman, the auction of the hero's property, and his end in Bedlam. Then we have added three other familiar myths: 1) the story of Mephistopheles—the protagonist Tom Rakewell engages a servant called Shadow; 2) a card game with the Devil which the Devil loses through overconfidence in himself; 3) the myth of the three wishes—in the opera Rakewell's first wish is to be rich, his second is to be happy, and his third is to be good. These three wishes are related to the three temptations, and so, respectively, to the wish for pleasure, the wish for absolute spiritual freedom through some gratuitous act, and the wish to become the savior of the world. The first of these wishes naturally leads him into a brothel; as for the other two, I do not want to give away any secrets that I would like to be a surprise, but I will say only that the second temptation leads him into marriage with a woman called Baba the Turk; and the third makes him preoccupied with a curious machine.

There is of course a virtuous young soprano, Anne, one of those operatic sopranos who would be a terrible bore to have to sit next to at dinner, but to whom on stage all is forgiven. In the scene in Bedlam the protagonist's madness consists in believing that he is Adonis and that Anne is Venus, while his mad companions are characters from Greek myth.

Because, like *Don Giovanni*, this is an *opera giocosa*, the death in Bedlam is followed by an epilogue in which the main characters appear in front of the curtain, take off their wigs and sing a happy moral.

And to conclude, a few words on the style of the libretto. I learned with great pleasure that Stravinsky did not want a music-drama but a traditional opera with recitatives, arias, and choruses, and that he therefore wanted a libretto which provided lots of opportunities for *bel canto*.

As far as the subject, which is from the eighteenth century, is concerned, we have tried to avoid historical solecisms in the diction without being boringly archaeological.

In the composition of the verses for the arias, anyone who has, like me, spent many years writing poetry is bound to find himself confronted by a fascinating problem, namely that of reversing completely his normal habits of mind. As a matter of fact, poetry is a reflective art, its existence is proof that man cannot be content with the outbursts of immediate sensation and that he wants to understand and organize what he feels. Music, however, is the most immediate of the arts, and in writing the words for an aria in which, to distinguish it from lyric and popular song, the words must be completely subordinate to the notes, the poet has to return to the immediate.

The Marschallin's monologue in *Der Rosenkavalier* is, in my opinion, too good as poetry, the details of the verse intrude too much on Strauss's attention; the words of "Ah non credea" in *La Sonnambula*, on the other hand, though they are of little interest to read, do exactly what they should, provoke one of the most beautiful melodies in the world.

The verses which the librettist writes are, so to speak, a private letter to the composer; they have their moment of glory when they suggest a melody to him; then they become as expendable as infantry to a Chinese general.

Complete Works of W. H. Auden: Libretti and Other Dramatic Writings, 1939–1973, ed. Edward Mendelson (Princeton, N.J.: Princeton University Press, 1993), 607–11. Copyright ©. Reprinted by permission of Curtis Brown, Ltd.

50

A FIRST REACTION TO POULENC'S *DIALOGUES DES CARMÉLITES*

The subject for Poulenc's only full-length opera was suggested to him in 1953 by the director of the Ricordi publishing house, while the composer was in Milan on a tour of Italy; it was Georges Bernanos's posthumously published scenario for a film, itself based on prior literary treatments of a true episode of the French Revolution: the martyrdom of sixteen Carmelite nuns who were guillotined on 17 July 1794, going to their death while singing the *Veni Creator*. Poulenc, who had been searching for a libretto, took to the suggestion eagerly and set Bernanos's words directly to music, after shaping them to his purpose. He worked with great enthusiasm, though not without interruptions due to personal as well as legal, copyright problems. The première, in Italian, took place at La Scala on 26 January 1957 and was hailed by *Le Monde* in Paris as "A great international event. A great French victory." The first performance in French took place on 21 June, after which Poulenc's *Carmélites* was on its way to a notable international career. Massimo Mila (1910–88), Italy's most distinguished music critic at the time, covered the Scala première for the weekly *L'Espresso*. His is by no means a rave review, but it helps to recreate for us admirably the effect Poulenc's opera had on sophisticated European ears, inured to the problematic musical scene of the late 1950s. The Darmstadt avant-garde was in full cry. How to account for a major work by a retrospective composer like Poulenc?

In the artistic lineup after World War I, Poulenc belonged to the forces of so-called modern music. Nothing strange about this, for a musician who was one of the most conspicuous elements in the "Group of Six," blessed at birth by Jean Cocteau and aiming to push French music along the path of antiromanticism marked out by Debussy and Ravel. But the odd thing is that Poulenc held that position while using a musical language filled with nineteenth-century reminiscences. Unlike Milhaud and Honegger, he didn't feel it his duty to provide himself with an original language: a duty that, in today's moralistic parlance, is defined as one of conscientious awareness of the problems of contemporary music.

Poulenc didn't give a hoot about the problems of contemporary music. He was filled with affection and gratitude for the masters of the past (and for some contemporary ones like Debussy, Ravel, and Stravinsky), and he made use of their example with an impudence that was his strength and his grace. He had become a master of the witty quotation, thrown in with a wink, as in a conversation among very cultivated persons, who, if they make use of quotations from Proust, Joyce, Gide, or Thomas Mann, do so not out of academic erudition, or for want of their own words, but because by quoting those specific words they intend to awaken immediately in the mind of the informed listener the whole complex of historical, ethical and social values that is connected with the meaning of those words in Proust, Joyce, etc. When he made use of musical turns typical of Debussy or, say, Massenet, that didn't make him their epigone, one who used their language because he was born and raised to it. No: he was, precisely, quoting them.

Poulenc was thus composing a music in which the values of taste surpassed those that are more properly creative; it could appear charming or irritating, depending on whether listeners were endowed with or devoid of taste and a sense of humor. The ballets *Les Biches, Aubade,* and *Les animaux modèles,* the *Concert champêtre* and the concerto for two pianos, the cantata *Le bal masqué,* some piano and many vocal pieces are small masterpieces of musical licentiousness.

His playful appearance prevented Poulenc from being taken as seriously as Honegger and Milhaud (while, of the "Six," his was perhaps the most authentic and gifted musical nature). But it was easy enough to sense that beneath it all there was a poetic sentimentality and that those jocular quotations palpitated with affection for music itself and for its great masters. In any case, there came a time when Poulenc decided to stop joking: without abandoning the simple structure of his apparently naive style, he attempted to express the grave thoughts that his maturity and the darkening European horizon suggested to him. He wrote some sacred choral compositions, a cappella, that caused much astonishment and were regarded with respect, but of whose actual success one may be dubious. Then, in memory of Garcia Lorca, he wrote a Sonata for Violin and Piano that renews, on a serious-pathetic plane, the usual sleight-of-hand of a work of art written in the language of fifty years ago, but treated with modern sensibility and intelligence.

Poulenc has been living off the interests on the thematic capital invested in this touching sonata for nearly twenty years, quoting impartially both from himself and from Ravel, Fauré, Stravinsky, and the others. He must be given due credit now, for, in undertaking the great task of setting to music, almost unchanged, the text of Bernanos's *Dialogues of the Carmelites,* he has for the second time in his life reinvented his musical wardrobe; and if he often seems to live in the shadow of Musorgsky's vocal melody, he has not plundered his Violin Sonata at all.

But what has he been able to substitute for that investment, which he has squandered down to the last penny? At a time like the present, when, no matter how diverse the musical tendencies and fashions might be, one thing is certain, namely the resurgence of deep polyphonic perspectives, Poulenc may well be the last musician to voluptuously savor the vertical arrangement of the notes of a chord. Indifferent to the problems of the contemporary musical language, he has shut himself up in a music that knows only two dimensions: that of the melody and that of the accompaniment.

It's quite true that in the nineteenth century an abundance of operas got written in only those two dimensions of music. But they were written with a melodic inventiveness that nowadays is rarer than a straight flush. Poulenc is a man of our century, full of sobriety and composure: his music is all generically melodious, but it does not provide great melodies. Perhaps, even if they did occur to him, Poulenc wouldn't utter them, as a matter of taste and good upbringing. He suggests melodies and keeps those hints floating like a cork on the rise and fall of methodical and traditional accompaniments: basses on the downbeat and a matching chord on the upbeat. Which, in mere words, reads: "oom-pah, oom-pah."

For Bernanos's text, which is full of psychological (and sometimes also verbal) subtleties, these twin resources of a chaste melody and a traditional harmonic accompaniment are really a bit too little. The composer uses them with exquisite refinement, and several of the sixteen musical episodes that make up the opera exhibit the jeweler's grace, the miniaturization that characterize the best Poulenc: especially in the large, homogeneous nucleus bestriding the first and second acts (illness and death of the Prioress, wake, bond of affection that forms between the proud and complicated Sister Blanche and the simple Constance). Here the music really captures that element of the subject which was most congenial to the natural gifts of Poulenc's art: the diverse fragrances of femininity that emanate from beneath monastic humility. But the music stops cold when confronted with Jansenistic verbal subtleties like: "What good does it do for a *religieuse* to be detached from everything, when she has not detached herself from her own self, that is, from her own detachment?"

Once the two leading motifs that seem to adumbrate the two aspects of the Carmelite order, humility and chivalric courage, have been exhausted, the monotony of the accompaniment and the tedium of the constant duple meter soon prevail over the generic melodiousness of the declamation. Granted, it is the nature of the subject that calls for this type of muted music—a very particular subject ("My daughter," says the Prioress to Sister Blanche, "the good people ask of what use we are, and after all they may be excused for wondering... Only prayer justifies our existence, and whoever does not believe in prayer can only consider us to be impostors or parasites"). Nevertheless it is permissible to remember that Erik Satie, setting to music long passages of Platonic dialogue [in his *Socrate*], had realized a music of this type, to be sure, but better able to convey the quintessence of those thoughts. Here we have a diligent, analytic representation of the events and the environment (more than of the characters): but fear, the true subject of this story of militant nuns, is not in the music.

A splendid collective performance at La Scala, with Virginia Zeani in the leading role, Nino Sanzogno the conductor, scenery by Georges Wakhévič, directed by Margherita Wallmann.

Massimo Mila, *Cronache musicali, 1955–1959* ([Turin]: Giulio Einaudi, 1959), 343–46. Trans. P.W.

51

EINSTEIN ON THE BEACH BY PHILIP GLASS

The following appreciation by Tim Page, Pulitzer Prize winning culture writer for *The Washington Post*, accompanied the 1993 CD recording of Glass's most famous opera.

Einstein on the Beach (1976) is a pivotal work in the oeuvre of Philip Glass. It is the first, longest, and most famous of the composer's operas, yet it is in almost every way unrepresentative of them. *Einstein* was, by design, a glorious "one-shot"—a work that invented its context, form and language, and then explored them so exhaustively that further development would have been redundant. But, by its own radical example, *Einstein* prepared the way—it gave *permission*—for much of what has happened in music theater since its premiere.

Einstein broke all the rules of opera. It was in four interconnected acts and five hours long, with no intermissions (the audience was invited to wander in and out at liberty during performances). The acts were intersticed by what Glass and Wilson called "knee plays"—brief interludes that also provided time for scenery changes. The text consisted of numbers, solfege syllables and some cryptic poems by Christopher Knowles, a young, neurologically-impaired man with whom Wilson had worked as an instructor of disturbed children for the New York public schools. To this were added short texts by choreographer Lucinda Childs and Samuel M. Johnson, an actor who played the Judge in the "Trial" scenes and the bus driver in the finale. There were references to the trial of Patricia Hearst (which was underway during the creation of the opera); to the mid-'70s radio lineup on New York's WABC; to the popular song "Mr. Bojangles"; to the Beatles and to teen idol David Cassidy. *Einstein* sometimes seemed a study in sensory overload, meaning everything and nothing.

A recording cannot capture the spectacular visual imagery that Robert Wilson devised for *Einstein on the Beach* but it should be said immediately that this was much more than the usual uneven collaboration between a librettist and composer. From its beginnings, worked out between Glass and Wilson over a series of luncheons at a restaurant on New York's Sullivan Street almost 20 years ago, this was truly a team effort.

At this time, Glass was writing long concert pieces for the Philip Glass Ensemble—most recently *Music in Twelve Parts* (1974) which might be considered Glass's *"Art of the Repetition"*—while working as a plumber and driving a taxi. "Foundation support was out of the question, of course," he recalled. "And most of my colleagues thought I'd gone completely off the wall." Still, by the mid-'70s, the Ensemble had built a cult following in the lofts and galleries of Manhattan's nascent Soho district, and Glass had begun amassing credits as a theater composer by providing scores for the experimental Mabou Mines Company (of which his first wife, JoAnne Akalaitis, was a founding member).

Glass became aware of Wilson's stage work during an overnight performance of the twelve-hour *Life and Times of Josef Stalin*, presented at the Brooklyn Academy of Music in 1973. He was attracted to what he called Wilson's sense of "theatrical time, space and movement." The two men promptly determined to collaborate on a theatrical opus based on the life of a historic figure. Wilson proposed Chaplin, then Hitler; Glass countered with Gandhi. Finally, Glass and Wilson agreed upon Albert Einstein, and the name of the as-yet-unwritten work became "Einstein on the Beach on Wall Street." The title was later shortened; neither creator now remembers when or why.

"As a child, Einstein had been one of my heroes," the composer reflected in his book, *Music by Philip Glass* (Harper and Row, 1987). "Growing up just after World War II, as I had, it was impossible not to know who he was. The emphatic, if catastrophic, beginnings of the nuclear age had made atomic energy the most widely discussed issue of the day."

"Philip and I immediately agreed on the overall length of time we wanted to fill—four to five hours," Robert Wilson said in a recent interview. "We decided that each scene would be about 20 minutes long and that we would connect the scenes together with what I call 'knee plays'—the knee is a joint that links two similar elements, hence 'knee plays.' I did a series of drawings and Philip set them to music."

Wilson stresses that this marked a complete break with traditional theater. "In the past, theater has always been bound by literature. *Einstein on the Beach* is not. There is no plot—although there are many references to Einstein—and the visual book can stand on its own. We put together the opera the way an architect would build a building. The structure of the music was completely interwoven with the stage action and with the lighting. Everything was all of a piece."

The Glass-Wilson opera was intended as a metaphorical look at Einstein: scientist, humanist, amateur musician—and the man whose theories, for better and for worse, led to the splitting of the atom. Although it is difficult to discern a "plot" in *Einstein*, the climactic scene clearly depicted nuclear holocaust: with its renaissance-pure vocal lines, the blast of amplified instruments, a steady eighth-note pulse and the hysterical chorus chanting numerals as quickly and frantically as possible, it seemed to many a musical reflection of the anxious, *fin-de-siècle* late '70s.

Einstein on the Beach brought the composer fame—and notoriety. It was presented throughout Europe in the summer of 1976, then brought to the Metropolitan Opera House for two sold-out performances in November 1976. Then, as later, audience response was mixed; Glass's works were presented to boos and bravos.

Jane Herman, the presenter responsible for bringing *Einstein* to the Met, has vivid memories of her first encounter with the Glass/Wilson opera. "Anthony Bliss had just taken over as the Met's general manager and he wanted something to fill the house when the company wasn't performing," she said. "Jean Rigg, the administrative director of the Merce Cunningham troupe, told me about Einstein and I went to see a runthrough in downtown Manhattan— five full hours, without break—and I liked it very much. So I reported back to Tony and he called [director] John Dexter in London who said if Robert Wilson wanted to do it, we should do it. So I flew over and we arranged a contract. And that, as they say, was that.

"I'll never forget that first night at the Met and the standing ovation after the 'Bed.' I'd never seen an audience rise to its feet just because it took something twenty minutes to ascend from the stage! This was clearly something new."

The flutist Ransom Wilson, who would later conduct and record some of Glass's music, has left a vivid impression of a New York performance of *Einstein on the Beach,* one worth recounting because it summarizes the reactions of many initiates: "As I listened to that five-hour performance, I experienced an amazing transformation. At first I was bored—*very* bored. The music seemed to have no direction, almost giving the impression of a gigantic phonograph with a stuck needle. I was first irritated and then angry that I'd been taken in by this crazy composer who obviously doted on repetition. I thought of leaving. Then, with no conscious awareness, I crossed a threshold and found that the music was touching me, carrying me with it. I began to perceive within it a whole world where change happens so slowly and carefully that each new harmony or rhythmic addition or subtraction seemed monumental."

For the 1978 recording of *Einstein on the Beach,* Glass abridged the score to fit on to four LP discs. The opening scene, for example, was cut from some forty minutes to a little more than twenty by reducing the number of repeats. (Glass likened the process to a friend after a diet: "It's the same person before and after; there's just a little less of him.") Still, that first recording, issued on Tomato and then CBS Masterworks (later SONY), won considerable attention and was long considered definitive. Why, then, a new version?

There are several reasons, according to Glass. "To begin with, the new recording is almost 190 minutes long, as opposed to some 160 minutes in 1978," he said. "We were prisoners of the technology of the time and could only fit so much music on an LP side. The CD has changed everything. And length is not a trivial matter in a performance of *Einstein* but very much a part of the total experience."

"And we just play the music so much more skilfully today than we could back in the 1970s. Back then, we were just learning the style. I imagine that the first performance of *Einstein* [at Avignon in 1976] was probably a total mess but everything was so unusual and so new that nobody noticed. We were on a limited budget, so we had to hire singers who could also move and dancers who could also sing. Our chorus this time around is far superior to that on the first recording. Moreover, synthesizer technology has improved so enormously that we are able to create a more beautiful, sensual sound than we could have dreamed of in 1978." . . .

Though he loathes the term, Glass is often classified as a "minimalist" composer. Much of his mature work is based on the extended repetition of brief, elegant melodic fragments that weave in and out of an aural tapestry. Listening to his music has been compared to watching a modern painting that initially appears static but metamorphoses slowly as one concentrates. Particularly in his early works, Glass limited compositional material to a few elements, which were then subjected to a variety of transformational processes. A listener quickly learned not to expect Western musical *events*—sforzandos, sudden diminuendos. Instead, one was immersed in a sort of sonic weather that twists, turns, surrounds, develops.

"I first saw Philip Glass playing with his ensemble at the Royal College of Art in 1969 or 1970," Brian Eno recently recalled. "This was one of the most extraordinary musical experiences of my life—sound made completely physical and as dense as concrete by sheer volume and repetition. For me it was like a viscous bath of pure, thick energy. Though he was at that time described as a minimalist, this was actually one of the most detailed musics I'd ever heard. It was all intricacy and exotic harmonics."

Since the mid-1960s, Glass had based much of his music on two central techniques: *additive process* and *cyclic structures*. Additive process involved the expansion and contraction of tiny musical modules; a grouping of five notes might be played several times, then followed by a measure containing six notes (similarly repeated) then by seven notes, and so on. "A simple figure can expand and then contract in many different ways, maintaining the same general melodic configuration but, because of the addition or subtraction of one note, it takes on a very different rhythmic shape," Glass explained.

Glass defines rhythmic cycles as the simultaneous repetition of two or more different rhythmic patterns, which, depending on the length of the pattern, will eventually arrive together back at the starting points, making for one complete cycle. "This has been described by some writers as sounding like wheels inside wheels," Glass explained, "a rather fanciful but not wholly inaccurate way of evoking the resulting effect."

With these two techniques as the basis of his style, Glass had already begun to build a music of increasing richness and complexity. *Einstein* added a new functional harmony that set it aside from the early conceptual works. (Indeed, some of the music in *Einstein* had been originally written for a long series of concert pieces called, appropriately, *Another Look at Harmony*.)

Einstein on the Beach may be said to represent the apogee of Glass's modernism. As the composer observed in *Music by Philip Glass*: "In its own way, the pre-*Einstein* music, rigorous and highly reductive, was more 'radical' in its departure from the received tradition of Western music than what I have written since. But as I had been preoccupied at that point with that more radical-sounding music for over ten years, I felt I could add little more to what I had already done. Again, it is surely no coincidence that it was at the moment that I was embarking upon a major shift in my music to large-scale theater works that I began to develop a new, more expressive language for myself."

Indeed, it is not *Einstein* but *Satyagraha* (1980) that marks the first of Glass's more-or-less "traditional" operas (insofar as an opera without linear narrative, with a text in Sanskrit and based directly on the Bhagavad Gita may be considered "traditional"). As opposed to the spartan *Einstein*, composed for the Philip Glass Ensemble, *Satyagraha* was scored for more conventional forces: strings, woodwinds in threes, organ, six solo singers and chorus of forty. While *Einstein* challenged ideas about what an opera—even an *avant-garde* opera—should be, *Satyagraha* neatly fit Glass into the operatic continuum. *Einstein* threw out the rules with modernist zeal: *Satyagraha* adapted the rules to the composer's own esthetic. It was difficult to find any historical precedent for *Einstein*; in *Satyagraha* one may find references to many of the composer's predecessors.

And yet Glass insists there is a strong connection between *Einstein*, *Satyagraha* and *Akhnaten* (1983). "Each of the three operas of this portrait trilogy has its own distinctive sound world," Glass said. "*Einstein on the Beach*, an opera about a great mathematician who loved music, is for amplified ensemble and small chorus singing a text comprised of numbers (actually the beats of music) and solfege syllables. *Satyagraha*, a work about one man leading his people to freedom, is a large choral opera with text taken directly from Gandhi's philosophical guidebook in the actual language in which he read it. In *Akhnaten*, my emphasis is orchestral, with choral and solo voices sharing common ground with the orchestra. . . . Should the three operas be performed within a fairly narrow time span (within the same week, for example) I believe their internal connection will become increasingly obvious and provide the audience with a coherent musical and theatrical experience."

Einstein on the Beach was revived in 1984, and then again in 1992, by International Production Associates for extended tours, culminating in residencies at the Brooklyn Academy of Music. In 1989, Achim Fryer attempted a new visual interpretation of the Glass music at the Stuttgart State Opera, which was generally judged unsuccessful. It is in its original form—as a joint venture between Glass and Wilson—that *Einstein* has become one of the most famous operatic events of the century.

Virgil Thomson, whom Glass admired and considered one of his few genuine forerunners, wrote a letter to Gertrude Stein after the first production of their *Four Saints in Three Acts*: "Of course there were some who didn't like the music and some who didn't like the words and even some who didn't like the decors or the choreography but there wasn't anybody who didn't see that the ensemble was a new kind of collaboration and that it was unique and powerful. . . . "

Much the same may be said for Glass and Wilson's collaboration, *Einstein on the Beach*. Its influence has been extensive—to a degree that Lucinda Childs, the dancer and choreographer, thinks may not be entirely healthy. "It's wonderful that people take it seriously and are influenced by it, but I see so much lifted out of context and it's hard to be positive about that."

"I don't think *Einstein* has lost a bit of its fascination," Harvey Lichtenstein, the director of the Brooklyn Academy of Music, said in 1993. "Indeed, I think I'm more interested in it today than I'd ever been. In the past I'd watch some of a performance, then get up and walk around for a while. The last few performances I've seen, I couldn't budge from my seat. I wish we were presenting it tomorrow night."

"It's had an enormous impact," Jane Herman says. "There have been rafts of material in the dance world, in theater, in music, that come directly out of *Einstein*. Every so often, I'll be in a theater and recognize some gesture and think—'Aha! Here we are again!' "

52

JOHN ADAMS ON *NIXON IN CHINA*

Nixon in China by John Adams and the poet Alice Goodman was given its première by the Houston Grand Opera on 22 October 1987 and was later seen in its original staging in New York, Washington, Amsterdam, Edinburgh, Los Angeles, Paris, Adelaide, and Frankfurt. A televised version was shown over the PBS network in 1988. The original productions were directed by Peter Sellars, who worked closely with Adams and Goodman on the concept and many details of the work. The opera has been revived several times in the United States and in Europe. Dubbed "headline opera" by the critics, *Nixon in China* is based on a historical event still fresh in the memory of its audience: President Nixon's official visit to the People's Republic of China in 1972, which established diplomatic relations between the two countries, nonexistent since the victory of the Communist revolution in 1949. The opera depicts episodes from the eight-day visit as reported in the press and seen on television: Nixon's plane landing in Beijing, Nixon's "historic handshake" on the airport runway with Chinese premier Chou En-lai, the meeting between Nixon and Mao Zedong, Chairman of the Communist Party, the banquet at the Great Hall of the People, a visit by Pat Nixon, the First Lady, to a model pig farm, the Evergreen People's Commune. In the original production the principal characters Nixon (baritone), his wife, Pat (soprano), Henry Kissinger (bass), Chairman Mao (tenor), Mao's wife, Chiang Ch'ing (soprano), and Premier Chou (baritone) were made up to look as much as possible like the historical figures they portrayed, several of whom were still alive at the time of the première. In the opera, plot is at a minimum: the characters interact in stylized exchanges and reminisce singly or in pairs about their personal histories and history in general. Critics called the musical style of *Nixon in China* minimalist because of its tonal harmonies and frequent repetition of text and musical patterns. However, in its use of jazz and dance rhythms and witty declamation of text, the opera resembles American pop music, and its vocal lines and goal-directed harmonies have a good deal in common with late nineteenth-century operatic practice. Although the staging is grandiose, the orchestra is quite small: a thirty-three-piece amplified ensemble consisting mainly of winds and percussion, along with a few strings and a synthesizer. In the following excerpts from an interview published nine years after its première, the composer presents his views on *Nixon in China*—and, in the last paragraph, on the future of opera, thus providing a fitting conclusion to this collection of documents.

QUESTION: *Peter Sellars approached you in 1982 at the Monadnock Music Festival in New Hampshire. Is that right? Now I read that initially you weren't so enthusiastic about the idea, but then you changed your mind.*

ANSWER: Yes. We were introduced to each other by a mutual acquaintance, and, of course, we got along immediately. Everybody who is introduced to Peter likes him. He was just crazy about my music. His enthusiasm for *Shaker Loops* was genuine. I could tell that he really understood it and loved it. We agreed, right then and there, that we were going to write an opera together, but he was already a step ahead of me: he even had the title. "Nixon in China" had a good ring to it, but I could only think of Richard Nixon as the usual butt of talk-show comedians. In subsequent communications I said that I wanted to do something more mythic, which shows how much I was missing the point! Of course, myth itself came to be the key that unlocked this story for me. All of those characters were intensely mythic. Mao had created a myth out of himself, and likewise his wife had mythicized herself during the Cultural Revolution. But it took me a while to sort these ideas out. Peter and I had very infrequent contact over the next couple of years. I actually don't remember what finally got the ball rolling... Maybe it was that I had written *Harmonium* and had finally set poetic text, something I had in fact never attempted. Sometime in early 1984 I called Peter and said, "Let's do this opera, and if it has to be *Nixon in China*, that's fine with me. But whatever it is, it has to have a verse libretto." Peter suggested Alice Goodman, who was a classmate of his at Harvard. He knew that she was one of the few people around who could write verse. That's a very rare thing these days. So we met for the first time in early December 1984 at the Kennedy Center in Washington. We were there because Peter, at an alarmingly young age, was already artistic director of the American Repertory Theater. I seem to recall that we had a three-day huddle. Alice and I had never met before. . . . But I remember those days, we sat in a conference room at the Kennedy Center, surrounded by a staff who could rummage through all the various Library of Congress and State Department libraries. We had an enormous seminar table literally piled high with videotapes to look at, a lot of Chinese literature in translation, Nixon's memoirs, contemporary accounts of the visit—everything ranging from left-wing journalism to the *Ladies' Home Journal, Newsweek, Time,* and thousands of photos. Over the course of the three days we developed the three-act structure and a lot of the casting. I know that Peter originally wanted the Kissinger role to be a dumb role—a certain vendetta which I stifled, because

I wanted to be able to have Kissinger sing. In the end, Alice gave him some memorable lines, and I believe we were all grateful that his role was not a silent one.

QUESTION: *What happened after that meeting?*

ANSWER: After that, Alice went back to Cambridge, I came back to California, and everyone started reading in earnest. That was a great experience for me—to read deeply. . . . Up to then I'd had only a very casual knowledge of Chinese history and the Communist revolution. Suddenly I was plunged into what seemed like a bottomless pit of material, but I loved this phase of the preparation.

I believe I started receiving sections of act 1 of *Nixon* the following summer [1985]. I still had another orchestral commission, which I had been postponing for years. I was so ready to start on *Nixon* that I decided I would kill two birds with one stone by writing a fox-trot that would function also as the main scene in act 2, where Madame Mao dances with the Chairman. But that piece [*The Chairman Dances*] soon got out of hand and very quickly took on its own unique personality.

QUESTION: *To what extent did* The Chairman Dances *represent your original intentions for act 3 of the opera?*

ANSWER: Of course, *The Chairman Dances* is for full orchestra and makes use of those forces to produce moments of grand, sweeping gestures and lush sonorities. I was thinking of Madame Mao's earlier life as a movie actress in the 1930s, and I thought the notion of movie music, specifically Hollywood movie music, might be a hidden key to her personality. You know, her public persona for Westerners was exclusively that of the shrill, unrepentant harpy of the Gang of Four. But we mustn't forget that she had a very different image as a young woman. She was, as far as we can tell, attractive, intelligent, and charismatic.

But when it came to the choice of the pit orchestra, I took a totally different tack. I asked myself, "What kind of music would the Nixons have listened to? To what music would they have fallen in love?" And the answer seemed obvious: white swing music from the 1940s. Glenn Miller or something similar. So I used what was essentially a big band for the pit orchestra: four saxophones, lots of brass, a trap set, etc. And to this I added strings, some other winds, and a synthesizer. It was an orchestra that allowed me to access that big-band sound but also provided the possibility of real power and thrust whenever it was required, such as when Air Force One lands.

QUESTION: *So that's the thinking behind the orchestra you use...*

ANSWER: This big-band sound was part of my birthright. In the 1930s my father played in a jazz band, and my mother's stepfather owned a dance hall in central New Hampshire. My parents met at that dance hall, under the umbrella of big-band music. The Nixons were roughly the same age as my parents. That seemed to be a useful means of musically getting under the skin of *Nixon*.

QUESTION: *Can you remember which part of the opera you composed first?*

ANSWER: I think my first sketches were of the "News" aria in act 1. Shortly after that I had the image of the rolling waves of a minor scale, and with that the opera started to come to life. . . .

QUESTION: *You have described your music as "postmodern."*

ANSWER: I haven't described it as that, but other people have. I think we are in a period when style has become diffuse, where no single style is dominant or carries the weight of an acknowledged prestige. One casts around for a rubric to define these periods in art history when no one overriding event or style is defining the language. *Postmodern*, a not very helpful term, came into usage about ten or twelve years ago. I don't like it, because it defines what is happening now only by negation: "We are no longer modern." I don't think that periods like the present one are necessarily bad periods. In fact, they sometimes produce the greatest art—periods when experimentation and exploration have given way to the need for assimilation. This is certainly the case with Mahler. Mahler was not the kind of vanguard thinker that Wagner was. *Tristan und Isolde* was one of those spasmodic events like *Le Sacre* or *Erwartung* in which the language underwent an enormous sea change. Now *Tristan* happened in the 1850s, and Mahler doesn't appear on the scene until the 1880s and 1890s, and most of his music doesn't even come close to matching the chromatic daring of *Tristan*. Yet Mahler had that special embracing ability to take everything in, whether it was academic fugues or village band music, or sentimental ballads. . . All kinds of music. I think that, in a sense, we are in a similar period now. Minimalism represented a very pure point of view, as did serial music, and chance music—all these were very highly defined styles. The rules were strict and the earmarks unmistakable. I remember this from my college years. It was really a pressing issue: either you were a Cagean, or you were a follower of the European avant-garde. It mattered intensely which party you joined. But this does not describe the scene now in the 1990s. . . .

QUESTION: *Whom are you working with now?*

ANSWER: I'm working [on *I Was Looking Up and Then I Saw the Sky*] with June Jordan, the poet and essayist, who lives here in Berkeley but grew up in Brooklyn. She has a completely different feel and approach to language, and her way of working is wildly different from Alice's. She writes with great speed and spontaneity. I actually haven't seen a word she has written for me yet. We've met and had several creative meetings with Peter. I know her poetry, and I'm really looking forward to it. It's going to be a completely different experience. . . . My plan, at the moment, is not to write for operatic voices but for singers who can work in a variety of pop styles—young people, very young people. . . . I have several reasons for wanting to go in this direction. I conducted *Mahagonny* (the Songspiel), and I was very taken with its economy and sense of rightness. Even though it is cast in the 1920s popular cabaret style, it just had a wonderful depth to it. I think my music veers toward that anyway, that *frisson* between art music and popular culture. There is also a tactical consideration, in that my operas are not getting out to the people I care about—young people. They don't play at universities, because they are too long and too expensive, so a lot of people still don't know who I am or don't know my work. I'm hoping that in a smaller production I'll get a larger number of performances. The big operas generated an enormous amount of media interest, but the actual number of people who saw them was quite small. The same thing happened with *Einstein on the Beach.*

QUESTION: *Where do you think the future of American opera lies?*

ANSWER: I've no idea, but I certainly think it will move out of the traditional realm of establishment opera. I might be completely wrong, but I just don't see new generations of innovative composers being drawn to the conventional operatic format, with a symphony orchestra in the pit and unamplified voices onstage, I am sure that music theater is in a somewhat reactionary phase right now, of which my two operas are probably a part. I haven't seen any of the Stockhausen operas, but I have the feeling that over the years those will probably provide a lot of models for other types of [musical theater] in terms of mixing media and really extending boundaries. But it is also possible that things could go in another direction, something far more ritual, like what Meredith Monk does, or something far more influenced by music theater from other cultures, like Gagaku or Noh, or ritual music theater from Sufi culture or Indonesia.

Matthew Daines, "An Interview with John Adams," *Opera Quarterly* 13 (1996): 37–54, passim.

Index

Boldface page numbers denote passages authored by the person indexed. Italic page numbers denote illustrations.